WRITING AND REBELLION

The New Historicism: Studies in Cultural Poetics
Stephen Greenblatt, General Editor

Number 27

Steven Justice, *Writing and Rebellion: England in 1381*

Of related interest in the series:

Nancy Armstrong and Leonard Tennenhouse, *The Imaginary Puritan: Literature, Intellectual Labor, and the Origins of Personal Life*

Caroline Walker Bynum, *Holy Feast and Holy Fast: The Religious Significance of Food to Medieval Women*

Stephen Greenblatt, *Shakespearean Negotiations: The Circulation of Social Energy in Renaissance England*

Samuel Kinser, *Rabelais's Carnival: Text, Context, Metatext*

Lee Patterson, editor, *Literary Practice and Social Change in Britain, 1380–1530*

David Harris Sacks, *The Widening Gate: Bristol and the Atlantic Economy, 1450–1700*

Debora Kuller Shuger, *Habits of Thought in the English Renaissance: Religion, Politics, and the Dominant Culture*

Gabrielle M. Spiegel, *Romancing the Past: The Rise of Vernacular Prose Historiography in Thirteenth-Century France*

WRITING AND REBELLION

ENGLAND IN 1381

STEVEN JUSTICE

University of California Press

Berkeley · Los Angeles · London

This book is a print-on-demand volume. It is manufactured using toner in place of ink. Type and images may be less sharp than the same material seen in traditionally printed University of California Press editions.

University of California Press
Berkeley and Los Angeles, California

University of California Press, Ltd.
London, England

© 1994 by
The Regents of the University of California

First Paperback Printing, 1996

Library of Congress Cataloging-in-Publication Data

Justice, Steven Victor.
    Writing and rebellion: England in 1381 / Steven Justice.
        p.   cm.—(The new historicism; 27)
    Includes bibliographical references (p.   ) and index.
    ISBN 0-520-20697-5
    1. English literature—Middle English, 1100–1500—History
and criticism.   2. Great Britain—History—Richard II, 1377–
1399—Historiography.   3. England—Intellectual life—
Medieval period, 1066–1485.   4. Langland, William, 1330?–
1400? Piers the Plowman.   5. Peasantry—England—Books
and reading—History.   6. Literature and society—England—
History.   7. Written communication—England—History.
8. Peasant uprisings in literature.   9. Tyler's insurrection, 1381,
in literature.   10. Literacy—England—History.   I. Title.
II. Series.
PR275.H5J87   1994
820.9'001–dc 20   93-558
                                                             CIP

Printed in the United States of America

For Jill

It is part of the insult offered to intelligence by a class-society that this history of ordinary thought is ever found surprising.

Raymond Williams, *The Country and the City*

Contents

Acknowledgments

This project was supported by grants from the W. M. Keck Foundation, which gave me a summer at the Huntington Library; the National Endowment for the Humanities, which supported the year I spent writing in St. Louis; and the University of California, whose Junior Faculty Research Grant financed research in London, Oxford, and Cambridge.

Grateful acknowledgment is rendered to the Bodleian Library, Oxford; the British Library; the President and Fellows of St. John's College, Oxford; and the Syndics of Cambridge University Library for permission to quote unpublished material.

Thanks are due the staffs of the Huntington Library, Olin Library at Washington University, Pius XII Library at St. Louis University, Concordia Seminary Library, Doe and Bancroft Libraries at Berkeley, and Green Library at Stanford in this hemisphere; and in the other, the British Library, the Bodleian, and the libraries of St. John's College (Oxford), Cambridge University, and the Institute for Historical Research.

Many people helped in all sorts of ways. William Chester Jordan started it all with a kind but pointed question about some remarks I made on 1381 during a lecture at Princeton. Audiences at Princeton (twice), the MLA (twice), and Santa Barbara did me the compliment of taking the ideas seriously enough to question and criticize. Thanks are due to Andrew J. Prescott of the British Library, for encouragement, advice, and permission to use his indispensable Ph.D. thesis; to my readers for the Press, Ralph Hanna III and Barbara A. Hanawalt, for their stringently intelligent comments (and for refusing confidentiality; if distinguished scholars like them continue to do so, perhaps we will soon see the end of that silliness); to Rita Copeland, Susan Crane, Paul Freedman, Gail MacMurray Gibson, Mary F. Godfrey, Richard Firth Green, Willis Johnson, William Chester Jordan, Seth Lerer, Clementine Oliver, Brian Stock, Ruth Shklar, and Katherine Zieman, who all read the manuscript at one stage or another; to Sarah Kelen, Kathryn Kerby-Fulton, and Carter Revard, who went far beyond the call of friendship and collegiality with their thorough and sometimes crucially helpful comments (and to Kathryn and Carter for spending an afternoon each at the British Library doing my codicological work for me); and to Anne Middleton, to whom I owe many of my thoughts anyway, and who engaged incisively and wittily with every argumentative move in the book.

My colleagues in the Berkeley English department have been entirely hospitable to this eccentric project; in particular, Stephen Greenblatt believed in this old-historicist project from the beginning and invited it into his New Historicism series. The six long and detailed critiques from unnamed internal reviewers for my fourth-year and tenure reviews have been crucial to me (I know who you all are, but must pretend I don't); the work and seriousness and sheer intelligence that went into them show why Berkeley's is the best English department in the country in which to be an assistant professor. My former colleagues at Washington University welcomed me back for the year I spent writing in St. Louis; and I must thank Carter Revard, again, for letting me pick his brain (one of the great resources for medieval studies in North America); George Pepe and Burt Wheeler, for letting me take over their library studies; and Naomi Lebowitz, for being brilliant and wonderful. Finally, I want to express my profound, abiding debt to my great teacher, John Fleming.

I wrote most of this book in the summer after my father's death. My parents both grew up in large families of small farmers in Kentucky—not bluegrass country, but the poorer east and north of the state. Like many of his generation, my father used the GI Bill to make a new life; he became a school teacher and administrator, first in Kentucky, then across the river in Ohio. Fleming Justice and Virginia Stevens Justice believed in education; they saw to, and saved for, their son's. They made it easy for me, and I guess that this book is an act of piety, to them and to the ambitions the country can nourish.

The book is dedicated to Jill N. Levin. She encouraged me to continue with the project when I wavered; she tolerated my moods and mitigated my compulsiveness; and she took a month off from her own research to edit the manuscript, recalling me from distant frontiers of syntax and sense. This is her book, but for bigger reasons than these. She is a better historian and exegete and writer than I am, and this was my attempt to live up to the example of scholarly elegance and conceptual inventiveness that her work and conversation have given me—and to realize her lesson that the ordinary is the secret that the extraordinary can be made to tell.

Abbreviations

AHR	*American Historical Review*
BIHR	*Bulletin of the Institute for Historical Research*
BJRL	*Bulletin of the John Rylands Library*
BL	London, British Library
Bodl.	Oxford, Bodleian Library
CCR	*Calendar of Close Rolls*
CJ	Chief Justice
CPR	*Calendar of Patent Rolls*
CUL	Cambridge University Library
CS	Camden Society
CYS	Canterbury and York Society
EcHR	*Economic History Review*
EETS	Early English Text Society
os	original series
es	extra series
EHR	*English Historical Review*
JEGP	*Journal of English and Germanic Philology*
JMRS	*Journal of Medieval and Renaissance Studies*
L	Latin
MÆ	*Medium Ævum*
ME	Middle English
MED	*Middle English Dictionary*

MLR	*Modern Language Review*
ModE	Modern English
MS	*Mediaeval Studies*
PRO	Public Record Office
Rp	*Rotuli parliamentorum*
RS	Rolls Series
SCH	*Studies in Church History*
SR	*Statutes of the Realm*
SS	Selden Society
TRHS	*Transactions of the Royal Historical Society*
VCH	*Victoria County History*
YLS	*Yearbook of Langland Studies*

Introduction

Official England first learned what was happening when some justices of the peace were fired upon with arrows. It was 30 May 1381, a Thursday (that Sunday would be Pentecost), and they were at Brentwood in Essex, collecting for the second time the poll tax levied a year earlier.[1] In 1380 parliament had granted a tax of 3*d.* per adult head, the third such tax in four years, but the revenues collected fell far below those brought in before; evasion was rife. The government of Richard II appointed commissions to inquire into payments and collect on arrears, commissions like the one that assembled representatives of southern Essex villages in Brentwood on 30 May. That day, the villagers of Fobbing told John of Bampton and John of Gildesburgh, Essex land-holders and justices of the peace, that they would make no further payments. Something happened then—it is not clear what—that resulted in the arrows fired on Bampton and his fellows, who fled to London while their attackers fled to the woods.

Things were quiet again for eight days (although later, in judicial retrospect, it would become apparent how much had really been happening) until 7 June, when a band from Essex and Kent took the castle at Rochester, released a prisoner there, and then moved across the county, breaking into the houses of sheriffs and escheators and burning the documents they held. The same pattern of action, more carefully planned, began in Essex three days later, on 10 June, when the sheriff at Great Coggeshall found himself confronted by a crowd that meant to seize his documents. Some from among this crowd then proceeded southwest, as some Kentish insurgents were proceeding (roughly) northwest, toward London both. Meanwhile, other insurgents spread through the two counties and beyond, making proclamations in the villages through which they passed, summoning the population, de-

---

1. That, at least, is how one important chronicle describes the situation. There are problems; see ch. 4, n. 18 below.

manding allegiance, swearing oaths to be true to each other and to King Richard. And they continued to extort money and burn archives.

On Wednesday, 12 June, they were at London (some of them, anyway, the others having dispersed to carry the insurgency to other locales): the Essex rebels at Mile End, the Kentish rebels at Blackheath. The king and his advisers saw that it was time to do something, and so they secured themselves in the Tower, from which they would venture several times, uncertainly, in the days to follow. By this time the violence was reaching other counties. On Thursday, 13 June—the feast of the Lord's body—Suffolk rebels under the leadership of the priest John Wrawe attacked the abbey of Bury St. Edmunds and with the apparent support of the town's burgesses executed the prior of the monastery and Sir John Cavendish CJ. On Friday, 14 June, the tenants of a great house nearer London, St. Albans, confronted their lord the abbot with their demands and sent a delegation to meet with the rebel leaders in the capital. Cambridge colleges were attacked; so was Dunstable abbey; and so were dozens of royal and manorial officials throughout the southern and eastern counties, as far west as Somerset, as far north as Derby. (There were also urban risings, not obviously connected with what was happening in the south, in York, Scarborough, and Beverley.)

But it was in London that the rebellion became the nightmare that the chroniclers remembered. The king's move to the Tower was preparation for his first attempt to deal with the rebels. On Thursday morning he sailed from the Tower to Greenwich, where the Kentish band had moved to meet him. At the sight of the crowd on shore, gathered to demand the execution of certain traitors, Richard, or his advisers, or all of them, quailed and returned to their stronghold. Then—the consequences of this act would become clear over the next two days—the rebels moved toward London. Someone for some reason opened London Bridge to them, and someone opened Aldgate. Some of the rebels (everyone later tried to blame everyone else) attacked and burned the Savoy, John of Gaunt's local residence; later they moved to the Temple and plundered it (they pointedly had not plundered the Savoy); they broke prisons and released the inmates; and they surrounded the Tower, where the king was hiding. Richard tried again to negotiate with them. He learned that they were demanding charters abolishing serfdom and that they could not be bought off with less. They again demanded the traitors.

Chief among those whose deaths they required were Simon Sudbury (the king's chancellor and the archbishop of Canterbury) and Robert Hales (the king's treasurer and prior in England of the Knights Hospitaller). On a generous reading of the king's actions, he tried the next day to let Hales and Sudbury escape by diverting the crowd; on a less generous reading, he sacrificed them. In any case he met the Essex insurgents, by agreement, at their Mile End encampment on Friday morning, 14 June. After he left the Tower, some rebels entered, seized Hales and Sudbury as "traitors, despoilers of the commons," and beheaded them on Tower Hill, along with the wealthy Franciscan physician Sir William Appleton; their heads ended up on display where the heads of traitors belonged, on London Bridge. Meanwhile the rebels at Mile End were asking the king again for an end to villeinage, a fixed rent of 4*d*. per acre, and charters confirming both grants. Richard agreed, with less ambiguity than he had to their demand for Sudbury and Hales. Chancery worked late that night, turning out copies of this charter (which circulated for months afterward, causing no end of trouble to lords throughout England); these were to be given to representatives of each village, on the understanding that the other insurgents were to return home.

That was to take care of half the rebels in London; and getting them out of London was evidently what the king and his advisers wanted; the city's safety and their own depended on it, and so did any possibility of quelling the violence in the counties. But the Kentish band was still at Blackheath, and Richard met with them on neutral territory, at Smithfield, on Saturday, 15 June. Wat Tyler spoke for the insurgents. He elaborated the demands of the previous day: abolition of villeinage, fixed rents, disendowment and dispersal of church goods, rationalization of the church hierarchy (one bishop thenceforth), abolition of outlawry, equality of status, and "no law but the law of Winchester." Something happened; William Walworth (mayor of London and, minutes later, *Sir* William Walworth) attacked Tyler and fatally wounded him. Richard, in a moment beloved of the chroniclers, rode before the rebels declaring himself their new captain, and led them to Clerkenwell. Walworth took the opportunity to muster London citizens to the king's defense; they surrounded the rebels and escorted them at the king's orders back to Kent. Richard immediately began appointing commissions for the pacification of the city and the counties and for the prosecution of the rebels. London was his first care; and while he was at work there, Bishop Despenser of Norwich freelanced his way through East Anglia doing what he liked best, confronting the enemy in open battle; the rebels he caught were summarily executed. After a week the king began his perambulation of the home counties, overseeing the suppression of the rebellion in Essex, and arrived, on 12 July, at St. Albans in Hertfordshire, where Tresilian CJ was leading the judicial inquiries. It was at St. Albans that John Ball—the chaplain from Colchester who preached equality to the insurgents at Blackheath—was tried, drawn, hanged, and quartered. The royal charters of manumission were of course revoked. The judicial commissions went on for months, as did sporadic acts of rebellion; but by the beginning of July, the government had resumed its work, and the rebels left alive had gone back to theirs.

Those, in brief and crude summary, are the events of the rising of 1381, but this book is only eccentrically about the events. It is rather about six short texts, which I transcribe in the first pages of chapter 1; though now that the project is finished, I see that it is only eccentrically about them as well. These vernacular pieces, preserved in two contemporary chronicles, originated among the rebels themselves around the time of the rising.[2] The mere existence of such texts is extraordinary, and offers extraordinary opportunities: to understand the thought of a rural revolt and of the rural communities that produced it; to trace what the English vernacular meant to those who spoke nothing else, and what writing meant to those who were not thought to read; to observe, from a startling angle, the development of vernacular literature, in the more usual and canonical sense of that word.

If these claims mingle political interests conventionally thought leftist with scholarly interests conventionally thought conservative, that is a part of my point, though I think neither designation interesting or accurate. To explain what I have meant to do in this book, it may help to begin with the final chapter. Chapter 5 describes how the rebellion was remembered by those who made the literature of Ricardian England, its historiographical literature and its poetry—Thomas Walsingham, John Gower, Geoffrey Chaucer, William Langland—and how they worked to contain the threat it posed to the privileges they enjoyed and

2. That these six texts are authentic—that they are what they claim to be, that they originated among the rebels, and that they reproduce the rebels' words with tolerable accuracy—is a contestable assumption, though it has only once been contested in print. Both internal and external evidence fully support it; that evidence will emerge in the first pages of ch. 1, and I address the question of authenticity directly in n. 28 of that chapter.

the literary vocations they pursued. This procedure will have a familiar ring for many, since it has been for a decade the procedure of choice for literary historicisms suspicious of a literary and historiographical record that purveys, after all, not "history," but only representation. But I hope it will matter that chapter 5 follows on four others, which describe a political culture in the countryside that the lords and chroniclers and poets barely knew *of* before the events of 1381 exploded it in their faces, and which, even then, they could not *know*; I hope that I will have reversed the usual perspective, will have viewed our canonical literature from its social outside, from great regions of rural experience and practice, so that its picture of the rebellion seems no longer an irresistible empire, but an anxious and sometimes ignorant attempt to compass what it did not understand.

The historian can look not only for the cunning of power, but also for its stupidity, or at least its lapses; to put it another way, circumstances sometimes allow us to call a representation not only a representation, but a mistake. (Such a mistake, made by the chronicler Henry Knighton in recording five of the six texts that concern me, begins my discussion in chapter 1.) And I'd suggest that this quaintly empirical judgment opens up more interpretative possibilities than it closes down, gives us more to interpret and more ways of doing it. The Foucauldian gloom of some recent historicisms—even those concerned to qualify or re-nounce their Foucauldianism—is self-imposed, restricted as they generally are to the traditional texts of literary study and an unwavering focus on their interpretation. Two pieces from the January 1990 *Speculum*, whose presentation of a "new philology" was haunted by the epistemological questions of the "new historicism," may help make my point. The first is from Lee Patterson, one of the most energetic and accomplished of our new literary historians, who has found worthy of celebration the "postmodern" insistence that "culture" be "no longer construed solely in terms of artistic masterworks."[3] But the drift of the proposals Patterson then offers for the deghettoization of medieval studies—"designing lecture series, conferences, and seminars that would attract nonmedievalists"; "encouraging nonmedievalists to teach medieval courses"; rejecting the isolation that follows from taking "interdisciplinary" as "a term of approbation"[4]—raises some questions. The

3. Patterson, "On the Margin: Postmodernism, Ironic History, and Medieval Studies," *Speculum* 65 (1990): 88.
4. Patterson, 104–5.

problem with our scholarship, he suggests, the obstacle blocking our participation in the wider culture of English departments, is the metastasis of preparatory disciplines that absorb the medievalist's time and attention: "not just languages, but paleography, philology, codicology, diplomatics, and a wide range of research techniques are thought to be essential possessions of the aspiring medievalist. . . . better to be dull than 'unsound.'" "That such a shift of emphasis" away from these disciplines, he concedes, "might well mean that students who know more about the human sciences as a whole will now know less about the Middle Ages is of course a cause for concern"; but "the alternative—remaining with the status quo—is impossible."[5] Since paleography and codicology had disappeared from the teaching of medieval literature at most North American universities before I began graduate school in 1980 (my hands had held my Ph.D. before they ever held a medieval manuscript), I assume that they do metaphorical duty for a whole cargo of what Patterson takes to be stultifying empiricist concerns. But I would suggest that it is precisely this sort of anti-empiricist mainstreaming that would leave us with a conception of medieval culture "constituted solely in terms of artistic masterworks" and conducted in the familiar ways.

Why it would do so is suggested in a passage from another article in the "new philology" issue. Discussing the claims of historical evidence in medieval literary and cultural studies, Gabrielle Spiegel briefly concedes a kind of priority to literary over other sorts of history: "While the [literary] text is an objective given, an existing artifact (in its material existence if not in its constitution as a specifically 'literary' work), the object of historical study must be constituted by the historian long before its meaning can begin to be disengaged."[6] Of course, there is an important sense in which this is true. But the assertion that the text—whether literary or historiographical—exists in any usable sense before it is constituted is just wrong. Some scholars constitute their texts for themselves; most of us work most of the time with texts constituted for us, first of all by those generations of scholars who have used "paleography, philology, codicology, diplomatics, and a wide range of research techniques" to edit texts, date them, place them, to render them comprehensible, usable, and accessible. My first point is that without these

5. Patterson, 106.

6. Spiegel, "History, Historicism, and the Social Logic of the Text in the Middle Ages," *Speculum* 65 (1990): 75.

disciplines, we remain bound to what has already been found appropriate for study; only by their practice can new material, or new sorts of material, become available for reflection, and the field itself be reconstituted to compass the lives or words of those who have not been thought worthy of publication. As long as canonical texts set the agenda of research, as long as they dominate the field of attention, "the middle ages" will be, at least for the literary historian, what canonical authors made it.

The second point is that these empirical disciplines (and I'll make free to call them *materialist* disciplines) can help us reconstitute not only the array of texts we might come to know, but also the texts we know already: they can become the tools of a skeptical historicism because they describe the material conditions of writing and mark the material limits of representation. The disciplines that search out the matter of which texts were made—the language, the hand, the book—insist on every text's secular character, its life as an object and an event constrained by moment, money, place, ideology, and body. They can also reveal the origins and dimensions and consequences of "mistakes" like Knighton's. This kind of "mistake" is of course something familiar to recent historicism and theory: it is the fissure, the gap, the aporia that registers the bafflement of discourse at its own contradictions. But fissures and gaps are things that one can see through and past. It is an antique and discredited faith that thinks writing transparent to reality; but it is merely a newer faith that thinks the fissure merely a witness to writing's opacity, without noting that the fissure is itself a break in that opacity. If we allow ourselves the antiquarian privilege of seeing representation as mistake, we can see it also as parapraxis: the slip of the tongue or of the pen that betrays not only the fact of repression (in both senses), and not only its incompleteness, and not only the anxieties that caused it— what recent literary historicisms have felt able to describe—but also, to a degree, its content, the repressed matter itself. No more than maybe a dozen of the following pages are "paleographical" in even the most casual sense, and there is one paragraph of brutally generalized dialectology. But these are pages that show (that showed me, at least) where the questions could be asked. Knighton slipped: and a whole world opens up, a rural political culture whose ideology was not only the ideology given it from above, whose deliberations were protected by the ignorance of its lords and can be discerned through the ignorance of its chroniclers. That known, the act of representation in historiographical and literary sources can be seen as something not just made but *being* made, made under the circumstances it has encountered and therefore altering to meet them; altering even the sources' own understanding of themselves.

I had not meant to write this book. It began as a few pages in another, longer book I am still working at, on the development of vernacular writing in Ricardian England. In June 1990 I chose to start my summer with those few pages, a small and well-defined task meant to give me some momentum; by August the first three chapters had written themselves (that is really the only way to describe it). Now that it has finished and I can be allowed an opinion on the subject, I can see a few things that ought to have been done differently or that need some explanation.

Most of all, if I had known where the argument of chapter 4 would go, I would have worked through the holdings of local record offices, especially manorial court rolls from Essex and Kent in the later fourteenth century. As it is, my arguments about the character of local political society rely on those rolls that have been edited and published, which are typically from the thirteenth century and from all over England. Earlier court rolls have enjoyed publication for good reasons; the entries are fuller and of more concentrated interest. It is unfortunate that the editing of such rolls for publication has almost ceased, for these documents are the stuff from which a new social history might be made. Easy for me to say, of course (since I am a literary historian and can never be expected to do it myself), but a historian wearied by the thought of another study of demographic patterns in a West Midlands village, or the career of another fourteenth-century bishop, might consider the usefulness of preparing such an edition. Edwin Brezette DeWindt's recent publication of the Ramsey rolls, with the introductory matter printed and the rolls themselves on microfiche, shows how interesting a centuries-long stretch of rolls can be (and how they can sensibly and affordably be published).[7] Similarly, L. R. Poos's study of Essex after the plague shows how information drawn from manorial records can be elaborated into a portrait of local culture.[8]

The ambition to escape the confines of "representation" has entailed

7. DeWindt, *The Court Rolls of Ramsey, Hepmangrove, and Bury, 1268–1600* (Toronto, 1990).

8. Poos, *A Rural Society after the Black Death: Essex 1350–1525* (Cambridge, Eng., 1991).

some perhaps eccentric treatment of evidence in this book, especially of the fourteenth-century chronicles. Without any articulated decision, without even any very extended argument, study of the revolt has come almost to ignore chronicle narratives in favor of judicial evidence. This historiographic turn has produced brilliant results for understanding the economic conditions that obtained, the social composition of the rebel bands, and the chronology of the rising itself; but something has also been lost, a curiosity about what drove the rebels, about what they thought and what they wanted.[9] There have been reasons for the turn. A more thorough recognition of the ideologically generated tendentiousness of the chronicles is the most important, along with a corresponding uncertainty of how we might then use them. These concerns are neither misplaced nor superficial: when a great and skeptical textual critic implies that we can take rough account of the chroniclers' distortions by trusting every second assertion,[10] we might feel that some thinking wants to be done. I cannot claim to have contrived a method (certainly not a theory) for interpreting historiographic narratives. Throughout I try to make clear why I accept particular narrations as approximately and usably factual. The efficacy of my treatment will appear (or not appear) cumulatively, in the persuasiveness (or lack of it) of particular readings, not in any theoretical or methodological justification; but the Epilogue offers a retrospective meditation on my procedures.

One assumption of this book is that taciturn records can be squeezed until they talk. But still, once squeezed, they can only say so much, and one of my persistent difficulties was deciding how far I should try to make the rebels live. The judicial records give us hundreds of names and dozens of isolated incidents attached to them. Most of them have been preserved for history at the single moment they assaulted a sheriff, or broke a house, or "joined"—simply—the burning of the Savoy; then they vanish. I decided against giving a probably spurious sense of

---

9. I could cite many examples, and all of them will appear eventually in the footnotes; a metonymic one, however, might be the indispensable *Past and Present* volume, *The English Rising of 1381*, ed. R. H. Hilton and T. H. Aston (Cambridge, 1984), whose index includes only three references to John Ball.

10. "And if only half of what the *Historia Anglicana* reports about John Ball and Walter Tyler is true, . . . Ball was to be sole archbishop of England, Tyler to be King of Kent, Litster King of Norfolk" (George Kane, "Some Fourteenth-Century 'Political' Poems," in Gregory Kratzmann and James Simpson, eds., *Medieval English Religious and Ethical Literature: Essays in Honour of G. H. Russell* [Cambridge, Eng., 1986], 83).

immediacy and concreteness by naming many of these names or by piggybacking on the work of Christopher Dyer and Andrew Prescott, who have worked back from indictments to manorial records and constructed short biographies of a few. Only in the aggregate do the rebels stay in sight long enough to be looked at carefully. I have talked about them mostly as a group, and that raises a question that has been asked by many who read the manuscript or heard my lectures on the topic: when I speak of "the rebels" as intending this or that, or possessing this or that form of knowledge, or carrying out this or that disciplined or ideologically informed act, whom do I mean? Leaving that question unanswered is a part of my point. It was the opinion of most contemporary chroniclers that the insurgents and their leaders were stupid, perverse, gullible, or out for booty or fun; it has been the opinion of modern historians (speaking in varying tones of voice) that the leaders were ideologically motivated, charismatic, and reasonably consistent, and that the rest were stupid, perverse, gullible, or out for booty or fun. The rising did produce acts of violence that seem to have been, from the point of view of its own articulated ideology, gratuitous or meaningless; in London, particularly, many grudges seem to have been pursued in the days of unrestraint, and in the insurgent counties opportunities for profit were occasionally seized. What is remarkable is the consistency and point of so many actions. Some of the mechanisms of insurgent discipline and information will be described in the chapters to follow; but it is impossible to know much. Look on the book, if you like, as a thought experiment: what might the rising look like if we resist infection from the panic of the chroniclers and assume a maximum (rather than the customary minimum) of discipline, consistency, purpose, and information on the part of those who made it?[11]

Concerning quotation of sources: those given in the text (with a very few exceptions) are always given in translation, and the originals in the notes (all translations, except those explicitly attributed, are my own);

11. As I was preparing this book for press, two very important essays appeared: Richard Firth Green, "John Ball's Letters: Literary History and Historical Literature," in Barbara A. Hanawalt, ed., *Chaucer's England: Literature in Historical Context* (Minneapolis, 1992), 176–200, and Paul Strohm, "'A Revelle!': Chronicle Evidence and the Rebel Voice," in his *Hochon's Arrow: The Social Imagination of Fourteenth-Century Texts* (Princeton, 1992), 33–56. Both are major contributions to the understanding of the rebellion, and I wish that I had known both earlier; as it is, I address some of the issues they raise in the footnotes, and discuss some of Strohm's claims in the Epilogue.

when, however, I quote a source only in the notes—corroborative or elaborative of a point in the text—I quote it in the original. Middle English sources appear without helps. But these consist mainly of the six rebel texts, which will become very familiar very quickly to anyone who keeps reading; Chaucer, probably familiar already to most of my readers; and Langland, who is available in the helpfully glossed editions of Schmidt (B-text) and Pearsall (C-text) and in two responsible translations (Goodridge and Donaldson, both of the B-text).

I

Insurgent Literacy

First the texts. They conclude the narrative of the rising in Henry Knighton's chronicle: "There were 20,000 men in this crowd of rebels. These were their leaders: Thomas Baker (the first mover and afterwards principal leader of the revolt), Jack Straw, Jack Milner, Jack Carter, Jack Trewman. Jack Milner spoke thus to his fellows":[1]

jakke mylner asket help to turne hys mylne aright. he hath grounden smal smal. þe kynges sone of heuen he schal pay for alle. loke þi mylne go ary3t. wiþ þe foure sayles. and þe post stande in stedefastnesse. wiþ ry3t & with my3t. wiþ skyl and wiþ wylle. lat my3t helpe ry3t. and skyl go before wille. and ry3t befor my3t. þan goth oure mylne aryght. and if my3t go before ryght. and wylle before skylle. lo. þan is oure mylne mys ady3t.

                                                                    (Henceforth Milner)

Jak Carter jakke carter preyes 3owe alle. þat 3e make a gode ende. of þat 3e haue begunnen. and doþ wele and ay bettur and bettur. for at þe euen men hery[e]þ þe day. ffor if þe ende be wele. þan is alle wele. lat peres þe plowman my broþur. duelle at home and dy3t vs corne. and i wil go wiþ 3owe and helpe þat y may to dy3te 3oure mete and 3oure drynke. þat 3e none fayle. lokke þat hobbe robbyoure be wele chastysede for lesyng of 3oure grace. for [3e] haue gret nede to take god wiþ 3owe in alle 3oure dedes. ffor nowe is tyme to be ware.

                                                                    (Carter)

Jak trewman jakke trewman doþ 3ow to understande þat falsnes and gyle haviþ regned to longe & trewþe. hat bene sette under a lokke. and fal[s]nes regneth in euerylk flokke. no man may come trewþe to. but he syng si dedero. speke. spende and spede. quoth jon of bamthon. and þerfore synne fareth as wylde flode. trew loue is away. þat was so gode and clerkus for welthe worche hem wo. god do bote for now3e is tyme.

                                                                    (Trewman)

1. "In illa misera multitudine recensebantur xx. mille. Isti fuerunt ductores eorum, Thomas Baker primus motor sed postea principalis ductor, Jakke Strawe, Jakke Mylner, Jakke Carter, Jakke Trewman. Jakke Mylner alloquitur socios sic" (*Chronicon Henrici Knighton*, ed. Joseph Rawson Lumby, RS 92 [London, 1895], 2:138).

Exemplar epi*stole* johan*n*is balle. Jon Balle gretyth ȝow wele alle & doþ
ȝowe to understande. he haþ runge*n* ȝoure belle. nowe ryȝt & myȝt.
wylle and skylle. god spede every [dele]. Nowe is tyme lady helpe to ih*es*u

4   þi sone. and þi sone to his fadur. to mak a gode ende. in þe name of þe
tri*n*ite. of þat [þat] is begu*n*ne. ame*n* ame*n* pur charite ame*n*.

(Ball₁)

Pri*m*a epi*sto*la johan*n*is Balle. John balle seynte marye pr*i*st greteȝ wele
alle man*er* me*n* & byddes he*m* in þe name of the tri*n*ite. fadur and sone
and holy gost. stonde manlyche togedyr in trewþe. and helpeȝ trewþe.

4   and trewþe schal helpe ȝowe. Nowe regneþ pr*i*de in pr*i*s. and couetys is
hold wys. and lecherye wiþ[outen shame] and glotonye withoute*n* blame
Enuye regniþ wiþ tresone. and slouthe is take in grete sesone. god do
bote. for nowe is tyme ame*n*.

(Ball₂)²

A sixth appears in Thomas Walsingham's chronicle, but not in Knighton's. Walsingham says that John Ball, the chaplain from Colchester,
"sent a certain letter, full of riddles, to the leaders of the commons in
Essex, urging them to finish what they had begun. It was later found in
the garment of a man about to be hanged for rioting, and its sense was
this":³

li*ter*a johan*n*is balle. missa comm*un*ibus estsexie
Johon schep som tyme seynte marie prest of ȝork. and now of colchestre.
Greteth wel johan nameles and joha*n* þe mullere and johon carter and

4   biddeþ hem þat þei bee war of gyle in borugh and stondeþ [togidere] in

2. Transcriptions from BL MS Cotton Tiberius C.viii, fol. 174a. All punctuation marks
from the manuscript (as also for the Walsingham transcription below), including emphatic
spacing, are given as low points. Boldface indicates material rubricated or underscored in
the original; italics and brackets indicate expanded contractions and editorial emendations,
respectively. I give no variants from the other Leicester Abbey manuscript of Knighton's
chronicle, Cotton Claudius E.iii, fol. 296b, because it is a direct copy of the Tiberius and
therefore without independent value. These texts transcribed here are printed, but quite
inadequately edited, in Lumby's edition, 138–40 (Lumby used the Claudius as his copy
text because it had been less badly damaged in the Cotton library fire); I have also taken
the opportunity to check them, and the text transcribed from Walsingham below, with
the edition by Green, "John Ball's Letters," 193–95.

Carter 3 heryeþ] MS heryþ
Trewman 3 falsnes] MS falnes
Ball₁ 3 every dele] MS every ydele; 5 þat þat is] MS þat is
Ball₂ 5 lecherye wiþouten schame and *Lumby*] MS lechery wiþ and *but marked for
correction*

3. "Miserat insuper ductoribus communium in Estsexia quandam literam aenigmatibus plenam, ad hortandum eos ut incepta perficerent; quae ex post inventa est in manica
cujusdam suspendendi pro turbatione praefata, cujus tenor talis est" (*Chronicon Angliae*,
ed. Edward Maunde Thompson, RS 64 [London, 1874], 322).

godes name. and biddeþ Peres plou3man. go to his werk. and chastise
wel hobbe þe robbere. and takeþ wiþ 3ow joh*a*n trewman and alle hijs
felawes and no mo. and loke schappe 3ou to on heued and no mo. joh*a*n
þe mullere haþ ygrounde smal smal smal þe kynges sone of heuene schal   8
paye for al. be war or [3]e be wo knoweþ 3our frend fro 3our foo. haueth
ynow. & seith hoo. and do wel and bettre and fleth synne. and sekeþ pees
and hold 3ou þer inne. and so biddeþ joh*a*n trewaman and alle his felawes.

(Ball₃)⁴

Walsingham continues: "John Ball confessed that he wrote this letter
and sent it to the commons, and that he made many others as well. For
which reason, as I said before, he was drawn, hanged, and beheaded
before the king at St. Albans, the ides of July; and his body was quartered
and sent to four cities of the kingdom."[5]

Who wrote them?[6] The question seems unpromising: quaintly empirical
and in any case insoluble. And it has not seemed to require an answer;
a casual, sane, but possibly mistaken scholarly consensus has assigned
all six to the hand of the enigmatic priest John Ball, writing both under
his own name and under the pseudonyms of Milner and the rest.[7]
Among historians medieval and modern, only Henry Knighton claims

---

4. Text transcribed from BL Royal MS 13.E.ix, fol. 287a; printed *Chronicon*, 322.

3 togidere] MS togidedre 9 3e] MS þe

5. "Hanc literam idem Johannes Balle confessus est se scripsisse, et communibus
transmisisse, et plura alia fatebatur et fecit; propter quae, ut diximus, tractus, suspensus,
et decollatus est apud Sanctum Albanum idibus Julii, praesente rege, et cadaver ejus
quadripartitum quatuor regni civitatibus missum est" (*Chronicon*, 322).

6. There can be no real question of their authenticity; see n. 28 below.

7. Most important, Konrad Burdach, *Der Dichter des Ackermann aus Böhmen und seine
Zeit*, vol. 3 of *Vom Mittelalter zur Reformation: Forschungen zur Geschichte der deutschen
Bildung* (Berlin, 1926); despite this faulty assumption, Burdach's discussion of the rebel
letters (167–203) is, along with that of Oscar Eberhard (see ch. 2, n. 21), the only extensive
study of them, and it is without measure the best. See also R. H. Hilton and H. Fagan,
The English Rising of 1381 (London, 1950), 100; Rodney Hilton, *Bond Men Made Free:
Medieval Peasant Movements and the English Rising of 1381* (New York, 1973), 214; R. M.
Wilson, *The Lost Literature of Medieval England*, 2d ed. (London, 1970), 196–97; R. B.
Dobson, *The Peasants' Revolt of 1381* (London, 1970), 379–80; and Anne Hudson, "Epilogue: The Legacy of *Piers Plowman*," in John A. Alford, ed., *A Companion to Piers
Plowman* (Berkeley and Los Angeles, 1988), 251–52. Rossell Hope Robbins does not commit
himself, but patently thinks so as well (in Albert E. Hartung, ed., *A Manual of the Writings
in Middle English* [New Haven, 1975], 1511–12). The assumption seems to be borrowed
from Walsingham, who does not say this in so many words, but reports Ball as confessing
to "many other" letters; this does not of course mean the other letters that have survived,
but, as will appear below, there is evidence that he did see at least one other, and that it
resembled a couple that appear in Knighton.

that four different rebels produced these texts; but a similar presupposition drives even his conclusion. The documents appear in the manuscripts of Knighton's chronicle as I have rendered them above: recorded in series, each headed by the name of a rebel, and without narratorial interruption. He introduces them by saying, "Jack Milner addressed [*alloquitur*] his companions thus." Knighton takes the words of Jack Milner to have been *spoken* to the assembled rebels (he has just mentioned a plenary meeting of "twenty thousand"). The same assumption seems to govern his report of the two that follow, which (like Milner's) he rubricates only with the names "Jakke Carter" and "Jakke Trewman": they too, Knighton takes it, are transcripts of spoken addresses.[8] Yet all three of them not only take epistolary form—beginning with the name of the signatory, followed by a greeting, request, or command—but are formally indistinguishable from the compositions ascribed to John Ball, both of which the rubrics (Knighton's own) identify as *epistolae*.[9] What Knighton can recognize as a letter when signed by John Ball he mistakes for a speech when signed by Jack Milner, Jack Carter, or Jack Trewman. Some category of discrimination has clicked in his mind, making difference where there is none.

The difference, of course, is that John Ball was—and was known to Knighton to be—a priest,[10] while the surnames of the three Jacks indicate (or at least tendentiously avow) that they are not just laity, but laborers. Knighton could not see how these five texts were the same because he knew they had to be different, knew that no layperson could write a

8. The assumption is repeated by Wells in the original *Manual of Writing in Middle English 1050–1400* (New Haven, 1916): "In Knighton's *Cronicon* under 1381, are three short English prose addresses . . . declared to have been delivered in London by the insurgent leaders, Jack Milner, Jack Carter and Jack Trueman . . . and along with them are a letter . . . purported to be from John Ball" (218). This description is corrected in Robbins's revised account in Hartung, *Manual* (New Haven, 1975), 1511. Wendy Scase also thinks them oral productions, calling them "the songs of the rebels" (*Piers Plowman and the New Anticlericalism* [Cambridge, Eng., 1989], 72).

9. They are his own rubrics in the sense that he himself included them: V. H. Galbraith follows Twysden, arguing persuasively that the manuscript "if not quite the author's autograph was nevertheless made under his direction" ("The Chronicle of Henry Knighton," in D. J. Gordon, ed., *Fritz Saxl . . . a Volume of Memorial Essays* [London, 1957], 142); see also Maude V. Clarke, "Henry Knighton and the Library Catalogue of Leicester Abbey," *EHR* 45 (1930): 103–7. Knighton, however, did not author these rubrics, as I argue below.

10. "Quidam Johannes Balle capellanus" is how Knighton introduces him to the narrative (Knighton, *Chronicon*, 131).

letter.[11] The priest writes and the rural laity speak; it is the way of the world.[12] The certainty that writing was what clerks did amounted in medieval England to what Kenneth Burke has called a "psychosis"—a systematic blindness productive of institutional stamina[13]—and Knighton draws his distinction between orality and writing across pretty undifferentiated written terrain in order to preserve it: John Ball wrote, while Milner, Carter, and Trewman spoke. And the distinction apparently survived Knighton. The historians who settle the authorship of all six texts on the cleric John Ball, unable to deny that "Milner," "Carter," and "Trewman" are letters, deny that Milner, Carter, and Trewman— laypeople, whatever their real names—wrote them. They, like Knighton, expect to find literacy only under a tonsure.

The suspicious thing about this assumption that clerics wrote and other people didn't is not that it makes no sense, but that it makes too much, tallies too well with the story that chroniclers and royal justices wanted to tell. Lee Patterson has recently observed that monastic chroniclers deny the rebels the marks even of fundamental human reasonability.[14] In the imaginative lexicon of the chroniclers, as of medieval latinity in general, the embodiment par excellence of reason is writing,[15] and their narratives of the rising are black fantasias about the victimization of written culture and its agents at the hands of those who could not coherently speak (much less think or write) and who could look at writing only with a rage for its destruction. The rebels in John Gosford's account of the revolt at Bury St. Edmunds act in a kind of bacchantic idiocy during their search for the prior of the abbey, obses-

---

11. It is the difference M. T. Clanchy summarizes in coupling the opposition *clericus:laicus* with the opposition *litteratus:illitteratus* (*From Memory to Written Record: England, 1066–1307* [Cambridge, Mass., 1979], 178).

12. The *rural* laity not only was included in this assumption, but was symbolic of it. Brian Stock points out that one of the antonyms for *litteratus* after 1100 was *rusticus*: "The *rusticus* was not only a serf, a villein, or simply a peasant; to speak *rustico more* was to communicate in an unlearned tongue for which there was no written counterpart based on grammatical rules" (*The Implications of Literacy: Written Language and Models of Interpretation in the Eleventh and Twelfth Centuries* [Princeton, 1983], 27).

13. "Given any pronounced social structure, there will be a 'psychosis' corresponding to it. That is, there will be a particular recipe of overstressings and understressings peculiar to the given institutional structure. And the tendency of the culture will be to see everything in terms of this particular recipe of emphases" (Burke, *A Grammar of Motives* [Berkeley and Los Angeles, 1969], 113).

14. Patterson, *Chaucer and the Subject of History* (Madison, 1991), 272–73.

15. Stock notes the high- and late-medieval "notion that literacy is identical with rationality" (*Implications of Literacy*, 31).

sively repeating the word "traitor"; when he is finally found and his head brought back, the townspeople cheer, "barking to each other."[16] Walsingham's final summary of the rebellion is this:

> Were they not full of devils, they would never have conspired to destroy holy church and the Christian faith, or worked for the destruction of the kingdom. . . . They must be judged by their works, because they murdered the father of the whole clergy, the head of the English church, the archbishop of Canterbury. What else did they do to damage the faith? They forced the teachers of grammar to swear that they would never again teach that art. What further did they do? They worked to give old muniments over to the flames; and lest someone might again be found who would be able to remember the old customs, or new ones, they killed all such. It was dangerous to be known a cleric; much more dangerous to be found with an inkwell: such rarely or never escaped their hands.[17]

Walsingham's rhetorical crescendo *begins* with the lynching of Archbishop Sudbury and intensifies until it reveals the most chilling of insurgent offenses, their attack on writing and writers. His rhetoric portrays the fury of the rebels as a ressentiment against writing itself. Walsingham imagines writing as a single thing that unites all forms of authority, manorial and state and ecclesiastical, and distinguishes them all from the mute idiocy of the peasant: even the attack on grammar masters and court rolls is action meant "to damage the faith" (*in fidei . . . detrimentum*). Both Walsingham and Knighton present the burning of documents as the wild efflux of rebellious mania, exemplifying and symbolizing peasant unfitness for meaningful action, for the ordered rationality of the writing at which they could only rage. However considerable John Ball's perversities to the minds of the chroniclers, they still allowed him literacy, indeed required it: "He taught the perverse doctrines of the treacherous John Wyclif, and the opinions he held, the false insanities, and more, which it would be long to recite," Walsingham

16. "Latrantes inter se invicem" ("Collectanea fratris Andreae Astone, Hostiarii Sancti Edmundi," *Memorials of St. Edmund's Abbey*, ed. Thomas Arnold, RS 96 [London, 1896], 3:127–28). On the authorship of this short chronicle (the *Electio Johannis Timworth*), see Antonia Gransden, *Historical Writing in England* (Ithaca, 1982) 2:166n.

17. "In fidei quoque detrimentum quid fecerunt? Magistros scholarum grammaticalium jurare compulerunt, se nunquam parvulos instructuros in arte praefata. Amplius quid fecerunt? Munimenta vetera studuerunt dare flammis; et ne de novo quis reperiri valeret qui vetera sive nova de cetero posset, vel nosset, commendare memoriae, hujusmodi trucidabant. Periculosum erat agnosci pro clerico, sed multo periculosius, si ad latus alicujus atramentarium inventum fuisset; nam tales vix aut nunquam ab eorum manibus evaserunt" (*Chronicon*, 308).

says,[18] and for Knighton, Ball was Wyclif's precursor, his John the Baptist:[19] a heretic, and therefore a known quantity, one whose perversity had at least rhythm and method, and therefore a category as well. A heretical cleric, rebellious and willful but within the pale of theological discourse and institutional expectation, could be imagined an author as no miller or carter could be.

But while Knighton is certainly wrong (in calling speeches what are clearly letters), must Petit-Dutaillis, Burdach, and Hilton also be wrong (in saying that Ball wrote them all)? That a chronicler could find it difficult to imagine peasants as authors does not, after all, mean that they *were* authors. Three kinds of evidence build a circumstantial case that more than one person was involved in the production of the letters. The first is simply retailed: while Walsingham and Knighton share the assumption that Ball was the one and only insurgent writer, they do not share it with the most nearly contemporary, and best informed, chronicle of the revolt, the one that originated around the court and has survived in the so-called *Anonimalle Chronicle* from York;[20] according to it, after the rebels of Essex made their first assault (and before they released Ball from prison), "The commons sent several letters to Kent, Suffolk, and Norfolk [urging them] to rise along with themselves."[21] Such a casual report cannot resolve the question—one cannot argue

18. "Docuit et perversa dogmata perfidi Johannis Wyclife, et opiniones quas tenuit, et insanias falsas, et plura, quae longum foret recitare" (Walsingham, *Chronicon*, 321).

19. "Hic [Wyclif] habuit praecursorem Johannem Balle, veluti Christus Johannem Baptistam, qui vias suas in talibus opinionibus praeparavit" (Knighton, *Chronicon*, 151).

20. Harriet Merete Hansen has launched the only real attack on the importance of the *Anonimalle Chronicle* ("The Peasants' Revolt of 1381 and the Chronicles," *Journal of Medieval History* 6 [1980]: 393–415), arguing that the London indictment of 20 November 1381 is, directly or indirectly, the source of every chronicle account. Her assumption that any coincidence between two accounts *must* indicate the derivation of one from the other, or of both from a common source, of course begs the question she poses. Her chart of relationships among the sources amounts to a ptolemaic system of epicycles saving the appearances of her premises.

21. "Puis les comunes manderent diverses lettres en Kent et en Southfolk et Northfolk pur lever ovesque eux" (*The Anonimalle Chronicle, 1333 to 1381*, ed. V. H. Galbraith [Manchester, 1927], 135). George Kriehn ("Studies in the Sources of the Social Revolt in 1381," *AHR* 7 [1901]: 266–68) originally suggested that the passage on the rebellion was lifted by the York chronicler from another source; Galbraith endorsed this opinion in the introduction to his edition (xxxiii–xxxiv, xliii–xlv), where he suggested that the author was Thomas Hoccleve, poet and privy-seal clerk. He has since withdrawn the suggestion and proposed instead William Pakington, keeper of the wardrobe in 1381, who was rumored by Leland to have chronicled English history from the reign of John to his present ("Thoughts about the Peasants' Revolt," in F. R. H. DuBoulay and Caroline M. Barron, eds., *The Reign of Richard II: Essays In Honour of May McKisack* [London, 1971], 48–51).

multiple authorship on the basis of a plural verb, or even assume that these "lettres" were necessarily like those the chronicles preserved—but the casualness itself is instructive: the chronicler can unreflectively think the *comunes* able to send (and receive, and construe) such letters. At the same time, he dates the appearance of *some* letters to the moment when Ball was incarcerated and presumably incommunicado.[22]

The second sort of evidence is more tenuous, and might seem at first to suggest common authorship rather than otherwise. This is a pattern of shared diction. The letters think in slogans and apothegms—"he hath grounden smal smal. þe kynges sone of heuen he schal pay for alle"; "wiþ ry3t & with my3t. wiþ skyl and wiþ wylle"; "make a gode ende"; "nowe is tyme"; "be ware"—phrases that are available to recombination and permutation because they are detachable and self-sufficient; they do not rely on narrative or sequential argument to give them their meaning. Across the corpus of the rebels' letters, the five in Knighton and the one in Walsingham, most such phrases in any given letter are duplicated, closely or approximately, in another (Trewman's is most independent). Three of these letters are signed by Ball, and three are pseudonymous.[23] The phrases in each of the three "lay" letters (as I will call them for the moment) that double phrases in another letter double only phrases in one of the three John Ball letters, and, with one exception, never phrases in the others. (The exception is "nowe is tyme.") Though the sample is small, the pattern is suggestive; one explanation is that the Ball letters were a source drawn on independently by the authors of the others. Then too, the similarities point up the differences: in Jack Carter's letter, the phrases "nowe is tyme" and "be ware" are combined to produce a meaning quite alien to what "nowe is tyme," with its call to action, means in the others: in them it celebrates opportunity, while in Carter's letter it warns of danger.[24] One guess these patterns might provoke is not that

22. There is also, entirely independent of the chronicle accounts, at least one 1381 indictment, from Estderham (Norfolk), that shows a letter used as an instrument of rebellion: "Item dicunt quod quidem Martinus Mannyngh manens in Sudberi misit litteras die et anno supra dictis apud Estderham per Robertum Agge de Yaxham [et al.] de eadem ex parte Johannis Wraw ut redderunt quoddam librum tenementum predicto Martino quequidem litere sunt in villa ista" (Edgar Powell, *The Rising of 1381 in East Anglia* [Cambridge, Eng., 1896], 133).

23. Of course the letter in Walsingham (Ball₃) formally gives as signatory "Johon Schep," but the information that follows ("somtyme seynt marie prest of 3ork and now of colchestre") effectively avows Ball's identity.

24. There is a similar, though more ambiguous case, in Ball₂ and Ball₃; see n. 29 below.

the letters issued from a common hand, nor (conversely) that they were produced independently of each other, but that an initial body of such letters incited a pattern of imitation, recombination, and distribution. This pattern of shared diction, of similarity and difference, suggests, though it does not of course prove, that the first letters, composed by John Ball and circulated perhaps among the commons of Kent, Suffolk, and Norfolk (as the *Anonimalle* claims), became the basis for a strange, and to Knighton unimaginable, epistolary practice among the rebels.[25]

The third piece of evidence is conclusive, in its way, and a little startling. The letters as they have come to us could not have issued from the same hand because they did not issue from the same dialect. Lumby's edition of Knighton's chronicle obscures this fact (though it does not efface it); Lumby chose as copy-text the Cotton Claudius manuscript rather than Knighton's own—Cotton Tiberius—of which the Claudius is a direct copy. The Tiberius is unambiguous on this point. In the matter of verb inflections, for example, Milner and Trewman favor the third singular indicative in *-t* and *-þ*, and Trewman the plural indicative in *-eþ*, while Carter shows the third singular in *-es* and the plural in *-eþ*. The Milner and Trewman inflections are characteristically southern forms; but Trewman also has the adjective *euerylk*, an unmistakably northern form which does, however, appear in Norfolk.[26] My point, however, is not to locate these texts by their dialectal differences, but to show what the differences mean. They do not necessarily mean separate authorship for these three "lay" letters: merely to notice the dialects

---

25. I wrote this passage before Green's "John Ball's Letters" appeared. The issue in this paragraph is complicated by Green's demonstration that many of these detachable phrases can be shown more or less persuasively to be related to sermon tag-verses; but it is not clear how it is complicated. Green takes it that the letters' relation to sermon verses confirms Ball's authorship of six (both because they suggest a technique common to all six and because a chaplain like Ball would be more likely than other rebels to collect such verses ["John Ball's Letters"]). This certainly is not an impossible conclusion, though some qualifications might be offered. As Green himself notes (183), such verses circulated in oral as well as written form; one of their functions was mnemonic, and one could know a certain repertory of such verses without possessing a collection of them, merely from hearing sermons. Whoever wrote the letters had presumably come to know some of the verses in this way; Green must cite over a dozen manuscripts to provide analogues for all the phrases in the letters (though it is not impossible that some one manuscript, now lost, contained them all). Green's argument nevertheless has force, and the scenario I am tentatively suggesting—that John Ball may have written the first letters and that other rebels may then have imitated what Ball wrote, borrowing elements from his and recombining them—fits with his evidence.

26. Angus McIntosh, M. L. Samuels, and Michael Benskin, *A Linguistic Atlas of Late Middle English* (Aberdeen, 1986) 2:47, 56, for the *-ilk* pronominal forms in Norfolk.

here is to shift the question to something other than authorship, something more directly of interest to the insurgent project. For while Milner, Carter, and Trewman vary among themselves, so do the John Ball letters. Ball₁ and Ball₃ have third singular indicatives in *-iþ* and *-eþ*, and Ball₃ the imperative in *-eþ*; Ball₂ has third singular indicatives in *-es* and imperatives in *-es*.[27] With the John Ball letters authorship is not in question: John Ball authored them. But he did not *write* the letters we have (at least not all of them): he did not hold the pen and make the marks on the copies that eventually reached Knighton and Walsingham.[28]

And that, I suggest, is what matters. Even if my guess above is wrong—that other insurgent authors employed John Ball's phrases and images in letters of their own—the letters were certainly and at least

27. The marks of dialectal instability within particular letters, like *regneþ* in Ball₂, do not affect the argument; they are only what one expects of a scribe, that he will regularize an alien dialect into his own, as the scribe of the Claudius manuscript of Knighton did, consistently, to all the letters; in Tiberius the scribe has normalized only spottily; what is astonishing is that he let the differences remain at all. One might explain away these dialectal differences by proposing that different (official) scribes, from different regions, copied the rebel letters into the form we have now, each regularizing the letters into his own dialect. This is not inherently impossible, but other internal evidence strongly suggests that this was not the case, as I argue below.

28. These dialectal relics have another consequence as well. One explanation of the letters has, for very good reasons, never been seriously offered in print (though it has been casually rebutted; Green, "John Ball's Letter's," 182): that they were a hoax, written by the chroniclers or someone else, presumably to mock or discredit the rebellion. That the chroniclers did not make them up is obvious enough: to suggest that they did, we would have to assume (since there is no evidence at all that Knighton knew anything of Walsingham's chronicling) that the two of them contrived independently the idea of foisting letters on the rebels; that Knighton wrote his letters without recognizing that he was writing letters; and that Walsingham, after finishing his, read it over and pronounced it *aenigmatibus plenam*. And it seems unlikely that Knighton would have introduced evidence of dialectal variation to authenticate his forgeries. It is similarly unlikely that someone else, for the same purpose, invented the letters that Knighton and Walsingham then copied, in good or bad faith: the dialectal differences pertain here too, as do questions of motive and effect. No one needed to "discredit" the rebellion, which was, to the mind of any imaginable chronicle reader, self-discrediting (for more on this point, see my Epilogue); and, though the letters were apparently introduced at Ball's trial, it would be naïve to assume that in order to hang Ball the justices *needed* any such evidence, and needed it badly enough to manufacture it. In any case, if the letters were manufactured, for either judicial or propaganda purposes, their author would surely have done a better, which is to say a more incriminating, job. Finally, the letters would have made for a very odd sort of propaganda, since (as I suggest at more length in chapter 5) one thing that everyone who wrote about the revolt wanted to be certain of was the absolute exclusion of the rebels from literacy and writing.

Some of these reasons also tell against Susan Crane's suggestion that the chroniclers, while not confecting the letters ex nihilo, were "reimagining rebel letters they saw or heard at an earlier time, using the topoi of clerical poetry" ("The Writing Lesson of 1381,"

copied and redistributed; the dialectal differences between the three John Ball letters put it beyond doubt that his letters were copied and recirculated by rebels other than himself.[29] But why? What and who were they for? One obvious procedure in answering such questions is to look for discursive connections, to listen for echoes of the letters in the actions of the rising, or for echoes of the actions in the letters. The destruction (on 13 June) of John of Gaunt's great London house, the Savoy, was one of the most memorable events of the rising, recorded by the chroniclers in punishing detail. It was also one of the most calculated: the insurgents carried out the destruction under severe discipline, forbidding themselves to plunder one of the richest palaces in the realm.[30] When one rebel tried to make away with some of the Lancastrian silver, the rest (Knighton says) threw him into the burning palace with indignant cries. Knighton's Latin version of their cry—*Zelatores veritatis et justitiae, non fures aut latrones*, "We are men zealous for truth and justice, not thieves or brigands"[31]—reflects the language of John Ball's three letters: "trewþe" (*veritatis*), "ryʒt" (*justitiae*), "robbere" (*fures*).[32] In this moment of choreographed discipline, the lan-

---

in Hanawalt, ed., *Chaucer's England*, 210). If this were the case, Knighton and Walsingham would then have "reimagined" them independently, the reimagination of each sounding very much like that of the other; Knighton would have reimagined what he thought were speeches, but accidentally given them epistolary form; and Knighton would have introduced the dialectal differences, though not consistently. Each of these is individually improbable; cumulatively, they seem nearly impossible.

29. One small difference between Ball$_2$ and Ball$_3$ may strengthen this assertion, though it is not as clear as the different uses of "nowe is tyme." An exhortation in Ball$_2$ ("stonde manlyche togedyr in trewþe") is closely paralled by one in Ball$_3$ ("stondeþ [togidere] in godes name"). I will suggest later that "in trewþe" has a force quite different from "in godes name"; this would suggest that the "scribe" of one letter understood the meaning of the exhortation quite differently from the "scribe" of the other. But since both are signed by John Ball, the variation (if it is a variation) must have been introduced by someone else, copying one of Ball's letters (and not under his supervision).

30. For a more extended discussion, see ch. 2 below.

31. "Unus autem illorum nefandorum sumpsit unam pulchram peciam argenteam, in gremioque abscondit, quod videns aliis et sociis referens, ipsum cum pecia in ignem projecerunt, dicentes, Zelatores veritatis et justitiae, non fures aut latrones" (Knighton, *Chronicon*, 135).

32. The testimony is the more credible because it is clear that Knighton is thinking of a phrase *in English*. "Trewþe," as we shall see—the only word he might have rendered as *veritas*—is a crucial term in the rising's vocabulary of self-description; it can be seen in the letters and in the reports of other chronicles. It is entirely believable that the rebels used it at this point. But in rebel usage, the word (ambiguous in ME as it only archaically is in ModE) invariably has a meaning rendered better by L *fides* than by *veritas*. "Robbere," though of course a concrete personal noun, is indeed a normative and nearly conceptual term in the vocabulary of insurgency; see chs. 2 and 4 below.

guage in which the rebels reminded themselves of, and announced to everyone else, their own justifying self-conception is the language of the letters.

This tells us very little; it shows only that there is some continuity between the thought of the rebel letters and the thought of the rebels, not that the letters helped to shape or disseminate that thought. It says nothing about why the letters were written, nothing about how they were published. It is this last question, in fact, that can help answer the question of motive, of what the letters were up to. Historians of the revolt used to speak of them as if they were secret communications ("lokke þat hobbe robbyoure be wele chastysede" meaning roughly "make sure you catch and kill that thief Robert Hales"),[33] but for the most part these texts would have been the merest didactic irrelevance to anyone wondering which archive to torch, which prelate to lynch. Clearly, they had to mean something more than and different from this to be worth the writing or the reading amid the violence of insurgency. Writing itself—both the activity and the product—was at issue in these letters: their composition and copying, recomposition and recopying were so many *acts of assertive literacy*.[34]

33. The particular identification of Hobbe with Hales belongs to Sir Charles Oman, *The Great Revolt of 1381* (Oxford, 1906), 44 ("It is curious that Sudbury's name is not bracketed with that of 'Hobbe the Robber': was Ball perhaps grateful to the primate for having dealt no harder with him in spite of their repeated collisions?"), and it was repeated in Hilton and Fagan, *English Rising*, 101; Robbins calls the letters "the organizational communiqués of leaders of the Great Rebellion" (Hartung, *Manual*, 1511).

34. To appreciate the importance of writing as a meaningful activity in itself requires a resolute gaze at historical difference, a constant awareness that (as is well known) reading and writing were separate and separable activities in the middle ages; that writing was (as Clanchy calls it) a "technology" requiring specific training. The laboriousness of writing—the recalcitrance of pen and the resistance of parchment (or, worse in some ways, paper), the variability of ink, and the jobs of sharpening, pricking and lining (for extended texts), drying—meant that the activity had to enter consciousness as something more than an extension of reading or thought.

Fredric Jameson helps to clarify the issues when he quite correctly issues the rebuke: "One cannot without intellectual dishonesty assimilate the 'production' of texts . . . to the production of goods by factory workers: writing and thinking are not alienated labor in that sense, and it is surely fatuous for intellectuals to seek to glamorize their tasks—which can for the most part be subsumed under the rubric of the elaboration, reproduction, or critique of ideology—by assimilating them to real work on the assembly line" (*The Political Unconscious: Narrative as a Socially Symbolic Act* [Ithaca, 1981], 45). But the flip side of his assertion that writing is ideological rather than physical labor (under present technologies) is that under different technologies, such as obtained in the middle ages, it might in fact *be* physical labor; and indeed—as in scribal craft, the only systematic means of textual reproduction—be alienated physical labor. (The relation of the works of scribal *littérateurs* such as Hoccleve to alienated scribal labor might be a promising line of inquiry.)

I might clarify what I mean by noticing an objection that may have occurred even to a reader persuaded by the argument so far: granted that the letters were copied by rebels other than John Ball, it hardly follows that they were copied by "peasants." It has long been known that clerics took part in the rising, and, since they would be an obvious source of any writing that was done, their presence might make the whole question moot. But even if priests did write the letters—and they may have—then the three pseudonymous letters staked a rhetorical claim altogether different: that lay rural workers had begun to write and were taking part in the culture of literacy, that the distinction Knighton so automatically drew between the literate cleric and the illiterate worker was itself an aspect of the oppressions and exclusions against which the peasants now rose. But if the hands that wrote the letters were hands touched by chrism, was this claim tendentious, a pretense of literacy on the part of those who still needed the clergy to make or construe marks on parchment? In what sense could these letters represent such a claim at all, and what sort of rural literacy might they represent? These questions imply others about what kind of experience these six pieces of rebel writing must have been to those who made and consumed them, and about how and where and by whom writing in general was met with and dealt with in the villages of rural England.

The question of the letters' material existence and their means of publication can clarify the deeper issues of meaning and intent: before deciding the motives and appeal of the letters, we need to speculate about the audience to which they were meant to appeal. This question resembles the sort often and usefully raised in literary history about, say, Langland's audience, or Chaucer's. But when put to the rebel letters, the question sounds strange, even oxymoronic: what might it mean to speak of an audience for the written word in the towns and villages, among those who were not supposed to be an audience for the written word at all? Again and more specifically, how did it reach them? The method of publication is a mystery, crucial to decode. Media of writing and publication have their own histories and associations, which is to say that they have social meaning; the medium, not necessarily *the* message, is *a* message that encodes the message. The oxymoron—the appropriation of literacy by those who theoretically had no business with it—has (and more important, had) the effect of bringing the medium itself to attention, visible because apparently so out of place:

of making the appropriation a gesture. Decoding the gesture means weaving together the message of the medium, the possibilities for its use, and the methods of its publication.

The letters come to us indirectly, surviving only in the chronicle transcriptions; no originals survive. This is unfortunate. But the transcripts in Knighton and Walsingham, and their surrounding matter, are open to surmise. Walsingham's transcript is the simpler case. He introduces it by saying that this letter, "full of enigmas," was "sent to the leaders of the commons in Essex . . ., and was afterwards found in the garment of a certain man about to be hanged for rioting"; Ball confessed to the writing of this letter and others, "and because of these [*propter quae*: the pronoun is plural]," he was drawn, hanged, beheaded, and quartered. Now the section of Walsingham's chronicle concerning 1381 is nearly contemporary with the event;[35] and though his account is subject to deep distortions, his testimony in this case is coherent—and informed, since Ball was tried and executed before his very nose, at St. Albans.[36] Since Ball confessed to writing "*this* letter [*hanc literam*]," the letter was evidently displayed during the inquest. The mysterious note in all this is the *propter quae*: Walsingham's assertion that Ball was hanged, etc., "because of these." Either he was executed *for the crime of* writing these letters (the one transcribed and the "many others" to which he confessed)—which is hardly likely[37]—or he was executed *on the evidence of* these letters—which means that the "many others," though unrecorded, were in evidence. This explains a small mystery in Walsingham's account: his summary of the letter he reproduces—Ball wrote "urging them to finish what they had begun" (*ad hortandum eos ut incepta perficerent*)—has nothing to do with the letter he actually transcribes. It does, however, quite precisely echo the phrase found in both Carter and Ball₁, "þat ȝe make a gode ende. of þat ȝe haue begunnen";[38] Walsingham had encountered, though he did not transcribe, at least one letter that included this phrase.

---

35. See V. H. Galbraith, "Thomas Walsingham and the Saint Albans Chronicle, 1272–1422," *EHR* 47 (1932): 12–30, and my discussion below, ch. 5.

36. For more detail on the circumstances in which Walsingham learned of Ball and his activities, see below, ch. 3; Burdach has been the only one to wonder about the implications of the text's retrieval and introduction into the trial (*Der Dichter*, 171, 171n).

37. After writing this chapter I discovered that the suggestion has once been made: Nick Ronan, "1381: Writing in Revolt. Signs of Confederacy in the Chronicle Accounts of the English Rising," *Forum for Modern Language Studies* 25 (1989): 306.

38. A fact also noticed by Green, "John Ball's Letters," 181.

This is more scrutiny than Walsingham's account would deserve on its own, since there is not much mystery about how he met with the letter. But it does suggest answers for two difficult questions that surround Knighton's transcriptions. First, how, fifteen years after the event, did documents that have not otherwise survived come into Knighton's hands? Second (and more important), what physical form must they have taken to make it possible for him to mistake Milner, Carter, and Trewman for speeches rather than letters? The answer to the second question should be obvious as soon as it is asked. If Knighton had found each of the letters in what was presumably its original form—a single sheet—it would have been impossible (rather than merely unlikely) for him to mistake any of them for anything but a letter; the object itself, in its mere physical presentation, would have declared its character unmistakably. If, however, Knighton found all three "lay" letters transcribed together, without interruption or further explanation (as in fact he presents them in his chronicle), on a single sheet or roll, or in a codex, mistaking the form of the first three would have been merely unlikely (rather than impossible). Knighton found the letters of Milner, Carter, and Trewman written continuously, together in a single place.[39]

That he does, however, recognize Ball$_1$ and Ball$_2$ as letters squares with this guess, and with two further facts about them. First, the rubrics to Ball's two letters, as Knighton reports them, differ from those to the other three, giving not simply Ball's name, but a description of the document; so Ball$_1$ and Ball$_2$ probably enjoyed a different provenance, more fully rubricated than Milner, Carter, and Trewman. Second, these two rubrics make no sense together: *Exemplar epistole johannis balle* and *Prima epistola johannis Balle* are no more commensurate with each other than with the other three (which are, however, commensurate among themselves). Nor are the rubrics accurate, since (as Knighton reproduces them) the *Prima epistola* comes second. Knighton, then, did not author these rubrics; he copied them verbatim from his sources. This in turn means that the source, in each case, has passed through other, more official hands on its way from its author to himself: neither John Ball

---

39. This observation should make it clear why I am confident that the dialects of the Milner, Carter, and Trewman letters are the dialects of those within the rebellion who copied them, and not the dialects of (three different) official clerks who copied them for judicial use: if they were copied continuously, they were presumably copied by the same person.

nor any presumptive rebel copyist wrote *Exemplar epistole johannis balle* across the top of his page. So Knighton has transcribed his five letters from transcriptions, *three separate* transcriptions: (1) the single source containing Milner, Carter, and Trewman, (2) the separate source containing Ball₁, and (3) that containing Ball₂. Knighton's five letters, like Walsingham's one, came from official sources; and so, like Walsingham's, they must have been presented to the special commissions prosecuting insurgents.[40] But Walsingham's account was contemporary: he saw the letter during the trials at St. Albans. It is not clear that such was the case with Knighton; if he saw any trials, they leave no trace on his narrative. And probably these letters had been presented at more than one trial: the same incommensurability that makes it unlikely that Ball₁ and Ball₂ were transcribed together makes it unlikely that they were presented at the same inquest. He was able to copy his five letters because they had been preserved, possibly in the archives of the sheriffs.[41]

But this hypothesis only pushes further back the question of how the documents were *first* acquired. If the letters survived for Knighton's use because they had been presented before royal justices, how did they come before the justices in the first place? We know that Walsingham says Tresilian CJ got Ball₃ from the garment of a man about to be hanged, but that tells us nothing about the provenance of the others, unless men all over England went to the gibbet hiding documents. The letters must have been diffused widely enough that they could have come into the hands of chroniclers at St. Albans and Leicester, and have been plentiful enough that the random fact of two chroniclers interested in transcribing them would secure the preservation of six;[42] but they must also have been visible and recoverable enough to have been preserved in these quantities in the first place. What circumstance could have met all these requirements? The answer, I think, is that these letters, or at least some of them, enjoyed a mode of publication current during Richard's reign, one that scholarship has virtually forgotten but that provoked the anxieties of church and state and often heralded collective

---

40. Or, if these letters came from Leicestershire where there was no special commission, they would have been presented before regular sessions of the justices.

41. For an example of the number and variety of enrollments in shrieval archives, see C. Hilary Jenkinson and Mabel H. Mills, "Rolls from a Sheriff's Office of the Fourteenth Century," *EHR* 43 (1928): 21–32.

42. A fact shrewdly noticed by Hilton and Fagan, *English Rising*, 100.

trouble. The letters were what official documents elsewhere call *escrowez* or *schedulae*, and what I will call broadsides.

Broadsides were single sheets or rolls posted in places of public business—church doors, for example, and town squares. Their history is hard to trace, since they were by nature topical and ephemeral; we usually know of them only at second hand, when they garnered enough public notice to earn mention in chronicles. The evidence, though sketchy, would not seem to date them back very far beyond the last quarter of the fourteenth century.[43] The earliest popular production I know of appeared in 1377 during the conflict between John of Gaunt and the city of London, following the duke's attempt to compromise the ancient liberties and titles of the city, subjecting it to the authority of the royal marshal. Not long after this infuriating encroachment, broadsides in verse (*rhythmos*) appeared, claiming that Lancaster was actually son to a butcher of Ghent. These were posted around the city.[44] Accounts of broadsides become more common during the 1380s: in 1382 the trial of Wyclif's followers Philip Repingdon, Nicholas Hereford, and John Aston produced a series of broadsides, including a bilingual production from Aston, which was countered by a Latin one by some member of the ecclesiastical hierarchy;[45] at about the same time, probably, Wyclif's (or "Wyclif's") eucharistic *confessio* appeared;[46] in 1387, in London again, the Austin friar-turned-Lollard Peter Patteshull posted on the doors of St. Paul's a broadside accusing his former confreres of murder, sodomy, and treason;[47] during the Merciless Parliament of 1388, anonymous libels against Archbishop Nevill of York were posted at Westminster.[48]

---

43. According to V. J. Scattergood, their extensive use did not begin until the fifteenth (*Politics and Poetry in the Fifteenth Century* [London, 1971], 25–26). For two earlier examples, see ch. 2, n. 30.

44. "Interea quidam, quibus talis dissensio placuit, non cessarunt in opprobrium ducis rhythmos componere et eos configere in diversis locis urbis" (Walsingham, *Chronicon*, 129); and see *Anonimalle*, 104–5.

45. *Fasciculi zizaniorum magistri Johannis Wyclif cum tritico*, ed. W. W. Shirley, RS 5 (London, 1858), 329–31.

46. The text is in Anne Hudson, *Selections from English Wycliffite Writings* (Cambridge, Eng., 1978), 17; on the possibility that it is in fact Wyclif's own, see Hudson's notes, 141–42.

47. Walsingham, *Chronicon*, 366–67.

48. One such is printed in William Illingworth, "Copy of a Libel Against Archbishop Neville," *Archaeologia* 16 (1812): 80–83; Nevill's family issued to parliament a complaint about three defamatory bills posted against him (PRO SC8/262/13079), quoted in Susan

The vernacular broadside embodied a claim as well as a message: merely by existing, it asserted, tendentiously or not, that those who read only English—or even could only have English read to them—had a stake in the intellectual and political life of church and realm. Wyclif's followers used the medium deliberately to create just this impression. That is matter for another book; but the Wycliffites also occasioned impressively detailed documentation of the possibilities of vernacular literacy—the ability to write as well as to read—below the level of the landowner and prosperous bourgeois. One of the best-documented early, nonacademic Lollards was the notorious William Smith of Leicester. According to Knighton (himself an Austin canon of that town), Smith "exploded into a feigned sanctity" after a woman rejected him; he renounced sex, meat, and wine, wandered barefoot for many years, "and in the meantime learned his abc's and taught himself to write with his own hand." Though an artisan, Smith had acquired a more than functional literacy.[49] Under examination by Archbishop Courtenay, Smith "handed over weighty books [*libros solemnes*] which he had written in the mother tongue, from the Gospels and from the epistles and bishops and doctors of the church, and which (he confessed) he had worked studiously at writing for eight years."[50] The inquisition was conducted in 1389;[51] the "eight years" of Smith's labor at his volumes date the beginning of his studies back to the beginning of the decade, just when Wyclif and his followers were working to create the impression of a wide and literate lay clientele for theology.

Woolfson Calkin, "Alexander Neville, Archbishop of York (1373–1388): A Study of His Career with Emphasis on the Crisis at Beverley in 1381," Ph.D. diss., University of California, Berkeley (1976), 299; and see Calkin's discussion, 245–46.

49. "Medio tempore abcedarium didicit et manu sua scribere fecit" (Knighton, *Chronicon*, 180–81). Knighton reports that Smith was, in fact, a smith ("Willelmus Smith . . ., ab artificio sic vocatus").

50. "Libros etiam solemnes quos in materna lingua de evangelio, et de epistolis et aliis episcopis et doctoribus conscripserat, et ut fatebatur per annos octo studiose conscribere laboraverat archiepiscopo coactus tradidit" (Knighton, *Chronicon*, 313).

51. As Hudson notes (*The Premature Reformation: Wycliffite Texts and Lollard History* [Oxford, 1988], 76). The official record of the visitation and inquisition is given in Joseph Henry Dahmus, ed., *The Metropolitan Visitations of William Courtenay, Archbishop of Canterbury 1381–1396* (Urbana, 1950), 164–67. The register names Smith as one of eight defendants, and implicitly suggests that the eight formed a community of sorts. As far as names may be taken as indications of vocation, five of the eight (including Smith) were artisans or of artisan origins (Nicholas Taylor, Michael Scryvener, William Parchemener, and Roger Goldsmyth); only one of the eight was a priest ("Ricardus Waystathe, capellanus," the man with whom, in 1382, Smith is said to have held his *gignasium* in an abandoned chapel on the outskirts of Leicester; see note 52).

Smith was exceptional for the thoroughness and enterprise with which he took to heart the possibilities of lay theology, but it was not his literacy, practiced undisturbed for eight years, that brought him to the archbishop's notice; his formation of a community (and school, *gignasium*) at St. John Baptist's chapel and his burning of the image of St. Katherine there did that.[52] Less noisily trumpeted, his literacy might never have come to Courtenay's attention, nor therefore to ours. Though exceptional, however, he was not unique; two years later, Bishop Trefnant of Lincoln examined Walter Brut ("a sinner, a layman, a farmer, a Christian," as he introduced himself), whose written Latin responses displayed a familiarity with continental millennial literature and caused a small committee of Cambridge theologians to be charged with answering him.[53] Exceptional again; but the very extravagance of Brut's example suggests, like Smith's, that more modest possibilities, in making script as well as deciphering it, were available to others. Literacy was a real and not impossibly distant ambition for large numbers in the countryside and in the towns.[54] This is well-worn ground now, and the secondary scholarship on medieval English literacy and education makes an extended discussion superfluous;[55] but even these surveys, impressive as they are, cannot convey the teasing, uneven texture of the evidence, the surprises that wait to be turned up in the most cursory perusal of official records.[56]

---

52. Knighton, *Chronicon*, 181–82.

53. *Registrum Johannis Trefnant episcopi Herefordensis*, ed. William W. Capes (London, 1916), 285–400. On Brut, see Hudson, *Premature Reformation*, 47–48, and K. B. McFarlane, *John Wycliffe and the Beginnings of English Nonconformity* (London, 1952), 135–38.

54. In addition to the scholarship on English schooling cited in note 55, see the fascinating and elliptical evidence in Richard W. Kaeuper, "Two Early Lists of Literates in England: 1334, 1373," *EHR* 99 (1984): 363–69.

55. See J. W. Adamson, "The Extent of Literacy in England in the Fifteenth and Sixteenth Centuries: Notes and Conjectures," *The Library*, 4th ser., 10 (1929): 363–93; Lynn Thorndike, "Elementary and Secondary Education in the Middle Ages," *Speculum* 15 (1940): 400–408; H. G. Richardson, "Business Training in Medieval Oxford," *AHR* 46 (1941): 259–80; Nicholas Orme, *English Schools in the Middle Ages* (London, 1973); Orme, *Education and Society in Medieval and Renaissance England* (London, 1989); M. B. Parkes, "The Literacy of the Laity," in David Daiches and A. Thorlby, eds., *The Medieval World* (London, 1973), 555–77; Ralph V. Turner, "The *Miles Literatus* in Twelfth- and Thirteenth-Century England: How Rare a Phenomenon?" *AHR* 83 (1978): 928–45; Clanchy, *From Memory to Written Record*; Jo Ann Hoeppner Moran, *The Growth of English Schooling 1340–1588: Learning, Literacy, and Laicization in Pre-Reformation York Diocese* (Princeton, 1985); on Europe at large (but especially France and Flanders), Henri Pirenne, "L'Instruction des marchands au moyen âge," *Annales* 1 (1929): 13–28.

56. The case of Anastasia, widow of William Spichefat—who appealed Richard of Capele and others for the death of her husband in 1312 (Herts) and who "herself *read out*

M. T. Clanchy has shown how tightly documentary writing was woven into the fabric of collective existence at all levels of society; by the beginning of the fourteenth century, for example, even smallholders could possess seals, ipso facto displaying some familiarity and capacity with documents.[57] The feudal custom that required the lord's consent before a villein family could send a son for formal schooling would have been pointless unless families did conceive that ambition. (Certainly there were some venues in which the peasant child might learn to read, and thereby acquire the skill necessary for more formal schooling; M. B. Parkes has given attention to accounts that were drawn up by reeves— peasants, and usually villeins—and to letters of instruction addressed to them by their lords.)[58] The custom was not a dead letter: villein families were sometimes amerced, and therefore thought it worth paying the fine to educate their children.[59] The students of New College, Oxford— indeed, the existence of that college—show that there was a rural (if not necessarily servile) clientele for university education.[60] There were practical reasons for artisans as well as merchants to be able to read, figure,

---

the appeal for the death of her husband, which was written on a sheet" (*ipsamet appellum suum in quadam cedula scripta oretenus legende de morte viri sui in hec verba*)—is not perhaps surprising, since she was free and her husband a "clerk" (*clericus*; G. O. Sayles, ed., *Select Cases in the Court of King's Bench under Edward II*, SS 74 [London, 1957], 43–44). And in the case of John Fox, who found pledges at the bishop of Ely's court at Littleport (8 December 1316) that he would return the martyrology belonging to the master of the Hospital of St. John, we should probably assume that it was taken (or entrusted) for its value rather than its contents (F. W. Maitland and William Paley Baildon, eds., *The Court Baron, Being Precedents for Use in Seignorial and Other Local Courts*, SS 4 [London, 1891], 130). But how did Aristotle, father of a juror in 1279 at the Ramsey Abbey manor of Little Stukeley, acquire his name? See Maitland, ed., *Select Pleas in Manorial and Other Seignorial Courts*, SS 2 (London, 1889), 96. (Another reference to Aristotle—"Aristotelum filium Willelmi"—appears in the abbey's cartulary; William Henry Hart and Posonby A. Lyons, eds., *Cartularium Monasterii de Rameseia* RS 79 [London, 1884], 1:392.) And how, or through whose agency, did John Stalker, a customary tenant in the same village, write a letter to the rector of the church concerning his vicar (the story is narrated and discussed below, ch. 4)?

57. *From Memory to Written Record*, 35–36.

58. Parkes, "Literacy of the Laity," 559–60. He notes that in the documents of the abbot of Westminster, edited by Barbara Harvey, the abbot writes to his own household servants in Latin, but to the bailiff and reeve in French: this act of condescension tells a great deal, since it implies that the reeve could read French.

59. Orme, *English Schools*, 52; and L. C. Gabel, *Benefit of Clergy in England in the Later Middle Ages* (London, 1928), 75–76.

60. In the seventy years following the college's founding (in 1379), a good half of the students there came from families that Guy Fitch Lytle classes as "rural smallholders," and there is one certain case of a student from a villein family ("The Social Origins of Oxford Students in the Late Middle Ages: New College, c. 1380–c. 1510," in Jozef Ijsewijn and Jacques Paquet, eds., *The Universities in the Late Middle Ages* [Leuven, 1978], 432–47).

and perhaps write, and apprenticeship indentures often record the master's duty to educate the apprentice.[61] Villeins might educate a son in hope of his promotion to freedom (the lord's permission was required because a son who became a priest would be lost to the lord).

How far any of this produced a viable and widespread rural literacy is of course uncertain. Nicholas Orme has suggested that, in order to raise some extra cash, village priests often taught the abc's and reading.[62] Some sort of elementary training had to have been commonly available; if there were no regular opportunities for peasant children to acquire the rudiments of literacy that they would need for more formal schooling, then the restrictions on villein schooling would make no sense.[63] And it is not apparent that it would have taken very much more than training in the alphabet and in pronunciation to yield some control of the written vernacular; so much only would be needed, and so much could probably have been passed along without any formal instruction at all. And one could have access to the written word without reading it oneself, since the literacy of one family member could be a delegated literacy for the entire family. Failure to consider such scenarios, and to sense the many "intermediate levels between complete literacy and complete illiteracy," can vitiate even the most sophisticated attempts to estimate "rates" of literacy.[64] So too can the failure to wonder why one

61. Orme, *Education and Society*, 2.

62. *Education and Society*, 6–7. Though the evidence he cites is from the fifteenth century, such arrangements are likely to have been informal and therefore to have escaped record; in any case, as Moran has said, it is clear that elementary education—in alphabet and reading—is almost universally underdocumented and therefore likely to be underestimated (*Growth of English Schooling*, 21–22, 93–95). A further complication is that one of the ways Moran has found to document the existence of such training is in testamentary bequests; schools that are more fully institutionalized, and that cater to a more prosperous clientele, are naturally more likely to leave this sort of record. Schools that amounted to no more than a local priest teaching a handful of local children at home—the likely venue of any relatively formal instruction any peasant children were most likely to receive—are most unlikely to leave any record at all.

63. It also seems likely that such informal schools might have trained many students who never continued to more formal education; basic economic rationality would suggest to peasant families that some evidence of capacity would be needed before they should commit themselves to the costs in money and lost labor involved in sending a child to school; but this is pure speculation.

64. Phrase quoted from Franz Baüml, "Varieties and Consequences of Medieval Literacy and Illiteracy," *Speculum* 55 (1980): 239. David Cressy's impressive attempt to estimate rates of Tudor and Stuart literacy from the ability to sign one's name (rather than set one's mark) shows several of the problems involved (*Literacy and the Social Order: Reading and Writing in Tudor and Stuart England* [Cambridge, Eng., 1980]). The sources he uses are all official (such as compulsory declarations of loyalty, wills, marriage licenses); his favorites are depositions in Courts Christian. These are not only official occasions of

would want to read, and what level of ability would be needed to do the reading one wanted.[65] For example, the ability to sound out, and therefore recognize, one's name and to know the equivalents of perhaps ten or twenty Latin words would be enough to allow minimally literate peasants to locate and recognize references to their lands in court rolls

---

signing: they are public occasions that put the signer under scrutiny in several ways, involving (with the exception of wills) an assumption of enforceable responsibility, in an alien and possibly threatening environment. The deposer, for example, avows the truth of her or his testimony in a matter before authoritative officials and signs a document written often in Latin, and in an expert hand. Cressy has commented on the awkwardness of the signatures of those who could write but rarely did; in such a venue, an uncertain or unpracticed signature made before those whose power was symbolized in their control of documents, *when there was an established and acceptable alternative*, might have been an unattractive possibility; a preference for the setting the mark might have been experienced as either deference or pride. (The procedures by which the witness was to be "set at ease" [111] would seem likely to do the opposite.) In any case, writing materials (as Cressy notes) were awkward before ballpoints, and one who had little occasion to write, even if she or he could read, might have found the mark an altogether more comfortable medium. All this is the more persuasive under the educational regime he describes. The sounding of the alphabet, reading, and spelling were all taught before the different, physically rather than intellectually demanding skill of writing. Since Cressy notes that "the stretch of a family budget could determine how long a child was sent to school" (28–29), it is at least probable that when children of less prosperous families did seek formal schooling, it would in their cases more likely be cut off early, before the confident acquisition of writing. Then, too, in the case of less formal education whose existence Cressy allows (and whose importance Orme has argued for the middle ages), it is not at all clear how important the skills of penmanship would have been. One could cite the case of John Croft, who abjured Lollardy before the bishop of Hereford in 1505. He confessed to reading and expounding heretical books, yet signed the abjuration with his mark (*Registrum Ricardi Mayew, Episcopi Herefordensis A.D. MDIV–MDXVI*, ed. A. T. Bannister, CYS 27 [Canterbury, 1921], 67). So some of those who made their marks rather than signed their names might have been simply unable to do the latter, though they had learned to read.

Cressy leaves a possibly distorting impression, since he treats only full literacy—the ability to write one's name, and indeed the confidence to do so even before the bishop's court—and makes only cursory allowance for the grades that intervene between it and full illiteracy. The impression given by such statements as "If you could not even form a signature your literacy was incomplete, although you might be able to manage some reading" (55) is rather strange, suggesting that *ordinarily* you would either pursue an education through to the acquisition of writing or not undertake it at all. His figures would have left a very different taste if, instead of saying that at the accession of Elizabeth there was perhaps 80 percent illiteracy among males and 95 percent among females, he had said rather that there was perhaps 20 percent *full* literacy among males and 5 percent among females (Cressy, 176).

65. To take Cressy as the example again: he suggests that "the writers who proclaimed the advantages of literacy" in early-modern England perhaps "overestimated its value to ordinary men and women" (*Literacy*, 1); in other words, there was little practical advantage in it. I will suggest later that in the fourteenth century there was. But it should be noted that there are other reasons, less insistently practical but still real, why one might want to read, and the difficulty in ignoring these is evident in Cressy's assertion that "in matters of religion there was [still] less reason for women to pursue literacy" (128), since their husbands did the thinking on these matters.

or extents, or to be aware of and articulate about the contents of charters they might hold. And I would suggest that this, not fluency or practice in reading books or writing letters, is the literacy that mattered to the rural communities that rebelled in 1381, the literacy that gave them their sense of familiarity with documentary culture and their determination to make it theirs.

The extraordinary collection of *Carte nativorum*—an early fourteenth-century register from Peterborough Abbey recording charters for land acquired by villeins—points to something still less easily explained, less immediately practical. From these charters, M. M. Postan was able to argue that the alienation by charter of land held in bond—theoretically illegal—began its slow development as early as the thirteenth century, becoming commonplace in the late fourteenth.[66] This is an area in which the literary historian is likely to blunder, but the evidence is suggestive: Postan's chronology of the progress of peasant charters matches Clanchy's chronology of the use and manipulation of documents on the part of the peasantry. This is nearly a tautology: land could not be formally transferred until the transfer was recorded, and obtaining records of transfer necessarily meant dealing with documents. But charters were not the only form of record available; customary tenants were supposed to enroll land transfers on the court rolls of the manor. There wasn't much to choose between the two forms as ways of securing one's rights; enrolling with the manorial court meant paying an entry fine, but then charters cost money, and the lord might always detect and exploit an illegally held charter.[67] Charters had one great advantage, both psycho-

66. *Carte nativorum*, ed. Postan and C. N. L. Brooke, Northamptonshire Record Society 20 (Oxford, 1960), xxviii–lxv. The points of Postan's argument that matter to my argument here remain unaffected by Edmund King's demonstration that the charters deal with a pretty narrow category of transfers (free land purchased from freeholders by prosperous customary tenants of assart land; *Peterborough Abbey 1086–1310: A Study in the Land Market* [Cambridge, Eng., 1973], 99–125); or by Paul R. Hyams's qualification of his chronology ("The Origins of a Peasant Land Market in England," *EcHR*, 2d ser., 23 [1970]: 18–31).

67. What follows is a very crude and speculative use of Postan's main arguments: that such transfers must have been a natural and necessary form of economic self-regulation throughout the history of the manor (on this issue, see Ian Blanchard, "Industrial Employment and the Rural Land Market 1380–1520," in Richard M. Smith, ed., *Land, Kinship, and Life-Cycle* [Cambridge, Eng., 1984], 227–75); that the (wholly illegal) use of sealed charters began in the late twelfth or thirteenth century; that the aim of using charters was not to legitimate the sale (since, in law, the charters only aggravated the offense), but to enter a permanent record of it for use in local disputes, locally mediated; that rising land prices at the end of the thirteenth century led lords to claim their share in the process—the entry fees they could collect and the higher rents which they could

logical and practical: they came from the royal chancery and were held independent of the lord and his authority. This sort of practice, and its acceptance by landlords, brought to villeins an increasing familiarity with the apparatus of documentary culture—a knowledge of how it worked and of what documents looked like, possession of their own seals, and (a corollary) the experience of "signing" their names—and the experience, *through* the use of these documents, of the privileges associated with, even evidentiary of, free status.[68] If writing was a socially charged symbol of freedom, the use of charters and other records brought the experience and possession of the symbol.

And also, it seems, the desire to make it actual: free status was what the 1381 rising (*pro libertate*) was all about.[69] The motive for the writing and copying of the rebel letters lay chiefly not in their contents but in the activity of their production: they made their most important claim merely by *being* written documents that came (or claimed to come) from the hands of *rustici*. I have cited evidence for rural literacy to assert not that the rebels were, as a group, more or less literate, but that literacy was something confidently possessed by some or a few of them, less confidently perhaps by a few more, and available, by one means or another, to almost all; that the letters announced the documentary competence of the insurgent population, a determination not to be excluded from documentary rule. The institutional "psychosis" that sorted literacy with social rank made social "fact" into social norm: the restriction of reading and writing to the governing classes of church, state, and manor was articulated as a principle of order.[70] It was in the nature of *clerici* that they should write and of rural workers that they should not, and this distinction in turn determined who might take a

---

set. The lords therefore (Postan argues) began bringing offenders to court, with an eye not to abolishing the use of charters, but to regularizing it and bringing it under their own control; this explains the regularization of the procedure and the creation of a "villein archive" such as the Peterborough cartulary. In effect, unable to beat them, the lords joined them, choosing to supervise what they could not suppress.

68. Hyams comments, of the thirteenth century, "In East Anglia, as elsewhere, possession of a charter would be considered by most ordinary people as *de facto* proof of freedom" ("Peasant Land Market," 24–25); and see his *King, Lords, and Peasants in Medieval England: The Common Law of Villeinage in the Twelfth and Thirteenth Centuries* (Oxford, 1980), 43–46, including the case of the tenant seeking to prove his freedom by producing a charter from his lord that remitted his customary services during the lord's absence (45), and the seizure in 1239 of villein charters at the Ramsey manor of Brancaster (Norfolk) (46).

69. Walsingham's phrase (*Chronicon*, 185).

70. See again Walsingham's comment on the rebellion, n. 17 above.

part in cultural and political reflection. Lords and freeholders possessed the artificial public memory of the cartularies and archives; clerics and educated nobles were free to reflect upon, not just practice, belief and ritual. The exclusion from writing of villeins and smallholders confirmed both their unfreedom and the rightness of it. And in the years just before 1381, the psychosis had become topical for the countryside, where a break with legal custom enforced the association of unfreedom and illiteracy in a matter of close concern to the rebels of 1381. One of the demands issued the king at Mile End was "that no one should be bound to serve another except voluntarily and by free contract":[71] this clause concerned the Statute of Laborers and its attempt to enforce labor on demand for fixed wages. The king's bench (the court of final and best appeal for complaints of free tenants against their lords) customarily heard only such actions for breach of contract as were based on written contracts; the "parol" contract had no force there. But in the enforcement of the 1351 statute, parol contracts between lords and their laborers were taken as binding, and since, as Putnam points out, it was an acceptable maxim for interpreting the statute that it had been "made for the advantage of the lords," the content of a parol contract was in effect what the lord said it was.[72] This decision made oral agreements as binding as written contracts, but of course left laborers without appeal to the documentary evidence that the written contract would offer. The apparent justification for this procedure was the consoling belief that laborers could not understand written documents.

If I am right that the circulation, imitation, copying, recopying, and recirculation of letters among the rebels produced the six texts recorded by Knighton and Walsingham and that these texts presented themselves to the world as posted broadsides, then their first and most important declaration surely resided simply in the gesture of writing and publication, in the visible and public declaration that *laici* and *bondi* had begun to occupy the cultural terrain of economic and intellectual privilege. The question of authorship with which I began has yielded no answers, but it has revealed a range of possibility invisible to official ideologies of the fourteenth century, and only fitfully visible to scholarly ideologies

71. "Qe nulle ne deveroit servire ascune homme mes a sa volunte de mesme et par covenant taille" (*Anonimalle*, 144–45); for a more extensive discussion of these demands, see ch. 4 below.

72. See Bertha H. Putnam, *The Enforcement of the Statute of Laborers During the First Decade after the Black Death, 1349–1359* (New York, 1908), 177–79, 200.

of the twentieth. The question has yielded no answers because the letters themselves proscribe the possibility of specifying their authorship, and that is part of their point: the pseudonymous character of Milner, Carter, and Trewman make authorship programmatically unlocatable, assert that these letters could have been written by anyone—any miller, any carter, any true man—and that now literacy and the privileges it symbolized were to be exercised by a new clientele.[73] But seeing what this meant, how it was specified into ideology, means looking more closely at the rebels' actions and words, and especially at their continuing and closely specified interest in archives and their contents.

Apart from the four-day conflagration in London, the chronology of the rebel activity is surprisingly hard to establish until its momentum had already slowed: only after the rebels had dispersed from London with the promise of manumission was the machinery of state justice, and with it the machinery of record, able to engage.[74] The first concern of the royal government was to establish guardians of the peace in London and to fill offices left vacant by lynchings;[75] on 20 June, Richard established commissions of oyer and terminer to inquire concerning the revolt, and shortly afterward local juries began returning their indictments.[76] Once the dramatic events of June were over, and discontent was driven underground to simmer in local secret societies and explode occasionally in acts of random violence, courts and chancery, tireless of record, began to catalogue events virtually as they happened, generating a detailed, almost week-by-week chronicle of dwindling and desperate conspiracies. About the days of concerted revolt, by contrast—up to and including the assault on London—we know chiefly what people were willing to say against each other before the royal justices (pretty much anything, if there was a score to be settled),[77] and what the

73. For more on the pseudonymous character of the letters, see ch. 3 below.

74. By the time (between 5 July and 30 August) the king issued letters close to the guardians and the justices of the peace in all the counties to hurry the indictments and records of processes concerning the rising to chancery, the parchment trail had grown long and thick enough to need consolidation (*CCR 1381–1385*, 7–8).

75. On 15 June, Richard II appointed Walworth, Knolles, Brembre, Philpot, and Launde to oversee the peace of the city, and two days later appointed Hugh Segrave to be chancellor pro tem (*CPR 1381–1385*, 18).

76. *CPR 1381–1385*, 23.

77. A point noticed at the time by the monk of Westminster: "Plurimi namque cernentes nullorum misereri quos conjuracionis macula aliquo modo infecerat, hiis singulis erga quos canescentis odii malicia movebantur tanti maleficii crimen imponebant, ut vel

chroniclers recorded (mostly the dramatic events in London). In the chronicles, the rising looks like a short-lived, contained eruption, extending over a couple weeks in June; the public records tell a different story. The royal amnesty excused breaches of the peace from 1 May— which would suggest a series of small explosions that came to a head rather slowly[78]—and jury returns testify that violence continued beyond the end of the year. Indeed, in many ways the chronicles and the judicial records seem to speak of different events entirely; the former give the impression of highly coordinated actions publicly executed by large crowds, the latter of local violence and theft only occasioned or colored, rather than motivated, by political complaint. Both kinds of source are necessary—the jury returns list names and give the only information about most local events, while the chronicles narrate events without regard to prosecutability—and neither can be privileged.[79]

---

tali objeccionis titulo diu affectatam in hos quos oderant explerent vindictam" (*The Westminster Chronicle 1381–1394*, ed. and trans. L. C. Hector and Barbara F. Harvey [Oxford, 1982], 16). Even under the pressure of public and state anxiety to quash every possibility of recurrence, a high proportion of acquittals was returned; this is possibly a measure of the very high proportion of tendentious accusations made for reasons of personal or local convenience. It may also be significant that on 12 September, the government suspended the inquests of local juries and transferred all remaining cases to the king's bench (Charles Petit-Dutaillis, *Studies and Notes Supplemental to Stubbs' Constitutional History* [Manchester, 1915] 2:301–2).

78. Petit-Dutaillis, Introduction to André Réville, *Le Soulèvement des travailleurs d'Angleterre en 1381* (Paris, 1898), lxx. For my own reconstruction of the chronology and its meaning, see ch. 4 below.

79. The distorting power of the chronicles is well known: they relied on hearsay information for distant events, were often executed years afterward, obeyed generic and ideological conventions, and pressed institutional interests. At the same time, to honor the judicial records while skirting the chronicles would display a bizarre naïveté, a faith that a state apparatus is more likely to give an undistorted account of events that threatened state apparatuses as such than monastic chroniclers did of events that threatened their own houses. Hilton makes a similar point (*Bond Men Made Free*, 179); but the issue is more complex, and the distortions of the record more systematic, than his comments would indicate. Aside from the problem the Westminster chronicler noted—that accusations of complicity with the revolt formed a ready and easy way to settle old scores or corner new markets (see n. 77 above)—the jury system itself was so constructed as to skew indictments seriously. Juries could not return answers of ignorance; the jury at St. Albans tried to tell Tresilian CJ "se nullum talem scire, nullum indictare juste posse, cunctos fideles et obsequentes Regi fore, semperque fuisse." Tresilian, catching the scent in the wind ("videns . . . quo tendebat ista responsio"), ordered them to reconvene and name names (Walsingham, *Gesta abbatum monasterii Sancti Albani*, ed. H. T. Riley, RS 28 [London, 1869], 3:348). They were under compulsion to provide evidence that they cooperated with the suppression of the rising. At the same time, it was in the interest of the entire community and of the jurors in particular (those most responsible for its continuing viability and its favor with the government), whether they were in sympathy with the rebels or not, to present the facts so as to minimize the offenses and evade the impression of cooperative, communal, treasonous action. Their interest lay in providing

However they disagree, they all witness to the crucial importance of
one insurgent tactic, illustrated in one of the earliest events narrated in
the Essex returns. An indictment given before Tresilian CJ concerning
one Ralph atte Wood of Bradewell alleges that on Trinity Monday, "he
voluntarily and feloniously rose up against the King's peace together
with others of his company with force and arms and went to the Temple
of Cressyng and overthrew the house there and took and carried away
armour, vestments, gold and silver, and other goods and chattels to the
value of twenty pounds, *and burned books there to the value of twenty
marks.*"[80] The fate of these books is an appropriate note on which to
begin the story told by the judicial records. All the sources, chronicles
and indictments alike, agree that the seizure and destruction of documents happened wherever rebellion did.[81] Manorial courts in years
following sometimes dated events of 1381 with the phrase *tempore rumoris
et combustionis rotulorum curie*—"during the uproar and the burning of
court rolls"[82]—and one of the first acts of parliament after the rising was
to provide for the replacement of important documents.[83] This destruction of muniments served as a focus, a disciplined intention that determined the objects and methods of attack, whether other violence was
carried out, was only threatened, or was absent altogether. According
to the Kent returns, some men of St. John's on Thanet appealed to their
fellows on Corpus Christi Day that they should "go to the house of

returns that atomized the violence, representing attacks on individuals as attacks *by*
individuals, and attacks motivated by vendetta or greed: rowdiness and theft counted for
less than treason.

80. Indictment quoted in J. A. Sparvel-Bayly, "Essex in Insurrection, 1381," *Transactions
of the Essex Archaeological Society* ns 1 (1878): 217.

81. Caroline Barron describes the characteristic actions in London as "attacks on
prisons and agents of the law, the burning of documents, and the hatred shown to
foreigners" (*Revolt in London: Eleventh to Fifteenth June 1381* [London, 1981], 3). With the
exception of the last—the foreigners in question were concentrated mostly in London
and Southwark, and in East Anglia, places concerned in the wool trade, and trade in
general—this is true of the rebellion at large.

82. R. G. E. Wood, "Essex Manorial Records and the Revolt," in W. H. Liddell and
R. G. E. Wood, eds., *Essex and the Great Revolt of 1381*, Essex Record Office Publications
84 (Chelmsford, 1982), 72.

83. "Item est assentuz, qe ceulx qui se sentent grevez par esloignement, arsure, ou
autre destruction fait de lour Chartres, Relees, Obligations, Estatuz-merchantz, Court-
roulles, ou d'autres lours Evidences perduz en cest derrain rumour & ryot, q'ils viegnent
par entre cy & la Nativitee de Seint Johan proschein a pluis oultre devant le Conseill
nostre Seigneur le Roi, & illoeqes facent suffisante proeve d'iceulx lours Munimentz issint
perdues, arses, & destruitz, & de la forme & tenure d'icelles; & le Roi, par l'advis de son
Conseil, lour ferra purvoier de remede, si avant come il le purra faire par la Loy" (*Rp*
3.114).

William Medmenham, and demolish his house and level it with the ground, and fling out the books and rolls found there, and to burn them with fire, and, if the said William could be found, that they should kill him." But once they got to his house, they "burnt the aforesaid rolls and books, and did no other harm to the said William."[84] This story, which is typical enough, says something about the relation of document burning to other forms of violence. Whatever threats were uttered, documents usually were destroyed while their surroundings and their owners remained intact, and the actions of these men of Thanet suggests that this destruction was in a way the kernel of intention that drove the violence, violence that could spill over into the destruction of persons or property, but did not always.

The rebels burned documents at the beginning of the revolt in Essex and Kent and London, and in the more distant counties as well; and wherever they did, they did so with a specificity that shows their familiarity and competence with the forms of literate culture. The insurgent animus against the archive was not the revenge of a residually oral culture against the appurtenances of a literacy that was threatening because alien and mysterious.[85] Both chronicles and indictments bespeak a precise targeting of legal instruments. In Kent, rebels attacked the castle and the *praetorium* of Canterbury, stealing "goods, chattels, and muniments"; at William Medmenham's house, they "burnt the Rolls touching the Crown of our Lord the King, and the Rolls of the office of Receiver of Green wax from the county of Kent"; at the house of Thomas Bedemanton, "the charters, writings, and divers muniments there found"; at John Colbrand's "columbare," the escheat rolls "of Green Wax"; from John Brode of Mersham, the "Escheat Rolls of our Lord the King, and . . . the receipt of the subsidy of the three groats" (that is, of the poll tax that prompted the rising); from the Kent sheriff William Septvantz, "the rolls of the Pleas of the County and of the Crown of our Lord the King"; the "Custumal of Petham, of the Lord

84. W. E. Flaherty, "The Great Rebellion in Kent of 1381 Illustrated from the Public Records," *Archeologia Cantiana* 3 (1860): 72.

85. For such an "anti-intellectual" reading of the rising (his word), see Alexander Murray, *Reason and Society in the Middle Ages* (Oxford, 1978), 214–16. Altogether, the image of indiscriminate, raging violence in 1381 is more a function of its chroniclers' anxieties than of the events themselves; as Richard W. Kaeuper has recently pointed out, the rising "was never a Jacquerie," and violence against persons was very specific and very rare (*War, Justice, and Public Order: England and France in the Later Middle Ages* [Oxford, 1988], 361).

Archbishop of Canterbury";[86] the "evidencias escaetie sue" of the escheators Elias Reyner of Strode and John Godwot. And in one mysterious phrase (in an indictment whose Latin is particularly bad and at the crucial point nearly incomprehensible), we are told that John Foxgrove and Roger Plomer took from the Savoy and burned "certain bookcases" (*certas armuras*) which are puzzlingly said to be *pro tubiis* (for rolls?).[87]

It is a miscellaneous set that includes the poll tax receipts; other documents of royal revenue (escheat and coroners' rolls, recording forfeits to the king by decease and felony); landholding and demesne records of the lords (custumals, cartularies, extents, manorial court rolls); and the records of local and royal justice, including commissions of oyer and terminer and of laborers. But the miscellaneity had its own logic, and a deeper specificity. Corpus Christi College, Cambridge, petitioned parliament concerning the burning of "Chartres, Escritz, Liveres, et autres munimentz" taken from its close;[88] these evidently concerned the college's landholding and the royal privileges granted to the college and university.[89] The complaint is as interesting for what is not there as for what is, since establishments like Corpus Christi possessed other stores of written documents, at least as visible, nearly as valuable, and certainly as symbolically significant as those taken: their libraries, which apparently remained untouched. The insurgents seemed to have purposed the destruction of certain kinds of documents and not of others, and—just as important—to have known the difference.[90] In London, the Inn of the Hospitallers of St. John was attacked and the records burned; a lodging for lawyers, it possessed collections of judicial actions and precedents.[91] The continuator of the *Eulogium historiarum* tells of "charters, muniments, and writings" taken and burned "in domo

86. These from Flaherty, "Great Rebellion," 82–95.

87. These from Edgar Powell and G. M. Trevelyan, *The Peasants' Rising and the Lollards: A Collection of Unpublished Documents* (London, 1899), 6–8. I am grateful for Carter Revard's suggestion that the *tubii* might be rolls.

88. *Rp* 3.108. According to the complaint and the finding of parliament, the trouble in Cambridge was instigated by the "burgesses and community," led apparently by a former mayor and bailiffs.

89. And apparently the privilege of levying wax for tapers burned in honor of deceased collegians (*First Report of the Royal Commission on Historical Manuscripts* [London, 1870], 65).

90. The complaint as I quoted it does mention the burning of "Liveres," but I take it that the locution "Chartres, Escritz, Liveres, *et autres munimentz*" shows that the "books" in question were most probably cartularies or the like.

91. Knighton, *Chronicon*, 135–36.

judicii" in Canterbury.[92] The *Anonimalle Chronicle*, finally, says that at Lambeth—the archbishop of Canterbury's London residence—"all the registry books and rolls of the chancery found there" were destroyed.[93] This last case shows that at least some of the rebels knew not only about the kinds and functions of documents and about the collections in their local communities, but also about the disposition of documents at the higher reaches of ecclesiastical government. They evidently went to Lambeth looking for parchment, since they did not destroy the palace (as they did the Savoy) and since the archiepiscopal prison was at Maidstone. Since the archbishop, Simon Sudbury, was also chancellor of the realm, he had responsibility for the documents of the royal chancery, but its London home was at Westminster.[94] But as archbishop, he also had an archiepiscopal *chauncellerie* located not in Canterbury but at Lambeth, and the rebels knew it.[95]

The chroniclers tell the same story, and—with anxieties ready to make metaphor—tell it better than their modern descendants. Charles Petit-Dutaillis thinks that the point of burning documents was to erase the memory of manorial customs and duties, and to vent rage over royal taxation;[96] Hilton that it was to undo serfdom and the accumulation of recently imposed services;[97] and J. R. Maddicott that it was to protest

---

92. *Eulogium (historiarum sive temporis)*, ed. Frank Scott Haydon, RS 9 (London, 1863), 354.

93. "Tout les livers de registres et rolles de remembraucez de la chauncellerie illoeqes trovez" (*Anonimalle*, 140).

94. Though there were local royal chanceries all over England, and some members of chancery would still sometimes travel with the king, Westminster was the central office; see T. F. Tout, *Chapters in the Administrative History of Mediaeval England* (Manchester, 1928) 3:57.

95. Irene Josephine Churchill, *Canterbury Administration: The Administrative Machinery of the Archbishop of Canterbury Illustrated from Original Records* (London, 1933), 7. This point has recently been independently made by W. M. Ormrod, "The Peasants' Revolt and the Government of England," *Journal of British Studies* 29 (1990): 6.
For further examples of document burning printed or mentioned significantly in secondary sources, see Powell, *Rising in East Anglia*, 132ff.; W. M. Palmer and H. W. Sanders, "The Peasants' Revolt of 1381 as It Affected the Villages of Cambridgeshire," *Documents Relating to Cambridgeshire Villages* 2 (1926): 20–21; Christobel M. Hoare, *The History of an East Anglian Soke: Studies in Original Documents, Including Hitherto Unpublished Material Dealing with the Peasants' Rising of 1381, and Bondage and Bond Tenure* (Bedford, 1918), 111–14; Bruce M. S. Campbell, "Population Pressure, Inheritance, and the Land Market in a Fourteenth-Century Peasant Community," in Richard M. Smith, ed., *Land, Kinship, and Life-Cycle* (Cambridge, Eng., 1984), 92–93. Christopher Dyer counts 107 incidents of destruction ("The Social and Economic Background to the Rural Revolt of 1381," in Hilton and Aston, eds., *English Rising*, 12).

96. Petit-Dutaillis, *Studies and Notes*, 278, 283.

97. *Bond Men Made Free*, 156, and see Ronan, "1381," 310–11. Hilton and T. H. Aston

corruption in the courts of justice.[98] These explanations do not differ strikingly from what Walsingham had to say, except that his analysis is—oddly, since he fantasizes violence that mostly did not happen—subtler:

> They began to show forth what they had premeditated and, utterly without reverence, they began beheading all lawyers and apprentices, as well as the justices themselves, and all jurors of the countryside that they could find, saying that the land would never rejoice in its original liberty until they were all dead. This pleased the peasants mightily, and (moving from small things to great) they ordered that all court rolls and muniments be cast into the flames, so that the memory of ancient things would vanish, and their lords would never again have a law to punish them with.[99]

It is this combination of shrewdness and hysteria that makes Walsingham always such a difficult and suggestive source. He claims that the rebels burned documents in order to wipe out the rule of custom and law in England altogether, even though he himself witnessed and recorded the attempt of the St. Albans rebels to recover customs and charters *more* ancient than those by which the abbot governed their lives.[100] At the same time, the insurgent ambitions in his account conflate distinct institutions—serfdom, the legal profession, the jury system, and the manorial court—whose common element was the documentary administration they shared: what the different levels of government had in common was the writing by which power was exercised, and recovering "ancient liberties" meant reforming all these modes of parchment bureaucracy.

---

make a more nuanced version of the same point in their introduction to the *Past and Present* collection: "Court rolls were burnt, evidently as a symbolic anti-seigneurial gesture in tenurially free Kent. 'Freedom' was conceived in much more general terms than freedom of tenure, being as much freedom from the tax-collector, from the royal official, from the justice of the peace or of trailbaston as from the local lord" (*English Rising*, 4).

98. Maddicott, *Law and Lordship: Royal Justices as Retainers in Thirteenth- and Fourteenth-Century England, Past and Present* Supplement 4 (Oxford, 1978), 59ff.

99. "Coeperunt facta monstrare quaedam quae mente conceperant, et omnes et singulos juris terrae peritos, tam apprenticios quam senes justiciarios, et cunctos juratores patriae, quos apprehendere poterant, sine ullo respectu pietatis, capitis truncatione multare; asserentes non prius quam illis occisis terram ingenua libertate posse gaudere. Placuit iste sermo vehementer rusticis, et, ex minoribus majora concipientes, statuerunt omnes curiarum rotulos et munimenta vetera dare flammis, ut, obsoleta antiquarum rerum memoria, nullum jus omnino ipsorum domini in eos in posterum vendicare valerent" (Walsingham, *Chronicon*, 287).

100. See the Epilogue, below, on the demand for the charter of Offa.

In revealing the range of purpose that motivated the rebels' destruction of documents, Walsingham unwittingly shows also how they made metaphor of them. Wat Tyler represented the Kentish band when he demanded that the king abolish "all serfdom and neifty," so that "all should be free and of one condition."[101] But there was not, nor ever had been, serfdom in Kent, which enjoyed the eccentric privileges of gavelkind tenure. (Even outside Kent, many of the insurgents were already freeholders,[102] to whom the abolition of villein tenure would have brought advantages at best oblique.) That this demand would be issued at all by the Kentish suggests that personal freedom and unfreedom were metaphorical as well as legal expressions for them.[103] Though they did seek a literal *libertas* for those who did not enjoy it (as the king's charter of manumission shows), *libertas* alone was not and could not have been their whole point; it did metaphorical duty for abolition of all the oppressions under which the countryside labored. The escheator, the coroner, the lord and steward, the lawyer and justice and jury did jobs separable and distinct when viewed from the inside, where the parceling out of office and jurisdiction mattered; viewed from the outside, they all worked together to hedge the sphere of rural action with documentary constraints. In lumping together the different institutions of different levels of government, the rebels offered a realistic assessment of how official writing of all sorts and in all offices could hobble them in their daily labor for subsistence and baffle their chances at prosperity. Their actions show what they were after. On the one hand, with a few explicable exceptions, there is what the rebels did not attack. The Cambridge libraries were spared while the archives were not. There is nothing to suggest the widespread burning of church service books, which would have been immediately to hand in many of the buildings broken by the rebels. There is nothing to suggest a wholesale assault on intellectual or ecclesiastical culture, even though houses of prelates and religious were invaded almost as frequently as those of escheators and

101. "Et qe nulle nayf serroit en Engleterre, ne nulle servage ne nayfte, mes toutz estre free et de une condicione" (*Anonimalle*, 147).

102. See Christopher Dyer, "Social and Economic Background," 9–42, "The Causes of the Revolt in Rural Essex," in Liddell and Wood, *Essex and the Great Revolt*, 21–36, "The Rising of 1381 in Suffolk: Its Origins and Participants," *Proceedings of the Suffolk Institute of Archaeology and History* 36 (1988): 274–87; and Andrew Prescott, "London in the Peasants' Revolt: A Portrait Gallery," *London Journal* 7 (1981): 125–43.

103. The demand also shows the importance of the rebels from Essex—where, Dyer has estimated, half the land was held in customary tenure ("Causes of the Revolt in Rural Essex," 26)—in formulating the program of the revolt; see ch. 4, below.

justices; records of their activities as landlords, not as clerics, met the flames. On the other hand, there is what they did attack: administrative records of all sorts and from all levels of ecclesiastical, royal, and manorial government. The variety among these objects of their anger suggests complaints not so much against particular oppressions in the matters of tenure, criminal justice, and royal prerogative, as against the entire documentary apparatus that defined their position with respect to the land and to the local and national community.

The actions of the rebels were as precise in their gestural significance as in their targets, and displayed intentions more complex than those just adduced. Walsingham and Hilton would be more persuasive if all that the rebels had done with the documents they seized was burn them. I have already cited the first recorded violence of the rising, when Ralph atte Wood burned papers at Cressingtemple. The same Ralph amassed a long recital of crimes, which included his service as "common leader of the perverse company of insurgents" who "went to the house of the said Edmund [de la Mare] and carried away a writ patent of the King with all the muniments touching the office of Admiral upon the sea, upon a [pitchfork], from the said house to 'La Milende' next London and so back to the said house in contempt of the king and of the office aforesaid."[104] The documents in question have no relation, at least no evident relation, to the motives usually given for the rebellion—admiralty documents touched on neither taxation nor manorial duties[105]—and the framing of the indictment suggests that Ralph or one of his companions knew what to look for, was handy enough with the ways of bureaucracy to know what could be found at Edmund de la Mare's house and what it would mean. Mere annihilation was not the only end in view when a particular parchment cache was seized. It is too early to say what Ralph's action meant,[106] but its evident gestural force shows

104. Sparvel-Bayly, "Essex in Insurrection," 217. Sparvel-Bayly translates *furca* as "gallows"; I give it as "pitchfork."

105. For a possible explanation of their complaints against the admiralty, see the largely persuasive argument of Eleanor Searle and Robert Burghardt that governmental inefficiency in protecting the seacoasts, and the devastating French forays that this permitted, was one motive behind the rising ("The Defense of England and the Peasants' Revolt," *Viator* 3 [1972]: 36–88). Ralph Hanna pointed out to me that admirals were sometimes farmed the "first fruits" of some future tax in return for arming fleets from their own funds; I have, however, been unable to locate in the *CPR* any such grant to Edmund de la Mare.

106. See ch. 2 below.

that the seizure of documents could be the symbolic matter of spectacle as much as the prosaic business of getting them out of the way.

Then too, there were documents that the rebels wanted to see created, not destroyed, like the charters of liberty that the commons of Dunstable demanded (in the king's name) of their prior, the abbot of Dunstable.[107] And there were still others that they wanted to preserve. In Bury St. Edmunds, a monastic borough, they demanded that the monks produce "in the sight of the commons" the charters of liberty for the vill "which Cnut, the founder of the monastery, once granted."[108] The next day, the monks brought all the charters they could find to the guildhall before the mayor, aldermen, "and the whole crowd of villeins." The rebels were dissatisfied with what they saw, and the monks promised to search their charters to find support for the liberties claimed; if they found none, new ones would be produced to serve the purpose.[109] Similarly, within Walsingham's ken at St. Albans, certain tenants of the monastery, led by Walter Grindcobbe, brought a royal writ to the abbot commanding him to hand over "certain charters in your keeping" concerning the liberties of the vill. The abbot reluctantly did so, and promised that new charters would be made at their pleasure. They burned what he handed over, but then demanded another, "ancient charter . . . with capital letters, one of gold and one of azure." Abbot Thomas said that he had never heard of such, but promised to hand it over if it should be found.[110]

This latter account offers problems. The king's writ indicates that the rebels wanted these charters because of the liberties they guaranteed. The abbot produced them, but they were burned; *then* the rebels asked for another, still older charter.[111] Evidently someone among the rebels read the charters enough to see that they did not contain what was desired. The abbot knew of no better remedy than newer charters, but the rebels did; they preferred a very old document to a very new one and were certain that it existed. Both incidents, at Bury and at St. Albans, followed the same course as the attacks on sheriffs and men of

---

107. *Annales prioratus de Dunstaplia*, in Henry Richards Luard, ed., *Annales monastici*, RS 36 (London, 1866), 3:417–19.

108. Walsingham, *Chronicon*, 303; Gosford, *Electio* ("Collectanea fratris Andreae Astone") 3:130.

109. They offered some of the monastery's treasures, worth more than £1000 (says Walsingham), as surety.

110. Walsingham, *Gesta* 3:307–8.

111. On the "capital letters," see the Epilogue, below.

law: a confrontation in which the rebels threatened force to extort documents. But now they wanted to display them, not destroy them. The reason for this difference is clear: the archives of great religious houses had what those of the sheriffs did not, charters of great antiquity, and while it could be taken for granted that recent issues would only confirm the status quo, older ones might testify to a status quo ante more favorable to rebel claims. Rosamond Faith has discerned a reverence for the documentary past in the "great rumor" of 1377, when peasant communities searched Domesday for evidence that they were ancient demesne of the crown (and therefore exempt from many customary duties).[112] Something of that reverence can be seen here. But the reverence was contingent on the ancient documents saying what the rebels wanted them to say; antiquity did not attest their authority, only the greater probability that they would be useful.

The rebels aimed not to destroy the documentary culture of feudal tenure and royal government, but to re-create it; they recognized the written document as something powerful but also malleable, something that, once written, could be *re*written. When they successfully demanded charters of manumission from Richard II—their most significant and public attempt to rewrite the government of Britain—they showed a precise understanding of the forms and procedures of document and archive. That they demanded them at all demonstrates their respect for the forms of official writing,[113] and also their knowledge of these forms. The series of events up to and including the issue of charters of manumission and amnesty which Richard granted on 14 June, and which his chancery worked feverishly to produce, was recorded closely

112. Faith, "The 'Great Rumour' of 1377 and Peasant Ideology," in Hilton and Aston, *English Rising*, 42–73; see also J. H. Tillotson, "Peasant Unrest in the England of Richard II: Some Evidence from Royal Records," *Historical Studies* (University of Melbourne) 16 (1974–75): 1–16. Hilton claims that this practice "was at least a century old" in 1377 ("Peasant Movements in England Before 1381" [1949], rpt. in his *Class Conflict and the Crisis of Feudalism: Essays in Medieval Social History* [London, 1985], 129).

113. So does the later history of these writs. Richard naturally revoked these charters as soon as the main body of rebels had dispersed; but peasants' possession of them gave headaches for months afterwards to landlords whose tenants refused customary services on their authority. See the letter patent of 22 July, in which the king orders the tenants free and neif of Langele Marreys that they are to continue their services as before the rising, claiming no privileges they had not enjoyed before; *and* (indicating the source of the trouble) that they are to return the charters of manumission issued after Mile End to the king and council (*CPR 1381–1385*, 2). For the revocation, its presentation in parliament, and the criticisms it occasioned from the commons, see *Rp* 3.99–100.

by the *Anonimalle*, whose author was close to the witnesses within the Tower and was perhaps there himself.[114] His account is detailed enough to show what both the rebels and the king's advisers were up to, and what each thought the other capable of. The chronicler reports that when Archbishop Sudbury and Sir Robert Hales persuaded the king not to come to the rebels, the rebels went to the king at the Tower. Richard at first merely offered amnesty if the crowds would disperse immediately; but to this

> they all cried, as with one voice, that they would not leave until they had the traitors staying in the Tower [Sudbury, Hales, and the others], and also charters declaring them free of all manner of service and all the other points they would demand. The king graciously granted their request, and had a clerk write a bill in their presence, which read:
>
> Richard, king of England and France, thanks his good commons heartily for their desire to see him and hold him for their king, and pardons them all manner of trespass and offense and felony made until this hour; and wishes and commands that each haste himself back to his own home, and wishes and commands that each send to him his grievances in writing; and he will, by counsel of his loyal lords and council, ordain such remedy as will profit him, and them, and the whole realm.
>
> To this he set his signet in their presence, and sent the bill, brought by two knights, to them near St. Katherine's, and had it read to them; the one who read it stood on an old chair among them so that he could be heard. All this time, the king stayed in the tower, to his own great distress. And when the commons heard the bill, they said that it was all trifles and tricks; and therefore they returned to London and announced throughout the city that all men of law, and all those of the chancery and exchequer, and all who knew how to write a brief or a letter, should be beheaded wherever they might be found.[115]

114. See n. 21 above for Galbraith's identification of the author as William Pakington. Galbraith's suggestion was incautious, but it is not clear to me that it deserves the drubbing it has received. Pakington was keeper of the wardrobe at this time, which was Richard's place of refuge after his return from Mile End and the lynching of Sudbury and Hales; even if he was not present in the Tower itself, he would likely have been in a position to hear reports of the previous day's events less than twenty-four hours later.

115. "Et toutz crierent a une voice qils ne vodroient aler avaunt qils avoient les traitours deinz la Toure et chartres destre free de toutz maners des servage et des autres maners des poyntes qils vodroient demander; et le roy les graunta bonement et fist une clerk escriver une bille en lour presence en ceste maner: Le roy Richarde Dengleterre et de Fraunce enmercy moult ses bones comunes de ceo qils ount si graunde desir pur luy vere et tener lour roy, et pardone a eux toutz maners des trespas et mespressiones et felonye faitz avaunt ces houres; et voet et comande desore en avaunt qe chescune soy hast a soun propre hostelle et voet et comande qe chescune ses grevances en escript et les facent envoier a luy

Though the other chronicle accounts differ from this report, none successfully contradicts it.[116] After several days of burning charters, the Essex rebels wanted to see one issued; they knew what to ask for; and they knew that what they wanted was not what they got, that the king's writ was just "trifles and tricks."

The real interest of the passage lies in a conjunction. The chronicler says that the commons, after rejecting the offered writ, *therefore (purceo)* issued a capital sentence against men of law and clerks of chancery and exchequer. He does not explain the causal connection, why *this* document touched off *this* threat, because to him it was obvious. The rebels recognized the course of action commended to them and knew what it was worth. Richard was temporizing. His suggestion that a written complaint would be considered by the "lords and council" of the king commended to them the most familiar, conventional means of redress for complaints against the actions of the king's lieges and ministers, the petition or bill—which could be brought either as a "partial" petition (concerning individual parties and their grievances) or a "common petition" (touching all the king's subjects).[117] Common petitions, and partial petitions of peculiar importance or requiring the king's discretion, were considered by the king and council, "in parliament" with the lords.[118] The king was issuing the promise, familiar in other times and places, that the grievances of the commons would receive most serious

---

et il ordenera par lavyse de ses loials seignurs et de soun bone conseil tiel remedy qe profit serra a luy et as eux et al roialme. Et a ceo mist soun seal de soun signet en presence de eux, et puis envoia la dite bille od deux des ses chivalers a eux denvers seint Kateryns et le fist leir a eux; et cestuy qe list la bille estea en une auncien chare amont les autres, issint qe toutz purroient oier; et en toute le temps le roy fuist esteaunt en la toure en graunde deseas a luy. Et quant les comunes avoient oie la bille, ils dissoient qil ne fuist forsqe troefles et mokerie; et purceo retournerount a Loundres et fesoient crier parmy la citee qe toutz les gentz de la ley et toutz ceuz de la chauncellerie et del eschequer et toutz qe savoient brief ou lettre escriver deveroit estre decolles ou ils purroient estre trovez" (*Anonimalle*, 143–44).

116. Both Knighton and Walsingham telescope the events to eliminate the colloquy between king and rebels at the Tower; either may be relying in part on the *Anonimalle* passage (Galbraith thinks Walsingham was ["Thoughts," 50, 50n]). The London inquest, concerned mainly with events in which officials of the city were concerned, omits everything happening about the king's person until Smithfield (two days later), in which mayor Walworth played a leading role (Réville, *Soulèvement*, 190–93).

117. The "common petitions" were not, as was once thought, petitions offered by the commons in parliament; they were rather matters, brought forward by anyone, touching on common concern. This is precisely what the petitions Richard was inviting would have been; see Doris Rayner, "The Forms and Machinery of the 'Commune Petition' in the Fourteenth Century," *EHR* 56 (1941): 198–233, 549–70.

118. On this, see Rayner, "Forms and Machinery," and Sir Goronwy Edwards, *The Second Century of the English Parliament* (Oxford, 1979), 46–48.

attention in due course. The rebels' reply—that they would execute clerks of chancery and exchequer—answered the king in his own terms. They singled out chancery because one of its jobs was deciding who in council or parliament was to hear what petition, and indeed to decide which petitions would be heard by king and council and which would not.[119] By pairing chancery with the exchequer, the rebels showed that they knew of another function, common to both offices: to act as courts of equity competent to redress grievances, chancery hearing claims against the king's ministers outside the jurisdiction of common law, the exchequer hearing matters concerning the land of the realm, manorial duties, and the rest:[120] the two major areas of rebel complaint.

The violence threatened—we are not told whether it was prosecuted—against chancery and the exchequer was not a non sequitur; the chronicler's "therefore" acknowledges as much. The decision to move against these offices was a move to preempt even the possibility that the rebels' grievances would become routine fodder for the machinery of government, shunted aside to parliamentary auditors other than the king, or even shunted out of parliamentary jurisdiction altogether. The "rustics" understood royal administration, and understood it better than the king's advisers expected.

The muniments and legal instruments burned in the attacks on manors and on lawyers were not an alien or mysterious presence to those who burned them, nor (to put it another way) was the act of burning them an exorcism of something threatening because incomprehensible. All the available sources—indeed, what the sources betray in their own despite—show that the destruction was informed, specific, and tactical. (Similarly, violence against persons was notably restrained, directed almost solely against the heads of departments in the royal service; only three local officials seem to have been killed.)[121] This is not, as I have

119. Only in the following decade did the keeper of the privy seal begin to share this work with chancery; see Tout, *Chapters* 5:52.

120. On chancery, see Bertie Wilkinson, "The Council and the Origins of the Equitable Jurisdiction of Chancery," in his *Studies in the Constitutional History of the Thirteenth and Fourteenth Centuries* (Manchester, 1937), 196–215. Exchequer's jurisdiction in equity was ancient.

121. As Ormrod has observed ("Peasants' Revolt and the Government of England," 13–15). Ormrod's suggestion that this apparent moderation "probably says more for the defensive measures taken by the gentry than for any lack of determination on the part of the rebels" (12) seems mistaken; as he himself notes, many sheriffs, escheators, coroners, and justices of the peace were confronted and harassed—which means that the rebels had

observed already, the picture of rural and town society usually drawn by historians of the rebellion or of the medieval peasantry. It is time to redraw the picture, to trace the paths of social experience along which bureaucratic culture traveled beyond its immediate home and its usual clientele. "Writing in the countryside" is not an oxymoron; even the chroniclers' assumption that writing would only baffle or enrage peasants expresses doubt not that writing would impinge upon a peasant's experience, but that the peasant could become part of its world, and therefore of theirs.

"Literacy," clearly, must mean something different from the mere ability to make and construe the written word. The literacy demonstrated in the acts of destruction is shallower, maybe, than the ability to read and write, though as I have already argued, these skills were perhaps more widely diffused than we have thought; but it is correspondingly broader, a savvy about the forms and functions and powers of documentary usage.[122] This is one reason why I shrugged off the question of whether the rebel letters were written by rebel clerics: the priest had very little advantage over his flock in the kind of documentary involvement that the rising displayed. The scope of the literacy the rebels claimed had more to do with their claims to familiarity with and investment in the documentary culture by which a realm was governed than with clerical bookishness: more to do with the place of writing in their collective lives, for the political culture of which these letters were a preliminary declaration must be traced in the culture of the village itself. The priest, however, is a good place to start; he will allow us to start sketching the shape of the rural community.

It has been conventional to speak of the rising's clerical sympathizers or "allies." Behind these casual locutions lies the assumption that those clerks who joined the insurgents joined them from outside, that ordination so translated a man from one world of thought and experience to another that he would thereafter be in his community but not of it.[123] Rodney Hilton, for example, notes that ordinarily a nonresident

---

gained access to them and therefore presumably could have killed them—but were allowed to go free.

122. What Parkes calls "pragmatic literacy" ("Literacy of the Laity," 557).

123. Hilton discusses clerical participation in the chapter he entitles "The Allies of the Rebels," and explains it by reference to the analogy between the effect of the Statute of Laborers on workers and on priests, and to theological dissent (*Bond Men Made Free*, 207–13); Dobson presents clerical participation as one of the "reasons for refusing to interpret the great revolt in terms of a crude class struggle" (*Peasants' Revolt*, 17). These

rector would engross the income of a church, hiring (at low rates) one
or more curates, "not necessarily drawn from the peasantry, but in close
contact with them." In the pulpit and in confession, these "were very
important conveyors of the ideology of the rulers of society to the
peasants."[124] To say that resident clergy were "in close contact" with the
peasants among whom they lived hardly describes what we see when
they surface in local records. In 1311, two Northamptonshire clerks join
in a fight between Richard of Aldwinkle and Richard of Molesworth;
the same year, William of Wenlington, parish chaplain of Yelvertoft,
beats Thomas le Soutere to death when Thomas refuses to sell him a
candle on credit.[125] When the chaplain of Sanford (Somerset) shuts the
door of the church against the lord who is fleeing a murderous conspiracy, perhaps he merely acts with prudence;[126] but when John Lelley,
vicar of the church of St. Michael in Derby, seizes the horse of Richard
of Makeney because it has run him down with a cart, he reacts in rural
fashion to a rural slight.[127] The abbot of Bec proceeds against the
"parson of the church" for allowing his cow to wander into the lord's
field (Thomas Guner and William Coke pledge for him).[128] The bishop
of Ely proceeds against Bartholomew, the chaplain at Littleport, for
carrying away the dominical sedge.[129] In the same court, Thomas Thame,
chaplain, has much business pending: he claims that the messuage of
which he and others hold two parts should be free of customary service;
he is amerced 2s. for failing to repair his section of the roadway; he is
faced with a claim that, along with four others, he has deforced Robert
Carter of a rood of land; he stands pledge for Elisote Jordan in the
assize of bread.[130] William the Chaplain is busy at Battle's court of
Brightwaltham in 1296 with more serious business: he wages his law

assessments follow Stubbs, who cited the presence of clerics as evidence of the variety,
even the incoherence, of the rising's aims (*The Constitutional History of England in Its
Origin and Development*, 3d ed. (Oxford, 1883), 2:469).

124. Hilton, "Medieval Peasants: Any Lessons?" (1974), rpt. in *Class Conflict*, 118.

125. These cases from Charles Gross, ed., *Select Cases from the Coroners' Rolls A.D.
1265–1413*, SS 9 (London, 1896), 59–60.

126. A gaol delivery of 1225 (F. W. Maitland, ed., *Select Pleas of the Crown*, vol. 1, *A.D.
1200–1225*, SS 1 [London, 1888], 115–16).

127. From 1331 (William Craddock Bolland, ed., *Select Bills in Eyre A.D. 1292–1333*,
SS 30 [London, 1914], 74).

128. Court baron of Deverill (Wilts), 1247 (Maitland, ed., *Select Pleas in Manorial
Courts*, 13).

129. Bishop of Ely's court and leet, 1316 (Maitland and Baildon, eds., *Court Baron*,
122).

130. Maitland and Baildon, *Court Baron*, 127, 130, 132, 138.

against a charge of defamation, is convicted of carrying off a rooster belonging to the lord and breaking his hedges, and is amerced for the trespass "of his brother Thomas" into the lord's garden.[131]

The point of these examples is not how fractious or grasping the local priest might be (court rolls rarely celebrate virtue), but how completely he was a villager: his crimes were like other villagers' crimes, his encroachments like their encroachments; he took part in the same fights, held plots in the same fields, sought the same exemptions. He was often local, one child of a family whose other children farmed the local fields, like the chaplain William above, whose brother also lived in Brightwaltham; the Ramsey manor court identified "Alan" of Nidding-worth-cum-Holywell as "brother of the parson."[132] The priest's church was where he preached and celebrated mass; it was also where he announced the beginning of pasturage and harvest and proclaimed waifs and strays, and where the villagers held meetings and stored grain.[133] He did not live in "close contact" with peasants; he lived with *other* peasants. What he said when he preached or heard confessions, whether he conveyed "the ideology of the rulers to the peasants," neither Hilton nor anyone else can know.[134] What he did when he was not wearing the priestly robe can be inferred from the evidences of court rolls and legislation, and it was more or less what any middling tenant would do, and unsurprisingly so: at the exiguous salary of four or five marks for

131. Maitland, *Select Pleas in Manorial Courts*, 172–73.

132. *Court Rolls of the Abbey of Ramsey and of the Honor of Clare*, ed. Warren O. Ault (New Haven, 1928), 188. The same relation obtains in the General Prologue of the *Canterbury Tales*, where the plowman is the parson's brother.

133. Warren O. Ault, *The Self-Directing Activities of Village Communities in Medieval England* (Boston, 1952), 15.

134. Hilton's evidence for the assertion quoted above and summarized here is as follows: "This was demonstrated very clearly in the limited ideology of the peasantry in times of revolt, when they found it impossible to break away from the traditional tripartite image of society which was promulgated by official ruling society mainly through the church" (Hilton, "Medieval Peasants: Any Lessons?" 116). There are a number of problems with this assertion, only the first of which is that this is very tenuous evidence on which to build any assertion about the contents of sermons and penitential injunctions. To limit the case to the English rising: on what basis does Hilton suggest that the rebels meant to preserve the three orders? Perhaps he means that by insisting "in future there should be no lordship, saving the lordship of the king" and that "there should be only one bishop in England," Wat Tyler was leaving in place the first estate (in the person of the lone archbishop of Canterbury) and the second (in the person of the king). But this ignores the inflection that the rising's ideology gave at least to the relation of king to commons, which I discuss in ch. 4. I hope that the following paragraphs, and the following chapters, will show that the idea of kingship that the rising promulgated was not drawn from the old tripartite ideology, but was a creative adaptation of common-law procedures and the customs of village self-government.

chaplains with cure of souls—the going rate before the plague, and the canonically fixed price thereafter—the stipendiary priest had to work his plots to keep body and soul together.[135] Orme would have us take seriously the possibility that many resident parish priests taught the abc's to children of the parish.[136] If we do, we must also acknowledge that those he taught were, with good or ill grace, his fellow villagers the rest of the time.

The priest's literacy, however attenuated, did mark him out from the other villagers; so did his sacramental function. But his economic and political interests differed little from those of a lay villager of similar means, and we might as well call "rebels" those clerics who joined the rebellion in 1381, as other peasants were rebels. And however far their literacy—their ability to read and write—was sorted to themselves alone, the insurgency displayed a literacy in that wider sense I described above—a knowingness in the ways and forms and occasions of documentary writing—in which they would have been no more expert than their fellows, and which they would have acquired from the same sources. The presence of clerics in the rising can explain a little of its cast—perhaps the diffusion of those ideas and texts I treat in the next two chapters—but it cannot explain the rebels' claim to documentary competence or the political imagination that underlay it. Explaining these things requires tracing the lines of contact between the local world of the village and the political culture of the realm, the places of public assembly in and around the villages: the places where those of similar and different stations negotiated common and rival interests and met with the world beyond the village. There are three such places, all in the immediate vicinity of every community. The first I have already described, the church. The second was the alehouse, often sitting next to it, and too often (to the church's proprietors) competing for the same clientele.[137] The third is the court: the manorial court held in particular villages under the lord's authority, and—what I am concerned with here—the county court or shire-moot.[138]

135. See Bertha Haven Putnam, "Maximum Wage-Laws for Priests after the Black Death, 1348–1381," *AHR* 21 (1915): 31.

136. See n. 62 above.

137. Barbara A. Hanawalt, *The Ties That Bound: Peasant Families in Medieval England* (Oxford, 1986), 28; Norman Tanner, *The Church in Late Medieval Norwich 1370–1532* (Toronto, 1984), 9–10.

138. We do not usually think of these places together because the study of them has been atomized, asymmetrical, and vertical, parceled out to historians of the larger

By the late fourteenth century, the strictly judicial labors of the county court were light,[139] but its monthly business meeting, the *plenus comitatus*, bustled with a variety of other business and allowed attendants to pursue a still greater variety themselves.[140] The court required the presence of the lords' representatives, major freeholders, the sheriff and coroners, and, the most important for our purposes, the "suitors," traditionally four men of each vill, who could be, and seem often enough to have been, villeins.[141] The court was where parliament met the population: it chose knights of the shire to represent the commons, heard these knights' reports on parliamentary business, and determined the sense of the community in their regard, processes in which the whole range of social classes there participated.[142] Royal writs, ordi-

---

institutions of which they were a part: the first to ecclesiastical, the third to legal and "constitutional" historians. The second has hardly been studied at all. A brief summary of scholarship—mostly on the legal, economic, and technological aspects of brewing and selling—is available in Peter Clark, *The English Alehouse: A Social History 1200–1830* (London, 1983), 20–38, which, as its subtitle suggests, uses the earlier period mainly to set up a discussion of later, better-documented centuries. But each of these venues also had a horizontal axis and convoked a local population even as it served an institutional function; the social historian would do well to think of them as sites of congregation and communication.

139. On writs and actions within its competence, see Robert C. Palmer, *The County Courts of Medieval England 1150–1350* (Princeton, 1982), chs. 7–8.

140. William Alfred Morris, *The Early English County Court: An Historical Treatise with Illustrative Documents* (Berkeley, 1926), 98–99, and generally 90–136; Palmer, *County Courts*, 16. See also the crucial discussion—on which much of this paragraph hangs—by J. R. Maddicott, "The County Community and the Making of Public Opinion in Fourteenth-Century England," *TRHS*, 5th ser., 28 (1978): 27–43. On its early judicial functions, see Frederick Pollock and F. W. Maitland, *History of English Law Before the Time of Edward I* (Cambridge, Eng., 1926) 1:532–56.

141. Maddicott shows, contrary to Morris's claim, that the reeve and four men of each vill were probably present at all meetings of the court, not just those before the justices ("County Community," 33). See also Hyams, *King, Lords, and Peasants*, 155.

142. On the choice of knights of the shire, see Palmer, *County Courts*, 293–94. A. L. Brown cites the fascinating common petition of 1376 which asks that the county knight be selected only by *les meillours gentz*, to which the king responded that elections were to continue to be by "common assent of all the county," which implies both that some wider constituency was the customary rule and that it was wide enough that those of higher rank worried about the influence of their inferiors. When a property requirement of 40s. for freeholders was eventually established in 1430, it was because of the disturbances that "lesser people" were said to bring to the elections ("Parliament, c. 1377–1422," in R. G. Davies and J. H. Denton, eds., *The English Parliament in the Middle Ages* [Philadelphia, 1981], 119). H. G. Richardson and G. O. Sayles argued massively and learnedly against the importance of the commons in the business or development of parliament; see, for example, Richardson, "The Commons and Medieval Politics," *TRHS* 28 (1945): 21–45. His point is that the commons were virtually without political initiative ("The commons become part of the machinery of government: they are the recognised channel through which certain kinds of business pass" [34]). But that point is not really at issue here. What

nances, and statutes would be proclaimed at the meetings and apparently kept on file with the sheriff (a practice that could help explain the familiarity of rebels with both contents and location of such writs).[143] The shire knights would bring news—sometimes on specific commission from the government, sometimes off their own bat.[144] Here, finally, the parliamentary petition (the course of action Richard recommended to the rebels) would be drawn up, and reports would be made on responses to petitions from the session just ended.[145] But the social functions of congregation and information probably consumed as much collective time and energy as other, more official duties: the court drew "a crowd of others who came to have their legal instruments witnessed in so public a place or merely to gossip and observe."[146] All of this displayed to those present the forms in which the royal government conducted its business, the issues it dealt with, and the documents that fed its official life.

And it did all this in a context that also displayed, openly, the configurations of local power. It would be silly to sentimentalize the court into a site where villein and freeholder enjoyed free colloquy and discovered their common interests. Though by the 1380s the court usually met in church or shire-hall, not in the castle of the lord, it was still the lord's territory and in a sense his property.[147] More important, it was in the more immediate control of those who formed the first and

---

is important is, first, the mechanism of deliberation and information around parliamentary business in the county and borough courts—even if this was mere pretense—and, second, the king's belief that public opinion was worth courting (which Richardson acknowledges: "They were . . ., on occasion, worth wooing and worth managing" [38]).

143. Morris, *English County Court*, 128–29; H. G. Richardson, "The Early Statutes," *Law Quarterly Review* 50 (1954): 545–46. Jenkinson and Mills show that over seventeen months, the sheriff in Bedfordshire enrolled about two thousand writs ("Rolls from a Sheriff's Office," 24).

144. J. R. Maddicott, "Parliament and the Constituencies, 1272–1377," in Davies and Denton, *English Parliament*, 61–87. Tout has demonstrated that the actions of both the king and the appellants in 1387–88 show that they all cared what the populace thought ("Parliament and Public Opinion, 1376–1388," in *The Collected Papers of Thomas Frederick Tout* [Manchester, 1934], 173–90). Thorpe CJ said in 1365: "Every one is bound to know at once what is done in Parliament, for Parliament represents the body of the whole realm" (quoted in F. W. Maitland, "The Crown as Corporation," in his *Collected Papers*, ed. H. A. L. Fisher [Cambridge, 1911], 3:247).

145. H. G. Richardson and G. O. Sayles, "The Parliaments of Edward III," *BIHR* 9 (1931): 12–13.

146. Maddicott, "County Community," 30.

147. Palmer, *County Courts*, 19–21. Morris, *English County Court*, 94. "Quality counted more than quantity," Maddicott says, "and the magnate unmistakably held sway" ("County Community," 31–32).

most lasting targets of violence in the rising: the gentry and prosperous burgesses who served as sheriffs and who chose and sometimes served as shire knights in parliament, the jurors, and the men of law. The royal provision of news, similarly, was not innocent; as Tout recognized, it was royal propaganda, disseminated in pulpit and court. Since the French war presented Edward III with the delicate task of scaring up money with threats of French invasion while simultaneously showing that money granted before had not been wasted, he worked the channels of public communication hard, touting victories, explaining away defeats, and cultivating francophobia. Shire knights brought home news carefully tailored to royal need, and sheriffs were charged with the public announcement of policy.[148] But news tailored is still news, news enough to keep English villages from suffering or enjoying a peaceful isolation; and such news, *especially* when tailored, implicitly tells the audience that its purveyor has an interest in its purveyance. News came in thick to the church pulpit,[149] and still thicker to the shire court.[150] These venues of local congregation offered a regular provision of exactly the information, and documents of precisely the sort—news of parliamentary deliberations and major events, the proclamation and display of royal writs, conferences on petitions, legal advice and instruments—that could enable the rebels' precisely articulated declarations and demands. These courts were part of the texture of local culture throughout the realm; they permitted (indeed required) some participation from both free-

148. H. J. Hewitt, *The Organization of War under Edward III, 1338–62* (Manchester, 1966), 159–60.

149. The king would order prayers for the English expeditions or against French invasions and at times even ordered that the motives of foreign policy be explained by the local clergy (Hewitt, *Organization of War*, 161–63; A. K. McHardy, "Liturgy and Propaganda in the Diocese of Lincoln During the Hundred Years War," *SCH* 18 [1982]: 215–27).

150. Thus covering two of the three "locales" I mentioned earlier. Partly for lack of information and partly for lack of study, a description of the alehouse and its role in the exchange of political information and opinion cannot be made. In the present state of information, it would require the sort of suppositious reconstruction of which Jusserand was master, and in which I will indulge, briefly, in ch. 3; still, one should assume that when gathered in groups people are likely to talk. The Cambridge inquisitions into the rising record one suggestive event. John Shirle of Nottinghamshire was hanged for his part in the rebellion; the jurors related that Shirle had declared the injustice of John Ball's execution "in a tavern in Briggestret in Cambridge, where many were assembled to listen to his news and worthless talk" (*Peasants' Revolt*, xxviii). For a discussion of this incident, see Ralph Hanna III, "Pilate's Voice/Shirley's Case," *South Atlantic Quarterly* 94 (1992): 793–812.

holders and villeins; they constituted a habit of information in the countryside.

This habit implicated everyone in particular moments of national history and particular institutions of national life; the English peasantry was not a "people without history"; they no more lived and acted through unreflective patterns of "primitive" communal impulse than did, or does, anyone else: to talk as though they did explains away more than it explains. For example, all the major chroniclers notice that the rebels called themselves the allies, almost the delegates, of the king. "With whom haldes yow?" was their challenge; the correct reply was "Wyth Kyng Richarde and wyth the trew comunes."[151] Hilton—as sympathetic to the rising as any historian—says of the rebels' appeal to the king for liberties that they knew his lieges would not grant, "The rumour was strong during the whole course of the rising . . . that the movement had the king's blessing. . . . They thought of the monarchy as an institution standing above individuals and classes, capable of dispensing even-handed justice": their trust, in other words, grew from their ignorance, from their innocent acceptance of what royal ideology wanted them, and everyone, to believe.[152] I would suggest that much of the trust, real or feigned, in Richard's person arose rather from their knowledge: knowledge of the forms of law (always on offer at the county court), supplemented by the persistence of local memory in the countryside; knowledge which, systematized and articulated, allowed them to appropriate the gentry's local administration to their own purposes.

---

151. "Et les ditz comunes avoient entre eux une wache worde en Engleys, 'With whom haldes yow?' et le respouns fuist, 'Wyth kynge Richarde and wyth the trew communes'" (*Anonimalle*, 139).

152. Hilton, *Bond Men Made Free*, 225. A classic and less self-conscious version of the same idea can be found in Petit-Dutaillis: "the rebels affected a high regard for the person of the king. A careful distinction was drawn between him and the 'traitors' who surrounded him. Several 'traitors' atoned with their lives for the humiliation and the misfortunes of England, but these murders were not the outcome of a calculated policy" (*Studies and Notes*, 275). For more of the same, see J. A. Raftis, "Social Change Versus Revolution: New Interpretations of the Peasants' Revolt of 1381," in F. X. Newman, ed., *Social Unrest in the Late Middle Ages* (Binghamton, 1986), 3–22; F. Graus, "The Late Medieval Poor in Town and Countryside," in Sylvia L. Thrupp, ed., *Change in Medieval Society: Europe North of the Alps* (New York, 1964), 319; Rossell Hope Robbins, "Middle English Poems of Protest," *Anglia* 78 (1960): 202. Eric Hobsbawm describes with more subtlety the process by which modern urban mobs personify their demands in a leader (*Primitive Rebels: Studies in Archaic Forms of Social Movement in the Nineteenth and Twentieth Centuries* [New York, 1959], 118–20).

The availability and usefulness of the petition was, even in the early fourteenth century, "realized by the very humble," and to judge from the servile tone and often spurious claims to poverty that can be found in "partial" petitions, was colloquially understood as a proper remedy for those who had few remedies of any other sort.[153] The petitioner conventionally addressed herself or himself directly to the king, who was, in form if not in fact, the dispenser of grace. Drawing up these petitions was part of the regular business of the shire court. But the shire court was also a court, and there was a legal form of access to the king's political person that might be said to encourage (rightly, for those with a sense of history) an identification with him by those who felt aggrieved. This was the procedure that developed into the law of trespass, that redress for wrongs—generally, violence or appropriation against the peace, usually on the part of a lord or an official—called the plaint.

The plaint was designed to induce some flexibility in the brittle structures of early criminal law. It had some peculiar characteristics.[154] First, it did not require a writ, thereby circumventing both the expense and the rigidly formulaic expression that hedged about common-law actions; the plaint was a fairly cheap and speedy way of getting justice against, say, a lord who extorted novel services without engaging him in trial by battle. Second, the plaint was neither quite a civil nor quite a criminal action, but partook of both. Third—and this, closely related to the last, is the point—the complaint was always joined by a second party: since it was an action of trespass, which was by definition a breach of the king's peace as well as a personal injury, the king figured as reserve plaintiff in every such action. Should the initial *civil* complaint wreck itself on the rocks of civil procedure—as it easily could, and was often even planned to do—the crown would immediately and automatically take it up again, this time as a criminal action. The maxim of the trespass law into which it developed was that the plaintiff sued *tam pro domino rege quam pro seipso*—on the king's behalf as well as on his or her own.

So the procedural form of the plaint, an action designed to prosecute the violence and extortions practiced by king's lieges and ministers, broadly implied that the king and the complainant were allied against

153. Maddicott, "Parliament and the Constituencies," 68–69.

154. For what follows, I rely largely on the discussion by Alan Harding, "Plaints and Bills in the History of English Law, Mainly in the Period 1250–1350," in D. Jenkins, ed., *Legal History Studies, 1972* (Cardiff, 1972), 65–86.

extortionate lords and ministers, that in fact the king, through his justices, *automatically* took the side of any party victimized by the arrogance of power; and the formulae used by such complainants show that the implication was taken seriously.[155] In 1381, the rebels' "trust" in the king derived less from the mysterious and mythicizing distance of the king's person than from the extraordinary accessibility of his name at law.[156] But this is not to say that this trust was a mere deduction of fact from the conventions of legal form; it preserved the memory of where those conventions had come from. Harding comments on the origin of the plaint, "I don't see how the law could ever have extended from the narrow field of land disputes to the substantially and socially far larger one of tort if thirteenth century kings had not taken the initiative and asked for complaints of such wrongs; not just because these wrongs infringed their authority in a general sense, but because they involved the misuse of their power by their officials."[157] His supposition fits with the historical concern of the monarchy to consolidate its own power in the countryside by providing paths of appeal to the throne over the heads of more local powers.[158] Royal justice in the twelfth and thirteenth centuries advocated the rights of the middling to

155. "Par dieu sire Justice pensez de moi kar io ay nul eyde for deu e vos"; "Cher sire joe vus cri merci issi com vus estis mis en la nostur seinur le Roy pur dreit fere a poueris e a riches"; "Et pur deu sere ke pite vous prenne pur Moy ke sun vn poueres home" (Bolland, ed., *Select Bills in Eyre*, 2, 6, 36). The editor comments, "It is obvious that most of these, at any rate, were composed without any assistance either from a professional lawyer or from one who was accustomed to express himself in Anglo-French. Apart from the actual script, most of them bear every sign of being the composition of illiterate people" helped, perhaps, by "some sort of professional letter-writers" (xix).

156. For a dramatic example of the personalization and dramatization of this legal form, see the following thirteenth-century poem on a conflict between the canons of Leicester Abbey and its tenants (Bodl. MS 57, fols. 191d–92; my emphasis):

Quando frui more captabant liberiore,
Gens dixit ville "patimur discrimina mille:

Nulli servire volumus: *dum possumus ire*
Ibimus ad regem qui nobis vult dare legem."

It is clear from the Coram rege rolls, as Hilton shows, that what this last line—"We shall go while we can to the king, who wants to give us right"—means nothing more than that the King's Bench is hearing a complaint by thirty of the abbey's tenants against the abbot for "illegal imposition of unjust services" ("A Thirteenth-Century Poem on Disputed Villein Services" [1941], in Hilton, *Class Conflict*, 108–12).

157. Harding, "Plaints and Bills," 69; see also Harding, *The Law Courts of Medieval England* (London, 1973), 87.

158. As in the establishment of the *iter*, the eyre, whose competence in the thirteenth century encompassed, in addition to questions of tenure, "the official misdoings of royal officers, sheriffs, coroners and bailiffs" (Pollock and Maitland, *History of English Law* 2:521).

check the power of the great, and it invited those with grievances to seek balm from the justices in eyre.

In fact, it seems to have been the enormous growth in accusations of trespass, from those too poor to purchase writs, clogging the path to the eyre, that brought its demise in the first decades of the fourteenth century.[159] By 1381, access to the king's justice was more difficult than it had been when Henry III invited complaints against his officials. The demise of the eyre brought a local judiciary more concerned to oppress than redress:[160] the keepers (later justices) of the peace were drawn from the gentry and larger landholders, and their powers became the subject of general criticism and even contempt for serving the private interests of those with large private holdings; after 1368, the justices of the peace were charged also with enforcement of the Statute of Laborers. The forms of law were still in place, and indeed the king's justice still stood as the best hope for outflanking seigneurially controlled juries; but such maneuvers took more ingenuity than in the past. The commons of the prosperous town of Abingdon came close to winning a long dispute with their overlord the abbot by "impeaching" him for the usurpation of royal rights. They thereby moved the case out of common law (where it would have been decided by jurors in the abbot's pocket) to council and chancery.[161] This "impeachment" had precisely the legal and imaginative structure of a plaint: Gabrielle Lambrick notes the same identification of the (collective) plaintiff with the person of the king. Lambrick is concerned to show that the idea of impeachment was not contrived ex nihilo in 1376, for the Good Parliament to use against the king's ministers, and that it was not a privilege just of the commons in parliament; and she suggests that the use of the word "impeachment" by the Abingdon tenants shows that it was already current by 1368. But none of her evidence shows that the concept was not, in fact, contrived ex nihilo by the lawyer for the Abingdon tenants. They wanted to get around the abbot's influence in local courts to gain access to the sort of

159. See Harding, *Law Courts*, 86–87.

160. Harding describes the manipulation of royal justice to the interest of landholders in "The Revolt Against the Justices," in Hilton and Aston, *English Rising*, 165–93.

161. See Gabrielle Lambrick, "The Impeachment of the Abbot of Abingdon in 1368," *EHR* 82 (1967): 250–76. The abbot won, but only by default, because there was not enough evidence for a reasoned decision; see Lambrick, 260. The contest had been going on for decades and would continue for decades beyond the eventual resolution of this moment in 1372; see G. D. G. Hall, "The Abbot of Abingdon and the Tenants of Winkfield," *MÆ* 28 (1959): 91–95.

royal justice once less tortuously available; they knew that common law no longer offered the protection it once had. The co-optation of the "king's justice" by local justices was a fiction that fooled nobody.

Solutions like this impeachment offered themselves only to groups (who could pool their resources to obtain legal help), and prosperous groups at that. But the tactic was an improvisatory way of recapturing an ordinary privilege recently lost, one that at the beginning of the century did not have to be pursued as an extraordinary circumstance but could be had, in theory, at least, from the nearest justice in eyre. For the Abingdon townspeople, the procedure was probably devised by the lawyer they retained; but there are excellent reasons for thinking that the possibility of entering a plaint before the king's itinerant justices, and of the royal invitation that initiated the procedure, lodged in local memory as markers of a time—idealized, but real—when the abuses of superiors could find remedy from the king, and when the king's part in the "double suit" of trespass was still meaningful, because the local gentry had not yet taken over the powers of justices. The villages of medieval England were tenacious of memory in the matter of privileges.[162] They manifested what might be called (collapsing two of Walter Ong's terms) the "homeostatic conservatism" of traditional cultures, preserving the memories that still matter while dropping out those that do not.[163] The close identification with the king that the rebels claimed was neither a blind acceptance of royal mythology nor a strategy for avoiding the charge of treason (by blaming the king's advisers rather than the king, a technique popular with parliaments both Good and Merciless). It was an extrapolation from the formal conventions of legal procedure. The rebels' blunt assertion that they were acting with the king against his ministers and lieges demanded that these conventions again be meaningful, when the recent evisceration of royal justice had rendered them meaningless. They asserted ancient legal privilege to

162. Rosamond Faith relates the episode of the tenants of Crondall (Hants), where the tenants claimed exemptions from certain manorial duties on the grounds that their land was ancient demesne—in the ordinary meaning, land held by the crown at the time of the Domesday survey. Crondall in fact appears in Domesday as land of Winchester's Old Minster; but it *had* been held of the crown twice, once in the ninth century and once in the tenth. "When the people of Crondall and Hustbourne Priors referred to 'the time when they were in the hands of the king's predecessors,' therefore, they must have been referring to a period which cannot have been nearer to their own time than the tenth century, and may have been as far back as the ninth" ("The 'Great Rumour' of 1377," 56–57). The crown accepted the tenants' claim.

163. Walter J. Ong, *Orality and Literacy* (London, 1982), 41–42, 46–49.

insist that the principle behind it—that the king sides automatically with
a wronged subject—become contemporary fact.

Familiarity, not ignorance, bred the rebels' contempt of official culture,
and that contempt was entirely provisional; they were ready to use its
language, and even to practice its exactions, in the name of their project.
The indictments relate actions which have been dismissed as opportunistic, self-interested, or worse, but which were in fact imitations of
state procedures with which the rebels, like all the king's subjects, were
only too well acquainted. When the Suffolk leader John Wrawe turned
state's evidence, he related a number of episodes like this one:

> John Wrawe, approver, accused Geoffrey Parfeye, vicar of the church of
> All Saints in Sudbury, and a certain Thomas, Geoffrey's chaplain . . .,
> Adam Bray, from the aforementioned parish of All Saints, and Thomas
> Munchesy of Edwardeston the younger, squire: that they (in the absence
> of the approver) went to the vill of Thetford, in the county of Norfolk,
> . . . and there feloniously and treacherously captured and extorted from
> the mayor and the greater burgesses of the said vill twenty gold marks,
> to save themselves and the aforementioned vill. And then they threatened
> the mayor and burgesses, that unless they delivered this sum, the afore-
> mentioned John Wrawe with his company . . . would come to destroy
> and oppress the mayor and the burgesses and burn down the vill. And
> from these twenty marks received from the mayor and burgesses, Geoffrey
> gave to Thomas Munchesy, for his part, twenty shillings; to Adam Bray,
> twenty shillings; and he kept, for himself and his chaplain Thomas, forty
> shillings; the rest, fourteen marks, he delivered to John Wrawe at Sudbury.[164]

This scene was repeated dozens of times throughout the counties in

---

164. "Item, idem Johannes Wrawe, probator, appellavit Galfredum Parfeye, vicarium
ecclesie Omnium Sanctorum de Sudbury, et quemdam Thomam, capellanum ejusdem
Galfredi . . ., Adam Bray, de parochia Omnium Sanctorum de Sudbury predicta, et
Thomam Munchesy, de Edwardeston, squier, juniorem, de eo quod ipsi, in absencia
predicti probatoris, iverunt ad villam de Thetford, in comitatu Norffolchie, . . . et ibidem
felonice et prodiciose ceperunt et depredati fuerunt de majore et capitalibus burgensibus
dicte ville de Thetford viginti marcas auri numerati, ad salvandum eos et villam suam de
Thetford predictam. Et tunc minabantur ibidem eosdem majorem et burgenses, nisi
voluissent eis deliberasse summam predictam, quod predictus Johannes Wrawe cum
comitiva sua predicta, eodem die veneris, veniret ibidem ad destruendum et opprimendum
ipsos majorem et capitales burgenses, ac villam suam predictam comburendum, etc. Et de
quibus quidem viginti marcis predictis de eisdem majore et burgensibus, ut premittitur,
receptis, prefatus Galfredus dedit predicto Thome Mounchesy, pro parte sua, viginti
solidos; predicto Ade Bray viginti solidos, et cepit penes se, pro se ipso et pro predicto
Thoma, capellano suo, quadraginta solidos, et residium [*sic*], videlicet quotuordecim
marcas, idem Galfredus postea liberavit predicto Johanni Wrawe apud Sudbury predictam"
(Réville, *Soulèvement*, 180–81).

revolt; but this testimony, which enjoys the fuller narrative latitude given to the stories of approvers, shows in more detail what elsewhere juries reported more concisely: "Also, they say that . . . John Wryde, of Osprenge, came with force and arms to Hugh Hosier and Thomas Perot, in Canterbury, and upon them did make an assault, and with violence feloniously compelled them to pay forty shillings."[165] In Wrawe's account, we can see what must have happened in incidents like this: the rebels arrived before some official or other wealthy person, declared that they would back up their demands with force, and extorted a specific amount from the victim, a part of which was kept for themselves while the rest was given into the trust of a leader. It was, mutatis mutandis, a familiar scene, familiar to every one of the men and women who took part in the rising, and the language of one indictment makes clear just what it most resembled. According to the jurors of St. John's on Thanet (in an episode already mentioned), certain rebels

> raised a cry . . . that every liege man of our Lord the King ought to go to the house of William Medmenham, and demolish his house. . . . and they ordered a taxation to be paid for maintaining the said proceedings against the lordships throughout the whole Isle of Thanet, except the tenants of the Priory of Canterbury and the franchise of Canterbury.[166]

"Raising the cry" (*levare uthesium*) was the immemorial privilege and duty of every subject, free or villein: if someone was found dead, or a trespass was witnessed or suffered, the hue and cry brought the community to the scene, to enforce the peace or to witness evidence of a crime. Its use was subject to close regulation: proceedings against those who falsely raised the hue and cry, and against those who failed to raise it when necessary, can be found in almost any session of any court. The community that responded became, in effect, the collective deputy of the court until the machinery of justice could engage. The rebels on Thanet used the alarm to gather the community in the old fashion, but once gathered, the community found itself asked not to bring an action before the customary authorities but to acknowledge new authorities from among its own numbers. And the chance report by this jury of the word the rebels used shows how specifically they imagined their authority, for what the other indictments (like John Wryde's) called

165. Flaherty, "Great Rebellion," 75.
166. Flaherty, "Great Rebellion," 72.

"extortion" the rebels called "taxation": the insurgency modeled its extortions after the three-groat subsidy, the poll tax that had sparked the rebellion in the first place. The rebels assumed for themselves the same right to compel payment by household to support their military objectives that the king had compelled to support his. They were, I have argued, well informed about the constitution of government and its written culture. They were also willing to imitate its procedures, to claim them for their own.

This action, in a way, summarizes what I have described so far as the technique of the rebels and their letters. It is worth recalling how Walsingham described their announcement that documents would be burned: "They ordered [*statuerunt*] that all court rolls and muniments be cast into the flames."[167] *Statuere* is the verb used for the royal establishment of a law (hence "statute"). Walsingham chose the verb he did, I suspect, to describe a kind of action, the props and bearing that the rebels used while making their proclamations, declaring them as if promulgating new legislation. The rebels sought command, command of their own collective lives and of the institutions that constrained them. And so they sought its medium: writing they could promulgate, could give effect in the political world. It is the sort of writing they took care to destroy, and also to create. How far "literacy," in any full and modern sense of that word, actually extended through the rural population, the insurgents claimed that they had it, had enough of it to claim the prerogatives of the literate and to govern for themselves. This placed them in what had been defined immemorially as a clerkly space, a space of writing and documentary record marked by specialized forms and formulae, by specialized languages and hands, by all the parchment that flowed into the royal chancery and back out again. The letters announced that they were taking over this space, and taking over the forms that went with it.

167. See above, n. 99.

2

Wyclif in the Rising

jakke trewman doþ ʒow to understande þat falsnes and gyle haviþ regned
to longe & trewþe. hat bene sette under a lokke. and fal[s]nes regneth in
euerylk flokke. (Trewman)

Trewman's first phrase is at once salutation and lèse majesté. As clearly
as anything else in his letter, it embodies the political ambitions of the
rising, for these opening words stake a precise and audacious claim.[1]
"Doþ ʒow to understande" is a near Middle English equivalent to Latin
sciatis and French *sachez*, the formulaic markers of the royal will: "Ricardus, Dei gratia, Rex Anglie et Francie, et Dominus Hibernie, omnibus
ballivis, et fidelibus suis ad quos presentes littere pervenerint, salutem.
Sciatis, quod. . . ."[2] So began the royal letter "patent," sealed on the
writing surface and therefore (in theory) open to anyone's inspection.
Letters patent were the medium of general announcement; they promulgated ordinances and statutes; they were among the writs proclaimed
at meetings of the county court. Like all products of chancery, their
language was elaborately conventional, and the opening *sciatis* was
particularly favored for those letters addressed to the realm at large ("to
all his bailiffs and all faithful whom the present letter may reach"). The
formula in Ball₁, where "gretyth ʒow wele alle" does duty for the Latin
salutem (which conventionally precedes *sciatis*) is still closer. Ball₂ ("John
balle seynte marye prist greteʒ wele alle maner men & *byddes hem . . .*")
recalls another, though less common, royal formula, *precipimus*; and
Ball₃ ("Johon schep som tyme seynte marie prest of ʒork. and now of
colchestre. Greteth wel johan nameles and johan þe mullere and johon

---

1. The beginning of Ball₁ makes the same claim: "Jon Balle gretyth ʒow wele alle &
doþ ʒowe to understande. he haþ rungen ʒoure belle."

2. *Rp* 3.78. This is an example from the year before the rising—issued during the 1380
parliament—but there are literally thousands of examples; the opening is formulaic at
least as far back as Henry I. See the array of exemplary letters patent in Hubert Hall, *A
Formula Book of English Official Historical Documents* (Cambridge, Eng., 1908), 60–74; for
a similar opening, see also the exemplary royal charters, 19ff.

carter and *biddeþ hem . . .*") uses the same locution in a letter patent addressed to particular individuals.[3] The rebel letters claimed documentary literacy; and they used it to claim the royal prerogative of documentary command.

This appropriation asserted that the letter patent was now available to common use, which in turn asserted that royal authority was common authority: it is the literary equivalent of the assertion made in several places during the revolt when the insurgents marched under royal standards.[4] The rebel John Cote, who turned approver in October 1381, told how the revels voiced this claim. He said that in September, rumor had reached Kent that John of Gaunt had manumitted his serfs; he and his fellows had decided that if the report were true, they would depose Richard and crown Gaunt *per realem potestatem suam*—"by their own royal power."[5] Behind the bland reportage of his testimony lies the extraordinary assertion that *realis potestas* was theirs to delegate as they pleased. Rebel bands asserted it by appropriating the symbolic instrument of the royal standard, the rebel letters by appropriating the instruments, also in part symbolic, of parchment, ink, and chancery formulae, the documentary forms of royal government. They prefaced their seizure of power by the seizure of the writing that mediated power.

The elaborate indecorum of the letters' claims shared motivation and meaning with the more openly contentious activities I have already described (invading religious houses and the homes of royal and local officials, seizing and burning documents, harassing lawyers). Trewman's

3. Letters patent, though accessible to all, did not necessarily carry a general address, as the briefest glance through the *CPR* will show. Richard's appointment (15 June 1381) of Walworth, Brembre, Knolles, Philpot, and Launde to oversee the safety of London, for example, is addressed to them alone (*CPR 1381–1385*, 18).

4. In law, this was a breach of the peace and an act of treason. All the official sources show some concern to discover how the commons got those standards. For example, the London inquisition of 20 November, which blames the entry of the rebels on treacherous aldermen, says that one of them, John Horn, went to a clerk of the city and claimed "unum standardum de armis domini regis" the mayor's authority (Réville, *Soulèvement*, 191); see also the indictments concerning the rising in Bridgewater (Réville, 283).

5. W. E. Flaherty, "Sequel to the Great Rebellion in Kent of 1381," *Archæologia Cantiana* 4 (1861): 76. Richard's pardon for Cote repeats Cote's *ipsissima verba*, only substituting "regalem" for "realem" (85). Flaherty mistranslates "realem," meaninglessly, as "real," and thinks the latter a "clerical error"; in fact, it is at worst a harmless scribal substitution of a synonym. A similar claim was recorded at the fringes of the revolt, when John Taillour of Morley and Henry Vepount and John de Derby of Horsley (Derby) were said by the jurors to have taken the royal castle at Horston, to have raised the banner of St. George there, "et posuerunt capiendo super eos *realem jurisdictionem* in preiudicium corone domini regis et terrorem totius patrie" (PRO KB 27/531, rex m. 20d, in David Crook, "Derbyshire and the English Rising of 1381," *Historical Research* 60 [1987]: 23).

image of "trewþe . . . sette under a lokke" precipitates the violence against documents into ideological metaphor. Describing the attack on the Hospitallers' Temple Inn, a lawyers' residence, Knighton says that the rebels "broke whatever chests [*cistas*] they were able to find in the church or in the chambers of the apprentices [of law], and they tore whatever books were found—both ecclesiastical books and the charters and muniments—in the locked chests [*cistis . . . securibus*] of the apprentices, and gave them as food for the flames."[6] Of the three usual ways of storing books in the middle ages—chained on shelves, locked in an "almery" (*armarium*, a book press), or locked in a chest (*cista*)—the first, a relatively late development, was most usual in great libraries; the other two were more common and were also used for storing unbound papers.[7] The "lokke" of Trewman's letter is, I suspect, the very material sort of lock that rendered the apprentices' *cistae* (in Knighton's account) "secure," rendered a figure for the exclusion of the rural laity from bureaucratic power organized as clerical literacy.

In the first chapter I argued that the insurgents not only destroyed documents but put them to meaningful symbolic use; Trewman's phrase suggests that their destruction was also meaningful and symbolic. A number of indictments say that muniments were burnt in public places.[8] The aim, it seems, was not just to get the documents out of the way, but also to display them outside the control of officials and in the control of the rebels, who could treat them as they liked. At Bury and at St. Albans, the rebels were willing to save old documents or preserve them, whichever suited their interests best;[9] the first point was to have, and

6. "Cistas in ecclesia sive in cameris apprenticiorum inventas fregerunt, et libros quoscunque inventos, sive ecclesiasticos, sive cartas et munimenta in cistis apprenticiorum securibus scindebant, et in cibum ignis dederunt" (Knighton, *Chronicon*, 135). There is at least one letter patent confirming this act of destruction; see Ormrod, "Government of England," 7.

7. For general descriptions, see Karl Christ, *The Handbook of Medieval Library History*, trans. Theophil M. Otto (Metuchen, N.J., 1984), 45–48; J. W. Clark, *Libraries in the Medieval and Renaissance Periods* (Cambridge, Eng., 1894); Richard Firth Green, *Poets and Princepleasers: Literature and the English Court in the Late Middle Ages* (Toronto, 1980), 93–94. An ornate medieval book-chest can be seen in Burnett Hillman Streeter, *The Chained Library: A Survey of Four Centuries in the Evolution of the English Library* (London, 1931), 4.

8. For example, "arserunt in plateis villarum predictarum" (Thomas atte Raven, in Dartford and Strode), Réville, *Soulèvement*, 185); "arderant en la fore du dite ville [Cambridge]" (*Rp* 3.108). Jury returns did not need to specify the locus of the action and usually did not; those that did always show it to have been a public place, a street or crossroads or square.

9. See above, ch. 1.

show, that the documents were available, subject to public deliberation, and disposable: to show that the "lokke" was broken. As the rebels opened up the letter patent to the use of the community (with its *realis potestas*), liberated it from exclusive possession by the single person of the king, they established a symbolic geography between the twin poles of the chest or almery—the place of secrecy and sequestration, of private control over public documents—and open, public spaces, where control belonged to the community at large.

The power of the claim that "trewþe. hat bene sette under a lokke" is its capacity to make the physical disposition of documents a metaphor for the oppressions the documents sustained, and the writing of the rebel letters, with their polemical appropriations of language and form, aimed to break the "locks" of clerical and bureaucratic culture. The clearest innovation in the rebels' imitation of royal letters patent was their language; royal letters were usually in Latin, sometimes in French, never in English. The rebel letters worked to undo the hermetic quarantine of authoritative forms, the conduct of state, ecclesiastical, and intellectual business in nonnative languages:[10] just by imitating the royal letter in the vernacular, they exposed and tweaked the institutional presuppositions of exclusion, expertise, and class difference that underlay it.

But the public experience of official documentary culture in late-medieval England, the experience that shaped its meaning in the countryside, made the symbolism of the rebels' appropriation more complex still. Rural communities most often met with royal letters patent in the assemblies I described in the last chapter, in county and borough courts.[11] The sheriff received a document in Latin or French; he proclaimed it in English.[12] These performances enacted social and political

10. For reflections on linguistically defined clerisies, see V. N. Voloshinov, *Marxism and the Philosophy of Language*, trans. Ladislav Matejka and I. R. Titunik (New York, 1973), esp. 74–77; for the middle ages in particular, see Michael Richter, "A Socio-linguistic Approach to the Latin Middle Ages," *SCH* 11 (1975): 69–82.

11. They were probably also read (the evidence is sketchier on this point) in the towns and villages themselves when special and urgent pronouncement was required, and possibly in churches as well.

12. Clanchy suggests that sheriffs translated impromptu (or after private rehearsal), the only way of explaining the total absence of surviving issues in English. The massively formulaic language of chancery productions eased the demands on the sheriffs' latinity, requiring of them chiefly a familiarity with a repertory of formulae. For the Latin literacy of sheriffs and other lower-level administrators in the reign of Henry II, see Richardson and Sayles, *The Governance of Medieval England from the Conquest to Magna Carta* (Edinburgh, 1963), 275–84. Clanchy suggests that such literacy had trickled down to village and

subordination in the subordination of languages and linguistic competence. Announcement in the mother tongue was only an act of information, an ephemeral act that emphasized the exclusion of its audience from the expertise (linguistic and otherwise) required to issue or manipulate documents. The clerical language, by contrast, was the medium of enactment: the sealing of the (French or Latin) instrument and its deposit in the archives of the realm made it the law of the realm, and the sheriff's translation merely apprised his audience of what had already been effected by this means.[13] The audience was left out of, or behind in, the action, belated witnesses to the language of record. When Jakke Trewman and his fellows issued their letters patent in the English vernacular, they did more than engross an authoritative documentary form; they attacked the linguistic exclusion it represented. They did not attack the assumption that authoritative action was written action. They aimed instead to make the language of record and official action identical with the language of information and everyday exchange, a language by definition open of access to those native-born. In chapter 1 I mentioned the case of Ralph atte Wood, who carried admiralty documents upon a pitchfork. In the late fourteenth century, the public and derisory display of a written document was a punishment for forgery;[14] Ralph and his comrades seem to have meant that offices like chancery and the admiralty had indeed forged the documents they shuffled back and forth—not that false signatures or seals appeared on the documents, but that the offices were issuing on their own account documents that ought to have been issued on everyone's.

The sense of exclusion from authority—especially linguistic exclusion—bespoken by the phrase "trewþe . . . under a lokke" is a gravitational center holding several of the diverse actions of the rebellion in

---

manorial officials as well by 1300 and traces evidence of sheriffs' linguistic competence (*From Memory to Written Record*, 186–87). Nevertheless, sheriffs had the assistance of clerks who were obviously necessary for dealing with the extraordinary influx of documents and for preparing instruments (on the receipt of royal writs, see ch. 1, n. 143 above), and such could obviously have given the sheriff some help in translation.

13. This is precisely the structure of linguistic hierarchy established by the 1362 statute requiring that pleas at law be entered in English, but still be enrolled in Latin: "qe toutes plees qe seront a pleder . . . soient pledez, monstretz, defenduz, responduz, debatuz & juggez en la lange engleise; et qils soient [entreez] & enroullez en latin" (*SR* 1.375–76).

14. The London Guildhall in 1380 punished one William Lawtone of Lyn (Chester) for forging a letter meant to cheat William Savage of London, by ordering him "put upon the pillory, there to remain for one hour of the day, the said letter being tied about his neck" (Thomas Henry Riley, ed. and trans., *Memorials of London and London Life in the Thirteenth, Fourteenth, and Fifteenth Centuries* [London, 1868], 442).

the same orbit. Walsingham's claim that the rebels "forced the teachers of grammar to swear that they would never again teach that art," a claim unparalleled among the other chroniclers, may well be a generalization from one or more incidents with which he was familiar;[15] if true, it is significant because grammar masters taught *Latin* grammar.[16] The anger behind this resentment can be heard in the cry of Margery Starre, of Cambridge, who scattered the ashes of burned documents, saying, "Away with the learning of the clerks, away with it."[17] Another very different action, the most disreputable of the rebellion, was the murder of Flemings, especially in Southwark. Hilton and Barron are perhaps right to say that resentment against the economic competition the Flemish offered (and perhaps exploitation of English journeymen by Flemish masters) created an atmosphere in which those attacks might happen,[18] but none of the major chronicle accounts, and certainly none of the indictments, even tries to suggest how their attackers explained the violence to themselves or what connection it might have had with the other, ideologically more transparent, events of the rebellion. A unique account in a fifteenth-century London chronicle offers a hint when it relates that "many fflemynges loste here heedes at that tyme, and namely they that koude nat say Breede and Chese, But Case and Brode."[19] Certainly Flemings enjoyed a privileged place in the weaving trade, a growth industry. But the story of the language test suggests that the rebels who attacked them sensed their exploitation in part through the symbolism of linguistic difference, and saw the Flemish— like men of law, government officials, and clerks—as figures of domination distinguished by a language the English artisan or rural worker

15. Walsingham, *Chronicon*, 208. It may, however, have derived from the threats made against chancery, exchequer, and men of law after Richard's first attempt to deliver a charter (see ch. 1, above), or indeed from the carrying out of those threats.

16. There is also the well-known evidence from Trevisa that French, also, was an acquisition of the schoolroom by the late fourteenth century (*Polychronicon Ranulphi Higden*, ed. C. Babington [London, 1896], 2:158–61). The point, however, is that the function of grammar masters was the inculcation of official and nonvernacular languages.

17. *VCH Cambridge* 3.11.

18. Caroline Barron speculates that the competition offered by the skilled weavers in London prompted the attacks (*Revolt in London*, 6); in this she follows the lead of Hilton (*Bond Men Made Free*, 195–98). Hilton, however, points out that the occupation of most of the Flemish victims is not known, that the first victims (according to the *Anonimalle*) were prostitutes, and that many of the Flemings were killed not in the cloth-making Southwark but at the East Anglian ports. Hobsbawm lists xenophobia as a characteristic of urban mobs (*Primitive Rebels*, 112).

19. In C. L. Kingsford, ed., *Chronicles of London* (Oxford, 1905), 15.

could not understand. Perhaps the attacks would be best described not as xenophobic, but as xenoglottophobic.

The linguistic specialization of official culture was a resentment suffered for generations; certainly it had always been an obstacle to be overcome; two hundred years before the rising, Walter Map complained that "serfs, whom we call *rustici*, are zealous to educate their useless and degenerate progeny in the arts."[20] Parents who educated their children sought, naturally enough, to play within the rules of the established game. Education in the "arts" was prelude to advancement in ecclesiastical or secular service, and those who sought it were looking to exploit the *cursus honorum* within the social hierarchy by helping their children across a linguistic divide that manifested and confirmed that hierarchy. The rebels had a different ambition: to create a properly *vernacular* authority underwritten by communal consensus, and to displace clerical privilege altogether. It was a timely aspiration in 1381, and its timeliness helps to explain the cast of the letters. For though the letters and the actions of the revolt show an awareness of the forms of legal and government documentation, and arrogate those functions to themselves, the language of the letters is not the language of law. The truth that has been held under a lock is something that no one can reach "but he syng si dedero," and the condition engages a pun that makes the line at once satirical and prophetic. "Singing *si dedero*," like "singing *placebo*," is a mocking statement of necessity: to get to *trewþe* (a thing already described as locked away in chests) you have to sing—promise—"I will give."[21] But *si dedero* (again like *placebo*) is also a liturgical text, the messianic Psalm 132, which promises "I will give no sleep to my eyes, or slumber to my eyelids . . . until I have found a place for the Lord, a fit tent for the God of Jacob." God "has chosen Zion, chosen it for his habitation," and has sworn, "I will dwell in this land because I chose it; I will bless its widows; I will fill its poor with bread; I will clothe its priests with salvation; and its saints will rejoice."

The letters commend to their addressees the vigilance the psalm promises ("nowe is tyme to be ware" [Carter]), and the similarity

---

20. Map, *De nugis curialium*, ed. M. R. James (Oxford, 1914), 7.

21. It was a conventional piece of satire. Oscar Eberhard points to an analogue printed in Wright's *Reliquiae antiquae* ("Dum cano 'si dedero,' protinus mea commoda quaero"; *Der Bauernaufstand vom Jahre 1381 in der englischen Poesie* [Heidelberg, 1917], 20–21n). Green prints an English example ("John Ball's Letters," 183).

between the language of the letters and the language of the psalm suggests that the rebels, or at least these epistolators, understood the rising to be theologically as well as politically reformist: "þe kynges sone of heue*n* he schal pay for alle," says Milner, and Trewman traces the "flode" of sin to the "welthe" of "clerkus." The gesture toward Psalm 132 in Trewman's letter suggests that the insurgency, prising truth from under its locks and assuming for itself the powers of kingship, meant to establish England as a fit house for the mighty God of Jacob. The language of the letters is, fitfully and perhaps randomly, the language of the psalter, and more generally of the liturgy, especially where it promises the revenge of the poor on the rich,[22] and enjoins vigilance and faithfulness. "Sekeþ pees and hold 30u þerinne," says Ball₃, echoing Psalm 34: "Keep your tongue from evil, and your lips from deceit. Turn from evil and do good. Seek peace and pursue it [*inquirere pacem, et persequere eam*]," a psalm that promises the just poor that they will see the rich reduced to hunger and need.[23]

If I am right about these allusions, the well-known gestures Ball₃ and Carter make toward *Piers Plowman* are neither random and uncontextualized snippings nor a devolution of the theological toward the political, but a programmatic, theologically inflected elaboration of the political. While the ideology of the rebellion began with the language and forms of common law and bureaucratic culture, it did not end there. Though the letters take a chancery form, they take nothing of chancery's language; though documentary bureaucracy provided the forms that the rebels reimagined into insurgent writing, it did not provide the terms or the processes by which the reimagination happened. Although the king's participation in double suits, the forms of parliamentary appeal, and the gatherings of the shire courts could suggest the ideology

---

22. As in the Magnificat, part of the daily routine of liturgy: "Deposuit potentes de sede, et exaltavit humiles."

23. "This poor man called, and the Lord heard him, and saved him from all his tribulations. . . . Fear the Lord, all his saints, for those who fear him will lack for nothing. The rich shall feel need and hunger, but those who seek the Lord will lack no good thing. Come, my sons, and hear me; I will teach you the fear of the Lord. Who is it that wants life, and loves to see good days? Keep your tongue from evil, and let your lips speak no evil. Turn from evil, and do good; seek peace and pursue it. The eyes of the Lord are upon the just, and his ear to their prayers. But the face of the Lord is upon those who do evil, and their memory will perish from the earth. The just cried out, and the Lord heard them, and freed them from all their troubles. The Lord is near those who are troubled in heart, and he saves the humble in spirit. Many are the tribulations of the just; and from all these the Lord frees them: the Lord guards all their bones, lest one of them should be broken. The death of sinners is terrible; and those who hate the just fall."

of reform, they hardly led inescapably to it—obviously enough, since for a century they did not. But in the late 1370s, there was a prominent, even clamorous voice that linked the issues of wealth, law, authority, and vernacular literacy in a scheme of theological and political reform.

Of course I mean Wyclif. That his teachings, if not his person, gave impetus to the rising was the view of contemporary chroniclers,[24] but its convenience in tarring the heretic with the brush of sedition has rendered it suspect. A half-century ago, scholars took it for granted that Wyclif was the true first mover of rebellion; since then—Anne Hudson's casual demurrers notwithstanding[25]—their notion has seemed increasingly untenable.[26] The old idea that Wyclif was ideologue to the revolt

24. Immediately following his account of the rising, Knighton moves to the subject of Wyclif: "In istis temporibus floruit magister Johannes Wyclyfe. . . . Hic habuit praecursorem Johannem Balle, veluti Christus Johannem Baptistam, qui vias suas in talibus opinionibus praeparavit, et plurimos quoque doctrina sua, ut dicitur, perturbavit" (*Chronicon*, 151).

25. "It is not within the brief for this paper to reinstate Wyclif as a cause, if not the cause of the Peasants' Revolt, though I believe that a credible case can be made for this now unfashionable view" ("Wyclif and the English Language," in Anthony Kenny, ed., *Wyclif in his Times* [Oxford, 1986], 85); "it seems possible that disclaimers of Wyclif's involvement [in the rising] may have gone too far" (*Premature Reformation*, 68).

26. "Modern scholarship has disposed conclusively of that myth," says E. B. Fryde (*The Great Revolt of 1381* [London, 1981], 17–18), and even Dobson referred in the same year to "the strenuous, disingenuous and at times positively absurd efforts of Archbishop Courtenay . . . to persuade lay opinion that the eggs hatched by John Ball had been laid by John Wycliffe" ("Remembering the Peasants' Revolt 1381–1981," in W. H. Liddell and R. G. E. Wood, eds., *Essex and the Great Revolt of 1381* [Chelmsford, 1982], 6–7). (However, Dobson ventured a slightly more measured opinion two years later [*Peasants' Revolt*, xxxvii–xxxviii].) Though Wyclif's pertinence to the revolt had been denied by some earlier scholars (Oman, *Great Revolt*, 19–20, and Petit-Dutaillis, for whom see n. 29 below), the decisive contribution was Margaret Aston, "Lollardy and Sedition, 1381–1431" (1960; rpt. in her *Lollards and Reformers: Images and Literacy in Late Medieval Religion* [London, 1984], 1–47. After her essay was published, the issue was treated rather gingerly; Michel Mollat and Philippe Wolff did allow the possibility of an indirect Wycliffian influence (*Ongles bleus, Jacques, et Ciompi: Les révolutions populaires en Europe aux XIVe et XVe siècles* [Paris, 1970], 208–9), and Rodney Hilton's uncharacteristic waffle on this question was nearly incoherent: "Perhaps the now discarded idea of a close link between Lollardy and the rising of 1381 was not after all so mistaken, provided that we regard Lollardy as something wider simply than the following of Wycliffe" (*Bond Men Made Free*, 213).

The proof text for these assertions has usually been Wyclif's *De blasfemia* (written shortly after June 1381), which says in effect, "That was not what I meant at all." The passage, and the entire work, is actually an ambivalent, strangely ironic exercise in minesweeping, capable of more than one reading (for a more moderate understanding of its implications, see Mariateresa Beonio-Brocchieri Fumagalli, *Wyclif: Il comunismo dei predestinati* [Florence, 1975], 27). What is most impressive about the work, however, is the mere fact that Wyclif felt the need to disavow the rising immediately, and apparently before anyone had publicly linked his name with it; he at least seems to have noticed some very clear resemblances between the rebels' ideology and his own.

had assumed that he had written the vernacular treatises edited in the last century under his name. Better scholarship took those treatises from him, and showed how comparatively academic Wyclif's activities were and how long it took for a widespread vernacular movement to develop from them. Wyclif could not have had anything to do with 1381, it seemed; there was neither means nor time. But a clearer understanding of the chronology of Wycliffism has emerged since 1972, through the work of Thomson, Mallard, McFarlane, Aston, and (preeminently) Hudson.[27] The rising was no concern of these scholars; but their work ought to make us wonder again whether Wyclif's teachings should be thought irrelevant to 1381. Petit-Dutaillis says that "the insurgents were not Lollards" because "they nowhere denied the spiritual powers of the clergy; they nowhere injured the statues or pictures of saints";[28] these things are true enough of the rebels, but they were also true of "Lollards" in 1381.[29] The clearer dating of Wyclif's works, and clearer understanding of his doctrines and audiences before 1381, makes it possible now to imagine his teachings as a public experience at the beginning of Richard

27. Williell R. Thomson, *The Latin Writings of John Wyclyf: An Annotated Catalogue* (Toronto, 1983), working from the notes and published writings of his father, S. Harrison Thomson; W. Mallard, "Dating the *Sermones Quadraginta* of John Wyclif," *Medievalia et Humanistica* 17 (1966): 86–105; K. B. McFarlane, *Lancastrian Kings and Lollard Knights* (Oxford, 1972); Margaret Aston, "Lollardy and Literacy," (1977; rpt. in her *Lollards and Reformers*, 193–217); Aston, "'Caim's Castles': Poverty, Politics, and Disendowment," in R. B. Dobson, ed., *The Church, Politics, and Patronage in the Fifteenth Century* (Gloucester, 1984), 45–81; Aston, "Wyclif and the Vernacular," *SCH* subsidia 5 (1987): 281–330; Anne Hudson, in the essays collected in *Lollards and Their Books* (London, 1985); Hudson, Introduction to *English Wycliffite Sermons* (Oxford, 1983) 1:189–202 (reworking her 1971 article, "A Lollard Sermon-Cycle and Its Implications," *MÆ* 40 [1971]: 142–56); Hudson, *Premature Reformation*, chs. 1–5.

28. Petit-Dutaillis, *Studies and Notes*, 276.

29. Wyclif was notably moderate about images, an issue that would, much later, become one of the determining tests in the episcopal investigations of Lollardy; his early followers say nothing about it. The earliest recorded act of iconoclasm was William Smith's and Richard Waytestathe's use of the St. Katherine image to cook their supper in 1382 (Knighton, *Chronicon*, 182–84), and this was a noted eccentricity even then. On the issue in general, see Hudson, *Premature Reformation*, 301–9; and Margaret Aston, "Lollards and Images," in her *Lollards and Reformers*, 135–92, and her extensive reworking of this material in *Laws Against Images*, vol. 1 of *England's Iconoclasts* (Oxford, 1988), 96–159. The question Petit-Dutaillis raises about "the spiritual powers of the clergy" is unanswerable because so vaguely framed; but there was nothing in Wyclif or the early Wycliffites to challenge the efficacy of ordination; indeed, later Wycliffites sometimes performed their own. Even Wyclif's eucharistic heresy, which began to draw attention in 1380, remained a thoroughly academic matter until the Blackfriars council of 1382. The word "Lollard" is itself an anachronism, since it was apparently first applied to Wyclif's followers at Oxford in 1382 by the Cistercian Henry Crumpe.

II's reign, to sort out not just what Wyclif thought but what his audiences, intended and unintended, seem to have heard.

I have already described the proliferation of posted broadsides in Ricardian England. I am aware of no records of broadsides posted before 1377;[30] by the early fifteenth century they were as common as dust.[31] But with the exception of the Gaunt libel, the earliest broadsides are all traceable to the activities of Wyclif and his followers after 1377, and I would argue that broadside publication of vernacular reformist theology formed a part of the cultural project of Wyclif's followers— and indeed of Wyclif himself.[32] There is one hint of vernacular publication even before Wyclif came to political prominence in 1376–77.[33] Shortly thereafter he produced a Latin treatise, addressed to the lay

30. There are occasional exceptions, of a very different character, from the century preceding, such as Archbishop Pecham's posting of a copy of Magna Carta on the doors of churches in the province of Canterbury, in 1280; see Decima L. Douie, *Archbishop Pecham* (Oxford, 1952), 113–20. No source makes it clear whether it was posted in the vernacular, though Pecham did order the charter explained to congregations during mass. This, however, was a one-time challenge to immediate royal policy, and I know of no evidence that it became a familiar tactic. Rather more interesting is the letter of Queen Isabella attacking the Despensers, which prefaced the deposition of Edward II; one copy "was posted in Cheapside and others soon began to appear in the windows of private houses" (May McKisack, *The Fourteenth Century 1307–1399* [Oxford, 1959], 84).

31. See ch. 1, n. 43.

32. The Neville libel of 1388 (see ch. 1, n. 48) is an exception that may in fact prove the rule. It clearly originated from among the clergy of York archdiocese and is no Lollard production (an approving reference to Thomas Becket is one proof of that). But it speaks of the greed, wealth, and "extorcione" of the "tirraunt" bishop, his abuse of office for personal aggrandizement, and his hypocrisy: "he maketh to his Kyng as her wer a saynt, but al þe world wot it wel, þe fayrer he speketh þe falsser he is" (Illingworth, "Copy of a Libel," 82). The document was posted at St. Paul's, where a celebrated and controversial Lollard bill had been posted a year earlier (Patteshull's; see ch. 1, n. 47). We seem to have here a broadside that uses some of the rhetorical techniques as well as the mode of publication that Wyclif and his followers had made their own, adapted for a less ideological, but equally controversial purpose.

33. In the early section of his *De nova prevaricancia mandatorum* (dated by Thomson c. 1375 [*Latin Writings*]), Wyclif casually relates that "certain ones" who considered the fact that Christ and his apostles taught in various tongues, and that the decalogue was available in brief vernacular form, decided on another project: "Intendentes autem brevitati doctrinam decalogi in quodam compendio aptaverunt, quibus dicitur in anglico, quod lex Cristi compilatur in quodam dyalogo, sicut decalogus per Mosem in duabus tabulis est collectum" (*John Wiclif's Polemical Works in Latin*, ed. R. Buddensieg [London, 1883], 1:117). In his *Dialogus* (late 1379), Wyclif says that, for the sake of both *pulcra alternatio* and wider publication, "visum est quibusdam quod sentencia catholica collecta fidelibus in vulgari reseretur communius in Latino" (*Iohannis Wycliffe Dialogus sive Speculum ecclesie militantis*, ed. Alfred W. Pollard [London, 1886], 1). Even Thompson has not noted these two passages, but they clearly refer to one and the same work and forcefully imply that the *Dialogus*—a polemical attack on ecclesiastical wealth—is in fact the (later) Latin version

nobility, in which he announced that he had found it necessary to issue the treatise "in the Latin language, as in the vernacular"—implying that a vernacular version was prepared either before or along with the Latin— and argued that the laity should receive vernacular instruction in theology.[34] More interesting still is the narrative of his skirmish with an unnamed critic, which Wyclif included in the *De veritate sacre scripture* (1379).[35] He says there that when questions were raised concerning the teaching of his *De civili dominio*, "I wanted this matter made clear to clergy and laity alike. So I gathered and published thirty-three conclusions about it in both languages [*in lingua duplici*]." These conclusions, he says, appeared "throughout a great part of England and of Christendom, all the way to the Roman curia."[36] It is possible that a lost vernacular version of these conclusions was posted; a similar series of conclusions by Wyclif's followers was posted in 1395.[37] His penchant for publishing his views in this way is suggested by the challenge he threw down in 1381, after the university had condemned his eucharistic doctrine (which taught that the substance of bread and wine remains in the consecrated elements at mass):

> Thus the people should be taught that the sacrament of the altar is by nature bread and wine, while by a miracle of the word of God it is the

---

of the "compendium" he mentions in *De nova prevaricancia*, which means that it was available probably by 1375 (his first mention of the project, which does not make it clear whether it has yet been carried out) and certainly by 1379.

34. "Necessitantur fideles sentenciam quam premittunt enucleare tam in lingua latina quam eciam in vulgari. Dictum est autem pro speculo secularium dominorum *in lingua vulgari* quomodo se debent regulare in toto conformiter legi Christi. Nec sunt audiendi heretici, qui fingunt quod seculares non debent legem Dei cognoscere sed sufficit eis noticia quam sacerdotes et prelati eis dixerint viva voce. Nam scriptura sacra est fides ecclesie et de quanto est nota planius in sensu orthodoxo, de tanto est melior. Ideo sicut seculares debent fidem cognoscere, sic in quacunque lingua plus nota fuerit, est docenda" (*Speculum secularium dominorum*, in *Johannis Wyclif Opera minora*, ed. J. Loserth [London, 1913], 74).

35. *De veritate sacre scripture*, ed. Rudolf Buddensieg (London, 1905), 1:345–50. The critic was probably William Barton, who as chancellor oversaw the Oxford condemnation of Wyclif's eucharistic teaching in 1380.

36. "Unde quia volui materiam comunicatam clericis et laicis, collegi et comunicavi triginta tres conclusiones illius materie in ligwa [*sic*] duplici" (*De veritate* 1:350); "per magnam partem Anglie et cristianismi et sic usque ad curiam romanam" (1:349). He refers here to the digest of the *De civili dominio* which takes the title *De paupertate Christi* (for which see n. 49 below). On this passage, see Aston, "Wyclif and the Vernacular," 286–87.

37. This is on the assumption, which I do make, that the English version contained the conclusions only, and not the supporting matter that appears in the extant Latin version; see n. 49 below. For the "twelve conclusions" of 1395, see the text and notes in Hudson, *Selections from English Wycliffite Writings*, 24–29.

body and blood of Christ. . . . This conclusion I mean to publish among the people [*propono publicare in populo*]. And let the worshipers of signs set next to it *their* conclusion [*iuxtaponant suam sentenciam*], that this sacrament is a pile of accidents without an underlying substance; and God, who gave the gift of knowledge and hates untruth, will multiply the truth according to the dignity of those capable of faith.[38]

If Wyclif means that he plans to *preach* his eucharistic doctrine, he has chosen an odd way to say so. *Publicare* is a most unlikely verb where the rest of the world would say *praedicare*; and for centuries, preaching to the public at large was called preaching *ad populum*. *In populo*, by contrast, is a localizing phrase that suggests writings issued in a public place, and the image implied in *iuxtaponant* ("set next to") confirms the suggestion. Toward the end of his life (1383), Wyclif tells of an incident in which "I made [*feci autem*] many reasons against this practice [the begging of friars] in the vernacular,"[39] choosing again a verb (*facere*) that could only awkwardly designate speech but was entirely conventional for writing.

Hudson, never given to hyperbole, says that the project of Wycliffite vernacular writing was "audacious, not to say dangerous: they were attacking the whole edifice of clerical domination in theology, in ecclesiastical theory, indeed in academic speculation generally"; elsewhere she describes their work as the first attempt in medieval England to create in the vernacular an intellectual idiom equal to clerical Latin for discussing theological and institutional topics.[40] This project of vernacular publication both demanded and offered to effect the delatinization of theological language: the medium itself symbolized Wycliffian claims that this language belonged to the public at large, and especially the poor, who (it suggested) were already entering into a full participation in public discourse.

By 1381 the broadside was a polemical gesture that asserted the rights of the laity to the intellectual, as to the material, goods of the institutional church. Insisting that theological discussion belonged in public ways and on church porches, as well as in universities and church pulpits, the broadside (itself an example of unrestricted discussion) enacted what it advocated and also purveyed the materials and examples that would

---

38. *De apostasia*, ed. Michael Henry Dziewicki (London, 1889), 253–54.
39. *Trialogus, cum Supplemento trialogi*, ed. G. Lechler (Oxford, 1869), 342.
40. Hudson, "Wyclif and the English Language," 90.

enable such discussion. It contentiously announced the beginnings of lay literacy, in the deepest and (for a medieval audience) most paradoxical sense of the phrase: *literacy*, meaning not just that laypeople could read and write, but that they could maneuver and manipulate the bookish resources of intellectual culture; and *lay* literacy, meaning not just that laypeople could ape clerics, but that precisely *as* laypeople they would take a rightful and informed place in the discussion of churchly and national issues. The claim was of course a fiction, since clerics wrote these broadsides that claimed to come from the laity;[41] but it was a fiction with resources. Among the Lollards, it would eventually find a kind of fulfillment in London and the towns, among artisans and servants who, having learned to read, would gather local communities of theologically informed dissent.[42]

We know (by the accidents of his own comments) that Wyclif published some works in vernacular digest (and there were probably others); we know from Walsingham and others that after Gaunt summoned him down from Oxford in 1376, he preached tirelessly in London, "running from church to church, sowing his lying insanities in the ears of many." Walsingham worried less about Wyclif's teachings in themselves than about their audience: "he began to communicate his excommunicate material so as to draw, not only lords, but even certain of the simple London citizens into the pit of his error."[43] The English hierarchy, too, did not formally censure disendowment proposals until Wyclif began to preach them publicly. Though proposals like Wyclif's had been made before, they had always in the past been offered for intramural discussion before council and parliament; it was Wyclif's novel strategy—or a novel aspect of Gaunt's—to offer proposals on the behalf of England's poor *to* England's poor, and as if from them.[44]

41. For example, the "twelve conclusions" (for which see n. 36 above), posted to great uproar at Westminster Hall during the February parliament of 1395, offered a particularly skillful example of this fiction, claiming to present the complaints of "poor men, ambassadors of Christ and his apostles," choreographing the meaning of public space to support a claim that the excluded were speaking.

42. See Hudson, *Premature Reformation*, especially her revolutionary chapter "Lollard Education," 174–227; Claire Cross, "'Great Reasoners in Scripture': The Activities of Women Lollards 1380–1530," *SCH* subsidia 1 (1978): 359–80; Margaret Aston, "William White's Lollard Followers," *Catholic Historical Review* 68 (1982): 469–97. And see my discussion of White and Brut, ch. 1 above.

43. "Quorum suffultus patrociniis multo audacius et animosius communicavit excommunicatam materiam, ita ut non solum dominos, sed et simplices quosdam Londoniensium cives secum attraheret in erroris abyssum" (Walsingham, *Chronicon*, 116).

44. I assume, and all the evidence agrees, that Wyclif's preaching was done with

The real question about popular heresy in these years is not so much what Wyclif said between his summons to London and the outbreak of eucharistic controversy, but what he was heard to be saying by those who did not have access to his Latin theological writings (which was almost everybody). Several sources give clues to how Wyclif published his doctrines and what they sounded like.[45] We can start with the chroniclers; although they tell us only how Wyclif's doctrines struck clerics in prominent religious houses, they have at least the advantage of telling us how the doctrines struck someone. According to the continuator of the *Eulogium historiarum*—a Franciscan friar of London or (more probably) Canterbury, and to my mind a most reliable witness—Wyclif "attacked the property of the church. . . . [He said] that Pope John [XXII] was nothing but a lawyer, ignorant in his theological pronouncements. He said also that the temporal lords and the founders of monasteries could withdraw temporal goods from delinquent churchmen."[46] According to Walsingham, "Among other unspeakable things he spoke, he denied that the lord pope had the capacity to excommunicate anyone. . . . He said further that no king or secular lord could give anything to any parson or church in perpetuity, for temporal lords could meritoriously withdraw what they had already given from such persons who live habitually in sin. . . . He also asserted that temporal

Gaunt's knowledge and to some degree at his behest. For a different view, see Joseph W. Dahmus, *The Prosecution of John Wyclyf* (New Haven, 1952), 10–17.

45. (1) The sermons which survive from this period, and especially the one that we know to have been given before a mixed public audience in London, in summer 1376; (2) the works of which we know Wyclif made vernacular digests; (3) Wyclif's "parliamentary address," or whatever that document represents; and (4) the reports of the chroniclers, especially Walsingham, whose chronicle account was written perhaps five years after the events he describes (see ch. 5, below). I do not include as an index of public knowledge the points alleged against Wyclif by the English bishops in 1377 and 1378; these are all drawn directly from his Latin works, and whoever selected them was less interested in what Wyclif had been saying in public than in assembling as damning a dossier as possible for the pope's condemnation.

46. "Eodeom anno, videlicet 1378, Johannes Wicclif magister in theologia dictus flos Oxoniae determinando disputavit contra possessiones immobiles ecclesiae. . . . Et quod Johannes papa fuit grossus legista, nesciens quid diceret in theologia. Item quod domini temporales et monasteriorum fundatores auferre possunt bona temporalia ab ecclesiasticis delinquentibus" (*Eulogium*, 345). Even though the chronicler is writing over thirty years after the events, he gives evidence that he is speaking of what Wyclif said specifically at the end of the 1370s. His assertion that Wyclif attacked possessioners while "religionem Fratrum Minorum multum commendans, dicens eos Deo carissimos" (*Eulogium*, 345) was true of 1375–1380, but most false thereafter. The assertion should be taken seriously, since the continuator—no friendlier to Wyclif was than any other chronicler—would presumably have preferred to tar antifraternalism with the brush of Lollardy than to tar his own order with the brush of Wyclif's admiration.

lords, if they needed, could licitly sell the goods of possessioners to relieve their own poverty."[47] According to the *Anonimalle Chronicle*, Wyclif "preached like a madman against the clergy."[48]

What all the chroniclers recall, then, is that Wyclif preached against clerical wealth, and that secular lords should liberate that wealth for the public good by disendowing churches and religious houses. These reports tally exactly with the "thirty-three conclusions" Wyclif published in the vernacular.[49] The argument of these conclusions begins from the axiom that Christ was *homo pauperrimus* and possessed his boundless spiritual wealth because he abjured all forms of secular ownership; that it is therefore the duty of all the clergy "to follow Christ in the poverty of the Gospel," and, like him, to refuse ownership. When they abuse their right to use goods by claiming them, that right ceases, and the duty of judging their spiritual superiors devolves upon the laity, who must ensure that the clergy receive goods only if they serve God. While the endowment of churches is a good thing, "the state of expropriation in which Christ established the church is more perfect, more meritorious, and more secure"; to return the church to this state, "secular rulers" may take away the goods of the church. Lords should not employ the clergy (including bishops) for secular business. Clerical luxury, avarice, and lechery have driven the peace of God from the realm. Scripture authorizes the laity to restore that peace by correcting the clergy, by seizing their wealth (which in any case "would be used to less evil by secular lords than by the clergy"), since "it is the office of the secular lords, and especially the king, to guard the law of the Gospel, and to observe it in their own behavior." The argument bears the impress of

47. "Inter cetera vero non loquenda quae dixit, negavit dominum papam quemquam excommunicare valere. Et si quidem concederetur ab aliquo, dominum papam posse in quemquam excommunicationis ferre sententiam, asseruit quemlibet sacerdotem absolvere talem in tantum posse, quam ipse papa. Dixit praeterea nec regem nec aliquem dominum secularem aliquid posse cuicumque personae sive ecclesiae dare perpetualiter, quia a talibus personis peccantibus habitualiter possent temporales domini auferre meritorie praeconcessa" (Walsingham, *Chronicon*, 115–16).

48. "Une meastre de divynite meastre Johan Wyclyff nome, avoit preche en Londres et aliours come homme arage diverses poyntes encontre le clergie" (*Anonimalle*, 103). It is not clear whether the chronicler believes him mad for holding such opinions or for pronouncing them within earshot of Bishop Courtenay.

49. "Conclusiones triginta tres sive de paupertate Christi" (*Opera minora*, 19–73). In the Latin version that survives, this is a long document. In form, it offers its conclusions first, followed by a marshaling of biblical, patristic, and legal authorities. It is possible that the vernacular version contained only the conclusions without the documentary matter.

Wyclif's employers, Gaunt and (through him) the royal court. Wyclif's *opusculum* permits the inference (indeed urges it, sotto voce) that the king and lords will themselves benefit from the confiscations: no surprises here, and at best only an ambivalent and qualified encouragement to insurgents.

But in 1376–1380, when he was attending to the reform of clerical wealth (and before he was derailed by the eucharistic controversy), Wyclif was also courting a public. The *De civili dominio* and the "thirty-three conclusions" offered a theological rationale for disendowment, but his public preaching and other vernacular writings offered other reasons with wider public appeal, drawing less on theological discourse than on common devotional imagery. These more popular writings were meant to incite a public demand for the seizure of church wealth by inscribing the imperative of disendowment within the images and stories that defined the church and its message. They provided the structure for a powerful reformist imagination that could subsist on its own, apart from Wyclif's specifications and from the purposes of the English government and nobility; one which, in fact, could even be turned against them. The reform Wyclif advocates in these works derives from his theological principles (which can be located throughout the *De civili dominio* and his other works of the period), but does not dwell on those principles. I will distill the thought chiefly from two of the works he offered to the public at large: a sermon securely datable to the summer of 1376 (published mistakenly as a treatise under the title *De demonio meridiano*),[50] and a treatise written specifically for the laity and circulated in English (though it survives now only in Wyclif's own Latin translation), the *Speculum secularium dominorum*.[51]

In Wyclif's writings, both academic and popular, the willed destitution of Christ, who "walked in painful poverty,"[52] is not just one position in his system but its starting point, and it grounds his entire notion of authority. The whole gospel points to it as its deepest purpose in narrating the life of Christ,[53] who is the "exemplar and foundation without which the Christian life avails nothing" and who became such an exemplar (Wyclif specifies a few pages later) precisely because of his

---

50. Printed in *Polemical Works* 2:417–25.
51. Printed in *Opera minora*, 74–97.
52. "Cristus autem ambulavit per penalem pauperiem renunciando mundo et eius glorie, in quo voluit suos sacerdotes maxime sequi ipsum" (*De veritate* 1:133).
53. "Totum evangelium redundat in istam sentenciam tamquam finem" (*Dialogus*, 11).

poverty.[54] That poverty is the axiom that initiates the "thirty-three conclusions," and throughout Wyclif's work it remains the touchstone, the one reliable mark of authority by which Christ signs and enacts the return to human sinlessness and the presence of divine wealth. It also measures the delinquency of the church, its neglect of Christ's commission to embody his life. Of course the conceptual and rhetorical difficulty Wyclif had to circumvent is that while king and nobles are no worse than ecclesiastics in the matter of wealth, and in any case are not bound solemnly to poverty as the clergy is, they are no better either; and in their wealth they can hardly claim the authority of destitution. Wyclif outflanked the problem, even turned it to rhetorical profit, by appealing to the canon-law maxim *Bona ecclesiae sunt bona pauperum*: the goods of the church are the goods of the poor. To canonists, this maxim meant that pastors and religious were to give relief where it was needed. But Wyclif made the phrase his own, giving it a literal inflection and the poor a literal claim on ecclesiastical *temporalia*.[55] They rightly own the wealth unjustly appropriated by the church, he says, and the lords are bound to render it to them again.

But not of course by direct grant, which would help royal finance not a whit. Wyclif needed to argue that the grant of ecclesiastical lands and rents to the realm at large was ipso facto a grant to the poor, and he did this in two ways, both of eventual importance to the rebels of 1381. He represented the oppression of the rural poor as a scandal because it abused the cherished poor of Christ and because it forced the state to tax the commons, putting the burden of public finance unjustly on those least able to bear it. In the *Speculum*, circulated in English around 1380, he rages against the necessity of taxing the poor:

No secular lord oppresses his tenants the way the clergy oppresses them through their monstrous ownership. Clearly, since ownership is thus

54. "Vita Christi est exemplar et fundamentum sine quo fundante et exemplante non potest esse christiani conversacio virtuosa, sed sine conversacione virtuosa non potest christianus venire ad patriam, ideo, nisi secutus fuerit hunc priorem" (*Iohannis Wycliffe Tractatus de civili dominio*, ed. R. L. Poole and J. Loserth [London, 1885–1904], 3:50); "Christus . . . oportet esse exemplar cuiuslibet vite laudabilis, qui vixit continue pro statu vie vitam pauperrimam" (ibid., 60).

55. For the origins of the phrase in canon law, see Brian Tierney, *Medieval Poor Law: A Sketch of Canonical Theory and Its Application in England* (Berkeley and Los Angeles, 1959), 26–58. In Wyclif, see, for example, "Bona ecclesie sunt pauperum et ecclesiasticis data non ad dominandum, sed ad gubernandum, dispensandum, et ministrandum" (*De veritate* 1:153).

withdrawn from the king and the nobles, they are forced to load the poor commoners [*plebem pauperem*] with unjust tallages. I ask: what greater injustice could be conceived, than that the king and his nobles should spare a treasury given over to the devil, in opposition to Christ; and, also in opposition to Christ, spoil his poor [*pauperes*] of the things they need to live? Secular lords should in prudence note how—just as the poor woman "gave more than the rest by putting a penny in the poor box"—a light injury done to a poor tenant is heavier, more intolerable than an injury a thousand times greater done to the king.[56]

In the sermon of 1376, Wyclif explicitly said that the lords had failed in this duty because they "require rents and services from the poor as always, but (because of hypocrisy, and bribes) they have not required rents and services from the clergy to ease the lot of the poor [*plebis*]."[57]

This passage names the second reason why the lords must seize the goods of the church. The devil "has led the three sects to burden the people beyond what God ordained—the monks, canons, and friars, who are obviously a burden to the poor of our realm," but "since the poor [*wlgus*] are the basis of the pillar of state, the realm of England must fail in its clergy and lords because it has failed its own people. Christ, though he was the eternal God, led the life of the poor for the relief of the people, and did not assent to the theft of their goods, but often helped them, in temporal as much as in spiritual goods."[58] The poor are the foundation—the *basis*—of the pillar of state.[59] Wyclif habitually uses

56. "Nullus quidem secularis dominus onerat gravius tenentes suos quam per istud monstruosum dominium onerat talis clerus. Patenter cum dominium a rege et potentatibus sic subtrahitur, necessitantur plebem suam pauperum iniustis pedagiis onerare. Quid quaeso cogitari posset iniustius quam quod rex et eius proceres parcant thesauro dato diabolo contra Christum et spolient suos pauperes de vite necesariis contra Christum? Debet enim prudencia secularium dominorum istud attendere quomodo sicut mulier paupercula *mittendo quadrantem in gazophilacium dedit plus ceteris*, ut Christus asserit Marci XII, 41, sic levis iniuria facta tenenti pauperi est sibi gravior et intolerabilior quam iniuria mole milecupla facta regi" (*Opera minora*, 82–83).

57. "Potentes enim, ut principes et seculares domini, ab ipsis requirunt redditus et servicia, sicut primo, et quid propter ypocrisim et quid propter occulta munera, in alleviacionem plebis a clero tales redditus non requirunt" (*Polemical Works*, 421).

58. "Et cum wlgus sit basis fulcimenti regnorum, necesse est, regnum Anglie pro defectu suorum wlgarium in clero et dominis terrenis deficere. Cristus autem deus eternaliter pro relevamine suorum wlgarium degit vitam pauperem, et non ipsos in rapina temporalium onustavit, sed tam in iuvamine bonorum talium, quam spiritualium multipliciter relevavit" (*Polemical Works*, 422).

59. Wyclif used the same language two years later to the same effect, in the *De veritate sacre scripture*: "plebeos pauperes, qui sunt dominis, clero, et artificibus fulcimentum, predari nunc taxis vel talliis, nunc pedagiis sive subisidiis"; he goes on to urge that the king should "capere bona sua ac eorundem pauperum, que per papam et cardinales, per

basis and *fundamentum* to denote fundamental *authority*, the authority on which judgment ultimately rests ("But scripture is the *basis* of any such judgment").[60] In what sense can the state be founded on the poor? Wyclif never explicitly says, but these works broadly hint that the poor, just by being poor and by suffering the depredations of the rich, share in the authoritative poverty of Christ, as when the *Speculum* refers to Christ and "*his* poor." They are the foundation of the state because they embody within it Christ's own authority and therefore are the ideal representatives of the realm. At the same time, Wyclif has managed the language of social distinction to eliminate all distinctions but one; his vocabulary slides back and forth between words that in fact have different connotative meanings—*pauperes, vulgus, plebs*—to speak as if all those who are not lords or clergy are the poor, and as if the poor are all rural workers, owing *redditus et servitia*, the old manorial phrase for the old manorial duties.

In these statements another element appears, more distinctly than in the "thirty-three conclusions." Because the rhetorical basis of disendowment is the injustice done to Christ's poor, directly and indirectly, by the oppressions of the clergy, and through them to the whole realm, disendowment is less a right than a duty. This is the canniest of Wyclif's rhetorical steps: the king and lords would not incur blame for seizing ecclesiastical goods because they *have no choice* but to seize them. Nobles are "despoiling" their tenants, overburdening them because (fooled by "hypocrisy" and silenced by "bribes") they have dropped the reins from the clergy. They "cannot be excused from damnation unless they exercise the power, the sword, they receive from God to defend . . . the law of Christ,"[61] and this means defending the poor of Christ:

> And thus secular lords must not unjustly burden their tenants or their poor neighbors, or let them be burdened by the disciples of Antichrist,

---

episcopos et abbates iacent irreligiose suspensa, ut sinit thezaurus anticristi ad destruendum proditorie se et suos" (*De veritate* 3:37).

60. "Si enim in scriptis et verbis se ostendunt [theologi] esse ignaros scripture, et in vita indicant se declinare a conversacione vite apostolice, plus credendum est aliis qui noscuntur in istis precellere. *Basis autem cuiuscumque talis iudicii est scriptura*" (*Tractatus de officio regis*, ed. Alfred W. Pollard and Charles Sayle [London, 1887], 125). For Wyclif's use of *fundatus*, and the Lollard Englishing of it ("groundid"), see Hudson, "A Lollard Sect Vocabulary?" in *Lollards and Their Books*, 171–72.

61. "Nec aliter excusari possent a dampnacione perpetua seculares domini nisi vel potestatem vel gladium quem a Deo habuerant exercuerunt ad defendendum secundum suam potenciam legem Christi" (*Opera minora*, 78).

because by the grace of their vocation God gave them the sword of earthly power. How will they be excused before the throne of Christ, in the Last Judgment, if their sword . . . is never drawn in the service of God, as he commands? . . . These [their pursuits of worldly gain] are the chief hindrances to that peace that the lords must especially defend, both in themselves and among the people; whence in the Psalm (33.15) that exemplary king and knight David says, "Turn from evil and do good; seek peace and pursue it."[62]

Lordly delinquency is no better than clerkly delinquency (the devil "has two torturers who suck the blood of simple subjects: tyrants of the world, and the simoniacal priests of the Antichrist"),[63] except in being more susceptible of reform.

The point of all this, Wyclif's point and Gaunt's, was to give to fiscal opportunity the urgency of an evangelical imperative, to present to the world what Gaunt and the royal government *wanted* to do as something they *had* to do: a government that wished to seize the goods of the clergy would not have to take responsibility for the action, for that precisely was their responsibility. For Wyclif's real audience, it was a kind of charade, in which the courting of the *simplices* and the installation of a theological imperative for disendowment were moves to outflank an ecclesiastical, papally authorized discourse, a charade that took no real account of its vernacular audience, as was dramatically illustrated a year after the rising. When the university chancellor at Oxford, Robert Rigg (for the moment a Wyclif sympathizer), invited Wyclif's lieutenant Nicholas Hereford to deliver the 1382 Ascension Day sermon in St. Frydeswyde's churchyard, Hereford knew, as everyone did, that Archbishop Courtenay was about to convene the Blackfriars council to condemn the teachings of Wyclif and his disciples, and that Courtenay's men were watching his sermon. Hereford concluded a comprehensive attack on the English clergy with the exhortation: "But alas, that the

62. "Et sic seculares domini non debent iniuste onerare suos tenentes vel proximos simplices vel sinere quod ab Antichristi discipulis onerentur, quia gracia huius ministerii Deus dedit illis gladium potestatis terrene. Quomodo ergo ante tribunal Christi in finali iudicio excusantur, quorum gladius propter causam conformem predictis trahit rubiginem nec evaginatur in Dei servicio sicut mandat? . . . Et ista sunt precipua fomenta pacis, quam domini debent in semetipsis et populo suo signanter defendere. Unde Psalmo XXXIII, 15 dicit ille egregius rex et miles David: *Declina a malo et fac bonum, inquire pacem et persequere eam*" (*Opera minora*, 79). Wyclif here quotes Psalm 34, quoted also in Ball₃.

63. "Nam Prov. XXX, 15 scribitur: *Sanguisuge due sunt filie dicentes: Affer, affer*, quod communiter exponitur de diabolo qui habet duos tortores sugentes sanguinem simplicium subditorum, scilicet tyrannos seculi et simoniacos presbyteros Antichristi" (*Opera minora*, 80–81).

king has no justices in his realm to pursue this act of justice, and that
there are no other justices specially commissioned for it. Therefore it is
necessary for you, O faithful Christians, to set your hands to bringing
this business to its proper end. And then, I am sure, it will proceed well,
because I know for sure that omnipotent God himself wants it done."[64]
The exhortation, offered without recommendations about how to proceed and with the knowledge that he was encouraging what the rising
had been crushed in attempting the year before, was intended for the
ears of the notary recording the sermon and eventually for the eyes of
Archbishop Courtenay, who hired the notary; not for the crowd, which
Hereford treated rather as a prop—symbols of the resentments that
would erupt against church and state if reform were further delayed.
And the same is true of Wyclif, who appeals to the sufferings of the
rural poor in order to recommend action, not to them, but to their
lords.

But if Wyclif's popular rhetoric of disendowment neglected its
popular audience, it also neglected to protect itself from them; his most
powerful and most conceptually informed demands were also the most
unstable, the most vulnerable to misunderstanding or appropriation.
Even in Wyclif's vernacular writings (if indeed the Latin versions are
fair witnesses to the original contents), the nicely hedged precision of
Wyclif's argument depended on the context of his language in academic
theology and canon law, and depended as well on his intended audience.
The following argument from the thirty-three conclusions has specific
and exclusive reference to clerics:

> It is clear that the pope, along with the priesthood, is not competent in
> civil law or lordship, nor has the law of the gospel or of nature. . . . It is
> clear therefore from the law of the gospel and of nature, that those who
> abuse wealth, to the harm of themselves or their neighbors, lack the right
> of using it [*ius utendi*] insofar as they lack the effort and purpose
> appropriate to the gospel [*labor evangelicus atque finis*]. That it [right of
> civil possession] is absent in the nature of alms [*ex titulo elemosine*], is
> obviously clear.[65]

64. "Set, heu! (inquit), heu! et ve! quod rex non habet aliquos iusticiarios in regno
suo ad hanc iusticiam exequendam, et ex quo non sunt alii iusticiarii ad hoc specialiter ex
officio deputati. Ideo oportet vos, O fideles Cristiani, manum apponere vt vos saltim hoc
negocium ad finem debitum perducatis. Et tunc firmiter spero quod bene procedet, quia
scio certissime quod ipse Deus omnipotens uult quod fiat" (Simon Forde, ed., "Nicholas
Hereford's Ascension Day Sermon, 1382," *MS* 51 [1989]: 240).

65. *Opera minora*.

All this is "clear" only if much else is clear: the distinctions between use and possession, civil and evangelical dominion, and gift and alms; the specialized sense of technical terms (*evangelicus* means "relating to preaching"); and the origins of the vocabulary in discussions of vowed poverty.[66] For an audience uninstructed in theological terms of art, an assertion like "those who abuse wealth, to the harm of themselves or their neighbors, lack the right of using it insofar as they lack the effort and purpose appropriate to the gospel" would mean not (as Wyclif means it) "clerics who abuse wealth, and harm themselves, compromising their discipleship and harming their neighbors by compromising the integrity of the church, lose their right of using (without legally possessing) wealth insofar as they fail to use it for the preaching of the gospel," but something more like "those who abuse their wealth, living in luxury and leaving others to starve, lose their right to the wealth if they act in a way not consonant with the teaching of the gospel," the latter of wider and not exclusively clerical application. Wyclif's meaning gains precision too from its intended audience, which silently renders general terms more specific. When he asserts that "it is lawful for the laity to withhold and take away the goods of the church from ecclesiastical superiors,"[67] "laity" means "king and lords," for these were the audience that mattered most to him. But his strategy of displaying the rural poor as his audience and clientele meant that inevitably they *overheard* his teaching, and could mistake the "laity" in question to be themselves.

"More than one prophet has made his reputation on what he did not say," Margaret Aston has said.[68] By invoking the rights and authority of the poor, Wyclif put into circulation a vocabulary that was available to purposes very different from his own.[69] Abstracted from its place in the

66. For the crucial dependence, mediated by FitzRalph, of Wyclif's vocabulary of dominion and reform on the refinements introduced by the Franciscan poverty controversies into the discussion of ownership, see James Doyne Dawson, "Richard FitzRalph and the Fourteenth Century Poverty Controversies," *Journal of Ecclesiastical History* 3 (1983): 315–44.

67. "Ex istis colligi potest sentencia, quam sepe inserui, licet sit mundo odibilis, scilicet, quod licet laicis in casu tam subtrahere quam auferre bona ecclesie a suis prepositis" (*De veritate* 3:1).

68. "Lollardy and Sedition," 3.

69. The point did not escape contemporaries. Between 1381 and 1383, the Cistercian William of Rymington attacked Wyclif's doctrines in his *XLIV conclusiones*. He allowed the possibility that the latter's teachings might have been behind the rising—"talis doctrina pestifera verisimiliter fuit causa nuper movens communitatem ad insurgendum contra

struggles between Gaunt and the bishops, it was ready for insurgent use. Wyclif's public rhetoric proclaimed that the lords had a responsibility to ease the oppressions of the poor; that their failure to do so sprang from a complacent enjoyment of their wealth, which was meant for the common good; that this irresponsibility increased the burdens of taxation in the countryside; that the nobility was therefore as blameworthy as the clergy; and that the poor, by virtue of their poverty, bore a natural likeness to Christ and the mark of his authority. The point about this rhetoric is that it could turn itself as virulently against those it was meant to serve as against those it attacked, and, indeed, put the blame for actions not taken precisely on the king and the lords. Wyclif had made this scheme to offer an opportunity to king and lords; but it could as easily level an accusation against them.

Though the rebels might have found some of this vocabulary in other sources (the next chapter will concern itself with one of them), no other likely and proximate source but Wyclif names disendowment as a responsibility owed by rulers to the poor. The rebels refused to remain merely the authenticating symbol for Wyclif's polemic; they made themselves its audience and agent, translating Wyclif's prescriptions into direct action against both sorts of "bloodsuckers," the "simoniacal clergy" and the "secular tyrants." The most notable and noted events in London—the executions of Sudbury, Hales, and Appleton, the burning of Clerkenwell, and above all the destruction of John of Gaunt's magnificent palace, the Savoy—show how the rebels shaped Wyclif's teachings into a vernacular program of disendowment.

The Savoy was "without its like,"[70] a singular monument to singular wealth, standing on the Strand at the western end of the Thames' London arc. Its destruction was one of the most memorable and disturbing events of the rising, provoking detailed narrative in the chronicles; the London city reports, in the Letter Book and the sheriff's inquisitions, were anxious to put the blame for that event particularly on the shoulders of uplanders.[71] There is one aspect of the event which

---

regem et proceres huius regni"—precisely because Wyclif's justification of disendowment would apply equally to secular lords: "Ex hac doctrina consimiliter sequitur quod licitum et meritorius est communi populo laicorum iudicare de peccatis et abusionibus imperatorum, regum, principum, et omnium temporalium dominorum, atque violenter auferre ab eis temporalia dominia" (Bodl. MS Bodley 158, fol. 201v–202r).

70. "Non habens sibi simile" (Knighton, *Chronicon*, 134).

71. The London Letter Book says that the men of Essex went straight for the Savoy

the chroniclers patently do not understand, though they all record it: by common agreement and under severe discipline, nothing was stolen.[72] The chronicles witness all the more credibly to this fact for their difficulty in explaining it. To the Westminster chronicler, it was a "thing unaccustomed in our days,"[73] while the *Anonimalle* chronicler reveals the fact only by way of turning the rebels into buffoons: he reports that at the Savoy they found three barrels, and "believing them to contain gold or silver," they threw the barrels into the flames. The barrels really contained gunpowder, and the results were catastrophic; this bit of slapstick at the rebels' expense reveals in passing that they were really trying to destroy gold, not make off with it.[74] Walsingham, dismissing their restraint as public relations ("so that it would be clear to the commons of the realm that they did nothing from greed"), adds the valuable information that they made a proclamation "that no one, under pain of beheading, should

---

when they arrived in London (Riley, *Memorials of London* 3:449); the sheriff's inquisition says they were led by Wat Tyler, who was most closely associated with the Kentish insurgents (Réville, *Soulèvement*, 192); and the *Anonimalle* lays the responsibility on the Londoners (141). The last assertion is accepted by Hilton, *Bond Men Made Free*, 193; Barron, *Revolt in London*, 3; and Bertie Wilkinson, "The Peasants' Revolt of 1381," *Speculum* 15 (1940): 30. The assumption seems to be that the city officials wanted as far as possible to exculpate the city itself and were particularly eager to avoid any rekindling of the dispute between the duke and the city that had flared four years earlier and had been suppressed only by the intervention of the queen mother; see Ruth Bird, *The Turbulent London of Richard II* (London, 1949), ch. 2. However, a good many rebels from the counties were indicted for actions in the city; see Prescott, "London in the Peasants' Revolt," 130; and the indictments in Sparvel-Bayly, "Essex in Insurrection," 215–16, and Powell and Trevelyan, *The Peasants' Rising*, 8. One document printed by Réville claims that the idea originated with a former servant of Lancaster's (*Soulèvement*, 202). While there is good reason to believe that London officials wanted to ensure the innocence of the city, their desire does not entail the city's guilt.

72. The jury presentments accuse Joanna Ferrour and her husband Thomas of stealing a chest worth £1000 and transporting it across Thames (Barron, *Revolt in London*, 3). (The documents given in Réville, *Soulèvement*, 199–200, show that a Middlesex jury acquitted her.) For chronicle accounts besides those I cite in this paragraph, see *Eulogium*, which says that the rebels threw the goods into the Thames, shouting "Nolumus esse fures" (352), and the Kirkstall chronicle, which says the same and adds, "nec fuerat quisquam eorum ausus aliquid alicuius precii salvare seu asportare" (*The Kirkstall Abbey Chronicles*, ed. John Taylor [Leeds, 1952], 111). (This account, incidentally, is a valuable though laconic witness, since it seems to be independent of other written accounts; in his narrative of the meeting with the king at Smithfield, the chronicler does not give Wat Tyler's name—referring to him only as *capitaneus eorum*—leaving the clear implication that he does not know it; any of the surviving chronicles, however, could have provided this detail.)

73. "Cerneres ibidem rem nostris seculis insolitam, nam dum preciosissima cernerent, tractarent, et colligerent, non audebat rustica manus preciosa furtivis manibus surripere, quia si quis in aliquo furto fuerat deprehensus, sine processu sive judicio ad mortem rapiebatur decapitandus" (*Westminster Chronicle*, 4).

74. *Anonimalle*, 141–42.

presume to take anything found there to his or her own use."[75] Knighton tells of a haplessly greedy rebel whom, found making off with a silver dish hidden in his garment, "they threw, . . . together with his dish, into the fire, exclaiming, 'We are men zealous for truth and justice, not thieves or brigands.'"[76]

Altogether, these reports are too unanimous in sense and too varied in detail to admit of doubt, and indeed no one doubts them. But at no other time or place during the rising do the rebels seem to have exercised this restraint. Walsingham was right to say that they adopted this discipline with an eye to a national audience, but they can hardly have meant thereby to excuse themselves from the charge of plundering, since they had been plundering publicly for days; the same crowd (apparently), on the same day, sacked the Temple Inn. Instead, it must have been a strategic symbolic action meant to declare their motives at one point of great public exposure. The cry Knighton attributes to them—"We are men zealous for truth and justice, not thieves or brigands"—deserves close attention. I have observed that its normative terms are those of the rebel letters: *veritas* ("trewþe"), *justitia* ("ry3t"), *fures et latrones* ("hobbe þe robbere"). "Hobbe the robber" appears twice in the letters (in Carter and Ball₃); both times he stands in symbolic opposition to Piers Plowman,[77] who in Ball₃ is to "chastise wel" the thief, and in Carter introduces the adjuration, "lokke þat hobbe robbyoure be wele chastysede for lesyng of 3oure grace. for [3e] haue gret nede to take god wiþ 3owe in alle 3oure dedes." The targets of the rising, the opponents of Piers and the rebels, are generalized into the collective figure of the thief. In declaring that they were "not thieves or brigands," the rebels were not evading an accusation but leveling one: that the goods being thrown into the river were the fruits of unjust possession.

But why did the rebels choose the Savoy, and it alone, as the scene for this gesture? They attacked Gaunt's palace on Thursday afternoon (13 June); the next morning, they executed Gaunt's protégé Archbishop Sudbury, and what they alleged against the one they alleged also against the other. Even Knighton's moralizing does not conceal the source of

---

75. "Et ut patesceret totius regni communitati eos non respectu avaritiae quicquam facere, proclamari fecerunt, sub poena decollationis, ne quis praesumeret aliquid vel aliqua ibidem reperta ad proprios usus servanda contingere" (Walsingham, *Chronicon*, 289).

76. Knighton, *Chronicon*, 135 (see ch. 1, n. 31 above).

77. For an extended discussion, see ch. 3 below.

the rebels' anger with the prelate and the charge leveled against him: Sudbury and his companions—Hales, John Legge, William Appleton— went freely and quietly to their deaths, and "unresisting, like lambs before the shearer, were brought forth with feet bare, heads uncovered, and hair disheveled, *as if they were guilty of homicide or theft.*"[78] It is hard to gauge the force of this last clause (is it Knighton's random simile, or does it recall some specific charge?), but other reports suggest that he may be recording the accusation the insurgents made. "Where is the traitor to the realm? Where is the despoiler of the common people?" was their cry as they searched for Sudbury, Knighton says.[79] The accusation of *furtum* is the one the rebels at the Savoy disavowed (and by implication leveled also at Gaunt), and which Carter and Ball use to figure the crimes that deserve the insurgency's revenge. Their declaration at the Savoy that theft was not their object was a deliberate counterpoint to the Sudbury execution, drawing the crucial line of moral judgment between those who steal and those who do not.

Bona ecclesiae sunt bona pauperum: Wyclif, as I have said, took this phrase in a peculiarly literal way. "The goods of the church belong to the poor, and are given to churchmen not to own, but to monitor, distribute, and serve";[80] when an ecclesiastic "unjustly consumes the goods of the church," he "defrauds both the living and the dead," is "an apostate, a seducer, and a heretic according to the laws of the church," and in such a case, "a layman must accuse and judge the delinquent cleric."[81] In Wyclif's rhetoric, ecclesiastical abuse of temporalities was, simply and factually, theft. "Hobbe the robber," identified as the figure against which the rioters were rioting, collapsed Wyclif's distinction between lordly wealth and prelatical wealth into a figure of wealth *simpliciter*. When the insurgents abjured plunder at the Savoy, ritually and communally proving themselves not "thieves or brigands," they

---

78. "Dum haec sic agerentur, ecce degeneres filii remanentes patrem suum archiepiscopum cum sociis antedictis absque vi vel impetu, absque gladio vel sagitta, vel quacunque alia oppressione, sed solum verbis minacibus et clamore turbido evocaverunt, et ad mortem invitaverunt, qui sponte non reclamantes, non reluctantes tanquam agni coram tondente se nudipedes, capite discooperto, cingulis abjectis, acsi homicidio vel furto rei" (Knighton, *Chronicon*, 134).

79. "Et post pusillum ingressi tortores, clamaverunt, 'Ubi est regni proditor? Ubi communis vulgi depraedator?'" (Knighton, *Chronicon*, 292).

80. See n. 55 above.

81. "Sic iniuste consumens bona ecclesie, fraudando vivos et mortuos, est apostata, seductor et hereticus"; "secundum leges ecclesie laicus debet in casu accusare clericum delinquentem et per consequens iudicare, quod sit malus" (*De veritate* 3:12, 13).

meant to demonstrate their moral right to the goods that they, unlike the lord and the prelate, refused simply to take. And this attempt to evade what Girard calls "acquisitive mimesis" underlies the rebels' claim to spiritual authority and therefore to political power; it allows Jack Carter, in his letter, to link prelatical theft to spiritual reform, to imagine insurgent actions not merely as a readjustment of maldistributed wealth, but as a spiritually reformist alliance with Piers Plowman. Hobbe the Robber's depredations are not merely or chiefly material: he is to be chastised "for lesyng of ȝoure grace. for [ȝe] haue gret nede to take god wiþ ȝowe in alle ȝoure dedes." Sudbury's "theft" deprives its victims not only of material goods but of "grace," just as Gaunt's theft must be not merely rectified but disavowed for the rebels to maintain their claim over lordly goods. Wyclif had insisted that the oppression of the poor not only was an empirical injustice, but disturbed the peace of God in the realm. So did the rebels.

The *veritas* for which they asserted themselves zealous, the "trewþe" with which Ball$_2$ urges them to ally themselves, is the normative term of Langland's *Piers Plowman* (which I discuss in the next chapter) and also of the insurgents' self-description. "Trewþe" is what they intend to repossess—what has been "sette under a lokke"—and what they already possess: the pseudonym "Jakke Trewman" is formed in parallel with the pseudonyms of the other letter writers ("Jakke Milner," "Jakke Carter," "Johon Schep"), all of which disavow singularity by claiming a generic identification with rural occupations. "Trewman," then, claims that this "trewþe" belongs to rural laborers as naturally as their rural occupations belong to them—the claim made by the rebels' "wache worde," "Wyth kynge Richarde and wyth the *trew communes*."[82] The "trew communes" are those who maintain their faith with the rest of the commons, and in being true *possess* truth, a truth with both political and theological inflections.

And with political and theological authority. Wyclif's teaching implied that priestly as well as political authority was derived from the laity, who were the true source of a church's faith and who were to

---

82. "Et les ditz comunes avoient entre eux une wache worde en Engleys, 'With whom haldes yow?' et le respouns fuist, 'Wyth kynge Richarde and wyth the trew communes': et ceux qe ne savoient ne vodroient respondre, furount decolles et mys a la mort" (*Anonimalle*, 139). Walsingham offers an inflection on what "trew" and "trewþe" meant to the rebels when he reports that they swore "ut regi Ricardo et communibus fidelitatem servarent" (Walsingham, *Chronicon*, 286).

judge and if necessary remove priests from their cures:[83] a communal responsibility that bespoke continuity, not division, of authority between the estates. When the clergy abuses its wealth, it ceases to be clergy altogether, and clerical authority devolves upon the unordained faithful.[84] Rebel actions and rebel letters alike located their political competence in theological prerogative. The most direct assertion of their theological competence during the riots in London was the execution of the advisers the king left in the tower while he met with the insurgents at Mile End, and especially Sudbury.[85] Sudbury was Gaunt's man, chancellor of the realm and (as such) an example of what Wyclif was apt to call the "caesarean clergy," clergy who held secular office. Ten years before, while bishop of London, Sudbury had become implicated in scandal when King Edward ordered him to reform abuses in his administration of the cathedral, which had been "spoken in popular report."[86] His claim on respect as a priest was already tenuous; Walsingham was not alone in his contempt (as Jonathan Hughes points out, it is some measure of Sudbury's diminished stature that no one tried to

83. This in an early, public sermon preached in London: "Christus ergo cognoscens eorum duriciam dure eos redarguit et medicinam mulcentem non eis apposuit nec cum eis sicut cum laicis in esculentis et interloquiis communicavit, sic patet ex cursu evangelii. Voluit enim Christus a laicis et feminis sustentari, ut patet in ingressu, in progressu, et in egressu" (*Sermons* 3:271).

84. "Et divertente clero ad seculum plus quam laici everti possit clerus in laicos et e contra, ita quod laici tam viri quam femine intendant postillacioni scripture, clerici autem tradicionibus humanis, bellis, contencionibus et aliis negociis secularibus" (*De veritate sacre scripture* 1:154).

85. All the major sources agree that Sudbury was taken, opportunistically, during the king's absence. Only two sources seriously dissent from this opinion. Gosford's Bury St. Edmunds chronicle says that the king was present when Sudbury was taken ("Collectanea . . . Astone," 126), but its testimony is negligible. The London Letter Book, however, gives a more interesting account: "at the prayer of the infuriated rout, our Lord the King granted that they might take those who were traitors against him, and slay them, wheresoever they might be found. And from thence the King rode to his Wardrobe . . .; while the whole of the infuriated rout took its way towards the Tower of London; entering which by force, they dragged forth from it Sir Simon, Archbishop of Canterbury, Chancellor of our Lord the King, and Brother Robert Hales, Prior of the said Hospital of St. John of Jerusalem, the King's Treasurer" (Letter Book H, in Riley, *Memorials of London*, 449–50; Riley's translation).

86. "Vulgatis relatis publicantur" (Thomas Rymer, *Foedera, conventiones, litterae, et cujucunque generis acta publica* . . . [London, 1869] 3:908). This was in 1371 and may have been a sort of preparatory exercise for the disendowment proposals that would be made starting the following year. The first of these proposals, which the crown seems to have instigated, was offered in the parliament of 1372 by two Austin friars. The language of Edward's letter patent—and it was, though addressed personally to Sudbury, a letter patent, and therefore public—anticipated with striking precision both the language and the arguments Wyclif would use five years later in advocating disendowment.

name him a martyr or establish a cult after his death).[87] But his death, though it brought him no greater respect than his life, was still the insurgent action that most terrified the government and bishops— innocence of participation in Sudbury's lynching was a sine qua non for the king's amnesty—and was a prime concern of the church hierarchy in the months after the rising.[88]

The rebels targeted Sudbury early in the rebellion for largely symbolic reasons. An unparalleled but credible report in the *Anonimalle Chronicle* says that before the rebels began to move toward London, they "came to Canterbury before the hour of noon, and four thousand of them entered the greater church of St. Thomas at the time of the high mass, and, kneeling, cried with one voice that the monks should elect a monk to be archbishop of Canterbury, 'because he that is now archbishop is a traitor and will be beheaded for his faults'; and so he was, five days later."[89] The right of selecting the archbishop had been contended for over a century; the prior and monks of the cathedral church nominally retained their right of election, and the pope his more recent right of provision, but by the latter half of the fourteenth century the office was in the king's gift,[90] and the king had chosen bureaucrats like Sudbury. In ordering the chapter to elect a new archbishop, the rebels ordered it to do what it wanted to do anyway, restoring its right to choose free from royal or papal interference, a right the monks had not been able to exercise for a century. The insurgents did not demand abolition of

87. Hughes, *Pastors and Visionaries: Religion and Secular Life in Late Medieval Yorkshire* (Woodbridge, Suffolk, 1988), 305. Hughes is possibly not quite right here; Walsingham refers to Sudbury's "martyrdom" and purveys a miracle story of the most recognizable sort, but the uniqueness and inconsequence of his effort, not to mention its contrast with his portrayal of Sudbury elsewhere, is nearly as eloquent as silence.

88. "Horpris ceux qi tuerent Symon l'Ercevesque de Canterbirs nadgaires Chanceller, le Priour de Seint Johan adonqes Tresorer, & Johan de Cavendish Chief Justice nostre dit seigneur" (*Rp* 3.103). The church, naturally, reacted as strongly as the government: see Bishop Brinton's announcement of excommunication for those involved in it (*The Sermons of Thomas Brinton, Bishop of Rochester (1373–1389)*, ed. Sister Mary Aquinas Devlin [London, 1954], 2:457).

89. "Et le lundy prochien apres le fest de la Trinytee viendrent a Caunterbury avaunt la houre de none et iiiior mille des eux entrerount en la meir esglise de seint Thomas en le temps del haut messe, et engenolauntz toutz a une voyce crierent a les moignes pur eslire une moigne destre ercevesqe de Kaunterbury, qar destuy qor est, est traytour et serra decolle pur sa iniquitee; et si fuist il dienz le v iour apres" (*Anonimalle Chronicle*, 137). Galbraith observes that the account of the events in Canterbury corresponds generally with what can be known from other sources (194).

90. See Churchill, *Canterbury Administration* 1:254–59.

the office or the election of one of their own.[91] They "knelt" to the monks; this chronicler, at least, thought that they had no intention of undoing the procedures of the church and every intention of abiding by the cathedral chapter's choice.

What they did regarding Sudbury in Canterbury contrasts with, but does not contradict, what they did to him in London. After leading him before the public "like a homicide or a thief," they beheaded him. As they did, "they cried with each stroke, 'This is the hand of the Lord.'"[92] This astonishing assertion can mean only that the rebels understood their collective action as the instrumental expression of God's imperative of reform. The execution and the election both display their faith that the "hand of the Lord" is present in collectivities of the disappropriated: the monks disenfranchised of their right to elect the archbishop, the commons of their right to the *bona pauperum*. But the claim is more

91. Walsingham's assertion that John Ball proposed to have himself appointed archbishop of Canterbury is an evident slander.

92. "Ad quemlibet ictum dicentes: 'Haec est manus domini'" (*Eulogium*, 353). This is rather a vexed matter, since Walsingham reports these same words but has *Sudbury* pronounce them: "Percussus vero in collo securi, sed non letaliter, apposita manu vulneri, ita dixit; 'A! a!' inquit, 'manus Domini est'" (*Chronicon*, 293). Further, one manuscript of the *Eulogium* gives the crucial participle as *dicētē* "dicentem," which would indeed assign the words to Sudbury (Dobson apparently assumes this to be the case, since he silently renders the passage to agree with Walsingham: "he said, as the stroke fell, 'This is the hand of the Lord'" [*Peasants' Revolt*, 207]); but the L sentence makes little sense read thus. Everything about the account in the *Eulogium* makes it clear that the continuator has drawn on a different and no longer extant report of the events in London. There are several indications that this is the case, like the vision of "a certain man" who saw devils among the rioting crowd. But there is nothing to suggest for certain that he draws on Walsingham at all (indeed, on some issues he has demonstrably better information even than the *Anonimalle*, as when he refers correctly to Wat Tyler as "de Estsex" [352], though the *Anonimalle* and others infer that he was from Kent; on this issue, see ch. 4, n. 30 below). This lost source, then, presumably reported the words as the continuator does. Walsingham's version is complicated by his unmitigated dislike of Sudbury. Recounting the story of Wyclif's first trial, Walsingham portrays the archbishop as a fool and a laggard: "Unde, licet sero, episcopi stimulati excitarunt patrem suum archiepiscopum quasi de gravi somno, et quasi potentem crapulatum a vino, vel potius mercenarium avaritiae inebriatum toxico. . . . Archiepiscopus vero, quamquam in bonis decrevisset dies suos ducere nec vigilias agere circa gregem suum, . . . tamen ne a compastoribus et collegis suis notari posset desertor ovilium, et per hoc pateretur dispendium suae famae sive nominis, misit qui invitaret filium prodigum ad respondendum his quae de eo dicebantur"—equating him, in his concern for his own reputation, with Wyclif himself, who, Walsingham says on the previous page, acted "ad unum finem . . ., ut videlicet ejus fame et opinio se inter homines dilataret" (*Chronicon*, 117). Walsingham's assignment of the words "Haec est manus Domini" to Sudbury expresses his sense that the prelate's death was God's punishment for such inactivity: "archiepiscopum vero, quamquam credibile est eum matyrio vitam finisse, tamen propter teporem curae quam adhibuisse debuerat in hac parte, horrenda mortis passione punisse" (311).

specific even than that and implies, by its choreography of utterance and gesture, a complex and articulable notion of how such authority might reside in the commons. For they gave the lynching the form of legal process. Walking bound and barefoot in ritual abjection, as Sudbury and the others were forced to do, was a customary humiliation; decapitation (forgoing the relative ease of rope and tree, far the most usual method) was the customary means of execution for those of Sudbury's rank.[93] In both these actions, the rebels mimed the legal procedures in a treason trial; like their proclamations, levies, taxations, and letters patent, the form of Sudbury's execution asserted by gesture the right of the commons to exercise royal prerogative, and their claim to be instruments in "the hand of the lord," the collective embodiment of the divine will and the collective source of royal power.

Immediately after the execution, the rebels used this judicial assertion of royal prerogative to contrive a gruesome, Wycliffian comment on the inadequacy of Sudbury's life to the demands of his office. Wyclif said, repeatedly and in both academic and popular writings, that only conformity to the life, poverty, and sufferings of Christ could confer priestly or prelatical authority,[94] and he characterized the passion as the final and summary expression of such poverty and suffering: "From the moment of his conception *to the hour of his death*, Christ was the poorest of humanity in order to give the example of poverty to his flock; and his example should be more peremptory than the decrees of all the popes—even John XXII—unless they are rooted in the teaching of the gospel," he says in the (originally vernacular) *Dialogus*.[95] Later on, even as he tried carefully to dissociate himself from the rising, he reasserted a favorite theme of his vernacular preaching, that the luxury of possessioners and prelates is a blasphemy against the example of Christ's sufferings.[96] Sudbury's fate after the falling of the ax gave expression to such sentiments, and showed the same mingling of royal justice and

93. On the predominance of hanging (and its relative ease), see John Bellamy, *Crime and Public Order in England in the Later Middle Ages* (London, 1973), 186–87.

94. E.g., his assertion that papal authority comes only from conformity to Christ's life (*De veritate* 1:152).

95. "Christus ab instanti sue conceptionis usque ad horam sue mortis fuit homo pauperrimus ad pauperiem suis ovibus exemplandum, et ista exemplacio debet esse precisior quam decreta omnium paparum, eciam Iohannis 22i, nisi in fide ewangelii sunt fundata" (*Dialogus*, 68).

96. *De blasphemia*, ed. M. H. Dziewicki (London, 1893).

theological commentary. On the unanimous testimony of the chronicles, Sudbury's head was taken, along with those of Hales and Appleton, to London Bridge, where it was fixed on a pole for all to view.[97] The commons thus continued to assert their judicial authority, imitating the usual postmortem humiliation of those executed for notorious offenses (especially treason), but they ornamented it with another and different assertion of authority, constructing a parodic tableau whose form we may deduce from the Westminster chronicler: "they fixed the head of the archbishop in the middle, and above the others, and (so that it could be the more readily distinguished from the others) they used a nail to secure the red cap on his head."[98] The configuration of the heads, with Sudbury's "in the middle and above the others," recalled the iconography of the Crucifixion, in which Christ hangs between the two thieves and is foregrounded, so that his cross stands higher than the others; on his head, often red with blood, is the crown of thorns—meant as a mockery but actually a proclamation of the true kingship displayed in his suffering. The rebel parody mocked the archbishop's pretensions to speak in Christ's name, projecting the image of the crucified Christ (which the rhetoric of later Lollardy would seek in the persons of the poor, the "quick images of God," rather than in the ornate and bejeweled crucifixes visible in church) behind Sudbury's exposed head, as the standard against which he was measured and found wanting. Christ's bloody crown of thorns, symbolic of suffering and authority, was replaced by Sudbury's red cap, symbolic of cardinalatial office and prelatical wealth.

The commons who tried and killed Sudbury called him *traditor*, a traitor to king and realm, before his capture, and after it they tried and punished him as such,[99] but the accusation simply does not make sense if it means something like collusion with the French.[100] The rebels were as precise in their use of the word *traditor* as they were in their appropriation of other official forms and terms. The treason statute of

97. "Capita vero illorum in lanceis et baculis transfixerunt ut a reliquis sic dinoscerentur" (Knighton, *Chronicon*, 134); *Kirkstall Abbey Chronicles*, 111; *Memorials of St. Edmund's Abbey*, 126; William Thorne, *Chronica de rebus gestis abbatum sancti Augustini Cantuariae*, in Roger Twysden, ed., *Historiae anglicanae scriptores decem* (London, 1652), col. 2157.

98. "Sacratum capud archiepiscopi in medio et eminenciori loco fixerunt, et ut specialius a ceteris capitibus agnosceretur capellam rubeam super capud cum clavo fixerunt" (*Westminster Chronicle*, 6); see also *Kirkstall Abbey Chronicles*, 111.

99. See *Westminster Chronicle*, 2; Walsingham, *Chronicon*, 292.

100. As Barron, for example, seems to take it; see *Revolt in London*, 6.

1352 had carefully defined the scope of the crime: treason was still and exclusively *laesio majestas*, the violation of the personal bond by which all owed loyalty to the king.[101]

In what sense, then, was Sudbury a *traditor* to those who executed him? "Ubi est traditor regni? Ubi est depraedator communi vulgus?" The pairing is, I suggest, apposition: Sudbury was a traitor *in that* he was the despoiler of the commons. They complained about Sudbury's treatment, not of the king, but of themselves; and yet, to have charged him with treason, they must have taken mistreatment of themselves to *be* mistreatment of the king, Sudbury's *laesio* consisting in his *depraedatio communis vulgi*. Underlying this assertion, giving it its consistency, is the point with which I began: the rebels' claim that the regnal person of the king resided in themselves. The trial and execution of Sudbury was the rebels' most schematic and spectacular assertion of their identity

---

101. See the "great statute" of treasons (*SR* 1.319–20). The parenthetical clause which closes the statute—"il y ad autre manere de treson, cest assavoir quant un servant tue son meistre, un femme qui tue son baron, quant homme seculer ou de religion tue son Prelat, a qi il doit foi & obedience; & tiel manere de treson donn forfaiture des eschetes a chescun Seigneur de son fee propre"—makes it clear that treason concerns not "king, or nation taken in the abstract," but "king or other personal lord." On this and the issues to follow, see J. G. Bellamy, *The Law of Treason in England in the Later Middle Ages* (Cambridge, Eng., 1970), 59–176. The specific range of *laesiones* consists of violence against the person, consort, or heir of the king, wars raised against him or comfort given to his enemies, the counterfeiting of the Great Seal or the king's money, or the killing of his major officers in the course of their duties. The statute also specifies what does *not* count as treason: in cases of open or secret warfare one against another, to kill or hold for ransom, "nest pas lentent du Roi & de son conseil que en tiel cas soit ajugge treson, einz soit ajugge felonie ou trespas selonc la lei de la terre auncienement usee" (ibid.). It is striking that in no case, by their own express pronouncements, could most actions of the rebels be taken for treason under the clear definitions in the statute. Murder of the chancellor, treasurer, or justices are included in the definition, but only "esteiantz en lours places en fesantz lours offices"; Sudbury and Hales were at mass when they were taken. The only usual act of the rising that *could* be so construed under the statute was the display of standards, which implied open war; as Andrew Prescott has pointed out, this is why standards appear so prominently in the indictments ("Judicial Records of the Rising of 1381," Ph.D. thesis, Bedford College, University of London, 1984, 101–2). And even there the claim to act in concert with the king and the use of the *royal* banners might have been thought to preempt charges of *laesio*, so that even a criminal classification of their actions would have prompted only the traditional charge of felony and trespass. (The justices' evident difficulty in rationalizing treason charges surely prompted the supplement to the statute in 1381: "Et le Roi defende . . . que nully desore face ne recomence par voie quelconqe celles riot & rumour nautres semblables. Et si nully le face et ce provez duement soit fait de luy come de Traitre au Roi et a son dit Roialme" [*SR* 2.20].) Since it could hardly be imagined that the use of the king's standards and the invocation of his name were strategic attempts to avoid treason charges—elementary game theory shows that if the rebels expected to face any charges at all, they would not have rebelled—they should probably be explained instead by a prior fit between the ideology that informed the rising and the ideology that underwrote common and statutory law.

with the king: just as the violation of his fidelity to the king was inflicted on the collective person of the commons, that same collective person passed judgment on and executed him according to the forms of royal justice. The "wache worde"—"Wyth kynge Richarde and wyth the trew communes"—bespeaks an identification that can tolerate substitution: the actions of the "trew communes" are the actions of the true king.

The rebels' assertions conferred on Wyclif's vernacular teachings of the late 1370s a consistency he himself took some pains to avoid. He had developed a coherent and compelling theological rationale for locating the authority of all just governance, including the king's, in the presence of the poor, who, by their poverty, constitute the political presence of the evangelical Christ; but he persistently denied the logic of his arguments, forestalling popular action by insisting on the imperative of obedience to the king. The fissure in Wyclif's political rhetoric was its tacit distinction between the authorizing fiction of royal power—that it was derived from its identification with "the foundation of the pillar of state," the poor—and the reality—that all the identification did for the poor was use them. Wyclif's attempt to bring politics under the roof of theology did not and could not work in the terms he provided: there is no way to locate authority in poverty and then assign it to the king. As has often been pointed out, he defined the king's power in the name of an evangelical imperative against which the clergy could be found wanting, but never applied the standard to the king himself. Instead, he left in place the working assumption of estates theory, that the estates live differently because they do different jobs.[102] The rebels in effect took him at his word about the identification of king and commons, and found in the identification their commission to exercise royal power—to create royal instruments, to execute royal justice, to impose royal punishments—and in doing so, they erased the distinction between the political and the theological.

102. In this sense, Paul A. Olson is right to stress the conservative and traditional, estates-oriented articulation of Wyclif's political imagination, but because this was a contradictory and inconsistent element in his thinking and rhetoric, it cannot be used (as Olson uses it) to ascribe a moderate reformism to Wyclif (*The Canterbury Tales and the Good Society* [Princeton, 1986]).

3

Piers Plowman in the Rising

For some years before 1381 (Walsingham says twenty), John Ball was preaching insurgency:

> He captured the good will of the common people (more than merit before God) by preaching in different places what he knew would please the crowd, attacking ecclesiastics and secular lords.
>
> He taught that the people were not to tithe a curate, unless the giver was richer than the vicar or rector receiving the gift;
>
> he taught that tithes and duties were to be taken away from curates, if it happened that the subject or parishioner was of better life than his curate;
>
> he taught further that no one was fit for the kingdom of God who was born out of wedlock;
>
> he also taught the perverse doctrines of the faithless John Wyclif.
>
> Because of all this, the bishops forbade him church pulpits, and so he began preaching in town squares, and villages. . . . After he was excommunicated for his refusal to cease and desist, he was committed to prison, where he declared that two thousand allies would come to liberate him.[1]

This account of Ball's recent heresies appears in the chapter "De presbytero Johannis Balle," in which Walsingham also transcribes Ball₃ and summarizes the Blackheath sermon ("Whanne Adam dalfe and Eve

---

1. "Hic per viginti annos, et amplius, semper praedicans in diversis locis ea quae scivit vulgo placentia, detrahens tam personis ecclesiasticis quam dominis secularibus, benevolentiam magis communis populi quam meritum penes Deum captabat. Docuit nempe plebem decimas non esse dandas curato, nisi is qui daturus esset foret ditior quam vicarius qui acciperet, sive rector. Docuit etiam decimas et oblationes subtrahendas curatis, si constaret subjectum aut parochianum melioris vitae fore quam curatum suum. Docuit insuper neminem aptum regno Dei, qui non in matrimonio natus fuisset. Docuit et perversa dogmata perfidi Johannis Wyclife, et opiniones quas tenuit, et insanias falsas, et plura, quae longum foret recitare; propter quae, prohibitus ab episcopis, in quorum parochiis haec praesumpsit, ne in ecclesiis de cetero praedicaret, concessit in plateas et vicos, vel in campos, ad praedicandum. . . . Postremo excommunicatus, cum nec sic desisteret, carceri mancipatur, ubi praedixit se deliberandum per viginti millia amicorum" (Walsingham, *Chronicon Angliae*, 320–21).

span, / Who was þanne a gentil man?"). It permits a few inferences. Walsingham, almost certainly a witness to Ball's execution at St. Albans, says that Ball had confessed and was *convictus*; though the trial—which sentenced him to hanging and quartering, with his body to be sent to four cities of the kingdom—may not have proceeded with justice's most deliberate care, a trial there certainly was.[2] Walsingham gleaned his information from the trial's proceedings; this is perhaps why it lacks the tone of tendentious precision with which Walsingham usually retails hearsay. In fact, the compressed syntax and the stylized, parallel format of the summary ("Docuit nempe. . . . Docuit etiam. . . . Docuit insuper") recall Walsingham's adjectival flurries less than the grim gerundial constructions of ecclesiastical justice found in formal catalogues of heretical articles that issued from episcopal inquisitions, like the one that presumably accompanied Ball's excommunication.[3] Such catalogues make their own distortions, often smoothing idiosyncratic heresies into formulae.[4] But Ball's at least have not been smoothed so far as to leave an undisturbed Wycliffian landscape: the charges *distinguish* his assertions that tithing is subject to the tither's judgment from "the perverse doctrines of the faithless John Wyclif." Walsingham's presumptive source

2. Although a royal writ pardoned all those "seignors & gentils" who "firent diverses punissementz sur les ditz villeins & autres traitors sanz due proces de loye & autrement qe les loys & usages de la terre demandent" (*SR* 2.20), its point was simply to protect those who—like Bishop Despenser—took quick action to restore order and to reassure the nobility in the case of further violence; judicial process seems to have been observed in all the prosecutions after the rising.

3. The only official notice of Ball's preaching in 1381 is a writ for his arrest in March 1381 for examination before Sudbury, which fits perfectly with Walsingham's account (Wilkins, *Concilia Magnae Britannie et Hibernie* [London, 1739] 3.103). There also exists a royal letter patent of 13 December 1376 to two Colchester rectors and others, instructing them to hand Ball over to the sheriff of Essex for his offenses against holy church (*CPR* 1374–1377, 415). As far back as 1366, he had provoked Archbishop Langham (Wilkins, *Concilia* 3.64). All of this tends to confirm Walsingham's account. For a survey of other known facts, see Brian Bird and David Stephenson, "Who Was John Ball?" *Essex Archaeology and History*, 3d ser., 8 (1977 for 1976): 287–88.

By 1381, the English church had not had much practice in dealing with heresy, a deficiency soon mended; the most noticeable activity had come in 1378, with the condemnation of nineteen articles drawn from Wyclif's teachings, chiefly from the *De civili dominio*. Whatever the actual connection between Ball and Wyclif, it is certain that the episcopacy wanted such a connection; the issuing of a public condemnation could have been, among other things, an attempt to make sure Ball remained an albatross around Wyclif's neck.

4. On this tendency in fifteenth-century England, see Anne Hudson, "The Examination of Lollards" (1973), rpt. in *Lollards and Their Books*, 125–40, and *Premature Reformation*, 32–40.

indicates what teachings might have helped shape rural resentment into a rebel program in 1381.[5] As Walsingham reports them, Ball's teachings implicitly define a dissenting, though not necessarily insurgent, community and its authority. Taken together, the first two—on the restriction of tithing to the prosperous and on the withdrawal of tithes from deficient clergy—establish a basis for implementing moral judgment independent of (and against) the clergy in practical decisions about the communal practice of parish life. They also make social and economic status the markers of moral authority: those poorer than the clergy and those better than the clergy—the groups that would benefit from the first two articles—are obviously the same group. Ball's doctrines specify the village community as an authoritative subgroup over against the clergy and the wealthier laity.

The drift of these two doctrines is easy enough to discern and to place within the ideology of the rising. The third is odd, in context or out. "He taught . . . that no one was fit for the kingdom of God who was born out of wedlock": it is not immediately clear why Ball might have thought so or what this might have to do with his other, more readily explicable, assertions. I believe that there is a source near to hand—both Ball's hand and ours—that explains both what this point meant and how it related to his others; and it offers an astonishing opportunity to watch a contemporary poem being processed to serve an ideology, and to exemplify a notion of writing, that are alien to its own. In *Piers Plowman* B, Passus 9, Wit—one of the many interlocutors encountered by the narrator in a search for "Dowel"—defines this "doing well" as honest labor, and adverts by contrast to those "fals folk, feiþlees, þeues and lyeres, / Wastours and wrecches" that "out of wedlok, I trowe, / Conceyved ben in [cursed] tyme as Caym was on Eue" (B.9.121–23).[6] After tracing the disastrous consequences of Cain's untimely conception (the marriage of the "daughters of men" with the "sons of God," the Flood), Wit returns, toward the end of the passus, to those born "oþergates" (otherwise, that is, than in wedlock), who

5. Springing Ball from prison was one of the first concerted actions of the rebels: his claim when he was imprisoned that "two thousand friends" would supply help proved realistic in the event. His liberation suggests that the rebels themselves not only knew of his preaching, but considered it important to their project.

6. Citations from the B-version are taken from the Kane and Donaldson edition (London, 1975); I retain the brackets that mark editorial emendations, but not the italics that mark expanded contractions. On occasion I restore well-attested manuscript readings; these are marked with angle brackets.

for gedelynges arn holden,
As fals folk, fondlynges, faitours and lieres,
Vngracious to gete good or loue of þe peple;
Wandren [as wolues] and waste [if þei] mowe;
Ayeins dowel þei doon yuel and the deuel [plese],
And after hir deeþ day shul dwelle wiþ þe same
But god gyue hem grace here to amende.

(195–201)

Here are Ball's bastards.

I will return in a moment to what Ball is reported to have said, to show how he reshaped Wit's speech into his distinctive doctrine; but I want to begin with something *not* reported. At the end of the Blackheath sermon, as Walsingham records it, Ball adjured the rebels to remain faithful to their mission. In response, Walsingham says, Ball's audience cried out that Archbishop Sudbury was a traitor and should lose his head—precisely what they would call him, and do to him, next day on Tower Hill.[7] As the report stands, this scarcely follows from what Ball was saying: evidently Walsingham or his source has left something out, some explicit charge of treason against Sudbury. From these words of the crowd and the presence of Wit's harangue in Ball's sermon (still to be documented), we can reconstruct some of what Ball said but Walsingham did not report, trace its origin in Langland, and incidentally confront a problem finessed in my discussion of Wyclif's influence on the rising.

The last chapter described how the execution of Sudbury choreographed the ideology of disendowment, how the charge of treason gave concrete expression to the Wycliffian charge that the wealth of the ecclesiastical establishment stole from the hands and mouths of those hardest pressed to keep on the near side of subsistence. But Wyclif himself does not speak of treason; the structure of thought that could equate episcopal theft with treason (treason to the royal authority collectively possessed by the commons) is there, waiting to be articulated. Was there some semantic prompt that suggested the connection? I think that there was, and that it can be found in Wit's speech. Thirty lines before speaking of the bastards, Wit describes the natural obligation of mutual care and the disappointing record Christians have compiled in this respect. He blames the bishops:

7. "Archiepiscopum, qui tunc superstes erat, communium et regni proditorem fuisse, et iccirco decapitandum" (Walsingham, *Chronicon*, 322).

Bisshopes shul be blamed for beggeres sake.
He is [Iugged wiþ] Iudas that ȝyueth a Iaper siluer
And biddeþ þe beggere go for his broke cloþes:

Proditor est prelatus cum Iuda qui patrimonium christi minus distribuit; Et alibi, Perniciosus dispensator est qui res pauperum christi inutiliter consumit.

(92–94a)

"He is a *traitor like Judas*, that prelate who too scantily distributes the patrimony of Christ; and elsewhere: He is a pernicious administrator who idly consumes the goods of Christ's poor." Here, I suspect, Ball found the epithet that dictated Sudbury's execution. For what Wyclif called theft, Langland called treason, and (like Wyclif) he found it a plague of the episcopacy.

Wit's denunciation of bishops thus lands (in Ball's sermon) in the middle of a disendowment proposal, where Langland never meant it to be: Wit himself imagines no remedy more profound than a better crop of bishops.[8] Yet Ball's rereading gives the passage a strangely persuasive coherence. Langland's susceptibility to adventitious recombinations like this one (I will argue) was both a consequence of his diffidence about any particular reform (indeed, about any particular course of action) and an invitation to those who would use *Piers* to underwrite their own particular courses of reformist action. This is only superficially a paradox, which (I will also argue) derives from distinct, institutionally embodied attitudes toward the written word. The kind of reading Ball brought to *Piers Plowman*, and the kind of writing he took from it, can explain how the rebels could appropriate the poem on their own terms and *at the same time* delegate its central character as the embodiment and authorization of their claims to power and how Wit's "bastards" could become elements in an ideology of rebellion.

For that problem still has to be untangled. Wit's concern about those born "out of wedlok" is a plausible source for Ball's condemnation of

---

8. Langland's relation to Wycliffite ideology has been the subject of successive scholarly orthodoxies, but the most recent discussions have rightly tended to distance them from each other; see Pamela Gradon, "Langland and the Ideology of Dissent," *Proceedings of the British Academy* 66 (1980): 179–205; Christina von Nolcken, "*Piers Plowman*, the Wycliffites, and *Pierce the Plowman's Creed*," *YLS* 2 (1988): 71–102; James Simpson, "The Constraints of Satire in 'Piers Plowman' and 'Mum and the Sothsegger,'" in Helen Phillips, ed., *Langland, the Mystics, and the Medieval English Religious Tradition: Essays in Honour of S. S. Hussey* (Cambridge, Eng., 1990), 11–31; David Lawton, "Lollardy and the *Piers Plowman* Tradition," *MLR* 76 (1981): 780–93; and Hudson, *Premature Reformation*, 398–408. On the particular issue of disendowment, the authoritative discussion is Kathryn Kerby-Fulton, *Reformist Apocalypticism and Piers Plowman* (Cambridge, Eng., 1990).

bastards, but this hardly explains why Ball or his audience would care. But if we read the passage in B.9 while wondering how one would have to read it to settle on the bastards as its central term, its centrifugal elements slot into place, nudged into a coherence they barely enjoy as Langland wrote it. The bastards of B.9 exemplify one pole of Langland's fundamental opposition, the distinction between "false" and "true" lives, and give one answer to its structuring question (what is "Dowel"?):[9]

> [Dowel in þis world is trewe wedded libbynge folk],
> For þei mote werche and wynne and þe world sustene;
> For of hir kynde þei come þat Confessours ben nempned,
> Kynges and knyȝtes, kaysers and [clerkes];
> Maidenes and martires out of o man come.
> The wif was maad þe w[y]e for to helpe werche,
> And þus was wedlok ywroȝt wiþ a mene persone,
> First by þe fadres wille and þe frendes conseille,
> And siþenes by assent of hemself as þei two myȝte acorde.
>
> (110–18)

Wit imagines "true" life as rural life: these "folk" have already been identified as the "trewe tidy men þat trauaille desiren," to whom God sends grace to work (107–9). From almost the beginning of the poem, "treuþe" has been the object of the narrator's inquiry, and Wit fixes its definition in its social meaning ("faithfulness"). Rural society, with its ties of kinship and obligation (the "fadres wille" and "frendes conseille") and its duty of familial and communal cooperation (the wife as helpmeet), embodies "trewþe" as the natural condition of laboring society. These folk "sustene" (109) the world not merely by populating it, giving birth to the "Confessours," "kynges," and the rest who are their offspring, but also by raising children within this nexus of social obligation, instilling in them the sense of reciprocal duty that makes authority and office matter. The bastards Wit imagines—"sherewes" like Cain—stand outside these local networks of reciprocity. They are "fals" because they "wandren"; lacking allegiance to any single locale and its imperatives, they are "wolues," outside of and threatening to society itself.

Wit attaches no *theologically* normative value to "trewe wedded libbynge," which is a natural phenomenon that enables both natural and

9. This distinction is how Holy Church, in Passus 1, explains the castles on the hill and in the dale, and it is what spurs Will's inquiry, "Kenne me by som craft to knowe þe fals" (B.2.4), prompting the appearance of Lady Meed, and through her, the rest of the *Visio*'s action.

supernatural authority.[10] Though Wit is speaking literally, and only, about those born out of wedlock (as his detailed strictures on marriage show), the "bastards" invite metaphorical annexations like Ball's, which reverse the force of the passage by reversing its social perspective. In Wit's account, the boundaries between those who maintain order and those who threaten it are clear. On the side of order, there are the aristocrats, autocrats, and hierocrats ("Confessours . . . / Kynges and kny3tes, kaysers and [clerkes], / Maidenes and martires") who supervise the political and spiritual life of the population, and the faithful laborers, married folk, "out of" whom they "come" (114); on the other side are rabble. This is society imagined from the top down, from the point of view of the confessors, kings, and knights themselves: they elaborate and preserve the social order that begins where they began, in the particular localities that in effect belong to them. But a rural audience (or their spokesmen)—looking from the bottom up—might draw the lines of demarcation differently, finding the invasive and destructive presence not the odd landless bastard but the prelates and lords whose coercions and exactions—manorial duties, tithes, and poll taxes—cut into villagers' marginal chances for prosperity. For Wit, the life of family and labor is not itself a term of theological thought, merely its social precondition; he does not even consider making the bastards into a metaphor. But for those villagers Wit is talking *about*—real villagers in real villages—the "natural" phenomena of marriage, kinship, labor, and social competition were the terms of theological practice and understanding.[11]

Ball's Blackheath sermon more elaborately translated Wit's imaginative vocabulary. Ball preached on his famous text—"Whanne Adam dalfe and Eve span, / Who was þanne a gentil man?"—and the burden of his speculative argument (as opposed to his practical prescription) is that "all were created to be equal by nature [*a natura*] from the beginning [*a principio*], and that serfdom had been introduced through unjust oppression, against the will of God; that if God had wished to create serfs, he would have fixed from the beginning who would be a serf and

---

10. "Those living the state of matrimony ordained by God are capable of the moral action necessary for salvation" (Robert Worth Frank, Jr., *Piers Plowman and the Scheme of Salvation* [New Haven, 1957], 53). One should add perhaps that for Wit they are also the necessary condition of that action.

11. As the researches of John Bossy, for example, have suggested; see *Christianity in the West 1400–1700* (Oxford, 1987), 14–87.

who a lord."[12] In Walsingham's report, Ball theorizes equality by equating the phrases "by nature" and "from the beginning": natural, rightly
ordered human relations are those God established before social stratification.[13] He drew these two grammatically parallel phrases, and the
rudiments of their application, from two grammatically parallel phrases
that Wit deploys very differently. Langland's Wit says that from the
"kynde" of wedded folk come the confessors, kings, and knights he lists
("of hir kynde þei come" [112]) and at the end of the list, he repeats the
assertion, with a different inflection: "out of o man come" (114). By
both phrases, Wit means merely that all derive "from human nature,
from undifferentiated humanity," that there is no *ontological* difference
between a king and a serf: "kynde" has the meaning "class" or "category."[14] When Ball said that all were created to be equal "by nature" (*a
natura*), he borrowed but completely redefined the phrase "of hire
kynde" (112). He fixed on the word "kynde" and saw there a different,
though also conventional, meaning: "nature" as the normative state that
God created.[15] So in the natural order God made, the confessors, kings,
knights, emperors, clerks, virgins, and martyrs *and* the wedded laborers
who populate the world are the same.

But if Langland's "of hir kynde" generated Ball's *a natura*, how did
"out of o man" generate *a principio*? Langland's phrase, as I said, makes
a point of metaphysical anthropology. But under the rubric of Ball's
thema ("Whanne Adam dalfe . . ."), it sheds its metaphysical inflection
for a historical one: the "o man" that humanity comes "out of" historically is Adam. And just as Langland makes "of hir kynde" and "out of
o man" synonymous, Ball equates *a natura* with *in principio*. Once
absorbed into Ball's understanding of its terms, the rhetorical trajectory
of Langland's sentence—from the undifferentiated human "kynde," to
the differentiations of social status and function, and then back to the

---

12. "Continuansque sermonem inceptum, nitebatur, per verba proverbii quod pro
themate sumpserat, introducere et probare, ab initio omnes pares creatos a natura,
servitutem per injustam oppressionem nequam hominum introductam, contra voluntatem
Dei; quia, si Deo placuisset servos creasse, utique in principio mundi constituisset quis
servus, quisve dominus futurus fuisset" (Walsingham, *Chronicon*, 321).

13. He theorizes well beyond any meaning the couplet had in other contexts; see Albert
B. Friedman, "'When Adam Delved . . .': Contexts of a Historic Proverb," in Larry D.
Benson, ed., *The Learned and the Lewed: Studies in Chaucer and Medieval Literature*
(Cambridge, Mass., 1974), 213–30. The examples he cites show that the ordinary function
of the *topos* was to humble the wellborn rather than to exalt their inferiors.

14. *MED* s.v. "kinde" (n.) 9 a, c; or possibly also 11 a.

15. *MED* s.v. "kinde" 8 a.

unitary "o man"—practically begs for a meaning different from Wit's, one that sees social difference as a disruption of the fundamental equality God put in place at the creation. Distinction of rank, then, is logically and historically subsequent to what God wanted and made, and is therefore *un*natural, a human and at best dispensable superimposition: "Whanne Adam dalfe and Eve span, / Who was þanne a gentil man?"

After borrowing in surprising detail from this passage, Ball (again, as reported by Walsingham) exhorted the Blackheath assembly in specifically Langlandian terms, urging them

> to act in the manner of a good paterfamilias cultivating his field, pulling out and cutting down the poisonous weeds that smother [*opprimere*] the corn: first killing the great lords of the realm; then executing the justices and jurors of the countryside; and finally removing from their land all they know to be harmful to the commons. Thus they would finally bring peace and security for themselves in the future if—once the great were removed—there would be equal liberty, the same nobility, equal dignity, the same power among them all.[16]

Hardly an exceptional simile for a rural audience, but the figure and its gloss point specifically to Langland's Passus 6, where Piers, Langland's authoritative plowman, announces that he will plow the half-acre, appears as paterfamilias (with his wife Dame werche-whan-tyme-is and their two absurd offspring), resolves to use his "cultour" to "kerue and ⟨clense⟩ þe furwes," and proceeds to oversee the hoeing up of the "wedes" (6.78–82, 103–4, 111).[17] This instance of theologically significant labor in Passus 6 becomes a symbol for it in Passus 19:

> For comunliche in contrees cammokes and wedes
> Foulen þe fruyt in þe feld þer þei growen togideres,
> And so doon vices vertues.
>
> (B.19.312–14)[18]

16. "Quapropter monuit ut essent viri cordati, et more boni patrisfamilias excolentis agrum suum, et exstirpantis ac resecantis noxia gramina quae fruges solent opprimere, et ipsi in praesenti facere festinarent: primo, majores regni dominos occidendo; deinde, juridicos, justiciarios, et juratores patriae, perimendo; postremo, quoscumque scirent in posterum communitati nocivos, tollerent de terra sua. Sic demum et pacem sibimet parerent et securitatem in futurum, si sublatis majoribus, esset inter eos aequa libertas, eadem nobilitas, par dignitas, similisque potestas" (Walsingham, *Chronicon*, 321).

17. Since the "cultour" was a knifelike attachment on the front of a plow, meant to remove weeds, I restore the manuscript reading of "clense."

18. I am not here interested in the question of whether the plowing in Passus 6 is allegorical or not; for opposing views on this question, see Guy Bourquin, *Piers Plowman: Étude sur la génèse littéraire des trois versions* (Paris, 1978) 1:19; David Aers, *Chaucer,*

In Ball as in Langland, "delving" is a figure for action, and the weeds are its frustration. Ball's *meaning* is outlandishly different from Langland's; where Piers (in 6) wants the nobles to "kepe holy kirke and myselue" (6.27),[19] Ball wants to kill them. But the *structure* of meaning is identical: both use the concrete vocabulary of labor as a vocabulary of reform. Ball has just substituted one referent of the (allegorical) weeding for another.

How can we describe John Ball as a reader of *Piers Plowman?* His appropriations are willful, at least tangential to and mostly at odds with Langland's purposes; yet his misreading of B.9 gives the passage a new and persuasive unity. He shows no interest in the enigmas, the shifts of direction and register in Wit's harangue, but cancels or recombines them to derive a command from Langland's underformulated speculations. But why should Ball have wanted to use a poem he had to read *against?* Or, conversely, why should he have had to read against a work he found of use? These questions require some scrutiny of *Piers Plowman* itself, beginning with Wit's discourse in B.9, to see what it was about Langland's writing that both offered Ball some resources of critique and made itself the first object of that critique.

From Passus 8, Langland's narrator Will wanders in search of "doing well," asking those he meets what it is and where it is found. In the characters he meets at the beginning of his search—Thought, Wit, Study, and the rest—Langland creates interlocutors whose interests and vocabularies are institutionally determined. Anne Middleton has established that Will's exchange with Thought at the end of B.8 represents, with witty compression, the *inceptio* of a university bachelor.[20] By Passus

Langland, and the Creative Imagination (London, 1980), 13–24; D. W. Robertson, Jr., and B. F. Huppé, *Piers Plowman and Scriptural Tradition* (Princeton, 1951), 79–91; and Margaret Jennings, C.S.J., "Piers Plowman and Holy Church," *Viator* 9 (1978): 367–74. The point here is that in Passus 19, allegorical interpretation becomes itself the literal articulation of the narrative. See Robert Worth Frank, "The Art of Reading Personification Allegory," *ELH* 20 (1953): 237–50, for a description of what I (not Frank) would call the rhetorical pretense of "personification allegory": that the conceptualization of experience forms the literal sense, as opposed to an imposed or interpreted allegorical one.

19. "Knight" in Langland's vocabulary of social relations characteristically refers to the *bellatores* in general, including the nobility; see Holy Church's description of their duties and possible failings in B.1, where Truth is said to have "kny3ted ten," of which Lucifer "[was þe louelokest of li3t after oure lord / Til] he brak buxomnesse" (105–13).

20. Middleton, "William Langland's 'Kynde Name': Authorial Signature and Social Identity in Late Fourteenth-Century England," in Patterson, ed., *Literary Practice and Social Change in Britain, 1380–1530* (Berkeley and Los Angeles), 39–40. She speaks of a

9, however, Will has graduated, and Wit, who takes over from Thought, represents the Aristotelian vocabulary of the arts faculty,[21] which is committed to philosophical deduction from the known world. Beginning from Kynde ("nature") as the "creatour of alle kynnes [beestes]" (B.9.26), and extrapolating social obligation from natural law, the unity of Wit's discourse, such as it is,[22] comes not from its doctrines (which neither follow necessarily from the anthropological premise nor are specific to it) but from its institutional investments, from Wit's claim to derive the moral imperatives Dowel, Dobet, and Dobest from the philosophical presuppositions and procedures of the university arts faculty.[23] How he defines Dowel is less important than his claim that his professional community has the authority to define it.[24] Wit's passage, and the speeches that follow, do not so much answer the question "What is Dowel?" as display professional jealousy and competition over the right to answer it. Dame Study, rebuking Wit (at the beginning of B.10) for teaching Will ("blamed hym and banned hym and bad hym be stille" [B.10.7]), proudly reveals the professional scholar's determination to engross knowledge, to control and restrict it. As it happens, Study reaches conclusions very similar to Wit's—on the destructiveness of

theology bachelor, but the same ritual obtained in the arts faculty as well; see James Weisheipl, "The Curriculum of the Faculty of Arts at Oxford in the Early Fourteenth Century," *MS* 29 (1964): 164. For a description of the institutional significance of inception, its place in the *cursus honorum* of university privilege, see Gordon Leff, *Paris and Oxford Universities in the Thirteenth and Fourteenth Centuries: An Institutional and Intellectual History* (New York, 1968), 157–60.

21. David Fowler has argued that Langland was a member of the arts faculty at Oxford (*Piers the Plowman: Literary Relations of the A and B Texts* [Seattle, 1961], esp. 185–205, and "Poetry and the Liberal Arts: The Oxford Background of *Piers the Plowman*," *Arts libéraux et philosophie au moyen âge*, Actes du Quatrième congrès international de philosophie médiévale [Montréal, 1969], 715–19)—but then he also thinks that Langland was John Trevisa. Janet Coleman sees continuities between the academic speculation and both Langland and Langland's audience (*Piers Plowman and the "Moderni"* [Rome, 1981]).

22. Frank calls it "the long and rambling speech of Wit" (*Scheme of Salvation*, 51).

23. This is the point of the favorable aside on the actions of the Jews (named here not as a stage in the Christian revelation, but merely as an example of a community from whom one would expect perfidy—"Iewes, þat we Iugge Iudas felawes" [87]). The question is why Christians cannot be "as *kynde*" as the Jews (89–91)—why, that is, they cannot act as *naturally*. This detouring around the usual historical mechanisms of revelation is rather a polemical move on Wit's part, since it outlines a doctrine on the use of "Christes goode" (89), or what Wit elsewhere calls (conventionally) the *patrimonium Christi* (93), independent of either theological or canonist discourse.

24. James Simpson suggests that it is not until Patience's exposition of the "Dowel" triad in B.13—as "*Disce . . . doce; dilige inimicos*"—that Will finally discovers an interlocutor who is not mortgaged to "the self-aggrandisement of the academic institution" (*Piers Plowman: An Introduction to the B-Text* [London, 1990], 148).

"Iogelours" (B.10.30–47), the failure of Christians to aid the poor (58–67), the spiritual precedence of "meene men" (71)—but she speaks the language of the theology rather than the arts faculty, beginning from the conceptual premise of redemption rather than creation.[25] But the similarity between their conclusions is not convergence, and their aggregation does not produce consensus. Will's next interlocutors, Clergy and Scripture, treat the same vexed questions—on the states of life and the treatment of beggars—in an explicitly theological context; here too theologians (contemptuous of uneducated "burel clerkes" [292]) recommend poverty, defined this time by reference to the communities, not of "wedded folk," but of the school and cloister. Even though Will's pedagogues pose similar questions and reach similar answers, their assumptions and procedures not only are distinct, but are unassimilable each to the other.

This is Langland's technique throughout the *vita*: to juxtapose theological vocabularies and presuppositions that are discontinuous with each other because of the conflicting institutional functions they serve; the fluidity and digressiveness of the poem signal not exactly a "decentering," but a proliferation of competing discourses, each of which tries to promote itself as the authoritative center to which all others must appeal. *Piers Plowman* eventually proposes not to resolve these institutional differences, but to make them coexist.[26] Digression is the principle of exposition, because each new organizing vocabulary is oblique to those that precede and follow, and all together serve to show not merely that each is limited, but that the origins and coherence of each lie chiefly in its attempt at self-validation and self-promotion, not in a coherent object or procedure of inquiry. Will finds no satisfactory definition of Dowel; he also finds no satisfactory norm for spotting such a definition if it were offered.

Recent criticism has described *Piers* as a self-canceling document, resisting the impulse to *know* in favor of the imperative to *do*; as Mary

25. While Harwood sees Dame Study as a figure drawn from the procedures of monastic *lectio* rather than of university disputation, he agrees that the *content* of her discourse marks a shift from the arts to theology ("Dame Study and the Place of Orality in *Piers Plowman*," *ELH* 57 [1990]: 11).

26. At the end of B.15, Anima imagines, as the consequence of a reformed Christianity, the "Sarȝens and also þe Iewes" joining in a progressive recitation of the Apostles' Creed, discovering a continuity of belief with Christians that lay latent, only needing to be expressed to be sensed (607–13). The model that underlies this vision is one in which a communal *practice*—here, the liturgy—produces a consensus in the fundamental tenets of the faith; this is enough to produce a community, in Langland's terms.

Carruthers has observed, the "meaning" of Dowel, Dobet, and Dobest is never specified and can be discovered only by action.[27] For all that, the poem is curiously and insistently literary, its reformist urgency inert because unparticularized.[28] Langland insists that one *do* (well, better, best) but does not say *what* one is to do. Because no institutional authority seems able to define Dowel, the poem exhorts the reader to action while it digressively worries what actions are called for and who has the right to say. As Langland suggests in Will's apologia to a later interlocutor, Imaginatif (B.12.20–28), writing is delay and compensation. Imaginatif has reproached the dreamer for wasting his time on poetry when he might be praying ("þow medlest þee wiþ makynges and myȝtest go seye þi sauter" [16]). Will first replies that literature offers holy recreation, citing saints who "pleyden þe parfiter to ben," but without provocation changes his argument ("ac" ["but"] signals the change of direction) to confront directly the function of his writing:

> Ac if þer were any wight þat wolde me telle
> What were dowel and dobet and dobest at þe laste,
> Wolde I neuere do werk, but wende to holi chirche
> And þere bidde my bedes but whan ich ete or slepe.
> (25–28)

On this revised account, his "makynges" are not recreations that ease the burden of prayer, but "werk" that marks time until prayer becomes possible, until he can learn the meaning of Dowel, Dobet, and Dobest.[29] When Will says that if he knew Dowel he would forgo "werk" in favor of continual prayer, he expresses a desire to do what Piers has already done, in Passus 7. After tearing the pardon that the priest has impugned, Piers resolves to "cessen of my sowyng . . . & swynke noȝt so harde," giving himself henceforth to "preieres and . . . penaunce" (7.121–23).

27. See Carruthers, *The Search for Saint Truth: A Study of Meaning in Piers Plowman* (Evanston, 1973), ch. 4.

28. Thus, for example, at what is arguably the climactic moment of Will's experience, brought face-to-face with "Kynde," he takes up the question he has been tracking throughout the poem and asks "what craft is best to lerne?" The answer he receives— "Lerne to loue" (B.20.207–8)—as unexceptionable as it is, is indistinguishable from the instructions received from Holy Church in Passus 1. It lacks at the end what it lacked at the beginning, the specification of what "love" entails. For more detailed arguments on what follows, see my essay "The Genres of *Piers Plowman*," *Viator* 19 (1988): 291–306.

29. On writing as labor, see John R. Bowers, *The Crisis of Will in Piers Plowman* (Washington, D.C., 1986), 191–218; I quite specifically disagree with Bowers on the force of the Imaginatif passage; see his discussion, 199–200.

Similarly, in the dialogue with Imaginatif, Will claims that he would give over *his* "werk"—his poetry—in order to pursue *his* prayers, if only he knew the meaning of Dowel. Piers seems already to know it, and that is his importance for the poem and for Will: he is the promise that Dowel can be known.

So in this passage, Will draws an analogy between his writing and Piers' sowing: both are forms of labor that would better be relinquished for prayer. Will would abjure labor to "wende to holi chirche": not simply to "go to church," since neither Middle English generally nor Langland in particular uses "holy church" to mean *a* church.[30] It means *the* church, and the problem (for Will) is to find it. Only when Piers again takes up his labor does the church finally appear. After a second course of plowing (19.267–316), Piers makes a barn out of the cross, the crown of thorns, and the blood from Christ's side, "And called þat hous vnitee, holy chirche on englissh" (19.318–28). And so it seems that Piers' promise will here be fulfilled: this authoritative but evanescent plowman constructs the Holy Church which, seven passus earlier, Will had re-solved to "wende to" after forswearing merely literary activity. But Piers' Holy Church is as literary a construction as Will's, and Piers becomes (in effect) an author at the moment of its building. Grace has instructed him to "*Ordeigne* þee an hous . . . to herberwe Inne þi cornes"; Piers echoes Grace's injunction: "ye moten gyue tymber, / And *ordeyne* þat hous" (319–20). *Ordeignen* recalls, by etymological proximity, the *ordinatio partium* that was a principle of manuscript compilation and that was (as A. J. Minnis has shown) a model for authorship among Ricardian English poets.[31] Piers' Holy Church amounts to no more than Will's, the "construction" on the page of a written church in default of a satisfactory institutional one.

I am borrowing Robert Brentano's phrase "the written church" in a

---

30. From the evidence of the *MED*, the expression "holi chirche," though it can have application to a local congregation, community, or church building, has as its usual sense the universal community or hierarchy of the church; see s.v. "chirche" (n.) 4a, and compare 1a, 1b. In Langland, the phrase invariably (unless in the instance under discussion) refers to the universal church.

31. M. B. Parkes, "The Influence of the Concepts of *Ordinatio* and *Compilatio* on the Development of the Book," in J. J. G. Alexander and M. T. Gibson, eds., *Medieval Learning and Literature: Essays Presented to R. W. Hunt* (Oxford, 1975), 115–41; A. J. Minnis, *Medieval Theory of Authorship: Scholastic Literary Attitudes in the Later Middle Ages*, 2d ed. (Philadelphia, 1988), 145–48, 162–210. In fact, Minnis cites Aquinas's use (in the commentary on the *Ethics*) of the building of a house to exemplify his maxim "sapientis est ordinare" (146–47).

way that does deliberate violence to Brentano's meaning, in order to distinguish Langland's text from Ball's understanding of it by distinguishing the different ways in which "writtenness" and writing could be imagined in late-medieval Britain.[32] Langland's "written church" exists on the page because it exists nowhere else; only in fictive construction can he make competing institutional voices coexist. Judson Allen liked to quote Morton Bloomfield's dictum that *Piers* reads "like a commentary on an unknown text"; the commentary shaped Langland's imagination of the kind of writing his poem was.[33] In medieval commentary, the written page is the model for and embodiment of understanding, which begins with writing—the Bible, the *Sentences*, the *Decretum*—as the source of its problems, procedures, and evidence, and ends with writing as well, generating more written pages as the witness and consequence of interpretative understanding. Langland, despite his tone of reformist urgency, produced—three times—yet more written pages and only an apology for the absence of action: a "written church."

Brentano's "written church" is something else, something closer to John Ball's understanding: the parchment produced in the course of ordinary ecclesiastical (as of state) business. These documentary forms, not the exegetical or literary structures that Langland used and produced, were the kind of writing that villagers, artisans, and minor clergy like Ball most often experienced. The written word in documentary record functions differently from the written word in Langland and the tradition of commentary. Each appointment, commission, promulgation, translation, provision, summons, condemnation, and definition executed by documentary writing operates under institutional conditions, and each *enacts* something, gets something done, whereupon the action becomes part of the life of the institution, and the writing a record of it.[34] A writ or charter can do its work only because of what I

32. Brentano, *Two Churches: England and Italy in the Thirteenth Century* (1968; rpt. Berkeley and Los Angeles, 1988), 291–345.

33. Allen and John Alford have developed a formal Langlandian poetics from the use of commentary sources and forms; see Alford, "The Role of the Quotations in *Piers Plowman*," *Speculum* 52 (1977): 80–99; Allen, *The Ethical Poetic of the Later Middle Ages: A Decorum of Convenient Distinction* (Toronto, 1982), 276–80, and "Langland's Reading and Writing: *Detractor* and the Pardon Passus," *Speculum* 59 (1987): 342–62.

34. The enactment might be proleptic (as when a commission is issued), performative (as when a statute is promulgated or a doctrine defined), or retrospective (as when a charter confirms a grant of land); but one persistent point in Galbraith's *Studies* is that the increasingly written character of the administration tended to make the document less a witness to than an embodiment of official action (*Studies in the Public Records* [London, 1948], e.g., 27, 64–77).

will call its *institutional presupposition*: it can successfully command action only within an institutional structure in which the *grounds* of command and action are already settled. If they are not settled, the document misfires, fails of its purpose, and must be repaired: only eccentrically could a faulty document be made, in its glorious indirection and indeterminacy, the object of contemplation.[35] Together, such documents collectively form the institution's "autobiography" (Brentano's term again), which is not a literature but an archive, not for contemplation but for reference.

Ball's conception of the written word owes more to this bureaucratic culture of instrumental writing than to the culture of theological commentary or the literary form Langland derived from it. Ball's reading, transforming elements gleaned from perhaps two manuscript pages of Passus 9 to produce the "kynde" equality of all Adam's descendants and the charge of *proditio* against Sudbury, conferred on Wit's speech a digressionless unity it does not itself possess, by reading it as documentary rather than contemplative writing, meant to prompt an action rather than discover a truth. Ball gave episcopal *proditio* a relation to common "kynde" it does not have in the poem; and the unifying element is the institutional presupposition, which exercises an interpretative force on the digressive passage in B.9. Langland's Wit is concerned with the common obligation of all to all, measured by the hard case of beggars. The Jews do not let their own starve, but English Christians do (B.9.84–91). Bishops set a bad example in this regard, paying useless minstrels (Langland's persistent worry) rather than supporting the poor (92–94). From there, the progress to the "trewe wedded . . . folk" is associative and problematic. The minstrels, who waste "speche" and "space of tyme" (100), motivate the mention of "trewe tidy men," who do not, but who are (Wit evidently thinks) a minority of the laboring

---

35. I take the nice term "misfire" from J. L. Austin; a background to this whole discussion is his description of "performative utterances"—which do not make "statements" (of fact) but accomplish actions (like the words "I do" at a wedding ceremony)—and their need for a system of social as well as linguistic conventions in order to accomplish their purpose (*How To Do Things with Words* [Cambridge, Eng., 1975]). As Austin expresses it in the second lecture, a problematic in such a performance is a *mistake*—about its form, its application, the social conventions that give it meaning, the intentions of those involved; because this sort of performance serves particular social functions, it does not have the leisure (so to speak) to confront ambiguities playfully or paradoxically. (Though the taxonomies of "speech-act" theory are of dubious stability—the point of Derrida's exchange with Searle—they do outline what certain kinds of performance are conventionally taken by the performers to be.)

population. It is a tortuous path from the beginning of this sequence to the last, but Ball makes crooked ways straight by a logic that is immediately apparent. He places the "trewe wedded libbynge folk," the settled, virtuous rural population, in the foreground. Not merely (as in Langland) the stock from which kings and knights and bishops are drawn, they become the norm against which kings and knights and bishops are measured. But Ball also makes them what Langland's beggars are, the victims of a rich prelacy whose abuse of the *patrimonium Christi* becomes for Ball a neglect of their duty to relieve, not beggars, but the "trewe folk" with whom they share common and equal origins. It is a duty the rebels seem to have felt that Sudbury—"despoiler of the common people"—had inadequately fulfilled.

And Sudbury lost his head: Langland's skeptical and evasive vocabulary became in Ball's hands a most decisive imperative. Even as he derived authority from *Piers Plowman*, Ball asserted authority over it, assimilating its language and imagery to a practical purpose already conceived and undertaken. The letters did the same:

> lat peres þe plowman my broþ*ur*. duelle at home and dy3t vs corne. and i wil go wiþ 30we and helpe þat y may to dy3te 3oure mete and 3oure drynke. þat 3e none fayle.
>
> (Carter)

> biddeþ Peres plou3man. go to his werk. and chastise wel hobbe þe robbere. and takeþ wiþ 30w johan trewman and alle hijs felawes and no mo. and loke shappe 30u to on heued and no mo.
>
> (Ball₃)

These cameo appearances have been the chief source of the letters' fame, suggesting dramatically the diffuse social presence that the idea of Piers had already achieved in Langland's lifetime. It was, Elizabeth Kirk has shown, an original idea: he resisted convention in choosing a plowman as the hook on which to hang an idea of Christian perfection.[36] In doing so he enjoyed, and in part created, a new kind of vernacular poetic readership, which formed an ad hoc community around the copies, and the copying, of the poem (just as he constructs a community within the

---

36. Elizabeth D. Kirk, "Langland's Plowman and the Recreation of Fourteenth-Century Religious Metaphor," *YLS* 2 (1988): 1–21. Though her investigations concern mainly clerical traditions of imagery, they nevertheless efficiently foreclose any suggestion that Langland based his Piers Plowman on an already extant "folk" character.

poem).[37] The appearance of Piers, Hobbe Robber, and Dowel in Carter's and Ball's letters is another, and the most surprising, instance of this new readership.

It is also the most challenging. For one thing, it is not clear which of the rebels might have known Langland's poem, or what they, or she, or he knew of it: was *Piers Plowman* (at one absurd extreme) the bedtime reading of a thousand insurgents or (at the other) John Ball's distant memory of an evening's conversation? This challenge is both historical and methodological, since it requires a history of literary audience, and implies textual consumption, among the rural working classes, where the ordinary empirical sources for such a history are wholly and almost by definition absent: if some of the rebels did have access to complete or partial manuscripts of *Piers Plowman*, those manuscripts—for reasons so obvious they don't even need listing—would have been most unlikely candidates for survival. External evidence of other sorts, it is true, gives witness to some knowledge of the poem,[38] and we can construct a hypothetical scenario for its transmission among rebel societies.[39] But

---

37. See J. A. Burrow, "The Audience of *Piers Plowman*," *Anglia* 75 (1957): 373–84; Lawton, "Lollardy and the *Piers Plowman* Tradition"; Anne Middleton, "The Audience and Public of *Piers Plowman*," in David Lawton, ed., *Middle English Alliterative Poetry and Its Literary Background: Seven Essays* (Cambridge, Eng., 1982), 101–23; A. I. Doyle, "Remarks on Surviving Manuscripts of *Piers Plowman*," in Gregory Kratzman and James Simpson, eds., *Medieval English Religious and Ethical Literature in Honour of G. H. Russell* (Cambridge, Eng., 1986), 35–48. Janet Coleman, in effect and rather less convincingly, suggests that this audience was already in place, a class of which Langland was a part instead of one he created (*Piers Plowman and the "Moderni"*). In future work I mean to discuss what can be known of Langland's audience and the circulation of his manuscripts—and therefore of his most immediate context—from the surviving *Piers* manuscripts.

38. In showing how extensively the rebel letters draw on the tag verses very conventionally used in vernacular sermons, Richard Firth Green aptly observes that one phrase which does *not* appear in such tag verses is "do wel and betre"—"confirmation," he says, "if any were needed, that this is a conscious Langlandian allusion" ("John Ball's Letters," 185). Kirk's demonstration of Langland's striking originality in drawing the figure of Piers Plowman (see n. 36 above) implies that, in using his name, the rebels could not have been drawing on a stock figure. In any case, if the images and phrases the rebels shared with Langland had indeed been part of a cultural *koiné*, it is hard to imagine why Langland, revising the B-version, should have felt the need to distance himself from the rising (that he did is a common and I think correct judgment, which I discuss below, ch. 5).

39. Nicholas Brooks has shown that to coordinate events in Essex with those in Kent, to select targets and arrange them so as to cover the ground (literal and metaphorical) that they covered in the week before they marched on London, required of the rebels an organization that was neither casual nor improvised ("The Organization and Achievements of the Peasants of Kent and Essex in 1381," in H. Mayr Harting and R. I. Moore, eds., *Studies in Medieval History Presented to R. C. H. Davies* (London, 1985), 247–70. The planning shows that the ubiquitous references in indictments and commissions to *congregationes* and *conventicula* did not derive from the authorities' fear of unsponsored pacts

these inferences and speculations only establish the probability that one person knew something about the poem, and the asymmetrical possibility that others might have known more—which gets us nowhere in particular. There is something absurd in the picture of villagers with their copies of *Piers*; but that is because it shoehorns an unaccustomed form of literary consumption into an accustomed one—the one we can trace among the propertied classes—when we are obviously dealing with a different phenomenon entirely. We can proceed only as we would in arguing a Dantean allusion in Chaucer, where no "external" evidence exists (no *Commedia* manuscript inscribed "liber Gaufredi Chaucer"), by showing that the allusion works; the procedure is compromised from the outset by the pitfalls of formalist analysis, but it is the only one we've got. While it is open to the objection that it always begs the question, the only alternative is summary denial, a refusal to entertain the possibility that the rebel epistolators *could* have known anything of the poem or made meaning of it, a refusal mortgaged to the assumptions about peasant literacy and intelligence behind Knighton's and Walsingham's representations of the rising. But the procedure has a corresponding advantage, for in trying to gauge the sense the rebels made of Langland, we must also reconstruct the *kind* of sense they looked for.

Piers' presence in the 1381 letters exemplifies a phenomenon recently described by Middleton: "The poem's fictive hero Piers Plowman . . . was widely taken to be the center and source of authority for the poet's powerful innovation, and in contemporary imagination Piers effectively supplanted the author as a putatively actual historical being, the origin of a mode of speech and action that abruptly found in his name a condensed rationale for its own continued articulation."[40] While correct,

---

and assemblies alone. These "conventicles" obviously planned actions; but those actions show that there was more than that. The importance attached to John Ball's liberation from jail, Wat Tyler's public demands, and the letters themselves all bear witness to the importance of ideological work at the outset; and programmatic oaths—like the one given at Bocking (Essex) on 2 June (see below, ch. 4)—were probably administered at such meetings. Likewise, the imposed discipline of many rebel actions, the evidence that Sudbury's execution was planned as an ideological trial, and the choreography of symbolic actions I will discuss in the next chapter show that their planning involved the articulation of rationale as well as of aims and tactics. It is hard to imagine copies of *Piers Plowman* circulating among such groups or the groups pursuing the program of reading and discussion that can be found among the town-dwelling Lollards of the next generations; see Hudson *Premature Reformation*, 180–200; Margaret Aston, "Lollardy and Literacy," and "William White's Lollard Followers." Still, such gatherings (also *conventicula* to the authorities) might offer a hint (no more than a hint) about what might have constituted the ideological work of the rebellion.

40. Middleton, "William Langland's 'Kynde Name,'" 16.

this does not precisely describe the case of the rebel letters. For though they invoke Piers Plowman among their own company, they treat him as having the malleability of a fictional creation, available for the creation and elaboration of other fictions, and indeed for his own *re*-creation: their Piers is their own Piers. "Lat peres þe plowman my broþur. duelle at home and dyȝt vs corne," Carter's letter adjures in the jussive subjunctive of the royal will. Though he is, as Middleton says, a "source of authority," he is also a subject, and is subject to command; and what they command him to do revokes both of the enterprises he announces in the *visio* of the poem. "I shal apparaille me . . . in pilgrymes wise / And wende wiþ yow [þe wey] til we fynde truþe" (6.57–58), Piers tells the knight, preparing to plow the half-acre. This is his first enterprise; the pardon Truth grants in Passus 7, and its subsequent destruction, prompt him to abandon it for a second:

> "I shal cessen of my sowing," quod Piers, "& swynke noȝt so harde,
> Ne aboute my [bilyue] so bisy be na moore;
> Of preieres and of penaunce my plouȝ shal ben herafter,
> And wepen whan I sholde [werche] þouȝ whete breed me faille."
> (7.122–25)

Choosing (1) to leave home on pilgrimage and then (2) to *stay* at home but give up plowing, the single action Piers does not consider is the one the letters command: that he stay at home and till his fields. It is also the one that, within the poem, Truth commands, bidding him to "holde hym at home and erien his leyes" (7.5) as the condition for the grant of the pardon. The letters in effect ally themselves with Truth against the poet; they enjoin Piers to stop being Langland's creation and become their own.

By appropriating Piers in this way, the letters define themselves in reaction to Langland's poem, but still in the poem's terms: their rejection of Piers' two enterprises forms a coherent, though still reactive, account of their ideology, and a coherent revision of Langland that rejects his ethic of penance and theology of pain.[41] The two possibilities, pilgrimage

41. On this aspect of Langland's devotional imagination, see Britton J. Harwood, "*Piers Plowman*: Fourteenth-Century Skepticism and the Theology of Suffering," *Bucknell Review* 19 (1971): 119–36, and Justice, "Genres." Both Harwood and I derive an identification with the suffering Christ from theological writing, Harwood to describe a means of cognition, and I to describe a rhetoric. While the identification of the individual with Christ through self-abnegation could produce an idea of authority independent of ecclesiastical control, in mainstream devotional practice the "suffering" resulting from the

and penance, are distinct in the poem, but also continuous,[42] the resolve of penitence clearly a reaction to the imperative "do wel and haue wel." But "having well," in Piers' ascetic lexicon, means having not at all, careless of "bilyue" and "bely ioye," trusting in the "liflode . . . ful esy" God will provide (122–30). Piers for a time abjures rural labor as a theological norm of ethical choice, forsaking the plow for something more like the anchorage.[43] Carter's letter, commanding Piers to continue his tilling, abjures the abjuration, commending labor as an ethical term that points toward the "ende" which will make "alle wele." Piers will "dyȝt . . . corne" at home, as the writer will "dyȝt" it with the recipients "þat ȝe none fayle," conflating material support with the symbolic and theological value of labor established by setting the two laborers as antitheses to "hobbe robbyoure."

This first revision of Langland's Piers—the rejection of penitential withdrawal—is relatively simple to parse; the rejection of pilgrimage is more complex: the image is snagged in the interpretative ambiguities that pervade Passus 6 (the account of the "pilgrimage"), and, once released, it expands to envelop Langland's rationale of authorship and the design of his poem. The "pilgrimage" in *Piers* has proved a puzzle: it is not clear whether it ever takes place, whether plowing the half-acre

---

identification was the willing acceptance of sin's just punishment. This is a zero-sum game in the acquisition of authority: if the merit of your suffering is expended in the cancellation of sin's debt, the suffering is no more than you deserve. The *arma Christi* rolls, for example, encourage an identification with the instruments of the Passion only as emblems for particular sins. (They also, by the force of their central metaphor, channel imaginative ambition into tracks parallel to, not in conflict with, those of social hierarchy.) These poems are particularly useful as measures of officially sanctioned Passion meditation, since their form as rolls—Huntington Library MS HM 26054, for example, is over six feet long—suggests that they were officially sponsored and meant to hang in church; see Rossell Hope Robbins, "The Arma Christi Rolls," *MLR* 34 (1934): 415–21. This penitential project treats taking part in Christ's sufferings as an identification to be sought, rather than an identity achieved, as it is in those aspects of Wyclif's preaching I describe in ch. 2.

42. See Denise N. Baker, "From Plowing to Penitence: *Piers Plowman* and Fourteenth-Century Theology," *Speculum* 55 (1980): 716–17.

43. It would not be far from the truth to suggest that in Langland's own imaginative lexicon, the plowman is a way of imagining anchoritic withdrawal without its institutional trappings and abuses, but this is itself complicated by his use of eremiticism as a metaphor for certain kinds of withdrawal from social participation. Morton Bloomfield has argued for the importance of the eremitic model for Langland's conception of Christian community; see *Piers Plowman as a Fourteenth-Century Apocalypse* (New Brunswick, 1962), esp. 69–72. For more extensive documentation, and consideration of its consequences, see Ralph Hanna III, "Will's Work," in Steven Justice and Kathryn Kerby-Fulton, eds., *William Langland and Piers Plowman* (forthcoming).

is itself the pilgrimage or only the preparation for it.[44] On the one hand, Piers, announcing that he will dress "in pilgrymes wise / And wende with yow [þe wey] til we fynde truþe" (57–58), puts on his work clothes, hanging "[his] hoper at [his] hals in stede of a Scryppe" (61) and promising later to be "pilgrym atte plow for pouere mennes sake" (102)—all suggesting that the plowing *is* the pilgrimage. On the other, he tells the folk that he "wolde" go on pilgrimage "hadde" he finished his plowing; and later he says that he will sow his field "and *siþenes* wol I wende / To pilgrymage as palmeres doon" (63–64)—all suggesting that the plowing *prepares for* the pilgrimage.

I have taken up this problem before and suggested that the inconsistency can be explained by seeing in it a typological overlay of the Exodus story (which Langland imitates in Passus 6–7): just as the Israelites must wander on their forty-year pilgrimage *in* the desert before making their pilgrimage *to* Canaan, the folk of *Piers Plowman* must pursue a pilgrimage *in* the half-acre before undertaking the pilgrimage *to* truth. It is a bookish solution with no obvious connection to the world outside the book, and it does nothing to suggest what Langland's point might be or what imperatives might issue from it. The Exodus typology solves one riddle only to pose others that in turn generate the succeeding action—which is to say that it yields yet another attempt to *write* an ecclesiastical community without offering any means to its empirical realization.[45] The pilgrimage Piers promises, "to wende . . . [þe wey] til we fynde truþe" (6.58), is dissipated in elaborating the very typology that explains it—at the end of Passus 7, Piers tears the pardon, as Moses breaks the tablets—and is finally forgotten. Because Langland will not commit himself to any version of the "search for St. Truth" that might reach its goal within the narrative, he must efface each version to make room for the next.

In ordering Piers to "duelle at home and dyȝt . . . corne," Carter's letter rejects pilgrimage ("duelle at home") and commends labor ("dyȝt . . . corne") as a model for community and authority. Pilgrimage, after

---

44. This paragraph and the beginning of the next pursue arguments more fully developed in Justice, "Genres."

45. Anne Middleton, "Narration and the Invention of Experience: Episodic Form in *Piers Plowman*," in Larry D. Benson and Siegfried Wenzel, eds., *The Wisdom of Poetry: Essays in Early English Literature in Honor of Morton W. Bloomfield* (Kalamazoo, 1982), 91–122, suggests that the poem's action is, from one point of view, just its own perpetuation.

all, implies a lack. Langland says as much in Passus 5, when the folk, after their confessions, pray "To haue grace to go [to] truþe," but in the attempt only "blustreden forþ as beestes ouer [baches] and hilles" (5.512–14): the deficiency in remedy of which they search for Truth is the same deficiency that defeats the search. Lacking any notion of who Truth is or how to find him, the folk are "beestes," lacking (as animals do) both autonomous reasonability and communal cooperation; Piers must guide them. "Beast" is of course a characteristic epithet for the rural laborer in virtually every genre of clerical and aristocratic literature;[46] it is also a figure for the untempered will. In either case, it symbolizes what lacks its own principle of order, coherence, or purpose; the folk need Piers Plowman to direct and govern them.

The rebel letters invert the relation: the folk govern Piers and, by telling him to "duelle at home," declare that pilgrimage is an unnecessary term of thought. The "truth" Langland's pilgrims seek is something the rebels need not leave home to get, because it is something they already have. "Stonde manlyche togedyr in trewþe," says Ball₂, "and helpe3 trewþe. and trewþe schal helpe 3owe": not *searching* but *standing together*—maintaining a place already occupied and a solidarity already forged—describes the rebels' relation to "trewþe." The epistolary pseudonyms themselves—Jakke Milner, Jakke Carter, Johon Schep—express this sense that truth is not something sought but something possessed: among those names, generalized expressions of rural labor, is Jakke Trewman's, which suggests that to be a miller, a carter, or a shepherd is to be part of the community of "true men."[47] These pseudonyms, in fact, say a good deal about both what the epistolators drew from and what they revised in *Piers Plowman*, and about why they jettisoned the pilgrimage metaphor altogether. With what names would they sign the letters? The king's letters patent, like all official letters, began with the

46. See Beatrice White, "Poet and Peasant," in F. R. H. DuBoulay and Caroline M. Barron, eds., *The Reign of Richard II: Essays in Honour of May McKisack* (London, 1971), 58–74. For both the tradition and its particular use in the historiography of the rising, see Patterson, *Chaucer and the Subject of History*, 262–65, esp. n. 56.

47. The phrase "trewe men" would shortly be taken up in vernacular Lollard writing with a similar structure of meaning, to designate particular people as "trewe" by virtue of their participation in a community; see Anne Hudson, "A Lollard Sect Vocabulary?" (1972), rpt. in *Lollards and Their Books*, 166–67. There is no way of knowing whether this was already Lollard usage in 1381, because no surviving vernacular Lollard texts, with the exception of the *confessiones* surrounding the 1382 Blackfriars council, can be clearly dated before the late 1380s. But it is, in its way, Wycliffian usage: *fideles* and *fideles christiani* are Wyclif's favorite ways of denominating Christians untainted by ecclesiastical corruption and revisionism; and *trewe* would be a quite precise rendering of *fideles*.

name under whose authority the document spoke (*Ricardus dei gratia rex . . .*)—so what name could replace the king's? How they called themselves would declare by what authority they spoke. The rebels claimed that the royal power lay ultimately with the whole commons; the signatures, in their programmatic banality ("Jakke Milner," "Jakke Carter") declared this generalized and common authority, insisted that precisely *everybody's* name could replace the king's.

These names perform another job of self-representation as well, also learned from Langland. Even in the counties where the rising first formed itself, not all the rebels were peasants.[48] Much has been made of this fact in recent years, and forswearing use of the phrase "peasants' revolt" is now a scholarly *topos*. Paul Strohm has gone further: the "highly interested characterization" of the rebels as *rustici* was a "strategy" of the chroniclers, which had "the practical political advantage of isolating and stigmatizing the rebels as beneath consideration and respect."[49] Strohm is certainly right about what this characterization meant for the chroniclers,[50] but they did not invent it; the rebels did. The articulated program of the rising, its most insistently theorized set of demands, addressed the concerns of the villein, the smallholder, the landless laborer: abolition of villeinage, fixed rent for land, employment by free contract, and the like. Actions of wider, more common concern or benefit—the attacks on justices and sheriffs, the agitation against John of Gaunt, even resistance to the poll tax—appeared rather as corollaries of these other, more public objectives than as fully articulated goals in their own right; the rebels, whoever they included, made their public case as peasants. Wyclif had located the authority for dissent in the rural laboring class, and in 1381 the rebels adopted this class identity as a focus around which they could arrange diverse ambitions.[51] The

48. See especially A. F. Butcher, "English Urban Society and the Revolt of 1381," in Hilton and Aston, eds., *English Rising*, 84–111 (on Kent), and Hilton, *Bond Men Made Free*, 176–213. Christopher Dyer, however, argues that "there is nothing . . . to contradict the traditional identification of the rising as the 'Peasants' Revolt'" ("Social and Economic Background," 17). Dyer is concerned mainly to show that the revolt had rural origins, not to argue that it was defined clearly by status and residence.

49. *Hochon's Arrow*, 38.

50. Though I will have occasion later to wonder about its "political advantage"; see below, Epilogue.

51. That is, whatever the particular motives of particular participants in the rebellion—however concentrated on larger issues of governmental reform or more local ones of personal vendetta and gain—they still expressed themselves in terms of rural oppression and its remedies, agreed in designating the image of the peasant as the justification for

peasant cast of the program was in part a rhetorical self-presentation, and the letters' signatures were personae that staged the rebellion under this ideologically informed image.[52]

The signatures locate authority in generic rural occupations. The names in Ball₃ (names of both sender and addressees) show the model on which they were formed, and show what Langland's Piers did for them: "Johon schep . . . johan nameles . . . johan þe mullere . . . johon carter . . . Peres plouȝman . . . johan trewman." As names formed after one customary model—baptismal name plus (rural) occupation—they proffer garden-variety peasant identities; as *symbolic* names formed after that model, they recapitulate the structure of, *and enter into authorship by means of*, the name of Piers Plowman. Wyclif's rural poor are a shadowy, underspecified aggregation of collective nouns (*vulgus, plebs, pauperes*). I would suggest that for the rebels, Piers condensed the theological and political authority that Wyclif conferred on the rural population into a meaningful image of rural labor, gave a name and a body to Wyclif's undefined but symbolically indispensable rural poor. When Piers first emerges into the narrative, arresting the folk's doomed attempt at pilgrimage, his labor is how he evades the distorting medium of clerical privilege to gain direct access to Truth:

> I knowe hym as kyndely as clerc doþ hise bokes.
> Conscience and kynde wit kenned me to his place
> And diden me suren hym [siþþen] to seruen hym for euere,
> Boþe sowe and sette while I swynke myȝte.
>
> (5.538–41)

---

and explanation of their actions.

Fredric Jameson describes the progressive and active—and therefore genuinely *conscious*—class consciousness of preindustrial working classes as a heuristic notion that becomes available to interpreters only when they focus on the "historic destiny of the class," rather than on the class origins of particular artifacts, since the latter can yield only an image of passive susceptibility to infrastructural forces: in other words, workers of the past must wait for academics of the future to interpret their actions into meaning (*Marxism and Form: Twentieth-Century Dialectical Theories of Literature* [Princeton, 1974], 389). But "historic destiny" is only (as the first chapter of *The Political Unconscious* recognizes) the place of an action in a historical narrative, and a class may have its own *contemporary* narrative about itself (whether that narrative is confirmed by the event or not); under these circumstances the class may become as fully symbolic to itself, and therefore able to focus the ideologies of several disparate and oppressed groups, as it can later become when functioning symbolically as a revolutionary "tradition." On the rebels' self-consciousness as a class, and a class with a "destiny," see the conclusion of ch. 4, below.

52. See Middleton, "William Langland's 'Kynde Name,'" 68–69, on the malleability of the rebel pseudonyms and their function in the rhetoric of solidarity; and pp. 66–73 generally for comments on their relation to *Piers Plowman*.

The books that clerks know "kyndely" are only mediations of the Truth that Piers knows "*as* kyndely," *without* mediation, through his "swynke," for which Truth gives the just reward that (by implication) earthly landlords do not: "þe presteste paiere þat pouere men knoweþ; / He wiþhalt noon hewe his hire" (551–52).

Piers offered an articulable model of the theological authority that the rebellion claimed for rural labor, but it was not (on its own terms) a realizable one. Here too the rebels used the poem's resources of critique first to criticize the poem. Piers' authority in the poem depends on the removal of the superfluous (and therefore obstructive) mediation of literate privilege. A serviceable flanking maneuver in the symbolic repertory of the poem, the image of authority that cannot write can work only in the realm of fiction, for writing is the mechanism of command. Langland's promotion of a limited and untrained literacy over clerical learning makes a comprehensible point about the spiritual precedence of experience over book learning, and about the importance of humility; but it makes that point to, and within the presuppositions of, a literate, book-owning audience, for whom the saintly laborer could be the metaphorical focus of an ideal they might pursue (simplicity, humility, perseverance) but could hardly represent something they might choose to become. Taken as a model for social authority—as Langland never meant it to be taken—the image is contradictory and self-defeating. In the documentary understanding of writing as enactment commanding realization in the empirical world, Piers' defectively literate authority is a losing proposition: authority claimed without writing would be no authority at all. This is rather a problem, since the Piers who surprises the Priest of Passus 7 with his biblical learning has offered the rebels an embodiment of the authority without traditional learning. It was, superficially, an odd choice for the rebel authors, to identify their authorship with the plowman who, although he reads, does not write.

Will writes. Langland's refusal to say so until Passus 19 ("Thus I awaked and wroot" [B.19.1]) does not, and is not meant to, hinder anyone's realization that he does. Will represents the "author-function" (in Foucault's phrase);[53] he offers a concrete exemplification of *auctoritas*

---

53. Throughout the A- and B-versions, the references to Will's poetic activity refer merely, and (in theory) ambiguously, to "making," as in Imaginatif's rebuke and Will's response in B.12.16–22 and the Prologue's "mynstrales," "japeres and jangleris" (B.prol.33–35). The figure of himself in C.5 (but is it himself?) sitting as a scribe is the first time he

as such in Langland's recurrent meditations on the mechanisms and authority of his own writing. Will's career as a pilgrim in the poem doubles his career as an author, figuring the processes of *inventio* and *dispositio* that generate the poem as inquiry and travel and revealing (for example) the willfulness of authorial choice. At the beginning of Passus 5, a celebration of "matyns [and masse and . . . þe mete] after" (5.2) seals the political reform accomplished in Passus 2–4. The confession of the folk that follows in Passus 5, which suggests that reform must come from the bottom up, follows only tenuously and maybe contradictorily from what has just transpired, which suggests that reform must come from the top down. Langland does not try to reconcile these models of reform or even to make them complementary; he just marks the conceptual break with a narrative break and confesses that only his desire to keep narrating carries him across it: Will wakes, expresses his wish to have "yseiȝen moore" (4), and returns, improbably, to sleep.

More pertinently, and more immediately concerned with the terms

---

imagines the scene of his writing (C.5.68–9). But even in the B version of the Imaginatif episode, the latter tells Will that his "makynges" are pointless "for þer are bokes y[n]owe / To telle men what dowel is" (B.12.17–18). (In any case, the use of oral-traditional "makynge" as a persona for authorship, lightly masked as bardship, had already been established within the alliterative canon by the *Winner and Waster* prologue.)

For a more extensive argument that Will figures the process of authorship in *Piers Plowman*, see Justice, "Genres." Foucault's phrase is of course from "What Is an Author?" in *Language, Counter-Memory, Practice: Selected Essays and Interviews*, trans. Donald F. Bouchard and Sherry Simon (Ithaca, 1977), where he uses it to denaturalize the (historically conditioned) notion that every text originates in a personal agency which is responsible (and can therefore be held responsible) for the production. I am deliberately misusing Foucault here to describe Langland's use of Will to figure the problems of authorship as such, without necessary autobiographical reference. (I might also note that "author-function" catches more of the impersonality implied in *auctor*, and more of the personality implied in *auctoritas*, than do ModE *author* and *authority*.) The question of apparently autobiographical detail (especially in C.5) has received a helpful *reductio* from George Kane, *The Autobiographical Fallacy in Chaucer and Langland Studies* (London, 1965), and J. A. Burrow's riposte in *Autobiographical Poetry in the Middle Ages: The Case of Thomas Hoccleve* (London, 1982), 393–95. Kane argues (correctly) that first-person histories, when entered in formal narrative and especially when cast in terms of conventional attributes, can be so conditioned by convention that they reflect it alone, and that in any case the governing motive will be their place in the fictional structure rather than verifiable detail. Burrow, by contrast, argues (correctly) that just because a detail reflects convention or "works" within a literary structure does not mean it could not be verified by other, more conventionally historiographic means. What this leaves is a free-floating, hypothesized subject for whom the question of empirical verifiability is unimportant not because the work carves out an autonomous aesthetic realm, but because the subject functions simply as a placeholder designating authorial agency. The importance of this point in understanding Langland is that he has constructed the figure of Will so as to embody certain problems of literary form and authority as generalizable problems of authorship itself. The question of how Will's reported career fits with Langland's is only the (here unimportant) question of whether Langland has created what he takes to be a generalized portrait of authorship or offered his own authorship as a generalizable example of it.

the rebels borrowed ("doþ wele and ay bett*ur* and bettur" [Carter]), Will's resolve to "seke dowel" (B.8.2) announces the ultimate project of the poem, the search for a satisfactory definition of "doing well." Explicitly in the *vita* and implicitly throughout, Langland represents the poem as inquiry; Will is a pilgrim, at first only metaphorically and by inference—he sets off "wondres to here" (B.prol.4)—but eventually by his own avowal, when he decides to seek Dowel.[54] Success in his search—finding someone "þat wolde me telle / What were dowel and dobet and dobest" (B.12.25–26)—would spell a gracious end to his authorial career ("Wolde I neuere do werk"). Insofar as he succeeds, he does so in a way that only displaces the problem. After the vision of the Passion and the Harrowing of Hell, Conscience in B.19 finally and authoritatively locates the meaning of Dowel, Dobet, and Dobest— quite unhelpfully, for Will's practical concerns—in the career of Christ: "comsede he do wel" (123) in the incarnation; his ministry of feeding and healing "was dobet" (129); "And whan þis dede was doon do best he [þoughte], / And yaf Piers [pardon]" (183–84). The "meaning" of Dowel and the rest turns out to be simply the gospel narrative, and the job of realizing it devolves again on Piers Plowman; Will's search for Dowel and his increasingly desperate search for Piers ("after Piers þe Plowman pried and stared. / Estward and westward I waited after faste" [B.16.168–69]) are in the end identical, and identically frustrated. The end of the poem does not complete the authorial project; it reassigns it: Conscience takes it over, vowing to "bicome a pilgrym / . . . / To seken Piers þe Plowman" (B.20.382–84). Authorship remains a waiting game, a pilgrimage toward a receding goal.

And so the rejection of pilgrimage in the rebel letters, their directive that Piers should remain at home, is a revisionist version of Langland's notions about writing and authorship. By taking Piers (not Will) as their authorial model, and at the same time eliding Langland's organiz- ing metaphor of pilgrimage, the letters situate their use of Piers (and *Piers*) within the nexus of established assumptions and obligations that Ball's preaching brought to Passus 9. "Doþ wele and ay bett*ur* and bettur," Carter can command,[55] "for at þe euen men hery[e]þ þe day.

---

54. That Will is a pilgrim is a critical commonplace; for example, see Rosemary Woolf, "Some Non-Medieval Qualities of *Piers Plowman*," *Essays in Criticism* 12 (1962): 111–25. For an attempt to read the entire poem through this lens, see Julia Bolton Holloway, *The Pilgrim and the Book: A Study of Dante, Langland, and Chaucer* (New York, 1987).

55. And likewise Ball₃: "do wel and bettre and fleth synne and sekeþ pees and hold ȝou þer inne."

ffor if þe ende be wele. þan is alle wele." He speaks in untroubled confidence that he and his audience already know what doing well and doing better *are*—which Will does not after twelve passus of asking. The "ende" that is "wele" is known to be "wele" in the collective judgment of those who "at þe euen . . . hery[e]þ þe day." This image of an evening conversation about a day just ended, with its picture of casual local consensus emerging from common local interests, suggests how a network of shared and established norms makes the content of "good" and "better" action immediately obvious. The letters, says Susan Crane, "do not communicate to us successfully."[56] But if they do not, it is not because the rebels were operating in a medium that did not belong to them (as Crane suggests), nor because they coded their writing for tactical purposes. The letters are elliptical because they did not need to be otherwise: they assume that their community of address, and its interests and purposes, sufficiently define the terms of their meaning and render them comprehensible to that community. They will not be meaningful to those who do not share those norms and interests, those who must still wonder about what is "good" and "better"—and who have the leisure to wonder about it.

Underlying the letters' rejection of pilgrimage, their identification of authorship with Piers (rather than Will), and their pragmatic reduction of Langland's speculative meditations to direct command, is an ideology of *locality*. Constructing their ethical vocabulary around the tenacious holding of ground already occupied ("stonde manlyche togedyr"), the rebel authors asserted the transparency of terms Langland made mystery of, asserted their availability to understanding and action within a particular local community whose norms were established and which was itself normative. In the poem, Piers is an evanescent presence (Will faints in joyful surprise at his sudden appearance [B.16.18–20] and is desperate at his departure); in the countryside, he is an immediately visible local presence, the collective instantiation of rural labor and its grievances, and can be conscripted as one of the rebels' fellows. *Their* schedule of rights and wrongs was already established; felt wrongs, and the retributive idea of right they generated, made the definition of "doing well" seem unproblematic and the need to do it urgent. Their knowledge of documentary forms gave them a model of writing that, unlike the skeptical shufflings of *Piers Plowman*, was enabling and performative.

56. Crane, "Writing Lesson," 210.

• • •

But though so much of the poem had to be stripped off on its way into the letters, *Piers Plowman* offered the rising more than the figure of Piers: it offered a new language of reformist and theologically informed legislation. Just as Walsingham's report let us watch how John Ball transformed the language and structure of Passus 9, the diction of the letters lets us watch the rebels plunder Langland's eccentric poetic lexicon and promote their own local and native vocabulary into an analytic, generalizable, and prescriptive one. The letters' momentary imitations of Langlandian prosody are, I think, only an accidental consequence of the different and more important influence Langland had on their social making; its very fitfulness suggests that it was an emblem of what *Piers* offered them, not the thing itself. It is hard to classify the letters formally: none of them is consistently in verse, and yet alliteration, rhyme, and isochronic measure form a persistent obbligato. There is not an alliterative long line of Langland's type (or indeed any classical type) in the group,[57] and the moments of verse recall more than anything else the alliterating rhymed stanzas of the Middle English lyrics. (Anyone who believes, if indeed anyone still does believe, that the alliterative revival witnesses to the persistence of alliterative measure in popular oral forms will receive little comfort from these crude imitations of Langland's line.)[58] And yet the disposition and use of vocabulary show the impress of Langland's idiosyncrasies. The relative crudeness of the imitation is valuable because it helps isolate what in his style seemed worth imitating, what promised functional operation in the rhetoric of the letters and their project of alternative literacy.

The letters concentrate on, and mimic, Langland's procedures of emphasis in alliterative staves, his superimposition of theological and social vocabularies, and his elevation of common words to quasi-technical status. It is a commonplace of *Piers Plowman* criticism that Langland eschewed the specialized and antique poetic diction of the revival in favor of an assertive colloquialism that uncovers conceptual resources in common language.[59] Though Langland criticism has en-

---

57. The closest is "and clerkus for welthe worche hem wo" (Trewman), which has at least the three alliterating lifts and the caesura, but the prosodic relation of the half-lines has been reversed, putting the nonalliterating lift in the first half-line.

58. Of course, these letters certainly originated in the south or east of England, almost certainly in Kent or Essex, while the surviving alliterative poetry is from the north and west.

59. See, for example, Burrow, "The Audience of *Piers Plowman.*" Thorlac Turville-Peter, *The Alliterative Revival* (Cambridge, Eng., 1977), 69–83; Woolf, "Some Non-

joyed repeated success in tracing such disingenuously artless constructions as "kynde wit" back to their theological sources,[60] Langland's purpose was not to prompt a search for Latin originals but to re-create their capacities in the vernacular; and even those readers who did not know the originals of Langland's technical vocabulary could not have failed to notice that it did function technically.[61] His diction displays continuities between clerical vocabularies and social experience, and declares the functionality of the latter as a moral and theological language. Langland opens the B-version with a textbook case, schematically setting out the principles of his lexicon and the privileges of social metaphor. There, the grammatically articulated contrast between those who "putten hem to plou3" and those who "putten hem to pride" and "apparailed hem þerafter, / In contenaunce of cloþynge" (B.prol.20–24) not only coordinates the concrete noun "plou3" with the abstract "pride," as Charles Muscatine has observed,[62] but also creates a language of analysis and criticism that is identical with neither the clerical language of theology nor the language of lay experience. The pairing inflects "pride" with a concrete social suggestion that invokes economic practice and statutory law.[63] At the same time, it establishes "plou3" as a conceptual term that can be mobilized with as much precision, and to the same analytic purposes, as "pride."

A more extended example, in the most familiar section of the poem, is the figure of Mede. Her name has no full equivalent in Latin, but Langland makes it an elaborated and coherent term of moral evaluation

---

Medieval Qualities of *Piers Plowman*," 90; Derek Pearsall, "The Alliterative Revival: Origins and Social Backgrounds," in Lawton, ed., *Middle English Alliterative Poetry*, 40. There is a fine analysis of Langland's self-consciousness about this matter in Simpson, *Introduction*, 5–14.

60. See, for example, Willi Erzgräber, *William Langlands Piers Plowman: Eine Interpretation des C-Textes* (Heidelberg, 1957); Randolf Quirk, "Langland's Use of 'Kind Wit' and 'Inwit,'" *JEGP* 52 (1953): 182–88, and "Vis Imaginativa," *JEGP* 53 (1954): 81–83; A. V. C. Schmidt, "A Note on the Phrase 'Free Wit' in the C-Text of *Piers Plowman*," *Notes and Queries*, n.s., 15 (1968): 168–69, and "A Note on Langland's Conception of 'Anima' and 'Inwit,'" *Notes and Queries*, n.s., 15 (1968): 363–64; Britton J. Harwood, "Imaginative in *Piers Plowman*," *MÆ* 44 (1975): 249–63, and "Langland's *Kynde Wit*," *JEGP* 75 (1976): 330–36.

61. Sometimes, in fact, there is no exact equivalent in intellectual Latin; there is nothing quite the same as "kynde knowyng," for example, or, more important, as "dowel," "dobet," and "dobest."

62. Muscatine, *Poetry and Crisis in the Age of Chaucer* (Notre Dame, 1972), 82.

63. The reference to clothing as a manifestation of "pride" recalls the vocabulary of the sumptuary ordinance of 1353, which sought to correct the "outrageous and excessive apparel of many people contrary to their station and degree" (*SR* 1.380).

and political critique.[64] *Mede* is a concrete noun in Middle English; for the most part her retinue consists of either abstract nouns (Symonie, Gile, Falsnesse) or collective nouns (Cyvylle); one is a common personal noun used as a proper noun (Liere), and one, the most characteristically evasive, an adjective hovering between abstract and concrete instantiation as a noun (Fals). Projecting all of these—the concrete noun *mede* and the abstract nouns in its train—as personifications acting on the same stage attaches an abstract vocabulary to social behaviors and renders the concrete "mede" conceptually workable as a term of analysis.[65] Mede first enters the poem as a synonym for an abstraction: Holy Church points to her when Will asks, "Kenne me by som craft to knowe þe false" (B.2.4). The three Mede passus that follow offer a sustained act of definition that creates a new term of institutional critique. The association of Mede with Falsnesse, Gile, and the others; her initial credibility with the king; Conscience's distinction between the "two manere of Medes" (B.3.231); her disruption of the complaint of Pees against Wrong—all of these elaborate a conceptual term that generalizes particular experiences of money's power to intercept policing and justice.

The most explicitly topical reference in the rebel letters echoes the central concern of the Mede passus, that "reward" has hijacked royal justice. "Speke. spende and spede," Trewman says, reporting the words of "jon of bamthon": John of Bampton, who, along with his fellow Essex justice of the peace John of Gildesburgh, appeared at Brentwood to reassess the poll tax in the event that sparked the rising.[66] The "trewþe"

---

64. The Latin quotations that appear in this part of the poem give *munera* as the prooftexting reference for "mede" (as at B.3.96–100, 3.240–41a, 3.350–53); by contrast, the line at B.3.252–54a offers *merces* as a synonym. The latter fits a little more closely with the range of the ME *mede*, but neither has the specificity that is developed for it in B.3.255–58: "That laborers and lowe [lewede] folk taken of hire maistres / It is no manere Mede but a mesurable hire. / In marchaundise is no Mede, I may it wel auowe; / It is a permutacion apertly." In any case, the important point is that neither Latin term has the conceptual expansiveness that Langland gives to *mede*.

65. I accept Anna Baldwin's recent revival of the suggestion that Mede originated in part as a roman à clef figure of Alice Perrers and agree that if correct, the suggestion is of considerable importance for understanding the reach of Langland's political thought; however, it is of no importance for the present discussion, which concerns rather the internal logic of the narrative (Baldwin, *The Theme of Government in Piers Plowman* [Cambridge, Eng., 1981], 34).

66. Lumby noted the suspension over the first vowel of "bathon" but still printed "Jon of Bathon"; I am probably not the first student of the rising who tried to discover what grievance the rebels might have had against John Harewell, bishop of Bath and Wells between 1366 and 1386.

no one may "come to" unless "he syng si dedero" is the "trewþe" that Trewman has said is "under a lokke": the royal justice that has been sealed away in clerical record. This justice is available only to the one who sings "si dedero": "I will give." Trewman's advice that speech ("speke") yields success ("spede") only when accompanied by payment ("spende") describes the real principles that have governed the law. The Mede episode leaves its trace in the letter's treatment of this subject, in the two partners who are twice associated in Passus 2 and who reappear, together, in Trewman. "Fettreþ [*Falsnesse* faste] for any kynnes ʒiftes, / And girdeþ of *Gyles* heed" (B.2.201–2), the king commands when Mede's marriage is first brought to his attention; when the vices flee the ordered arrest, "*Falsnesse* for fere fleiʒ to þe Freres; / And *Gyle* dooþ hym to go agast for to dye" (213–14). Their appearance together in Trewman's letter—"*falsnes and gyle* haviþ regned to longe & trewþe. hat bene sette under a lokke"—retains its Langlandian association, since the adminis-tration of justice is one of the two foci of complaint in the letter (the other is ecclesiastical corruption, the "falsnes" that oppresses every "flokke"). Trewman borrows not just the phrase, but the mode of thought enabled by its grammatical form: the confident promotion of "falsnes" and "gyle" as partial personifications that can *reign* provides a metaphorical language that analyzes particular complaints into structural criticism, and therefore permits significant political statement. The mode of speech *articulates* opposition: both speaks it and gives it structure. Langland's "falsnes" and "gyle" distribute rebel complaints within a generalized category and find the structural bonds that link them: the absorption of justice by clerkly profit and the preemption of grace by clerks emerge as analogous and related problems. And the grammatical logic of the articulation generates further articulations: "falsnes" prompts its antonym "trewþe" (a term crucial in Langland's vocabulary as well) and thereby calls up a term of social organization in the countryside that suggests an alternative mode of government.[67]

To contrive the demands issued at Mile End, the discipline at the Savoy, the choreography of Sudbury's execution, and the various treat-ment of official documents, the rising needed something the countryside did not have, an accessible and public vocabulary capable of generalized critique. Aron Gurevich has given substance and evidential elaboration to a truism, the more credible because for Gurevich it describes an

---

67. I discuss this principle of rural government at length in ch. 4.

absence that is not a *lack*: the "disinclination for abstract concepts" among medieval *illiterati* was not in itself a deficiency, but simply a mode of organizing experience in language.[68] But in the attempt to produce meaningful *and public* critique, it was a deficiency; merely empirical criticism has only the resources of enumeration. The early fourteenth-century "Song of the Husbandmen" shows what a skilled and eloquent complaint from the period before the rising could, and could not, accomplish.[69] It catalogues the oppressions of the "hayward," "bailiff," and "wodeward" (15–17), the depredations of the "ryche" who "pileþ the pore and pykeþ ful clene" (25–26). The poem's empirical cast of thought reveals itself and its limitations toward the end, when it adds a complaint against the "wickede wederes" (70) that, like the appropriations by royal officials, cut into the margin of subsistence. But the "wederes" negate the possibility of critique; the object of the complaint becomes just "things, human and otherwise, that cause suffering," which implies that the human phenomena are no more open to change than the others.

Langland, I think, showed how the concrete and empirical language

---

68. Gurevich, *Medieval Popular Culture: Problems of Belief and Perception*, trans. János M. Bak and Paul A. Hollingsworth (Cambridge, Eng., 1988), 11. Gurevich's particular achievement is to have elaborated a class-specific schedule of popular convention by drawing on the evidence of clerical Latin works; he builds on the methods of the Bakhtin circle and their insistence on what Bakhtin himself calls "the internal dialogism of the word": the cleric who spoke to a laboring population gives evidence of his audience's beliefs and perceptions merely by the cast he had to give his statements in order to render them meaningful. The problem with this procedure is of course that it assumes both the transparency of the audience's mind and the probability that no distortion interfered with the cleric's understanding of *what* was meaningful to his audience and *how* it was meaningful. One might suggest alternatively that the clergy perpetuated and anatomized its own sense of cultural superiority in the assumption that their hearers could not make sense of an abstract conceptual language, or treat it *as* abstract and conceptual. But this does not materially affect my point here, which is not about the capacity for analytic thought, but about the possession of an analytic language.

69. Text in Rossell Hope Robbins, ed., *Historical Poems of the Fourteenth and Fifteenth Centuries* (New York, 1959), 7–9. The poem is obviously not a peasant production. The unspoken but undoubted threat of the poem—whose speaker complains "to seche seluer to þe kyng y mi seed solde, / forþi mi lond leye liþ & leorneþ to slepe" (63–64)—is: this year peasants starve; next year we all starve, since the seed corn is being sold off for grain to pay the king's taxes. The poem threatens that unless the burden of taxation is reduced, we will all be starving peasants. Peasants, however, were not the only people who would profit from a reduced taxation, and the most striking aspect of the complaint is the relative importance of royal exactions (and the relative *un*importance of manorial ones; on this, see J. R. Maddicott, "Poems of Social Protest in Early Fourteenth-Century England," in W. M. Ormrod, ed., *England in the Fourteenth Century: Proceedings of the 1985 Harlaxton Symposium*, [Woodbridge, Suffolk, 1986], 132). In any case, the point at issue here is not so much the origin of the author as the resources available for the articulation of political complaint.

of complaint might be rendered systematic and conceptual, promoting empirical images into a meaning as generalized and precise and analytical—and therefore as available to conceptual deployment—as abstract nouns (the "plou3" that is opposed to "pride"). But in the case of the rebel letters, it is not a plow, but—a more contentious image—a mill: "jakke mylner asket help to turne hys mylne aright. he hath grounden smal smal. þe kynges sone of heuen he schal pay for alle. loke þi mylne go ary3t. wiþ þe foure sayles. and þe post stande in stedefastnesse." As the revolt at St. Albans dramatically witnessed, milling rights were a perpetual irritant between tenants and landlords. Lords had the right to license mills and tallage their (mandatory) use.[70] Tenants would sometimes evade this costly arrangement by using handmills small enough to be concealed from the bailiff: at St. Albans, these mills had been confiscated "in the time of Abbot Richard" and been put to a symbolic use that proclaimed the abbey's right to multure.[71] With its "post" and "foure sayles," Milner's letter claims a technology more ambitious than the peasant handmill: it imagines rebels possessing a mill of their own and the lordship that milling rights belonged to. At the same time, the letter's mill diagrams the moral basis of the rebels' claim in a schematically allegorical image which (like similar images in Langland—Kynde's "castel" [B.9.1–24], Haukyn's coat [B.13.273–14.15], the Tree of Charity [B.16.22–896], the barn of Unite [B.19.319–28]) resolves its component parts into abstract statement. The next sentence in the letter anatomizes the "foure sayles": "wiþ ry3t & with my3t. wiþ skyl and wiþ wylle. lat my3t helpe ry3t. and skyl go before wille. and ry3t befor my3t. þan goth oure mylne aryght. and if my3t go before ryght. and wylle before skylle. lo. þan is oure mylne mys ady3t." The permutations, a little pedantic in their completeness, insist on the necessity of corporate discipline (like the enforced ban on plunder at the Savoy) for the revolt at large and also for the meaningfulness of this very image. The limits that justice places on power ("ry3t be for my3t") and clear judgment on desire ("skyl . . . before wille") have an obvious relevance to the public justification, and self-justification, of revolutionary violence. But it also makes possible the image of the mill itself: if power and desire overcome justice and reason, the mill will be "mys

70. See Marc Bloch, "The Advent and Triumph of the Watermill," in *Land and Work in Medieval Europe: Selected Essays*, trans. J. E. Anderson (Berkeley and Los Angeles, 1967), 136–68, esp. 156–59.

71. For the importance of these handmills in the St. Albans rising, see below, ch. 4.

ady3t"—badly constructed, no longer "stedefast"—and therefore will sacrifice its normative, prescriptive power.

For the central passage of the letter claims just that power for the image: "he hath grounden smal smal. þe kynges sone of heuen he schal pay for alle" (Milner). I assume that this chilling couplet has the force of the more elaborate version in Ball₃: "johan þe mullere haþ ygrounde smal smal smal þe kynges sone of heuene schal paye for al. be war or [3]e be wo knoweþ 3our frend fro 3our foo." In the latter, the grinding of the corn passing through the mill figures the discrimination and judgment that separate "frend" from "foo,"[72] so that in Milner's letter the turning of the mill "aryght," the communal enterprise for which he "asket help," is the location and execution of enemies, the mill grinding the largest grains down to equal size ("smal smal"). The ambiguous promise that Christ "schal pay for alle" insists that lords will be punished (and their victims rewarded) for the lordly oppressions represented metonymically by the restriction of milling rights. But of course the retribution is precisely what is specified by the image of the grinding itself. The rebels who will do literal grinding at the mill they appropriate will *by that very appropriation* work as God's deputies (as in Sudbury's execution) and perform the metaphorical grinding of Christ's revenge.

Piers Plowman gave the rising a language and a style, an imaginative model of rural articulacy that conferred on empirical language a conceptual utility and a public force. The poem's doctrines were less important. The vision of the Prologue in which royal power is created by "might of þe communes" (B.prol.113) may have helped shape the rebels' assertion of identity with the king,[73] but Wyclif's early preaching offered a more elaborate and revolutionary version of the same assertion; and in any case, it is impossible to specify anything in the letters or the words of the insurgents that derives from Langland's line. What Langland offered was the example of a conceptual language that could be formed ad hoc out of the common tongue to serve particular interests and to be mobilized against others. This model meant something to the rebels that it could not have meant even to Langland: that when a particular

72. The locution itself suggests the imagination of "locality" I have discussed. The social relations suggested by "frend" and "fo," as John Bossy has argued in his analysis of the sociology of liturgical prescription, were heavily inflected with senses of kinship and of communal interest; see "The Mass as a Social Institution 1200–1700," *Past and Present* 100 (1983): 29–61, and my further discussion of this passage in ch. 4, below.

73. Langland perhaps worried that it did. Susan Crane has offered a brilliant reading of the ambiguities in this passage and its revision ("Writing Lesson," 211–13).

oppression was shared by a class, the oppressed could protest it as a class, and, once resistance began, could use these generalizing vocabularies to organize their action and critique. When Langland's deliberately evasive locutions entered the rebel letters, they became definite and precise—"do wel" most significantly, but also "falsnes and gyle"— because the movement wielding them had (or at least wanted to seem to have) a shared standard of judgment to make them meaningful.

There is one exception to that last generalization. "Truth" is not structurally one of *Piers Plowman*'s most complex terms. As a name of God, it catches that divine attribute that offers to creatures the guarantees, and imposes on them the duties, of faithfulness, but the axis of obligation and faithfulness is set by God and the creature; the "trewþe" that binds people in reciprocal obligations is not portrayed as continuous with the "trewþe" that binds them to God.[74] There is nothing in *Piers* like the statement of Ball₂, "stonde manlyche togedyr in trewþe. and helpeʒ trewþe. and trewþe schal helpe ʒowe." Langland uses "trewþe" most prominently to mean "God." But that meaning is implausible in its first appearance in Ball₂ and impossible in its second.[75] "In trewþe" has an adverbial force: stand together faithfully. In its second appearance—the command "helpeʒ trewþe"—its function as object of the verb requires a fully nominal sense, which would apply "trewþe" as a quality of persons to the relations between persons: help the community to which you owe fidelity. But by the third—"and trewþe schal helpe ʒowe"—it seems to have achieved the theological sense that is almost its only sense in Langland: God will help you. Absorbed so deeply into the vocabulary of the rebels that it became half of Trewman's name, *trewþe* was an organizing term of the rebels' expression and thought. The letters brought to bear on the word a social context and common experience that elaborates it beyond Langland's usage. In *Piers*, "trewþe" is an attribute of God and a duty of his creatures toward him. In the letters, it is the mutual obligation of human beings that manifests the

74. The locus classicus for the meaning of "truth" in the poem is Holy Church's discourse in B.1. The corollary of God's act of creation is a bond of obligation between God on the one side and humanity on the other:

> For he is fader of feiþ, and formed yow alle
> Boþe with fel and with face, and yaf yow fyue wittes
> For to worshipe hym þerwiþ while ye ben here.
> (B.1.14–16)

75. Ball₃, however, makes a parallel statement—"stondeþ [togidere] in godes name"— where the divine name does find a place; see ch. 1, n. 29 above.

will of God. Their conception of "truth" is not something they brought away from Langland, or from Wyclif; it is something that they brought to both.

This last point raises a problem in the letters and the rising that baffles conventional historiography, literary and otherwise. The meaning of the rebels' letters, like the meaning of their actions, cannot be traced back to a textual origin: the textual sources that informed the lexicon of the rebels were appropriated and transformed along the way. If the rebels were able to wrest Wyclif and Langland from their purposes to serve the thought of the insurgency, there had to be an ideology *on the basis of which* these appropriations and translations were performed. That ideology must be sought where no one has thought to seek it: in the lives of the villages themselves.

4

The Idiom of Rural Politics

Some of the tenants of St. Albans went to London during the revolt; there the king, momentarily pliant in the matter of writs, granted them a letter directing their lord, the abbot, to release the ancient charter they were demanding and to observe the tenants' rights in commons, pasture, and fishing. Presented with the royal command, Abbot Thomas "tried to remind the rebels that all these cases had been decided in their fathers' time, and that the decision was recorded in the royal rolls at Westminster."[1] It is obvious what he had in mind: if the villeins really cared what old documents said, chancery was full of old documents that would show they had no claims. The rebels' spokesman, Richard of Wallingford, replied "that the commons were the lords now, that they cared not a whit for the laws, and neither expected nor accepted excuses like these."[2] "Heu! heu!" responded the abbot.

Thomas de la Mare was a capable and politic man who had already governed St. Albans for thirty years, adding to his monastery's wealth, winning royal favor (he served on Edward III's council), and earning some reputation for piety.[3] But in 1381 he could not do anything right:

1. "Dominus autem Abbas, recepta cum reverentia debita et perlecta littera, informare nitebatur et commonere eos, qualiter omnia talia per placita fuerunt suorum patrum temporibus terminata, et exinde recordum esse apud Westmonasterium in rotulis regiis; unde juxta leges regni, antiquitus usitatas, asseruit eos nullum jus vel clameum habere debere in omnibus quae petebant" (Walsingham, *Gesta* 3:306).

2. "Ricardus de Walyngforde, omnium prolocutor, respondit ad haec, dicens communes jam pro tempore dominari, leges penitus non curare, nec rationes tales velle vel expectare vel acceptare" (Walsingham, *Gesta* 3:307). The exchange is one of Walsingham's set pieces—Richard's speech continues in direct discourse after this—and so need not be taken as an indecorously accurate report; Richard is as unlikely to have said that they cared nothing for the laws as the commons were to have called the abbot (as Walsingham here says they did) "a just and peaceful lord" ("Fatemur . . . vos et aequum et placidum nobis fuisse dominum, et idcirco nequaquam proposuimus in diebus vestris vos pro causa hujuscemodi molestasse" [307]). However, Walsingham, with his profound transference to Abbot Thomas, would hardly have contrived a scene in which he performs so badly.

3. See the sketch by Dom David Knowles, *The Religious Orders in England* (Cambridge, Eng., 1957) 2:42–48.

he was blindsided again and again, mistaking the situation and misjudging his response. He was not alone; the rising surprised everyone, and everyone was caught looking the wrong way once it came (the only lordly strategy that really worked was Bishop Despenser's blunt expedition through East Anglia).[4] Why did Richard think that an amnesty would satisfy the rebels? Why did Sudbury and Hales stay in London to lose their lives? Their mistakes suggest more than deficient preparation; they suggest blank ignorance before the thought of the countryside, almost bafflement at a foreign tongue. Landowners had been predicting rebellion since the new king took the throne: when some villages in 1377 tried to prove themselves ancient demesne of the crown (and thereby escape some manorial duties), the commons in parliament worried that "unless a quick remedy is imposed, war may break out within the realm because of these acts of rebellion,"[5] and Gower warned that the "nettle [*urtie*]" of the "common people" would "sting" landowners like himself.[6] But even as their predictions registered rural discontent, they confessed their poverty in understanding it. The commons in 1377 took it that the trouble came "through the advice, procurement, maintenance, and abetting of certain persons": the lawyers put them up to it.[7] Gower's metaphor—"nettle"—uses a familiar biblical image for heresy.[8] The only motives they could imagine behind rural fractiousness were motives from their own world, the world of law and heresy, and therefore the only minds they could imagine behind it were those of lawyers and heretics.[9]

4. The king pursued the same course as soon as he could; see his summons of troops to London and the home counties printed in G. O. Sayles, "Richard II in 1381 and 1399," *EHR* 103 (1988): 826–27.

5. "Issint qe l'ein doute, qe si hastive remedie ne soit mis, qe de leger gere purroit sourder deins mesme le Roialme a cause de lour Rebellion susdit" (*Rp* 3.21). The petition also shows that the landowners feared the repetition in England of the French Jacquerie: "Et pur eschuere tiel peril come nadgairs sourdy en la Roialme de Fraunce par tiel rebellioun & entre-alliaunce des Villeins encontre lour Seigneurs."

6. "Cil qui pourvoit le temps present / Se puet doubter procheinement, / Si dieus n'en face son aïe, / Qe celle urtie inpacient / Nous poindra trop soudainement" (*Mirour de l'omme*, 26491–95, in *The Complete Works of John Gower*, ed. G. C. Macaulay (Oxford, 1899), 1:293). For still earlier examples of such worries and warnings, see Kaeuper, *Law, Justice, and Public Order*, 349–50.

7. "Par conseil, procurement, meyntenance, & abettement de certeines persones" (*Rp* 3.21).

8. Herbert B. Workman, *John Wyclif: A Study of the Medieval Church* (Oxford, 1926) 1:327.

9. In fact the commons insinuate—a little incoherently, given their earlier reference to the Jacquerie (see n. 5 above)—that it all might be traceable back to the French and

The point is not that they thought peasants stupid, though they did. It was a seigneurial maxim that villeins possessed *nihil extra ventrem*—nothing outside their own bellies.[10] The phrase explicitly concerned the villein's constitutional incapacity for ownership,[11] but it implied a whole anthropology of the peasant. Open the peasant up and you find emptiness, hunger, desire; close him back up again and he will take the shortest and bluntest course to satisfaction.[12] Administrative writers could imagine two such courses. *Fleta*'s idealized plow-drivers ("not . . . melancholy or irascible, but cheerful, singing joyously so that through their melodies and songs the oxen may take joy in their work") and shepherds ("prudent and wakeful and kind") supply their wants in conscientious harmony with, and under the direction of, their lord, not

---

worry that at least it would abet an invasion: "ou q'ils soy aherderont as Enemys de delaa pur soy venger de lours Seigneurs, si sodeyne venue des ditz Enemys y fuist" (*Rp* 3.21).

10. As the abbot of Burton-on-Trent solemnly said in the presence of the sheriff of Derbyshire, his assembled free tenants, and his villeins, after a dispute with the villeins in 1280 (G. Wrottesley, ed., "The Burton Chartulary," *Collections for a History of Staffordshire* [William Salt Archaeological Society] 5 [1884], 85). For commentary, see Hyams, *King, Lords, and Peasants*, 17–24.

11. Or, as the abbot's court at Halesowen put it, "nativus nichil amittere potuit nisi ad dampnum domini," since the neif's chattels were in fact the lord's (*Court Rolls of the Manor of Hales*, ed. John Amphlett [Oxford, 1910], 1:203).

12. There is a corresponding attitude in the economic history of the English manor, an attitude that lives within a narrowly Malthusian world: that the only motivations that count in the countryside, the only ones that determine economic *or* political behavior, are related *directly* to fluctuations in the availability of resources. In its most global form, this attitude was one of the chief stakes in the "Brenner debate," where the polemics at once polarized and muddied the issue. Postan and Hatcher's claim that "neo-Malthusians" such as themselves did in fact consider the social and political conditions of the medieval economy is certainly true ("Population and Class Relations in Feudal Society," in T. H. Aston and C. H. E. Philpin, eds., *The Brenner Debate: Agrarian Class Structure and Economic Development in Pre-Industrial Europe* [Cambridge, Eng., 1985], 64–66; a glance at Postan's *Medieval Economy and Society: An Economic History of Britain 1100–1500* [Berkeley and Los Angeles, 1972], shows that he does consider them); and Brenner's claim that in the "neo-Malthusian" model, such conditions are without serious consequence is also true ("Agrarian Class Structure and Economic Development in Pre-Industrial Europe," in *Brenner Debate*, 13–24). The point at issue is not whether the relation of the population to the productive capacity of its land is of fundamental importance (all agree that it is), but whether that relation is the explanatory key to political formations, whether (in other words) demographic factors leave room for the exercise of political will on the part of anyone, lords or peasants. It will be evident that my sympathies (they amount to little more than that) are more with Brenner than otherwise, but this is of small importance to my discussion, for I am concerned not with the macroeconomic (and macropolitical) world of the debate, but with the microlevel adjustments that particular communities could make to particular, *and experienced*, situations. Malthusian determinism is sometimes on offer at this level as well—for a particularly clear example, see J. Z. Titow, "Some Differences Between Manors and Their Effects on the Condition of the Peasant in the Thirteenth Century," *Agricultural History Review* 10 (1962): 1–13—an application I would rather distance myself from, in part because of its superficial resemblance to my own

in a determination to outstrip starvation and certainly not in conscious and regulated cooperation with each other.[13] By contrast, Walter of Henley's treatise on husbandry pictures servants (here, as in *Fleta*, demesne workers) whose "frawde" the master must guard against.[14] The obedience of an undifferentiated will or the grasping of an unregulated one: either way the peasant has only will, without mind or notion. If they have notions, they have only the notions they are taught; if they act with sustained purpose, they proxy for sowers of discord.

Confusion possessed the lords and royal government in June 1381 largely because the violence issued from a collective life in the countryside that was invisible to them. Their confusion might remind us of Henry Knighton, who thought the letters of Milner, Carter, and Trewman were speeches because he could not conceive the possibility that such persons might write letters. The actions of the rebels must be read through the gaps in the accounts, the bafflements of the justices and chroniclers; and the letters (it should be clear by now) cannot simply explain those actions: they too issued from a life that for the most part was recorded only as it interested those who kept the records, and their lexicon developed in the shadows that surrounded and protected the political culture the villages built for themselves. At the end of the last chapter, I said that the insurgents used Wyclif and Langland to their own purposes, and I asked: but what was the ideology *on the basis of which* they performed these appropriations, what notion of themselves and the authority they wielded? Where did it come from? And then what kind of textual interventions did the letters make, what functions

---

notion that the pressures of subsistence forced rural communities to a political creativity. The points that differentiate my slant from the Malthusian one are first, a respect for that creativity, for the ability of communities to meet the uncertainty of resources not just with competition over or regulation of those resources, but with a large adjustment in their ways of life; and second, an assumption that the struggle for resources is, and is felt as, inseparable from the experience of common life as a whole. By this latter, I have in mind something like William Roseberry's reading of the *German Ideology*: material production (including agricultural production) entails the "production of a whole way of life that is itself part of a historical process" (*Anthropologies and Histories: Essays in Culture, History, and Political Economy* [New Brunswick, 1989], 37–39).

13. "Non enim esse debent melancolici vel iracundi, set gauisi, cantantes et letabundi, vt per melodias et cantica boues in suis laboribus quodammodo delectentur"; "Pastores autem expedit habere discretos et vigiles et benignos, ne oues per suas iras torqueantur set vt pacifice in leticia suas depascant pasturas" (*Fleta*, ed. H. G. Richardson and G. O. Sayles, SS 72 [London, 1955], 2:251–52).

14. *Walter of Henley and Other Treatises on Estate Management and Accounting*, ed. Dorothea Oschinsky (Oxford, 1971), 317. On other views, see Rodney Hilton, *The English Peasantry in the Later Middle Ages* (Oxford, 1975), 24.

did they play in the imaginations of those who wrote and copied them? This chapter will be the most diffuse and indirect of the book because it will try to move through the shadows to find the rising's political imagination. A key term will be *trewpe*. This word is, as I have said, crucial in the letters, and its meaning unexhausted by the "sources" I have examined; but there is more to it than that, for it names the tie by which political community was established and maintained. Discovering its meaning is a task only obliquely philological: the real task is to isolate and reconstitute the elements of rural life that gave the word its content. To that end, I will go back to the beginning.

The rising began on 30 May at Brentwood, when the village of Fobbing refused further payment toward the poll tax and fired arrows on the commission sent to collect it. Thomas Baker spoke for them; Knighton honored him with the distinction of being "first mover" of the rebellion,[15] and indeed he was the first mover in the sense that he made the first public move.[16] But the record of Hugh de la Zouche's inquest at Chelmsford includes an odd fact:

> Numerous persons of Fobbyng, Stanford, Mokkyng, and Horndon, with a certain weaver dwelling in Billerica, and one John Newman of Rawreth, a common thief, and many other men of the vills of Rammesden, Wate, Herwardstok, Gynge, Bokkyng, Goldhangre, Reynham, Welde, Benyngton, and Gyng atte Stane rose up against the king and gathered many malefactors and enemies of the king, and made congregations in Brendewode on Thursday after the Ascension [30 May] 4 Richard II, and they made an assault on John Gildesburgh, John Bampton, and other justices of the peace with bows and arrows, pursuing them to kill them.[17]

The odd fact is in the list of villages. Virtually all are in the immediate vicinity of Brentwood, within or just over the borders of Barstable hundred; like the representatives from Fobbing, residents from these

---

15. Knighton, *Chronicon*, 138. Petit-Dutaillis follows out the implications of what Knighton says: "la dureté du commissaire royal John Leg . . . excita une indignation générale en Essex, et quelques gens du peuple, entre autres un boulanger de Fobbing, Thomas Baker, *organisèrent* une agitation" (Réville, *Soulèvement*, lxxi; my emphasis).

16. In fact, Knighton may simply have misunderstood a locution conventional in legal documentation; as Prescott points out, far too many people were named in the indictments as the "prime mover" of the rising to allow the phrase any literal application; he suggests that it merely indicates the accused's voluntary participation ("Judicial Records," 104).

17. Sparvel-Bayly, "Essex," 218.

other villages were at Brentwood to meet the tax commission.[18] Bocking, on the other hand, lies a good twenty miles to the north, far from any other village represented that day. In itself, the presence of persons from Bocking would be no more significant than that of persons from Benington (Herts) or Goldhanger (on the Essex coast), towns also represented and also at a distance from the event. But this Thursday was the last the rising saw of Benington and Goldhanger. Bocking was different: the next recorded event was a *congregatio* there three days later (2 June).[19] No public action was taken at or after this Pentecost meeting; an oath was sworn, of which the indictments give two versions.[20] In one, the rebels swore "to be of one assent in killing and destroying various lieges of the lord king and that they wanted no law in England except for ones proposed by themselves"; in the other, they swore "to be of one assent in destroying various lieges of the lord king, and his common law, and even the dominion of the lords."[21]

These have a familiar ring. When Richard II met the rebels at Mile End eleven days later, they demanded "that he allow them to take and keep all the traitors who were against him and the law," and that "no one should be a serf, or do homage or any service to any lord, but should give four pence for an acre of land, and that no one should owe

18. As the *Anonimalle* explicitly says: "et avoit somonde devaunt luy une hundrez des villes prochiens, et vodroit avoir levee de eux novel subside, comandaunt a les gentz de les villes enquerre diligentment et doner lour respouns et paier lour paiement" (134). What exactly Bampton and Gildesburgh were doing is less certain than I make it out to be here. Tout pointed out that Bampton had not been appointed poll tax inspector in 1381; he casually guesses, "Perhaps he was acting simply in his capacity of justice of the peace" (*Chapters* 3:366–67). Prescott, on the strength of the indictment quoted above, asserts that they were "sitting as justices of the peace" ("Judicial Records," 128, 134). Brooks, however, seems less certain that the *Anonimalle*'s account can be dismissed, suggesting that perhaps Bampton had replaced one of the inspectors ("Organization and Achievements," 251). There is a good deal to say for this opinion. For one thing, the other named victim, John de Gildesburgh, *was* a poll tax inspector. And although the 4 July indictment from Chelmsford does speak of Gildesburgh, Bampton, and "other justices of the peace," it does not say that they were acting in this capacity at that time.

19. The sequence of events in Essex and Kent has been mightily clarified by Prescott, "Judicial Records," 128–50. Brooks, building on Prescott's research, puts a different construction on some of the testimonies ("Organization and Achievements," 251–54); and I differ somewhat from both.

20. PRO KB 145/3/6/1; Brooks, "Organization and Achievement," 252n.

21. This last phrase reads "etiam [ad destruendum] omnia dominia diversis dominis spectantia." It is possible that it should be translated "and [destroying] the lordships of several lords"—that is, particular demesnes rather than the institution of lordship. But though this would account for the plural *dominia*, it makes nonsense of the *etiam*: they swore "to destroy certain lieges of the lord king, the common law, *and even* a few manors"?

service to anyone but by his own will and covenant";[22] that is, they asked for the death of certain lieges of the king and an end to the lordship of the lords.[23] But the really curious clause in the oath made at Bocking is that there should be "no law but certain laws proposed by themselves" and "[destruction of] the common law"; this has no obvious parallel in the demands Richard faced at Mile End. To see its importance we have to go back to 2 June and widen our scope. There were actually two different congregations that day, one at Bocking, the other across Thames in Kent. One Kentish rebel who later turned approver, Abel Ker of Erith, confessed that he had "gathered conventicles" and made the abbot of Lessness swear to join their company. The next day he crossed into Essex and raised a hundred men, whom he led back to Kent.[24] When Brooks speaks of Ker's "recruiting drive into Essex,"[25] he mistakes the case: why not recruit in Kent?[26] Ker went to Essex because

22. "Qil vodroit soeffrer qils purroient prendre et avoir toutz les traitours quels furont encontre luy et la ley. . . . Et . . . qe nulle homme ne deveroit estre nayf, ne fair homage ne nulle maner de servys a ascune seignur, mes doner iiii d. pur une acre de terre et qe nulle ne deveroit servire ascune homme mes a sa volunte de mesme et par covenant taille" (*Anonimalle*, 144–45).

23. The sense in which the rebels demanded an end to lordship is clear from Richard's letter patent revoking the concessionary charter he had granted the rebels. In listing the concessions he was revoking, Richard first said that the charter had released everyone "ab omni bondagio et servitio"; further down, he said that the charter had declared "that no acre of land held in bondage or villeinage, in the aforementioned counties, should be had for more than 4*d*." ("quod nulla acra terrae, in comitatibus praedictis, quae in bondagio vel servitio tenetur, altius quam ad quatuor denarios haberetur, et, si qua minus antea tenta fuisset, imposterum non exaltaretur" [Rymer et al., *Foedera* 4.126]). But what did it mean to fix the rent of land held in bond or villeinage when a few lines before, everyone was *released* from bondage and villeinage? The answer, I think, is that the charter does not say that Richard had declared that *rents* should be no more than 4*d*., but that no more than 4*d*. *should be required for the holding of land*: that is, that rents be fixed at that level *and* all other forms of service abolished.

I am inclined to trust the versions of the oath given in the indictments; they accord well with each other, and their extreme vagueness suggests that neither the jurors nor the commissioners were reading later events or formulations back into the Bocking assembly.

24. "Et dicit quod ipsemet, simul cum . . . [aliis] . . . prodiciose, ex unanimi consensu, insurrexerunt contra dominum regem et populum suum, conventiculas malefactorum congregantes, et abbathiam de Lesnes in comitatu predicto intraverunt, et abbatem ejusdem loci essendi de eorum comitiva jurare co[e]gerunt. . . . Et predictus Abel dicit . . . [quod] in eo assensu pertransierunt aquam Tamesye, de Earhethe usque comitatum Essexie, et ibidem ex sua falsa et prodiciosa allegancia insurrexerunt, levaverunt, quandam conventiculam centem hominum et pluris de eodem comitatu Essexie congregaverunt" (Réville, *Soulèvement*, 183–84).

25. Brooks, "Organization and Achievements," 254.

26. The "recruiting" of large numbers of villagers uncommitted to or ignorant of the rebellion followed a familiar pattern: the villagers would be assembled and proclamation made; sometimes threats were directed at those unwilling to join. Such proclamations are always mentioned in the judicial records, since in the ad hoc redefinition of the treason

he knew that he would find there what did not yet exist in Kent: an assembly ready to take action.

A Kentish force did assemble shortly thereafter, part of which helped carry the revolt to London on Corpus Christi Day; the king spoke with them at Smithfield on Saturday, as he had with the Essex rebels on Friday.[27] The *Anonimalle Chronicle* records the demands made at Smithfield:

> that there should be no law but the law of Winchester, and that there should be no outlawry through any process of law thenceforth; and that no lord should have lordship, but that it should be portioned out among all people, excepting only the king's lordship; and that the goods of holy church should not be in the hands of religious, or of parsons and vicars, or of any churchmen, but that they should have their sustenance alone, and the rest of their goods should be divided among parishioners; that there should be no bishop in England but one, and no prelate but one; and all the lands and tenements of the possessioners should be taken from them and shared out among the commons, excepting a reasonable sustenance; and that there should be no serf in England, and no service of neifty, but that all should be free and of one status.[28]

As different as these demands look from those made by the Essex contingent the previous day, they are nearly identical in all the ways that matter. Tyler, it is true, said nothing of traitors; after the executions of Sudbury and Hales on Friday, he may not have felt the need. When he spoke of disendowing the church hierarchy, he merely gave the insurgent position on lordship a specific application to prelates and religious, which he then elaborated with the Wycliffite matter on the church hierarchy. Like the Mile End rebels, Tyler demanded the abolition of lordship and serfdom. That leaves only one difference between the Mile

---

statute to cover the case of the rebels, the making of public proclamations was in itself evidence of sedition. Ker uses altogether different language to describe his actions of 3 June: "conventiculam . . . congregaverunt," which suggests rather a quiet, even secret levy of those already willing.

27. Barron, *Revolt in London*, 7; Fryde, *Great Revolt*, 23.

28. "Et adonqes le dit Wat rehersa les poyntes queux furount a demander, et demanda qe nulle lay deveroit estre fors la lay de Wynchestre, et qe nulle ughtelarie serroit en nulle processe de laye fait de ore en avaunt, et qe nulle seignur ne averoit seignurie fors swelment estre proporcione entre toutz gentz, fors tansoulement la seignurie la roy; et qe les biens de seint esglise ne deveroient estre en mayns des gentz de religione, ne des parsones et vikeers, ne autres de seint esglise, mes les avances averont lour sustenance esement et le remanent de les biens deveroient estre divides entre les parochiens; et nulle evesqe serroit en Engleterre fors une, ne nulle prelate fors une, et toutz les terres et tenementes des possessioners serroient pris de eux et partiez entre les comunes, salvant a eux lour resonable sustenance; et qe nulle nayf serroit en Engleterre, ne nulle servage ne nayfte, mes toutz estre free et de une condicione" (*Anonimalle*, 147).

End and Smithfield demands, Tyler's insistence "that there should be no law but the law of Winchester, and that there should be no outlawry through any process of law thenceforth." Later in this chapter I will show that this demand had a precise content; I will only assert now, in anticipation, that it is virtually identical to the insurgents' resolution to abolish all laws not initiated by themselves—the point sworn to at Bocking. So the specifically political demands put to the king by rebels from *both* Essex and Kent find their first expression in the oath taken at Bocking on 2 June; and they find such explicit expression nowhere else, and nowhere before.

All of this suggests that two important details of the *Anonimalle*'s report of the beginnings of the rising are close to the truth. First, that chronicle says that "the commons of Kent" spent the first days of the rising "without a chief or captain."[29] That Abel Ker and his fellows made their first move on the same day as the congregation at Bocking, and yet had to find their first helpers in Essex, suggests that the initiative was coming from the northern county. When they got a captain, they got him from Essex. Some chroniclers say, and historians have repeated on their authority, that Wat Tyler was from Kent, but they apparently deduced this because he first appeared at Maidstone. In fact, the best witnesses, in the judicial records, say that he was from Essex.[30] Second, these details also make plausible the assertion quoted in the first chapter: that the Essex commons "sent letters to those in Kent, Suffolk, and Norfolk, asking them to rise along with them."[31] The rising began in Essex; proceeded there more widely and intensely;[32] and received there the statement of aims that would be spoken to the king in London.[33]

29. "Saunz test et saunz chieftayne" (*Anonimalle*, 136).

30. The *Anonimalle Chronicle* says that after the attack on Rochester (7 June) the Kentish rebels "firent lour chieftayne une Watt Teghler de Maydenstoun pour les mayntener et conseiller" (137). Because Tyler did not survive to be tried by the royal commissions, there are no judicial records concerning him and therefore no jury's statement of his name and home village. But the continuator of the *Eulogium historiarum* identifies him as "unus tegulator de Estsex" (*Eulogium*, 352). More important, the juries in the hundreds of Faversham and Dounhamford independently relate that "Walter Teghelere, of Essex," with others, led the Kentish rebels in Canterbury, and it is clear from the Faversham indictment that this man was the leader of the band: they "forced the Sheriff to go to his manor of Milton, in custody of the foresaid Walter, and made him swear that he would deliver all the rolls and writs that were in his custody . . .; he, under the fear of death, delivered up all the rolls and writs . . . as beforesaid; and the said Walter, with consent of the foresaid John Hales and his conventicles, burnt those rolls and writs" (Flaherty, "Great Rebellion in Kent," 92–93).

31. *Anonimalle*, 135; see ch. 1, n. 21 above.

32. The rising transpired differently in the two counties, as Prescott has shown: the

Essex had the idea, and Essex is the place to track it down. But we can be more specific still. The presence at Brentwood of representatives from Bocking on 30 May, and the meeting at Bocking three days later, are not the village's only distinctions. One distinction lay decades in its past: earlier in the century the free tenants of Bocking had petitioned their lord, the prior of Christ Church, Canterbury, complaining of his bailiff.[34] Their petition was assertive, resourceful, and savvy.[35] A second distinction lay in the more recent past: when Archbishop Langham, in 1366, cited John Ball for his subversive preaching (whatever that may have been at this early date), he sent his order to the dean of Bocking.[36] The third was very shortly to come. Brooks observes that for a week after the Brentwood attack there were no acts of public revolt in Essex; only on Thursday, 6 June, did open insurrection and public proclamation begin,[37] and the first act, on 6 June, was carried out by those who had met at Bocking.[38] Thomas Baker and the villagers of Fobbing, first to act at Brentwood, were neither the first nor the most important to organize.[39] They appear again only on 7 June—the day *after* Bocking and its neighbors assaulted the Essex sheriff—sending to the village of

---

violence in Essex was diffuse and nearly simultaneous, many incidents happening in many places at about the same time, suggesting that many different groups were at work; the events in Kent were "less extensive and more derivative than . . . in Essex," suggesting rather the progress of a single company ("Judicial Records," 141–50).

33. On behalf of this last, it might also be urged that of all the counties of England, the least likely to think of demanding an end to villeinage would be Kent, whose gavelkind knew neither serfdom nor the duties entailed elsewhere by customary tenure: the Kent custumal (1293) begins with the principle "that all the persons of Kentishmen should be free, as much as the other free persons of England"; the document is translated from an early manuscript in *VCH Kent* (London, 1932) 3:325.

34. Discussion and translation in John F. Nichols, "An Early Fourteenth Century Petition from the Tenants of Bocking to their Manorial Lord," *EcHR* 2 (1930): 300–307. There is not, to my knowledge, any significant scholarly work on Bocking, or indeed on Hinckford Hundred, in the absence of the *VCH* volume which should deal with it. W. F. Quin's *History of Braintree and Bocking* (Lavenham, 1981) is very inadequate; its sketchy discussion of medieval Bocking can be found on pp. 11–29.

35. Its particular clauses show (as its editor says) "conscious[ness] of their rights and of their common interests, and . . . a very real grasp of the legal niceties involved." The most striking passage of the petition complains that they have been denied the right to set each other's amercements "against reason and Magna carta" (Nichols, "Petition," 306).

36. Wilkins, *Concilia* 3.65.

37. Brooks, "Organization and Achievements," 255.

38. It was an attack on the house of the Essex sheriff at Great Coggeshall, about four miles from Bocking (Sparvel-Bayly, "Essex in Insurrection," 217; Prescott, "Judicial Records," 134; Brooks, "Organization and Achievements," 255).

39. Indeed, if the *Anonimalle Chronicle* is credited on this point, their response to the first action at Brentwood was to flee to the forests that lay in the west of the county (*Anonimalle*, 134).

Rayleigh "to raise the people of that vill against the king's peace."[40] Now the villagers of Rayleigh were at Brentwood on 30 May and therefore knew roughly what was up. So this message was an announcement that it was time to begin open resistance because the villages of north Essex had begun it: only after the action at Great Coggeshall was the rising proclaimed in the south of the county. Proclamation went on for three days, 7–9 June. When, on 10 June, the rebels began concerted and direct action, they followed the same north-to-south vector: at Cressing Temple on 10 June, at Chelmsford on 11 June, and at Mile End outside London on 12 June.[41]

Their first public action was the burning of archives, and I want to return to this action, to the flames themselves this time rather than the documents they consumed. Rebels from all over Essex gathered in the area of Bocking on 10 June; they destroyed buildings belonging to the Hospitallers at Cressing Temple, and they entered the sheriff's house at Great Coggeshall again, seizing documents this time, as they did also from the escheator at Feering. They carried the documents to Chelmsford for a ceremonial public burning the following day.[42] Thus began a pattern that would be taken up throughout the regions of revolt: at Dartford in Kent, for example, and at St. Albans, where "certain obligations" and rolls belonging to the archdeacon "were burnt at a Cross in the town, as they say."[43] The burnings were usually public, and in most villages, lacking a formal "square" and often even a green, they would have happened at a crossroads, or just the main (or only) street in the settlement.[44] By setting fires in the streets during Corpus Christi

---

40. "Thomas Bakere de Fobbyng et Willelm Goldebourn felonice miserunt Robert Berdon de Orsete ut nuntium eorum ad villam de Reyle die veneris proxima sancte Trinitati . . . ad levandum homines ville predicte contra pacem regis" (PRO KB 145/3/6/1; Brooks, "Organization and Achievements," 255n.).

41. Prescott, "Judicial Records," 134–36; Brooks, "Organization and Achievement," 255–64.

42. See Prescott, "Judicial Records," 135–36.

43. For Dartford, see ch. 2, n. 8 above. The St. Albans burning is taken from the abbey's petition to the king for compensation: "Et issint furent les obligacionez deliverez a eux, et mayntenant par eux furent ars a un Crois en la ville, com ilz diount" (Walsingham, *Gesta* 3:292).

44. A detailed and very useful typology of village plans is given in B. K. Roberts, "Village Patterns and Forms: Some Models for Discussion," in Delia Hooke, ed., *Medieval Villages: A Review of Current Work*, Oxford University Committee for Archaeology Monographs 5 (Oxford, 1985), 7–25. The fires would be constructed *in* the streets because rural streets were characteristically very wide and sunk well below ground level, and thus the safest places for fires; see Hanawalt, *Ties That Bound*, 26–27.

week, the rebels anticipated what would happen in a couple of weeks' time anyway. Midsummer Eve (23 June, vigil of the Nativity of St. John Baptist) was celebrated all over England with communal "watches" lit by bonfires in streets, in squares, and on hillsides.[45] The fires celebrated community as locality: in the towns, they called a neighborhood "a bonfire."[46] John Stow describes how it was remembered in London. The "Bonefiers in the streetes" were constructed by common labor; the "welthier sorte" would furnish forth feasts "whereunto they woulde inuite their neighboures and passengers also to sit, and be merry with them in greate familiarity. . . . These were called Bonefires aswell of good amity amongst neighbours that being before at controuersie, (were there by the labour of others) reconciled, and made of bitter enemies, louing frendes."[47]

What was this ceremony to the rebels, that they should take the trouble of carting the Great Coggeshall documents to Chelmsford to re-create it? Midsummer fostered "amity amongst neighbors" by cele-brating enmity against the lord, from whose lands the firewood seems to have been poached in symbolic contempt of a resented seigneurial privilege:[48] the reservation of woods and ponds and the animals, wood, and fish therein, resources that would have been most welcome to the peasants from whom they were reserved.[49] Cultivation of even a healthy

---

45. On its forms in the last two centuries, with some historical documentation, see A. R. Wright, *British Calendar Customs: England* (London, 1938), 6–12; for medieval and early modern evidence, see George C. Homans, *English Villagers of the Thirteenth Century* (1947; New York, 1975), 369–70; Charles Phythian-Adams, "Ceremony and the Citizen: The Communal Year at Coventry," in Peter Clark and Paul Slack, eds., *Crisis and Order in English Towns 1500–1700: Essays in Urban History* (Toronto, 1972), 57–85; and Keith Thomas, *Religion and the Decline of Magic* (New York, 1971), 48, 72. Mirk's sermon for the day bore unwitting testimony to the ceremony's power and popularity, urging return to a presumptive devotional vigil of the past instead of the "songys and daunsys, . . . lechery and gloteny" into which he says the celebration had devolved (*Mirk's Festial: A Collection of Homilies*, ed. Theodor Erbe, EETS es 96 [London, 1905], 182).

46. Phythian-Adams, "Ceremony," 65–66.

47. John Stow, *Survay of London* (London, 1598), 74.

48. Phythian-Adams, "Ceremony," 68, and *Local History and Folklore: A New Framework* (London, 1975), 26.

49. "Le seneschal deit a sa venue as maners enquere de mefesaunz e dez trespas fes en parks, en vivers, en wareynes, e en conyngeres, e de tutes autres choses ke fet sunt a damage son seygnur en la baillie" (*Seneschaucie*, in Oschinsky, *Walter of Henley*, 268). A thoroughly representative example of the enforcement of these privileges is provided by the proceedings of the Ramsey abbey court over two days in 1294. On 11 January at Broughton, Walter Gernoun was presented for carrying an oak branch from the lord's wood; John Gernoun and John son of Ralph Everard were each convicted of carrying brambles from the lord's wood; during the view of frankpledge at Wistow the next day,

yardland—thirty acres or so—left a peasant family in customary tenure only a slim margin of safety, and cultivation of a smaller holding only a slim margin of subsistence.[50] The animal and vegetable life reserved to the lord held resources of supplemental provision (especially supplemental protein) available to less labor- and resource-intensive work than cultivation (which peasants were maximally practicing anyway). But demesne rights were central to the idea of lordship, and the lords insisted on their inviolability. Poaching animals and fish drew heavy fines—firewood lighter ones—and incited astonishing excuses.[51] The same evidence shows how frequently peasants did it.[52] The conflict illustrates a point argued for years by Rodney Hilton and refined by Robert Brenner: the economic rationale of lordship was extraction of surplus value from the tenancy; and though such a rationale theoretically *could* produce an equilibrium (the lord extracting as much as he could without endangering the health or lives of his productive force), it did not, because the lord felt pressures other than the constraints of productive capacity (he, after all, was not going to starve): competition for status and influence, for example, had a force that could push the lord to push his tenants beyond what they could comfortably bear.[53] For the lord,

---

one Godfrey was presented for carrying branches from the lord's wood, and Robert Patrick for bringing his cart in at night to carry away *spinae* and trees for burning (Ault, *Court Rolls of the Abbey of Ramsey*, 206–10).

During the revolt at St. Albans, the rebels gave serious and direct expression to this grievance, demanding common pastures, woods, and ponds; "ut, videlicet, novis gauderent bondis circa villam, in quibus libere sua pascerent animalia, et piscationem sine calumnia in certis obtinerent locis, necnon venationes et aucupationes iterum haberent in certis locis" (Walsingham, *Gesta* 3:299).

50. For example, the incremental demand on resources represented by the levy of royal taxes (which were irregular, granted at need, and therefore could not be budgeted for) could force agricultural families to sell off seed corn—the most desperate measure short of selling land (J. R. Maddicott, *The English Peasantry and the Demands of the Crown, 1298–1341*, Past and Present Supplement 1 [Oxford, 1975], 4–5). For a careful balance of profits against costs in the budget of a prosperous peasant family, see Christopher Dyer, *Standards of Living in the Later Middle Ages: Social Change in England c.1200–1520* (Cambridge, Eng., 1989), 110–18, 148–50.

51. See, for example, the affecting story (in *La court de baron*) of the man who could not resist the combination of his sick wife's craving for a tench, and the allure of one ("so beautiful and bright") he happened to see in the lord's pond (Maitland and Baildon, *Court Baron*, 54–55). The fines for poaching were not like, for example, prosecutions for breaking the assize of ale; in the latter, the same people paid fines year after year as tacit licensing fees, a silent agreement between tenants and lord on the organization of trade. The relative uniformity of the amercements in the assize, and the relative absence of attempts at defense or excuse, confirms their contractual character.

52. See Hanawalt, *Ties That Bound*, 116–17, 132–33; and her "Men's Games, King's Deer: Poaching in Medieval England," *JMRS* 19 (1988): 175–93.

53. See Rodney Hilton, "Feudalism in Europe: Problems for Historical Materialists,"

prohibition of poaching was maintenance of his prerogatives; for the peasants, it was a restriction on their livelihood.[54]

But if the midsummer bonfire expressed the resentments that fueled violence in 1381, its annual celebration did not have much practical consequence: it did nothing to loosen lords' control over resources, as indeed the lords must have realized, since they seem to have tolerated the midsummer thefts.[55] Recent discussion of popular ceremonies has tended to decide that their contained, seasonal character necessarily undermined any oppositional stance. Bakhtin's delineation of carnival— in which the mass of anonymous villagers thumb their noses at "official culture" (roughly "the church" and "the state"), opposing its claims for the timeless naturalness of its order with a celebration of impermanence, angularity, and corporeality[56]—has caused some to wonder whether *scheduled* disorder could be subversive, or whether, after all, the people who suffer domination blow off steam and then go back to work.[57] The

---

New Left Review 147 (1984): 84–93, *The Decline of Serfdom in Medieval England* (London, 1969), 40–43, "A Crisis of Feudalism," *Past and Present* 80 (1978): 11–12. Brenner's summary runs like this:

> The system of surplus extraction tended to develop according to its own logic, so to speak, and, to an important degree, without reference to the requirements of peasant production—as a function, in particular, of the lords' growing needs for *politically-motivated consumption*, arising from their needs both to maintain a dominant position *vis-à-vis* the peasantry and to protect themselves *vis-à-vis* one another. If it is true that lordly surplus-extraction was ultimately restricted by peasant-based production, it was also the case that the system of lordly surplus-extraction could limit, even govern, the development of peasant production itself. (Brenner, "The Agrarian Roots of European Capitalism," in Aston and Philpin, *Brenner Debate*, 232)

For the importance of what Brenner calls "politically-motivated consumption" in determining the expenditures of the lords, documented by a historian with no discernible investment in the Brenner thesis, see Dyer, *Standards of Living*, ch. 3.

54. Throughout this chapter I assume that the apparent increase in prosperity that followed the plague of 1349 substantially changed neither the contingency of rural life nor peasants' perceptions of it. Some justification of the assumption can be found below, nn. 123, 124, 128, 132.

55. Phythian-Adams, "Ceremony," 68.

56. "The feast was a temporary suspension of the entire official system with all its prohibitions and hierarchic barriers. For a short time life came out of its usual, legalized and consecrated furrows and entered the sphere of utopian freedom. The very brevity of this freedom increased its fantastic nature and utopian radicalism. . . . During the entire medieval period the Church and state were obliged to make concessions, large or small, to satisfy the marketplace" (Bakhtin, *Rabelais and His World*, trans. Hélène Iswolsky [Bloomington, 1984], 88–90).

57. Terry Eagleton makes Bakhtin a foil for Benjamin's political realism: "Bakhtin's utopia . . . could not be more bulging with positive life. Indeed carnival is so vivaciously celebrated that the necessary political criticism is almost too obvious to make. Carnival,

point is well made, but it is as confined and confining as Bakhtin's. Both he and his critics take it that the ambition of carnival is to be opposi- tional; they disagree about whether the ambition is fulfilled. Neither asks whether the festivities might serve, and the opposition therefore be subordinate to, some other purpose internal to the community, defined independently of (not in response to, and not therefore in the terms of) the power that rules it. For that is the case here. The bonfires evidently drew energy from the expansively wasteful encroachment on the lords' forest, but the encroachment was just as evidently not their point; rather, it was instrumental to the purpose of the festivities, as indeed was the expansiveness. They celebrated and enabled reconcilia- tion just when the fields demanded it. Midsummer marked the beginning of harvest,[58] and harvest, the most labor-intensive season of the year, demanded cooperation.[59] At the season when village custom required the work of every able body and enforced close supervision on each to maintain the yield of all, division and rancor were real temptations and unwarranted luxuries.[60] The common grudge against lordship relieved internal pressures by scapegoating (not all scapegoating is unjust; some- times it just acknowledges fact) and presumably celebrated the self-

---

after all, is a *licensed* affair in every sense, a permissible rupture of hegemony, a contained popular blow-off as disturbing and relatively ineffectual as a revolutionary work of art" (*Walter Benjamin, or, Towards a Revolutionary Criticism* [London, 1981], 148). According to Allon White and Peter Stallybrass, most "thoughtful political commentators" find carnival simply "a form of social control of the low by the high" that "therefore serves the interests of that very official culture which it apparently opposes" (*The Politics and Poetics of Transgression* [Ithaca, 1986], 13).

58. Homans, *English Villagers*, 370–71.

59. W. O. Ault, *Open-Field Husbandry and the Village Community: A Study of Agrarian By-Laws in Medieval England*, Transactions of the American Philosophical Society 55.7 (1965), 12–14.

60. On the by-laws of the harvest, see below. The "community" in medieval com- munities was maintained with difficulty; see John Bossy's deliberately provocative sug- gestion that the parish priest was "there, socially speaking, to assist in the creation of peace" in the natural state of feud that characterized rural society ("Blood and Baptism: Kinship, Community, and Christianity in Europe from the Fourteenth to the Seventeenth Centuries," *SCH* 10 [1973]: 139). Throughout, when I speak of the rituals of community and cooperation in the medieval village, I mean rituals created to foster a cooperation that, though necessary, was hard to maintain, a peace always threatened with violence; otherwise, indeed, the rituals themselves would have had little purpose. Bossy implies a different model: that the church and clergy brought to the community—from the outside—the means of peacemaking in a situation that would otherwise be hopelessly rancorous. I find it hard to accept this assumption, if only because popular rituals that were manifestly not contrived by the church or clergy seem to have had much the same point.

sufficiency of the community, its ability to resolve its differences and manage its affairs independent of the lord.

The rebels in 1381 translated the symbolic resistance of midsummer into actual resistance, building their fires not from the underbrush of the manorial forests but from the literate underpinnings of manorial rule. They made a point about what sustained privileges like enclosed forests: the parchment they burned recorded customary rents and services, payments and defaults, records of landholding, manorial privileges, amercements, and appointments to office—the artificial memory that sustained the mechanisms of extraction. But the focus of *their* bonfires was, like the fires at midsummer, as much the community that surrounded them as the lord they served. Communal autonomy, the mechanisms of *self*-rule in the villages, were also celebrated around these fires: the community defined by the fire rendered the documents superfluous.

To put it another way, the rising in 1381 focused local practices developed in the service of subsistence—practices that included but were not dominated by either ceremonial or guerrilla action against the lord—as expressions of political and social reform; to put it yet another way, the ideology on which the insurgency drew was concerned not with rebellion but with order and survival. Festivities form a clue to this ideology, since they are a community's articulation of itself to itself; this is why I think it important to distance myself from the debate over carnival. The world imagined by that debate—a world in which rulers want people to work and people want to break things—is, materially speaking, oddly unconstrained. For in the late-medieval countryside the object of ordinary attention was food. This was the source of most legal actions among tenants and between tenants and others; it was the motive of most assaults and trespasses and crimes; it determined the forms of sociability and the conventions of family organization. It set the criteria for social acceptability and shaped its vocabulary: the parasites of village society—the idlers and beggars, wastrels and prostitutes whose banishment the communities themselves sought, indeed all those who would not do their proper work—were unwanted not because they were corrupting, unsightly, or troublesome, but because they were "useless."[61] To act as though these communities, in their moments of

61. See, for example, John Bundeley, miller, of whom the court and *visus* at Nidding-

play, should have attended entirely to those who ruled them is to insist that they should have given these rulers a greater power than they already had, the power to absorb the imagination and attention of their subjects, and to pretend that the subjects had no resources deeper than anger and reaction.[62]

On the other hand, the system under which they lived was, not to put too fine a point on it, stupefyingly unjust, and coping with it did not change it. Thus the complexity of the bonfires of documents, which both drew on an annual ceremony to express the autonomy villages had marked out for themselves in the shadowy corners of manorial jurisdiction, and made the ceremony itself a public challenge to that jurisdiction; and thus the complexity of all such traces of ritual and festivity in June 1381. The bonfires at midsummer proclaimed the ability of the community to resolve differences in the face of threatened dearth and to resolve them without the assistance of the lord's court, or the king's. The spin the insurgents gave to the ceremonies in their creative and often violent translations—what it took to make yearly rituals into symbolic articulations of a new order—also yields clues to what the new order was imagined to be, and what it had to do with the old.

The rising happened in the season of festivity.[63] One testimony to the cloud of unknowing that interposed between the rising and those who prosecuted and recorded it is the blindness of the narrative and judicial records to the meaning of their own chronology. Chronicles and court rolls routinely date the events in the usual way, by reference to church feasts, betraying no suspicion that the feasts had anything to

---

worth-cum-Holywell in 1288 said, "Non est idoneus ad opus villate quia non custodit fideliter bladum hominum villate ad molendinum missum" (Ault, *Court Rolls of the Abbey of Ramsey*, 189); and the cases of Cecilia Tannatrix, cited before the eyre at Ramsey in 1287 "for receiving Philip Tixtor who is useless to the vill, outside the assize"; and of "Beatrice, wife of Stephen de Walsokne," cited at the same session for "regularly receiving Henry, cleric of Aldwinkle, and other useless people and foreign prostitutes, without the knowledge of her husband, who is blind" (*The Court Rolls of Ramsey, Hepmangrove, and Bury, 1268–1600*, ed. and trans. Edwin Brezette DeWindt [Toronto, 1990], 34–35).

62. Indeed, as Andrew Taylor has suggested (drawing on Michael Camille), "carnival" might best be regarded as "medieval dream work," the political unconscious of the literate class at work redrawing popular thought and speech into a nightmare grotesquerie ("Playing on the Margins: Bakhtin and the Smithfield Decretals," paper delivered at the International Congress of Medieval Studies, Kalamazoo, May 1992).

63. For other instances of popular ceremony in the actions and thought of the rebels, see Christopher Dyer, "The Rising of 1381 in Suffolk," 281.

do with the events.[64] The rising occupied what Charles Phythian-Adams calls the "ritual half" of the late-medieval year and even seems to have marched in the approximate rhythm of the major feasts.[65] Ascension week with its rogation processions, 20–26 May in 1381, preceded the initial assault on the justices at Brentwood; the Bocking oath was taken on Whitsunday—Pentecost, the feast of the church's founding; court rolls were first burned on Trinity Monday; and of course the rising reached its climax around the greatest of all these feasts, Corpus Christi, the celebration of community, body, and food.

In these celebrations, and preeminently Corpus Christi, we can catch rural communities in the act of self-description. Though the feasts had ecclesiastical origins, they made their meaning within the communities that celebrated them; or rather, the communities discovered meanings within them: after all, "the church" itself was not present to contain the spin of multivocality; only the local priests were there, and they, as I argue in chapter 1, dwelt more often within the concerns and the imaginative world of their communities than in those of pastoral theology or episcopal discipline. The feasts were subject to what Michel de Certeau calls "poaching," consumption to unauthorized ends.[66] But again, it is not at all clear that the appropriation was itself the point, that it was particularly defiant or even conscious: rather, the relation between the community and liturgies contained possibilities of meaning that resistance detonated in 1381. The great Corpus Christi plays have dominated study of the feast.[67] But the plays belonged to the towns, not to villages like those where the rising started and grew. (One urban

64. The exception is Walsingham, who, in his characteristically overdetermined way, saw the correspondence between the rising and its liturgical occasion, but understood the conjunction not as evidence of the rebels' meaningful action, but as a sermon from God on the dangers accruing to the realm through the unhindered publication of Wyclif's eucharistic heresy: "misisse creditur a multis Deum tribulationem praefatam, eo praecipue tempore quo specialem de transubstantiatione Corporis Christi facit sacrosancta ecclesia mentionem" (*Chronicon*, 311).

65. Phythian-Adams, "Ceremony," 74.

66. Certeau, *The Practice of Everyday Life*, trans. Steven F. Rendall (Berkeley and Los Angeles, 1984), ch. 12, the term designates the kind of casual and unofficial reading that violates the "proper" sense that is circumscribed within the "*readable* space" of literal (official) meaning (171). (I am poaching on Certeau's terminology here myself, since he uses it in a historical argument about postindustrial capitalism.)

67. Most important, Mervyn R. James, "Ritual, Drama, and Social Body in the Late Medieval English Town," *Past and Present* 98 (1983): 3–29. But see Miri Rubin's ambitious study of the ritual and social functions of the Eucharist, *Corpus Christi: The Eucharist in Late Medieval Culture* (Cambridge, Eng., 1991). Unfortunately, I obtained Rubin's book after I had written this chapter, but I have drawn on it for confirmatory evidence.

rising in 1381 perhaps used a dramatic form to construct its public self-characterization.)[68] The feast itself gave the rebels an instrument of expression in meanings it already encapsulated and practices it already sponsored. Throughout the southern counties the *societates* of rebels transformed the feast's clerical concerns into a public language of their own. What made the feast of use to them makes it of use to us, in tracing back and down the notions of community, authority, and government they brought to the rising.

The revolt at St. Albans provides a spectacular starting point from which to explore the feast, its subject, and its season, in order to return again to the rising. Walsingham says that while some of the rebels negotiated with the abbot about the ancient charter (with capital letters in azure and gold), others were busy elsewhere:

> Meanwhile [*interim*] the disorderly rustics broke into the cloister with their tools, and into the parlor where the handmills had been placed as paving stones, to document and record [*in munimentum et memoriam*] an old dispute between the villeins and the monastery at the time of Abbot Richard. They tore these up, carried them out, and brought them to the commons. They broke the stones into small pieces, giving some to each, just as it is customarily done in parish churches on Sunday to break and distribute the blessed bread, so that, when they saw these pieces, they would see for themselves that they had been victorious in their case against the monastery.[69]

Walsingham uncharacteristically credits the rebels with a sense of decorum here. The sharing out of the millstones imitated (he claims) an informal, quasi-liturgical ritual, in which parishioners, who received communion only once or thrice a year, received bread which had been prayed over, but not consecrated, and which was shared out after Sunday

---

68. This was at Bury St. Edmunds (Suffolk). I will discuss this event, and its implications for the understanding of religious drama, in a forthcoming essay, "Urban Guilds and Religious Drama in 1381."

69. "Tamen interim ribaldi, cum instrumentis claustrum ingredientes, de locutorio forinseco lapides molares, qui in pavimento ostii locutorii, in munimentum et memoriam antiqui placiti inter villanos et Monasterium tempore quondam Abbatis Ricardi, locati fuerant, levaverunt, asportaverunt, et ad communes detulerunt, et ibidem minutatim confregerunt, dantes partem cuique, ut panis benedictus Dominicis diebus partiri et conferri in ecclesiis parochialibus consuevit; ut, videlicet, videntes easdem particulas, apud se recognoscerent sese olim in ea causa de Monasterio vindicasee" (Walsingham, *Gesta* 3:309). Middleton has remarks on this incident that overlap with mine, in "William Langland's 'Kynde Name,'" 69–70.

mass.[70] These "ribalds and rustics" (as Walsingham elsewhere calls them)[71] might have sought the abolition of all law, the annihilation of memory and custom, and the destruction of the faith; but they would not have mocked the Eucharist.

But how, from hearing of or even seeing the action, could Walsingham have told the difference? He couldn't, and neither can we. We can only trace an ethnographic trail around it, and might begin by noting that the rebels made this gesture, whatever it was, two days after the feast of Corpus Christi, which has some claim to be thought not only the occasion of the rising, but also a source of its public idiom. That trail will lead through the feast, the Eucharist it celebrated, the popular ceremonies with which it shared a season, and the concerns that all of these addressed, back finally to St. Albans and its millstones. St. Albans must hold pride of place in any discussion of rebel strategy and ideology, simply because Walsingham's eyewitness account in the *Gesta abbatum* gives uniquely full and detailed information, day by day, for the weeks of insurgency; from him we have to infer what we can about what went unrecorded in the dozens of venues unsupplied with chroniclers. In some ways this is too bad. St. Albans did not rise together with the villages of Essex and Kent, but only after learning that they had; it was not part of the original network of activity and did not join the march on London. Walsingham is not the Bocking or Brentwood chronicler I might wish to uncover. But in some ways he is better. When the commons of St. Albans decided to rise against the abbot, they took care to get, in detail, the best counsel to be had: they went to London to be instructed and deputized by Wat Tyler.[72] Their techniques of insurgency (it will appear) recall closely the actions in Essex and Kent, as did their

---

70. Rubin, *Corpus Christi*, 73–74. Rosamond Faith, whose discussion of this event is responsible for bringing it to recent attention, translates *benedictus* as "consecrated." Although, as I will argue later, this translation accurately describes what the *rebels* thought they were doing, it does mistake what *Walsingham* thought they were doing ("'Great Rumour,'" 66).

71. *Gesta* 3:299.

72. "Et ut celerius optatum consequerenter effectum, quidam laudaverunt Walterum Tyler adeundum, ducem ribaldorum et rusticorum de Cantia, ut, accepta ab eo potestate, . . . domum redirent, et strictis conditionibus expeterent quae volebant" (*Gesta* 3:299); "Ipse [William Grindcobbe] etiam in primis prolocutor principalis pro istis negotiis ipsi Waltero, idolo rusticorum. . . . commover[u]nt ipsum Walterum, quanquam non fuisset propositi sui recedere de Londoniis, nec quemquam a se de suis sequacibus mittere, ad promittendum eis adventum suum ad radendum barbas Abbatis et Prioris, et caeterorum monachorum; id est, ad decapitandum eos; . . . ita duntaxat, ut ipsi in omnibus mandatis ejus parerent, et nihil praeterirent de universis quae mandaret" (*Gesta* 3:300).

demands and the ideas behind them (one of their number may even have used a pseudonym like those in the letters).[73] The rebellion at St. Albans consciously followed Wat Tyler's prescriptions, creating an elaborate symbolic choreography which Walsingham records with varying proportions of mystification and disgust: an authorized edition of the rebellion, so to speak, and one that followed the ceremonial patterns of the Corpus Christi season.

For Corpus Christi was not just a feast; it was a season of outdoor ceremonies lasting from Eastertide to midsummer, a season whose most extravagant celebrations were associated with this central feast. By itself, the celebration of Corpus Christi cannot tell us much about what it meant to those who celebrated, because it presupposes the other festivities with which it was seasonally associated. But by looking around it (at its season) and behind it (at the Eucharist it commemorated), we have some hope of understanding how it was experienced, in the sparsely documented countryside as well as in the towns, and perhaps even of answering the question that Mervyn James's classic essay never puts— why did *this* feast become a popular, almost universal, expression of corporate identity?

The density of symbolic meaning that accrued to the eucharistic bread is a commonplace of medieval scholarship; to put some life back into it, to see why it elicited the passions it did, we have to leave the altar, where most historians of the liturgy have (both metaphorically and literally) stood, and join the congregation in the nave. What they experienced in the first part of the mass was an at least minimally

73. When Walsingham narrates the story of the millstones in the parlor floor, he mentions no names (I have given the passage complete). He next alludes to the incident when he tells of the arrest of the rebel leaders at St. Albans: "Secrete vero seorsum convocatis ballivis et constabulariis, jussit [Sir Walter Lee] ex parte Regis, ut mox, post subtractionem turbae quae ad villam convenerat, elaborarent circa captionem Willelmi Gryndecobbe, Willelmi Cadyndon, et Johannis Barbitonsoris, (qui, videlicet, ut supra retulimus, petras molares abstulerunt de locutorii pavimento)" (*Gesta* 3:339). Grindcobbe we know, and likewise William Cadingdon, whom Walsingham mentions early in the account as a second leader of the local insurgency. But the mysterious *Johannes Barbitonsor*—John Barber (strictly, John Beardcutter)—appears only here, not to be mentioned again; and Walsingham has *not*, as he claims, mentioned these names, or any names, in relation to the millstones. I am inclined to connect Barber's name, and his elusiveness in this eyewitness account, to a fragment of Wat Tyler's conversation that Walsingham seems to have reproduced: Tyler promised to come to St. Albans "to shave the beards [*ad radendum barbas*] of the abbot and prior and certain other monks; that is, to cut off their heads" (*Gesta* 3:300).

participatory exchange with the celebrant: a greeting from the priest (facing the people through this part of the liturgy), prayers, readings, a vernacular sermon sometimes, announcements and marriage banns, the vernacular bidding prayers, an offertory. Then silence: the priest gave his back to the congregation, turned to the altar (which stood against the wall, as it had for centuries), and continued his prayers mostly in an undertone only partially audible to those behind him. Everyone knew what his movements would eventuate in, knew that the priest was making God from bread, but the particular actions were something the congregation could not ordinarily observe. A longish silence, a couple of minutes at least from the *secreta* to the consecration, was suddenly broken by the church bell, or a little "sacring" bell within the church, or both; candles were brought forward, and the priest, his back still to the congregation—the action in some churches set off against a black cloth behind the altar—raised God over his head.

This was the elevation. It produced jostling, accesses of communal enthusiasm, calls of encore.[74] Cranmer's protégé Thomas Becon presented a snide but persuasive picture of it in a later age: "When the bell once rings (if they cannot conveniently see), they forsake their seats and run from altar to altar, from sacring to sacring, peeping here and touting there, and gazing at that thing which the pilled-pate priest holdeth up in his hands. And if the priest be weak in the arms, and heave not up high enough, the rude people of the country in divers parts of England will cry out to the priest: 'Hold up, sir John, hold up; heave it a little higher.' And one will say to another: 'Stoop down, thou fellow afore, that I may see my Maker: for I cannot be merry except I see my Lord God once in a day.'"[75] Becon's sixteenth-century scene (which is expressly rural: "the rude people of the country") was close to what Wyclif had in mind in the fourteenth, when he attacked the "idolatry" of the Eucharist.[76] The bell rang the consecration to those outside the church,[77]

74. Joseph A. Jungmann, S.J., *The Mass of the Roman Rite: Its Origins and Development*, trans. Francis A. Brunner, C.SS.R. (New York, 1955), 2:206ff.

75. Thomas Becon, *The Displayeng of the Popishe Masse*, in John Ayre, ed., *Prayers and other Pieces*, Parker Society 4 (Cambridge, Eng., 1844), 270.

76. Jeremy I. Catto, "Wyclif and the Cult of the Eucharist," *SCH* subsidia 4 (1985): 269–86.

77. "In elevatione vero ipsius corporis domini pulsentur campane in uno latere, ut populares, quibus celebrationi missarum non vacat cotidie interesse, ubicunque fuerint seu in agris seu in domibus, flectant genua, indulgentias concessas a pluribus episcopis habituri" (from Pecham's Lambeth Council; F. M. Powicke and C. R. Cheney, eds.,

and often rang them in: the Lollard preacher William Thorpe lost one audience at midsermon when the sound of the bells sent them running for the altar.[78]

Why the commotion? The elevation lasted only a moment,[79] and it was as close to the host as the congregation, which seldom took communion, usually got. After the elevation, the host vanished on the far side of the priest, not to appear again; when he turned back to face the congregation, he had eaten the bread, drunk the wine, and washed the paten and chalice. The sacrament was virtually invisible, kept from the laity whose unity and community it was said to epitomize—as homilists would frankly admit. A versified Corpus Christi homily in the Vernon manuscript takes as its devotional theme the priest's monopoly over the consecrated elements and his gradual separation from the laity whom he had once faced across a common table; the homily narrates how that former intimacy had been chipped away, papal decree by papal decree, as the priest and the table were moved away, vested, and turned around.[80] The laity's posture had come to differ from the priest's; rood screens interposed.[81] But the most dramatic change was the silence in which the canon was pronounced, a silence doubled by the Vernon homily, which translates and explains most elements of the mass for the laity's better understanding, but which conspicuously omits the words of consecration; the canon itself was always kept secret, with the more or less explicit rationale of withholding it from those unqualified to speak it, for fear that they *would* speak it to unofficial or superstitious

---

78. "As I stood there in the pulpit, busying me to teach the commandment of God, there knelled a sacring-bell; and therefore mickle people turned away hastily, and with great noise ran from towards me. And I seeing this, say to them thus, 'Good men! ye were better to stand here full still and to hear God's Word'" (*The Examination of Master William Thorpe, Priest . . .*, in Alfred W. Pollard, ed., *Fifteenth Century Prose and Verse* [New York, n.d.], 130). See also Rubin, *Corpus Christi*, 152.

79. Episcopal legislation in the thirteenth century actually limited the time the host should be shown to the people; see Jungmann, *Mass of the Roman Rite* 2:209. On the liturgical history and rationale of the elevation generally, see Jungmann, 205–10, and Adrian Fortescue, *The Mass: A Study of the Roman Liturgy*, 2d ed. (London, 1955), 338–42.

80. "De festo Corporis Christi," in *Minor Poems of the Vernon MS*, ed. Carl Horstman, EETS os 98 (London, 1892), 168–97.

81. On posture, see Jungmann, *Mass of the Roman Rite* 1:128; those outside the church were also encouraged to kneel at the ringing of the elevation (see n. 78 above). On rood screens, see C. N. L. Brooke, "Religious Sentiment and Church Design in the Later Middle Ages," *BJRL* 59 (1967): 13–33.

or blasphemous purposes.[82] The altar was separated from the congregation, reserved for the priest's solitary action and spectacle. Even the reserved sacrament, even when stored above the altar, was ordinarily so enclosed as to be invisible.[83] The glimpse of it at the elevation was offered to the faithful as a guarded revelation of something too precious to be long exposed to the common air.

But the exclusivity that surrounded the host does not explain why congregations could enthuse tumultuously at its sight. A popular idea of the Eucharist's physical and spiritual efficacy was reflected in and fostered by the hundreds of miracle stories that sermons offered to the laity. Caesarius of Heisterbach, for example, tells of a woman who placed a consecrated host (secreted at mass) in her beehive, in the hope that the bees would produce more honey; they built a tabernacle around it instead.[84] Manning tells of a man buried in a mine collapse. His wife placed a daily offering of bread and wine on the altar, skipping Good Friday alone;[85] a year later, when the mine was opened again, the man emerged, saying that he had fed well on the bread his wife had sent him through her "curteysy" (l. 10780) and that he had had to fast only on Good Friday.[86] Caesarius's story of the beekeeper would be pointless if the woman's hopes had no connection with the audience's: she thought that this sacramental food would make more food—only slightly literalizing the preachers' assertion that after sight of the host one "schal wonte no bodely fode."[87] Manning, too, expects his readers to think the same: the bread the miner's wife places on the altar is evidently eucharistic,[88] and though offered to God, feeds her husband.

82. Bossy, *Christianity in the West*, 68.

83. See Archdale A. King, *Eucharistic Reservation in the Western Church* (London, 1965).

84. Caesarius of Heisterbach, *Dialogus miraculorum*, ed. Joseph Strange (Cologne, 1851), 2:172–73.

85. Robert Mannyng of Brunne, *Handlyng Synne*, ed. Idelle Sullens (Binghamton, 1983), ll. 10733ff.

86. Lest the audience draw the wrong moral, Manning warns, "But for al þys tale, yn ȝour lyues / Truste ȝe not moche on ȝoure wyues, / Ne on ȝoure chyldren for no þyng, / But makeþ ȝe self ȝoure offryng" (10799–82).

87. From Mirk's Corpus Christi sermon (*Festial*, 169); in the *Instructions*, where he also includes this "benefyce," the list is attributed to St. Augustine (*Instructions for Parish Priests*, ed. Gillis Kristensson [Lund, 1974], ll. 314–19).

88. Not only because it *is* bread and wine and *is* placed on the altar, but more specifically because she does not put it there on Good Friday, the only day in the liturgical year when no mass was celebrated and no elements consecrated.

Popular ideas, images, and stories associated the Eucharist not just with salvation but with *salus*: security, health of body as of soul, prosperity and fullness.[89] The Vernon homily interrupts its discourse on the mass to attack forestallers speculating in grain: "He buggeþ Corn aȝeyn the ȝere / And kepeþ hit til hit beo dere" (51–52). The digression shows what these miracle stories expected their audiences to worry about: dearth. To merely human production, the homilist and the audience oppose the timeless abundance of the heavenly bread, a dream of provision without shortage. The host was made locally of local grain,[90] the same stuff that parishioners ate every day (or hoped to),[91] but produced in its most luxurious form: it was the inefficiently ground white flour so widely desired.[92] In its eucharistic transformation, bread was both symbol and promise to those who spent their lives working to produce it.

Hence the enthusiasm that could erupt at the brief sight of the host. Corpus Christi celebrated the sacrament itself and used the affect it excited to promote a sense of corporateness. In theological terms, the host symbolized and incorporated all the faithful; the eucharistic body of Christ was identical to the church, the "mystical" body of Christ.[93]

---

89. Piero Camporesi's description, though it concerns early modern Italy, is pertinent: "La 'carne divina' . . . era diffusamente percepita anche come misteriosa, sovrumana sostanza nutritiva: midolla divina generosa nel distribuire insieme salvezza e salute (*salus* era il termine ambiguo in cui si allacciavano i due significati non facilmente disgiungibili), manna e balsamo celeste, farmaco soprannaturale" (*La casa dell'eternità* [Milan, 1987], 197).

90. For evidence on the baking of hosts, and that parishioners were required to contribute grain for the purpose, see Rubin, *Corpus Christi*, 42–43. The evidence of the story from Manning (about the woman whose offerings fed her trapped husband) makes sense only if its audience were expected to understand that the offertory at mass was originally an offering of the bread and wine that would be used at the consecration.

91. Peasants grew wheat chiefly as a cash crop; it rarely graced their tables, which would have bread made from barley, oats, rye, or whatever was most efficiently grown and would bring least profit on the market; see Postan, *Medieval Economy and Society*, 122–23, and Dyer, *Standards of Living*, 151–60. Dyer, however, notes that wheat consumption by the peasantry grew in the fourteenth and fifteenth centuries. Still, a pretty clear association between status and grain can be seen in the households described by Dyer, where the family would get wheat bread, but the lower servants bread made from beans and lesser grains (*Standards of Living*, 57).

92. A point nicely made by Rubin, *Corpus Christi*, 147. See, for example, the statutes of Exeter (1287): "Sint autem oblate candide, integre, et rotunde, nec per tantum tempus custodiantur quod in sapore vel aspectu abhominabiles habeantur" (Powicke and Cheney, *Councils and Synods* 2:990). On white bread, see Dyer, *Standards of Living*, 57, and Hanawalt, *Ties That Bound*, 54.

93. On the development and theology of the analogy, see Henri de Lubac, *Corpus mysticum: L'eucharistie et l'église au moyen âge. Étude historique* (Paris, 1949), esp. chs. 3–4.

Village festivities on and around the feast expressed this same sense in a different and more pertinently material way. Though the vernacular plays and pageant-wagon tableaux of Corpus Christi Day were the prerogative of prosperous towns, rural parishes had their own, more modest processions: the people of each church would perambulate the parish boundaries, the priest displaying the host at the rear.[94] The force of the procession derived in part from the summer concerns of agricultural society, from the fear of dearth and the desire for plenty that grew more urgently topical as harvest approached. Other seasonal ceremonies resembled and informed the Corpus Christi procession and allow us to understand something about why this feast became such an important celebration of community. The three days before the feast of the Ascension (which preceded Corpus Christi by three weeks) were "rogation days" on the church calendar. In the village, they were the days for "beating the bounds," making procession to significant boundaries, feasting and drinking at each in a communal mnenomic that preserved the precise definition of locality from year to year against insensible encroachments.[95] At the same time, the Rogation procession made the community visible as a *population*—displayed the village to itself—while recalling and making visible the community as a *locality*, a place and a unit of production, the source of subsistence whose integrity and equilibrium was essential to survival. The community was a community because of the place that sustained it.

Another, less well attested ceremony bears some resemblance to these boundary ceremonies (and incidentally to the sharing out of the St. Albans millstones). There is some evidence that at midsummer, the bonfire of "good amity" was divided among the villagers to be carried through the fields,[96] a practice nearly unintelligible without reference to the fields they were carried through and to the open-field systems whose

94. Miri Rubin, "Corpus Christi Fraternities and Late Medieval Piety," *SCH* 23 (1986): 100.

95. Homans, *English Villagers*, 368; Thomas, *Religion and the Decline of Magic*, 64–65; Dorothy M. Owen, *Church and Society in Medieval Lincolnshire* (Lincoln, 1971), 108. "Maintenance of boundaries elicited strong emotional responses. Fights with neighboring villages occurred at the beating of the bounds, and people who lived outside the village were called strangers and foreigners and were treated with suspicion" (Hanawalt, *Ties That Bound*, 23). And see Phythian-Adams, *Local History and Folklore*, 19, for observations on the social importance of geographical boundaries.

96. Homans, *English Villagers*, 369. Stow's report that the St. John Baptist watch fire entailed "also a marching watch" might suggest an urban version of the same procedure (*Survay*, 75).

shape still marks much of the English countryside with its curving ridges. Individual farmsteads were not the only or usual form that family holdings would take in rural England. More often (the frequency varied with the region),[97] each family's holdings would be parceled out into small strips (each defined by the throw of dirt from the plow) mixed in with strips belonging to other families in the large undivided fields that surrounded the village.[98] The strips could be tiny: at Warboys (Hunts), a Ramsey Abbey manor, one eighteen-acre holding—a middling size— was held in forty-three strips in the common fields; another eight acres were held in sixteen strips. The means of identifying these little parcels is instructive: "1/2 a. on Long Flexlond next Simon Lone; 2 r. at Middilgrove Yerdes next William Brandon; . . . 1/2 a. on Longewold between Rector of the Church and Richard Gerold jun.; 2 r. on Watercroft between Hugh of Eydon and Geoffrey"; and so on.[99] The names here of course belong to the holders of adjacent strips, and this emphasizes one of the striking aspects of strip farming, how much of each family's land immediately bordered on other families' lands. This closeness encouraged ad hoc cooperation, such as the sharing of plows, and more formal coordination of crops, fallow, and grazing schedules. But it also required a self-protective vigilance, since a holding in, say, forty-three strips offered as many as eighty-six opportunities for en- croachment. The integrity of their holdings was as important to the

---

97. For field systems in the regions concerned in the revolt, see below, n. 139.

98. The subject has been massively studied. The extent of strip farming remains a relatively uncontroversial topic: it was found throughout England except in the extreme southwest and northwest, somewhat less concentrated in the north and in Kent and the East Anglian fens. Based largely on the discoveries of A. R. H. Baker (see especially "Open Fields and Partible Inheritance on a Kent Manor," *EcHR*, 2d ser., 17 [1964]: 1–23), Joan Thirsk has insisted on the necessity of distinguishing between *common-field* systems— systems in which holdings were parceled out through large fields and where common rules of grazing and crop rotation governed—and *open-field* systems—any systems in which holdings were scattered, whether or not common rules were observed. (Older literature used "open-field" to designate what Thirsk has more precisely called "common- field" husbandry.) While common fields were regionally bounded (occupying the central strip in the old maps, stretching from southwest to northeast England), open fields could be found throughout the land; see n. 138 below.

The standard and still indispensable work on the mechanisms and organization (though not the origins) of common-field work remains C. S. and C. S. Orwin, *The Open Fields*, 3d ed. (Oxford, 1967); Thirsk's preface to the third edition contains a review of scholarship to the mid-1960s. Thirsk's own arguments about the origins of common fields appear in "The Common Fields" (1964) and "The Origin of the Common Fields" (1966), both reprinted in R. H. Hilton, ed., *Peasants, Knights, and Heretics: Studies in Medieval English Social History* (Cambridge, Eng., 1976), 10–32, 51–56.

99. Raftis, *Warboys: Two Hundred Years in the Life of an English Mediaeval Village* (Toronto, 1974), 162–63.

family as the integrity of the fields was to the village, and since the threat of encroachment concerned all equally, all had an interest in maintaining a mutual respect and restraint about lands and boundaries; rights were tenaciously maintained and infractions severely punished by village jurors. When the brands were carried through the fields at midsummer, they were separate brands taken from a common fire, illuminating separate strips of a common field: the division of the fire mimed the structures of tenure and cultivation and acknowledged the dependence of each holding on the larger field.

In the perambulations of the rogation days and the bonfire ramble of midsummer, the community as a productive unit celebrated the land as the instrument of production and the source of its livelihood. The perambulation of Corpus Christi echoed that of the rogation days three weeks earlier, but this time the procession culminated in the unveiled display of the lasting Bread. That body of Christ represented the whole community of the faithful; and for these rural communities and their celebrations, there was a natural juncture between the eucharistic and the social bodies: the former was food, and the latter was the means of producing it. In beating the bounds, food marked festivity as it marked in memory the extent of the land and its integrity; the wholeness of the community expressed itself, and found need for its expression, in land and grain. In the Corpus Christi processions, the perambulation proceeded under the sponsorship of the miraculous food of God, which appeared, this one time each year, not in the confined and discontinuous space at the altar, but in the open, carried by the priest who exercised his sacramental function as a part of, visibly continuous with, the community.

All this is of course speculative, bringing to bear what clues we have on an experience of community that has left only fragmentary and unintended testimony. What is not speculative is my assertion that the rebels used the language and ceremonies of Corpus Christi and its season. "takeþ wiþ ȝow johan trewman and alle hijs felawes and no mo. and loke schappe ȝou to on heued and no mo" (Ball₃): Ball's injunction depends on the commonplace analogy between the eucharistic body and the social (or "mystical") body under the headship of Christ. The emphatic parallelism of the clauses (". . . and no mo . . . and no mo") suggests that this eucharistic image of community makes a natural appositive to the central normative term of the letters—*trewþe* ("johan trewman and alle hijs felawes")—so natural that he does not trouble to explain it. How then is it to be explained? What is the relation between the eucharistic images and the vocabulary of *trewþe*, and what does the relation mean? These questions lead back to Walsingham and St. Albans, to the most explicit and the most riddling account we have of Corpus Christi during the revolt: the millstone communion to which I now, finally, return.

"Meanwhile [*interim*] the disorderly rustics broke into the cloister with their tools, and into the parlor where handmills had been placed as paving stones, as a document and memorial [*in munimentum et memoriam*] of an old dispute between the villeins and the monastery." These rebels invaded the parlor while others negotiated with the abbot about the old charter, which, they claimed, the monks had hidden because of the liberties it guaranteed to the abbey's tenants. But the handmills themselves—surrendered "in the time of Abbot Richard" and used as paving stones to declare the abbey's right of multure—served the function of written testimony: they were there *in munimentum*, "as a document."[100] What the rebels did to the parlor floor was just a special case of what they did to documents of the parchment kind: they removed them from a place of private reservation, displayed them publicly, and destroyed them. In appropriating the millstone "documents," however, they also appropriated eucharistic sacramentality (distributing the pieces like the bread at mass) and displayed the structural similarity between documents and sacraments: two forms of clerical privilege, each of which, though formally matters of public concern, had been withheld from the community to which they rightly belonged. The rebels generalized their complaint about documentary culture—its reservation of record and command to a self-perpetuating clerisy—into a complaint about culture as such, about clerical control of the central expressions of common existence and belief.

Later, when the game was up, the abbey demanded, among other signs of submission, the return of the millstones. The villeins brought back "six, as many as they had carried away,"[101] which means that they

100. *Munimentum* was used in medieval England almost exclusively to denote written records: "munimenta dicuntur probationes et instrumenta quae causam muniunt," as Du Cange says (*Glossarium mediae et infimae Latinitatis*, nova editio [Niort, 1885], s.v. "munimina").

101. "Circa horam Vesperarum allati sunt lapides molares sex, quot, videlicet, asportaverant" (Walsingham, *Gesta* 3:347).

had kept the fragments of the stones after breaking and distributing them, still carrying for them a symbolic force. In seizing the handmills ("in the time of Abbot Richard"), the monastery had translated them from tools into signs (*in munimentum et memoriam*). In taking them back, the rebels demonstrated that they were participating in the culture of documentary symbol on their own terms, not retrieving the mills from it in order to restore them to practical use (the millstones, once broken, were useless not only as flooring tiles but also as millstones). Choosing the sacrament of signification as their medium ("signis tantum et non rebus," says the Corpus Christi sequence of the bread and wine),[102] they announced that they were translating the millstone documents into a different register of meaning and (by extension) that the documents were theirs to translate as they pleased.

The millstones also represented and declared the rebels' clear awareness of how cultural forms like eucharistic ritual depended on their own labor. What they broke and distributed was not bread, eucharistic or otherwise, but the instruments of its production, the millstones used to make flour from grain.[103] In reclaiming the *munimenta* of an abbatial victory, they engaged a kind of institutional pun. As they laid claim to the documentary memory of the monastery (the millstones as *munimenta*) and the sacramental ministry of the priesthood (the millstones as "holy bread"), they also announced a regime of peasant lordship: destroying handmills made sense only if they planned to possess a mill of their own, with "foure sayles" like the one described in Milner's letter. Those who jimmied them up from the floor made the stones mean more than the monastery had, even as they seized the meanings for themselves. The documents (the stones) belonged to them, and so did the sacrament. The millstone eucharist emphasized the agricultural work without which the mass was impossible (no mass without bread); but it *was* a eucharist, which located Christ not in the miracle of transubstantiation but in the task of subsistence.

What they announced in the millstone eucharist they announced again, and differently, by a perambulation the next day. After receiving the charter of liberties from the abbot,

---

102. The sequence attributed to Aquinas (*Analecta hymnica* 50:584–85).

103. "The compacted metonymies implicit in the millstones' new symbolic function are no less daring: they are made by ceremonial imposition to stand for the commodity, bread, in whose production they are instrumental" (Middleton, "William Langland's 'Kynde Name,'" 72).

without waiting for the charter to be sealed, they made perambulations around the vill in a great crowd and with much noise and shouting; following them were carts full of bread, beer, and such provisions, which were poured out generously at the point of each boundary mark, as a more effective memorial and evidence to their neighbors and children of the seisin [*seisinam*] they had gained over the liberty.[104]

Andrew Galloway has shown how this reportage consigns the rebels, ignorant in the ways of documents (they do not wait for the seal), to an impoverished world of memory and oral tradition;[105] but it is in this very hostility that Walsingham, savoring their haste, allows the complexity of the rebels' own symbolism to emerge. Interested only in what he thinks the rebels' mistakes, he unknowingly outlines a chronology that betrays the real point of their actions. This perambulation on Sunday could not have meant (as Walsingham thought) to announce that the insurgents had gained seisin of the liberty; by their own claim (disseised grantees of the crown that they were), they had regained this three days before, on Thursday.[106] And the day before, they had already traced the route they took again on Sunday: on Saturday, rebels from the abbey manors met those from St. Albans, who offered "to lead them to the places that should be destroyed, or be made secure."[107] Progressing together as one group, they destroyed houses ("as they had learned from Wat Tyler in London"), unfurled the royal banners, "and made proclamations that watches should be placed close around the vill to prevent any monks from entering or leaving."[108] The Saturday procession apparently stopped to proclaim *each* watch where it was to be placed (*proclamationes* is plural), proceeding "around the vill." And yet this was not a perambulation. It was, with some creative amplification,

104. "Villani igitur praedicti, chartis libertatum praedictarum, ut praemittitur, sic adeptis, non expectata earum sigillatione, cum maxima turba et pomposo clamore et tumultu, perambulationes suas circa villam praedictam fecerunt, subsequentibus eos carectis cum pane, cervisia, et aliis victualibus, refertis, et ad positionem cujuslibet metae largiter expensis, ad majorem memoriam et evidentiam eorum posteris et vicinis de adquisitione et seisina libertatis praenotatae" (Walsingham, *Gesta* 3:320).

105. Galloway, "Gower and Walsingham on 1381 and the Profession of the Late Medieval Author," paper delivered to the Medieval Association of the Pacific, Tucson, March 1988.

106. See Maitland's discussion of seisin (Pollock and Maitland, *History of English Law* 2:29–40).

107. "Adducent ad loca diruenda, vel certa facienda" (*Gesta* 3:312).

108. "Praesumpserunt insuper, sub vexillo regio displicato, proclamationes facere de vigiliis locandis circa villam in numero copioso . . . ne ullus exiret ibidem monachus, vel intraret" (*Gesta* 3:313).

what Walsingham says it was: the setting of a watch, as the Statute of Winchester (1285) gave villages the right and duty to do.[109]

The Saturday ramble had a practical aim and a symbolic import I will discuss in a moment.[110] The Sunday perambulation was different, a specific response to the new charter they had just obtained. For although Walsingham does not say so or apparently care, his narration makes it clear that they carried the charter on the perambulation. Their walking of these bounds did announce their claim to the town's liberty, as Eileen Roberts has pointed out, since the abbot and monks alone enjoyed the right of perambulation.[111] But after the perambulation—a detail again not explicit, and again impossible to avoid—the rebels returned immediately to the abbot, to demand once again the ancient charter of Offa, of which the abbot claimed never to have heard.[112] The perambulation was not (as Roberts claims) their climactic celebration of a definitive victory, but their specific response to the new charter, to its virtues and defects. They beat the bounds of the land whose common freedom they demanded; but they believed that land and that freedom to be theirs already by ancient right, withheld from them only by the documentary manipulation of their monastic lord. The *real* charter, the charter of Offa that attested their rights, was still, they thought, kept from them, metaphorically and perhaps literally "under a lokke." The new charter was only a proxy, important to them because it witnessed the abbey's

109. "E desoremes est comaunde, qe veylles soient fetes, issi cum auncienement soleyent estre, ceo est asaver del jour de la Ascenciun deqes le jour Seint Michel, en chescun Cite sis homes, en chescune porte, en chescun burgh par xij. homes, en chescune vile [en terre] par vj. homes or iiij. solom numbre des genz qi abitent, e facent [la veille] continuelement tute la nuit del solail rescusse jeqes al solail levaunt" (*SR* 1.97).

110. Walsingham notes the practical aim: to spot any military aid that might be coming to help the monks, and to see that none could leave to call for help; see Réville, *Soulèvement*, 25.

111. When the monks made their perambulations, the relics of St. Alban himself brought up the rear (Eileen Roberts, "St. Albans' Borough Boundary and Its Significance in the Peasants' Revolt," in *The Peasants' Revolt in Hertfordshire: The Rising and Its Background* [Stevenage Old Town, 1981], 128–31).

112. Walsingham is not at his clearest here, since the chronology seems not to matter to him, but he does say clearly (1) that the villeins made their perambulation "without *waiting* for the charters to be sealed" ("non expectata earum sigillatione"), implying that they left for the perambulation without delay (as far as he was concerned, in comic haste), and (2) that they again demanded the ancient charter *after* they had possession of the new charters ("Obtenta autem charta secundum voluntatem propriam, de villae libertatibus chartam exquirunt, qualem saepe memoravimus Abbatem aut monachos nullatenus habuisse" [*Gesta* 3:320]). The only chronology his account permits is this: the charters were written out; before they were sealed, the villagers left for the perambulation; then they returned for further negotiations.

acknowledgment of rights they already had. This is why they carried it away unsealed: the abbot's authority really was not pertinent in this matter. By taking the charter, unsealed, on a beating of the bounds, the St. Albans rebels carried clerkly expertise into the landscape of common authority and common memory. Like the millstone eucharist (and associated with it in the imaginative lexicon of the Corpus Christi season), their perambulation marked the passage of clerical privileges into the regime of local political culture.

The actions of the St. Albans insurgents on Saturday and Sunday show that their opinion (their "stupid" opinion, to Walsingham's mind) that "in future there would be no lord, but only king and commons" was what the insurgents elsewhere meant by allying the "trew communes" with "kynge Richarde."[113] "They judged no name more honorable than the name *communitas*," says Walsingham,[114] and they knew what they meant by this name, which was neither vague nor randomly chosen: it was established legal usage and the core of what they demanded. *Communitas* designated the village population—even when made up partly of villeins—as a political corporation with rights and responsibilities before the common law, derived immediately from the crown.[115] By "commons" they did not mean "commoners in general," and by "king and commons" they did not mean "the king together with commoners." "King and commons" meant the agents of royal authority within particular localities, which were those localities, the populations who acted as largely self-governing bodies. The same demand was voiced in a very similar way among the main body of Kentish rebels, if the *Anonimalle*'s account is trusted: at Smithfield, that chronicle relates, Wat Tyler demanded "that there be no law but the law of Winchester, that there should be no outlawry in any process of law, and that no lord should have dominion in future, but that dominion should be divided among all, excepting only the king's."[116] The Statute of Winchester

113. "Nec quemquam de caetero reputaturi fuerunt dominum, juxta aestimationem suam stolidam, nisi Regem solummodo et communes" (*Gesta* 3:305); see ch. 2, n. 81 above.

114. "Ita enim tunc temporis gloriabantur eo nomine, ut nullum censerent nomen honorabilius nomine 'communitatis'" (*Gesta* 3:305).

115. The indispensable study is Helen M. Cam, "The Community of the Vill," in her *Law-Finders and Law-Makers in Medieval England: Collected Studies in Legal and Constitutional History* (London, 1962), 71–84.

116. "Qe nulle lay deveroit estre fors la lay de Wynchestre, et qe nulle ughtelarie serroit

deputized each community for the keeping of the king's peace,[117] and Tyler's insistence that dominion be "divided among all" has to be understood in terms of that statute: he did not mean that each individual should hold a moiety of power, but that the localities deputized in the statute, where the villagers made their lives and livings, should each exercise plenary local lordship, saving only the authority proper to the king himself.[118] The rising's notion of the new political order, if utopian, was at least not vaguely so: it was that local communities should continue to exercise their acknowledged and conventional authority *in place of*—not, as was already the case, in addition to—the authority of the lords.[119]

The "community of the vill," the local organization fitfully recognized as a corporation by royal authority, was not created by royal authority: it was self-created, from necessity. The necessity arose, it has been suggested, from gapping and overlapping jurisdictions, as when a village, divided among several manors, owed suit to the courts of

---

en nulle processe de laye fait de ore en avaunt, et qe nulle seignur ne averoit seignurie for swlement estre proporcione entre toutz gentz, fors tansoulement la seignurie la roy" (*Anonimalle*, 147).

117. See n. 109 above.

118. It is also significant that the community was directly responsible to the crown, manorial lordship notwithstanding, in many of its functions; see Cam, "Community," 73–74.

119. As Dyer notes (concerning the Suffolk rebels), "It would be a grave error to assume that the rebels were behaving lawlessly; rather they were establishing a new law" ("The Rising of 1381 in Suffolk," 275–76).

Paul Strohm has recently taken his place in a long line of historians who claim that the insurgents (in his words) "appear never to have developed a comprehensive associative or communitarian ideology" (*Hochon's Arrow*, 54). Like Hilton (see ch. 1, n. 134 above), he believes that their thought was trapped within a three-estates model (an elite, bookish ideology whose pertinence to popular thought has probably been overestimated). As evidence for their deficient or undergeneralized notion of community—unable to make alliance "with other, nonmonarchic sources of social authority" because it excluded "the effective centers of potential armed opposition to monarchic power" (55)—he cites a story from Walsingham, who says that the insurgents in the Tower "treated with" the garrison guarding it "with familiar words, now about joining their numbers, now about keeping faith with those ribalds, now about swearing an oath that along with them they would seek the traitors to the realm" (*Chronicon*, 291; "but," Strohm continues after citing this passage, "few or no alliances appear to have been consummated. For this reason alone, the conclusion at Clerkenwell, or something like it, may be regarded as foregone" (56). It seems unlikely that the king's household knights (paid, Robert Brentano tells me, from chamber accounts) would have constituted "potential armed opposition to monarchic power," or that anyone would have thought them so. The passage from Walsingham is part of a larger, highly rhetorical denunciation of the social indecorum of the rebels' actions in the Tower, and if it is based on fact, the "familiarity" they showed the knights may have been the kind of tongue-in-cheek friendliness sometimes displayed to those who ordinarily wield power or command when their hands are tied.

different lords.[120] But the necessity arose more from the material challenges of provision and subsistence than from the feebler imperatives of jurisdictional tidiness. England's agriculture, conservative and low yield, was a grudging provider.[121] While everyone acknowledges that the countryside enjoyed a higher standard of living after the plague, it is not clear that the exigencies of subsistence were much relaxed, or (to the extent that they were) that they *felt* much relaxed.[122] On Christopher Dyer's calculations, even a virgate holder (with reasonably extensive lands, about thirty acres) could manage only a slight margin of profit by ordinary means in an ordinary year; holders of half-virgates and less could often break even only by doing wage work besides.[123] Maintaining their slightly higher standard of living required constant adjustment of

120. "The sense of unity at Harlestone [Northants], its corporateness, has come from the very fact of its divisions" (Joan Wake, "Communitas Villae," *EHR* 37 [1922]: 407–8).

121. See Postan, *Medieval Economy and Society*, 61–64; Dyer, *Lords and Peasants in a Changing Society: The Estates of the Bishopric of Worcester, 680–1540* (Cambridge, Eng., 1980), 128–33. But see also Bruce M. S. Campbell, "Agricultural Progress in Medieval Society: Some Evidence from Eastern Norfolk," *EcHR*, 2d ser., 36 (1983): 26–46.

122. It is evidently impossible here, and mostly beyond my capacities, to discuss the competing and contradictory claims about standards of living in the countryside. It has often been assumed that postpandemic England enjoyed an explosion of prosperity as the bottom fell out of land prices, but several questions might be put to the assumption. Grain and meat prices remained high, and the prices of manufactured goods apparently rose; the shortage of labor after the plague meant a shortage of goods as well, and quite possibly widespread poverty; see, for example, E. B. Fryde and Natalie Fryde, "Peasant Rebellion and Peasant Discontents," in Edward Miller, ed., *The Agrarian History of England and Wales*, vol. 3, *1348–1500* (Cambridge, Eng., 1991), 747–50, and Harry A. Miskimin, *The Economy of Early Renaissance Europe, 1300–1460* (Englewood Cliffs, 1969), 47–51. At the very least, the demographic changes that followed the plague allowed, and may have partly caused, crop shortages and their attendant anxieties; there seems to have been a "dear year" around 1369 or 1370; see C. E. Britton, *A Metereological Chronology to A.D. 1450* (London, 1937), 146. Some confusion about rural "prosperity" after the plague may be caused by some confusion about how short-term and long-term effects of tenurial changes were related. It is widely acknowledged, for example, that the commutation of customary services to money payments contributed in some degree to the eventual end of villeinage; for a cautious summary, see Hilton, *Decline of Serfdom*, 29ff. But commutation did not in itself constitute any great advantage to the villeins, who were now forced to raise the cash to pay their commuted services, something they would ordinarily have had to do by performing wage labor for someone else; see Fryde and Fryde, *Peasant Rebellion*, 787. Peasants do seem to have preferred commutation, but the advantages may have been no more than a greater freedom to arrange one's own work schedule, the psychological benefit of not being *commanded* to labor, and perhaps some slight measure of profit; these do not necessarily make for prosperity. Even older historians thoroughly committed to using commutation to explain the decline of villeinage show that it was an extremely complex process that did not necessarily redound to the immediate benefit of tenants; see, for example, Frances G. Davenport, "The Decay of Villeinage in East Anglia," *TRHS* ns 14 (1900): 123–41; on the Norolk manor she studies, a combination of commutation, term leases, and the flight of customary tenants brought the complete disappearance of

demands and resources. And often in the lords' despite: Dyer notes that peasant, not seigneurial, initiative lay behind most assarts and technological adaptations,[124] but the scope of innovation was limited, since (as Brenner observes) manorial tenure did nothing to encourage capital investment on the tenants' part.[125] Expanding individual holdings by purchase, or common land by reclamation, was in any case limited by the population required to exploit the lands under available technologies. Recurrent attacks of the plague after 1349 caused a labor shortage for peasants as well as lords, to the extent that some prosperous peasants made use of the Statute of Laborers to compel work and to enforce contracts.[126]

Landlords after the plague were astonishingly unmindful of the need to leave their tenants the resources to consolidate their position when faced with rising prices and labor shortages: they kept rents as high as ever though their tenants were less able to pay, and they worked out new tenurial arrangements to the tenants' disadvantage.[127] The villagers could not be so cavalier, since the productivity of each depended to some degree on the productivity of all: to exploit their holdings, they needed a population healthy enough to work, and those with holdings

---

villein families.

In any case, it is the phenomenology of economic life that is really at issue, how peasants and peasant communities experienced economic change. One mystery about postpandemic England is the low rate of population replacement; after the devastation of their numbers in the plague, the English peasantry seem not to have worked at restoring them, as would ordinarily happen in a period of markedly increased prosperity. Georges Duby believes that peasant families, having tasted prosperity (or at least stability), tried to consolidate their position by limiting family growth (*Rural Economy and Country Life in the Medieval West*, trans. Cynthia Postan [Columbia, S.C., 1968], 310; but see John Hatcher, *Plague, Population, and the English Economy 1348–1530* [London, 1977], 56). An equally plausible hypothesis along the same lines would simply be that such families did not *feel* more prosperous or secure, or that if they did, they also felt the prosperity to be fragile.

123. Dyer, *Standards of Living*, 117–49. J. Z. Titow has slightly happier estimates, (*English Rural Society 1200–1350* [London, 1969], 78–90).

124. Dyer, "Documentary Evidence: Problems and Enquiries," in Grenville Astill and Annie Grant, eds., *The Countryside of Medieval England* (Oxford, 1988), 25.

125. Brenner, "Agrarian Class Structure," 233.

126. L. R. Poos, "The Social Context of Statute of Labourers Enforcement," *Law and History Review* 1 (1983): 27–52.

127. On rents, see G. A. Holmes, *The Estates of the Higher Nobility in Fourteenth Century England* (Cambridge, Eng., 1957), 114–15; for examples of lordly creativity in maintaining the disadvantages of villein tenure, see Barbara A. Harvey, *Westminster Abbey and Its Estates in the Middle Ages* (Oxford, 1977), 244–61; Rodney H. Hilton, "A Rare Evesham Abbey Estate Document" (1969), rpt. in his *Class Conflict*, 101–7; and in general, Hilton, *Decline of Serfdom*, 36–43.

too small to support them needed the work to afford necessities on the market.[128] The communities themselves had to ensure the health and survival of the rural work force, which is to say their own.[129] This required, among other things, guarding the integrity of everyone's product. The fear of dearth and the need for bread, which generated a deep and echoing devotion to the eucharistic host in rural communities, generated also an ethic and a legality independent of, though often confirmed by, seigneurial administration and royal law.

Discussing these forms of self-regulation means abandoning the ritual and spectacle of Corpus Christi for the duller business of food and vesture. But the peasants themselves had to return to such business after each feast; though festivals show most resonantly how communities wanted to understand themselves, work was what their lives were mostly made of.

The active peasant land market of the later middle ages shows how finely peasant families had to calibrate resources and how communities consciously and collectively absorbed slippages and changes in relative prosperity. It also shows the political and ethical imagination by which they kept body and soul together. In theory there should have been no land market among villeins, since the land they tilled belonged to the lord.[130] This rather academic point was virtually without application: an acre here, a half-acre there, this strip and that strip would change hands, small exchanges that can be traced in any year on any manor where we can trace anything at all. Freeholders would come to own parcels in villein tenure, and villeins, parcels in freehold. Manorial courts kept vigilance over this brisk shuffle of plots, since a clandestine sale deprived the lord of entry fines (payable when taking up land in customary tenure). On the tenants' part, there was reason to enroll sales with the court, since enrollment gave proof of right. While the lords took care to profit from the transactions, it was a more local system that regulated the sometimes desperate dumping of land. In Cottishall (Norfolk), during the Malthusian nightmare of 1300–1350 (rising pop-

128. See, for example, Dyer, *Standards of Living*, 117–18; Hanawalt describes the activities by which supplementary income could be acquired (*Ties That Bound*, 115–20).

129. However, Harvey speculates that the abbot and monks of Westminster opposed fragmentation of villein holdings not merely to ensure against a loss in customary services, but also to ensure a working population for the demesne lands (*Westminster Abbey*, 212).

130. Pollock and Maitland, *History of English Law* 1:382.

ulation combined with crop failures), land transfers rose with grain prices: people sold land to buy food.[131] An obvious act of desperation (what do you do for grain the next year?), the practice shows just how inadequately buffered against contingency rural families were. The few buffers they had grew not from natural economy or lordly policy, but from village custom, which cushioned these disasters with guarantees.

Cyclical landholding—which allowed a family to shed land it could not farm and reacquire it when necessary—was a common pattern.[132] Ian Blanchard has wondered about the *quondam* clauses that often occur in enrolled land transfers ("A holds X amount of land once [*quondam*] held by B"): whose interest did these clauses serve? He found that in his Derbyshire villages families routinely repurchased the very land they had earlier sold: the alienation, though absolute in legal fact and in the nominal control of the lord, was to the mind of the village temporary. Blanchard thinks the *quondam* clauses witness to a "collective memory";

---

131. Campbell, "Population Pressure." In Cottishall the situation changed after the plague: land transfers no longer fluctuated with prices, and transfers tended to be in larger parcels than the quarter- and half-acres seen before it. Studies of other communities also find larger sales later in the century (I know of no others that collate sales with prices); see Marjorie Keniston McIntosh, *Autonomy and Community: The Royal Manor of Havering, 1200–1500* (Cambridge, Eng., 1986), 122–23; Rosamond Faith, "Berkshire: Fourteenth and Fifteenth Centuries," in P. D. A. Harvey, ed., *The Peasant Land Market in Medieval England* (Oxford, 1984), 119. On the other hand, Rodney Hilton, studying West Midlands society after the plague, still finds many sales involving "most often a few detached acres of arable or meadow" (*The English Peasantry*, 48), as does Barbara Harvey for the Westminster estates in the late fourteenth century (*Westminster Abbey*, 328). It is not clear, however, what these data mean. Strictly speaking, Campbell shows only that after 1350 conveyances *enrolled with the court* were larger and less evidently tied to prices; he does not show that land was no longer sold for food, or even that small transfers became less common. First, the records do not allow comparison of land *prices*. If, after the severe population drop, they fell (with the sudden increase of supply and loss of potential buyers), then more land would of course have been sold to realize the same profit. At the same time, grain prices remained high, around preplague levels, until the mid-1370s, so that roughly the same amount of cash was indeed required for the same provisions. Second, that fewer sales of small parcels after 1350 does not mean that sales in fact decreased. Faced with the need to recruit tenants, landlords significantly lowered entry fines, which were their real reason for enforcing enrollment in the first place (see Faith, "Berkshire," 115–17). And during just this period (and in connection with just this issue) Dyer observes, "On some manors one gains the impression of some administrative slackness in the two decades after the plague, followed by more stringent controls in the 1370s" ("Social and Economic Background"). On Campbell's own evidence (111) these years show the greatest discrepancy between alienations of land and barley prices. It is possible that with entry fines low and administration generally confused, lords did not find it worthwhile to monitor the traffic in small parcels of land.

132. For a close description of these patterns, see Edwin Brezette DeWindt, *Land and People in Holywell-cum-Needingworth: Structures of Tenure and Patterns of Social Organization in an East Midlands Village 1252–1457* (Toronto, 1972), 117–21.

I will quarrel with his phrase later, but they do witness to a collective *ethic* protecting villagers from a permanent loss of land because of a temporary need for cash.[133] It is hard to say why villagers preferred established tenures: their notorious suspicion of strangers might have had something to do with it, their suspicion of accumulation of land within the community perhaps more.[134] But it is worth noting that no one could be certain of avoiding forever the desperate sale of land; the reversionary rights of all functioned as insurance for each. And the first concern of the community was to keep land under plow; villagers themselves disciplined those who left land uncultivated.[135] Those who did not have to sell, but who could not for the time being afford to cultivate their entire holding (whose children were not old enough to help with tillage and harvest, for example), might sell land only if they could be sure of retrieving it in better days: without the guarantee they might be slow to sell and thereby leave land untilled. Reversionary rights stated in effect that the community was bound to maintain each of its members, because its collective fortunes depended on it; they allowed individual families to adjust their holdings to their ability to cultivate and assured the village that no land would be left pointlessly fallow.

The sentiments of friendship and kinship that underlay this collective ethic were economically functional and were accompanied by a corre-

133. Blanchard, "Industrial Employment," 241–48. Blanchard goes on to point out that village jurors oversaw and enforced these informal reversionary rights. Before Blanchard, DeWindt offered a different explanation: *quondam* and *nuper* imply "that the holding of the property had not been continuous but that it had reverted to the direct control of the [lord] for a period of time in the absence of immediate claimants" (*Land and People*, 130). Though this explanation could account for the *meaning* of the clause, it cannot explain its *motives*, why the lord or anyone else would want this information. There is a better explanation for the lord's motives in recording the *quondam*: it provides a reference that keeps manorial documents up-to-date, so that a parcel of land now held by B but "once" held by A—and which appears in a survey, say, under A's name—could be traced in the survey. This explanation, unlike DeWindt's, can accommodate Blanchard's data and interpretations.

134. On the former, see Hanawalt, *Ties That Bound*, 236; on the latter, see Hilton, *English Peasantry*, 41.

135. On this issue, see Hilton's nuanced observations: "On some issues, the village notables acted strongly. This must normally have been in collaboration with the lord's authority, though by no means necessarily as a result of the initiative of the lord, his council, or his steward. As one would expect, non-conformity with the expectations which the village community had of its members as cultivators led to intervention. At Moor in Worcestershire, as a result of presentment by the homage in 1374, William Heyne forfeited his half yardland for not maintaining it, and his children were refused their inheritance. . . . At Cleeve Prior in 1435, nine tenants were presented for not cultivating their holdings" (*English Peasantry*, 55).

sponding suspicion and surveillance: festivities like midsummer and Corpus Christi, fostering "good amity" by making the community visible to itself in its relation to the land, were matched by more coercive demands for mutual visibility on workdays. Areas of open-field farming have left sets of regulations concerning tillage, pasture, and harvest: "the usage throughout the land called Bie-laws" as a royal justice called them in the 1370s.[136] These by-laws, formulated "by the consent and agreement of the whole community," as the phrase often went, were sometimes enrolled with the lord's court, but were created by the villages themselves to address their own needs.[137] They regulated the seasons and schedules required by a fully developed common-field system—the pattern of field rotation, the dates when beasts could be grazed on the stubble of the fields, the times for plowing—and they addressed problems of discipline that throw light on rural self-understanding, on the vocabularies by which villagers explained themselves to themselves.[138] A few examples from regulations concerning harvest: No one is to give another grain while in the fields.[139] There is to be no open path from a

136. Warren O. Ault, "Village By-Laws by Common Consent," *Speculum* 29 (1954): 379.

137. Ault, "By-Laws," 383–84.

138. Surviving by-laws come exclusively from areas of common-field farming (where land was held in interspersed strips, rotation was agreed upon, and the arable was common pasture between growing seasons)—as opposed both to mere open fields (where the arrangement of holdings was similar, but where there was no common grazing or rotation) and to enclosed and separate farmsteads. True common fields were regionally distributed, found most commonly outside the main centers of the 1381 rising: not at all in Kent, only in the northwest of Essex, rarely in Suffolk and Norfolk, more commonly in Cambridgeshire and Hertfordshire. But there are several reasons for taking the evidence of by-laws, and common-field tillage generally, into account when discussing the ideologies of agriculture throughout England. First, while common-field systems were regionally specific, open-field arrangements were "liable to be found in any part of England, wherever people lived in close proximity to one another, in hamlets or villages" (Joan Thirsk, Preface to Orwin and Orwin, *Open Fields*, x). Second, those areas of southern England untouched by rebellion—the weald of Kent and Surrey, for example—were also those virtually without open fields. Third, open-field (as opposed to common-field) systems, though they required no regulations regarding pasturing and rotation, nevertheless required attention to the problems I am about to discuss. The absence of *recorded* by-laws does not mean their nonexistence, particularly in those areas (such as southeast England) where manorial records are slighter. Fourth—and most tenuous—now that common fields are seen as a comparatively late response to the problem that feudal arrangements imposed on agriculture generally (rather than as a deep, distant, racial characteristic of the Germanic peoples; see Grenville Astill, "Rural Settlement: The Toft and the Croft," in Astill and Annie Grant, eds., *The Countryside of Medieval England* [Oxford, 1988], 37), they can perhaps be seen as exemplary forms of the strategic adaptation to lordship.

139. Great Horwood (Bucks), 1322: "Et quod aliquis ipsorum non det alicui aliquod bladum in campo" (Ault, *Open-Field Husbandry*, 60).

close to the fields.[140] Those carting grain are to leave the fields only by highways.[141] And—probably the most common injunction—grain may be carted away only by daylight.[142] The point of all these was to keep everybody visible to everybody else during harvest and to keep the ownership of all grain clear at all times: where the strips under cultivation were mixed together, it was only too easy to sneak away with stolen sheaves. Thus they required everyone to work alongside everyone else and in the daylight, to move the grain in an easily observable way (in carts) and by easily observable paths (the common highway), and to handle only their own sheaves. The presence and observation of the whole community served both to check and to protect each of its members, to ensure the integrity of each family's production: to forestall (in a word) theft.

"Lokke þat hobbe robbyoure be wele chastysede" (Carter): this image of delinquency in the rebel letters, and the charge of theft (theft that was also treason) for which Archbishop Sudbury lost his life, issued from deep in the thought-world of village communities. Just how deep can be measured by the rural repertory of actionable insults, of which the manors of Ramsey Abbey provide some fine examples. At Little Stukeley in 1288, Hugh Greling complained that John Dike had "called him thief [*furem*] and other enormities"; at King's Ripton in 1290, Henry of Swindon complained that John Stalker had defamed him, calling him "thief [*latronem*], traitor [*seductorem*; Maitland suggests the translation], homicide, and other enormities."[143] More instructive than particular instances from manorial courts are the examples of defamation chosen for precedent books used by bailiffs in such courts: these treatises, guides to conducting court business and formularies for enrolling it, were copied from actual court rolls to teach the bailiff how to hear and record the business he would most often meet with. In one treatise, a tenant complains that one Stephen Carpenter "assailed him with rustic words [*vileynes paroles*], such that he called him a thief and a false man [*laron e deleaus*]."[144] Another, the *Modus tenendi curias*, gives this for-

140. Newington (Oxon), 1348: "nec quis habeat semitam apertam extra clausum suum" (Ault, 65).

141. Great Horwood (Bucks), 1357: "Item quod nullus glaniator eat de campo nisi per iiijor altas venellas sub eadem pena" (Ault, 66).

142. E.g., Great Horwood (Bucks), 1357: "Item quod nullus cariabit nec cariare faciet blada sua de campo nocturno tempore" (Ault, 66).

143. Maitland, *Select Pleas in Manorial Courts*, 109, 116.

144. Maitland and Baildon, *Court Baron*, 27.

mula: "A complains of B that on such-and-such a day and place he insulted the said A with contentious words, calling him false, perverse, and an outlaw traitor [*illegalem traditorem*], and accused him of committing theft of such-and-such a thing [*imposuit ei furtum fecisse de tali re*]."[145] "Thief" and "theft" were fighting words, formulaic insults that implied other, corollary insults: "traitor," "false man," "disloyal man."[146] The thief of the rural imagination was not the open bandit but the appropriating sneak: a man *plenum* (or a woman *plenam*) *fraudibus*, a *falsum virum*, as other litigated insults put it.[147] You don't get any worse than a thief, the village bosom-serpent who cheats neighbors of their scarce resources. A thief is a "traitor"; and suddenly the taunts launched against Sudbury ("Where is the traitor to the realm? Where is the despoiler of the common people?") make concrete sense, their Wycliffian articulation rooted in experience;[148] and Carter's opposition between "peres þe plowman" (adjured to "dyȝt . . . corne") and "hobbe robbyoure" reveals its origin in the village.

But if "theft" held a central place in the moral and social lexicon of the village, it must have had an antonym. Abjuring theft, what were you and what did you do? There is more to the story, mentioned above, of John Stalker and Henry Swindon, the scandal of King's Ripton. Swindon complained that Stalker "did not content himself" with merely spoken abuse, but "the next Sunday sent a letter to Lord Roger of Ashridge, clerk of our Lord the King and rector of the church at King's Ripton; the letter violently defamed this Henry with the words reported above, and even claimed *that he was not worthy to live in the village of Ripton, or in any village*, since he was a homicide, having killed Nicholas [Stalker]; for which cause the said Lord Roger took three years from [Henry's] term at the church of King's Ripton, which he held in farm from Lord Roger."[149] The passage is interesting, and not only because it reveals that the contumelious Henry—who had been accused of assault the previous April and was amerced the following December for assault and theft—was vicar of the village church. It also shows what was pretty

145. Maitland and Baildon, *Court Baron*, 83.

146. This last point is clear from the final example, where the asymmetry of the syntax shows that the first three terms were the product of an actual accusation of theft.

147. From Ogbourn (Wilts), 1290 (Maitland, *Select Pleas in Manorial Courts*, 36); and Smithscroft (Hunts), 1287 (Anne Reiber DeWindt and Edwin Brezette DeWindt, eds., *Royal Justice and the Medieval English Countryside* [Toronto, 1981], 466).

148. See ch. 2, n. 78 above.

149. Maitland, *Select Pleas in Manorial Courts*, 116; my emphasis.

much the worst that could be said of people: that they should leave. To the accusation of theft was now added a closely related accusation of homicide.[150] Another case in another Ramsey manor, Broghton (Hunts), makes a less specific charge by way of an equally specific vocabulary. The pledges there say that John son of Agnes Metheu "is not at all faithful [*non est omnino fidelis*], and he withdrew. Therefore let him be seized if he come within the liberty."[151] The charge was vague—they knew what they meant and evidently there was plenty to know—and the vagueness is interesting in itself: their shorthand for one so offensive that he was advised to refuse himself the village before others did it for him was *non est omnino fidelis*. Of course the chief pledges did not really say that he was not *fidelis*; that is the bailiff's Latin. But we can guess what their word was: they said he was not *trewe*.

Or maybe they said he was not *trewe man*, but in either case it becomes clear why the rebel letters found in "Trewman" a name as recognizably rural as "Milner" or "Carter." The opposite of being a thief was not just *not* being a thief, because theft was not just theft (to rehearse this again, with one last nuance): within the "knowable community" of the village, any offense was a personal offense against those whose names and faces and lives one knew, a violation of the trust everyone had to put in everyone else: a violation of *trewpe*.[152] Some people had to be millers and carters; all people had to be *trewe men, trewe women*.[153]

150. This is one of several cases I have seen in which someone leveled an accusation of homicide that was either obviously and purely formal (as in n. 144 above) or was patently false (Nicholas Stalker was apparently still alive); those who have worked more with court rolls have perhaps seen others. Since it is hard to imagine that anyone would seriously have made an accusation of murder when the supposed victim was walking the village streets, I take it that homicide too functioned as a formulaic insult, habitually joined with an accusation of theft. I have no idea exactly what it meant, or how it related to the other insults I have mentioned. It might be significant that Knighton describes the rebels leading Sudbury to his death "as if he had been accused of theft or homicide"; see ch. 2 above.

151. Ault, *Court Rolls of the Abbey of Ramsey*, 199–201.

152. "Knowable community" is of course Raymond Williams's phrase, which I like because it suggests that everyday experience is informed by station and custom: "But a knowable community, within country life as anywhere else, is still a matter of consciousness, and of continuing as well as day-to-day experience. In the village as in the city there is division of labour, there is the contrast of social position, and then necessarily there are alternative points of view" (*The Country and the City* [Oxford, 1973], 166).

153. The Ramsey view in December 1297 yoked the judgment of untruth with the charge (n. 62 above) of being "useless," when Alan cum le Gere's pledges for good conduct were rejected because Alan "is useless and unfaithful" (DeWindt, *Court Rolls of Ramsey*, 91). Robert Mannyng, adapting the *Manuel des pechees* at the beginning of the fourteenth century for lay audiences of all ranks, explains the unworthy reception of the Eucharist

Trewþe was a practical necessity of common life and had to be enforced; the need for enforcement created practices, both informal and institutional, that gave form to the year's work and enabled it. One advantage to open-field husbandry, less often mentioned now but hardly abandoned, was that less prosperous smallholders could share the plow (an indispensable and quite expensive tool);[154] its efficient use would have required cooperation between those who needed it, that cooperation in production which, in 1381, Milner's letter used to figure insurgent solidarity ("jakke mylner asket help to turne hys mylne aright"). Though to the bureaucratic formalism of the courts such arrangements would have looked ad hoc, they belonged to what DeWindt has nicely called the elaborately "contractual" character of the village, where mutual dependence and cooperation were routinely and publicly embodied in formal agreements,[155] in an institution woven so completely into the texture of village life that its appearance in court rolls only hints at its ubiquity. This is personal pledging, a practice so broadly employed and so precisely defined that it has some claim to be thought a principle of local organization.[156] It required finding one or more (usually two) neighbors who would vouch for something: good behavior, appearance in court, payment of a fine, performance of a service, repayment of a debt. Some pledges offered themselves (the noun "pledge" designates the person, not the promise) in court business, but many, and probably many more, were employed without the court's mediation: pledges for debt, for example, turn up on the court rolls only when lenders sued for collection. In the king's courts a pledge was sometimes called a *fideiussor*,[157] and the term appears occasionally on manorial court rolls to describe peasant pledges as well. A *fideiussor* guaranteed *fides*, stood surety for another's *trewþe*. A pledge for debt fell liable if it went unpaid;

---

with exactly this normative opposition: "And ȝyt men seye here synne ys gref / þat brynge a trewe man on a þef" (*Handlyng Synne*, ll. 10269–70).

154. Orwin and Orwin, *Open Fields*; Ault, *Self-Directing Activities*, 5; Lynn White, Jr., *Medieval Technology and Social Change* (Oxford, 1962), 41–57.

155. DeWindt, *Land and People*, 256, 256n.

156. For discussions of pledging and pledging patterns in particular communities, see J. Ambrose Raftis, *Tenure and Mobility: Studies in the Social History of the Medieval English Village* (Toronto, 1964), 95–104; DeWindt, *Land and People*, 242–64; Elaine Clark, "Debt Litigation in a Late Medieval English Vill," in Raftis, ed., *Pathways to Medieval Peasants* (Toronto, 1981), 261–62; Edward Britton, *The Community of the Vill: A Study in the History of the Family and Village Life in Fourteenth-Century England* (Toronto, 1977), 27, 103–9; R. M. Smith, "Kin and Neighbors in a Thirteenth-Century Suffolk Community," *Journal of Family History* 4 (1979): 219–56.

157. A term from civil law (Maitland and Pollock, *History of English Law* 2:191).

a pledge for a fine owed it if the delinquent defaulted; a pledge for court appearance or good behavior could be amerced for the other's failures. Only a small minority of pledges secured the faith of relations; pledges were sought outside the family.[158] Doubtless the powerful sentiments of connection, of "good amity among neighbors" expressed around the bonfire and the consecrated bread, underwrote the reciprocal willingness to stand risks; but good amity or not, that willingness would have been short-lived if pledges had often found themselves holding the bag.

In fact, the system implied its own guarantees, besides the obvious one that a bad risk might never obtain another pledge.[159] She or he would also have to live among the villagers between securing pledges and—if only by semantic deduction—defaulting on a *fideiussor* displayed inadequate *fides*, insufficient *trewþe*. Defaulters probably found other areas of cooperation closed; in any case, the system unmistakably depended on coercive communal sanctions and on the presumption that a person's good faith was a matter of common concern. Pledging, like the harvest by-laws, created a formalized means of mutual surveillance by which villagers enforced *trewþe* and organized production. It was a political practice that regulated the relations within the village community.

But it was also a practice of the lord's court, where fines, court appearances, good behavior, restitution, and performance of repairs were guaranteed by pledge; manorial custom used pledging to make peasants themselves the lord's occasional enforcers, as the appointment of tenants as reeves made them the lord's regular enforcers. In fact, lords used the same language of communal fidelity in trying to secure the submission of their villeins. One precedent book gives the form of a tenant's fealty. Kneeling and kissing the book, the tenant is to swear: "Hear this, Lord Bailiff N. etc. that I, N., will not be a thief [*latro*], nor a friend of thieves, that I will conceal no theft or thief [*furtem nec furem*], but will report it to those in charge, that I will keep faith [*fidem*] with our lord King Henry of England and to my lord Lord N., and will be obedient to the instructions of his bailiffs."[160]

---

158. See n. 166 below.

159. On which, see Britton, *Community of the Vill*, 27. Explanation of some cases might be had from the suggestion, offered by Martin Pimsler, that prosperous villagers would sometimes *sell* their truth, thereby mitigating the risk in advance ("Solidarity in the Medieval Village? The Evidence of Personal Pledging at Elton, Huntingdonshire," *JBS* 17 [1977]: 1–11, and Dyer, *Lords and Peasants*, 267). But in the nature of the case, this must have been a subspecies of the practice.

160. Maitland, *Court Baron*, 76–77.

Looked at in one way, the lords thus insinuated their power into the relations of their villagers, using the self-interest of each to lever them all against each other: a Foucauldian nightmare of power internalized. But, as Dyer has observed in another connection, there is always another way to look at such seigneurial conveniences.[161] The lords' reliance on pledging, and indeed all their delegations of authority to the community, allowed their tenants to edit what would be done before the court and therefore what would reach the ears of the lord or his officials. For example, Barbara Harvey has described Westminster's Abbey's experiments with term leases after the plague, when depopulation had sunk land values and lords could get tenants only by arrangements disadvantageous to themselves; the abbey apparently wanted to lease its customary land for fixed terms, so that it could lease them again, more profitably, once land values rose. But the abbey itself soon tried to abandon the practice; as Harvey observes, peasants would only have leased for term if they could in fact expect to hold the lands indefinitely.[162] She thinks the experiment failed because of a "customary" preference for renewing leases, but custom does not attach so rapidly to novelty without someone's agency. What probably happened was that local officials (who were drawn from among the villagers themselves) saw to the protection of their fellows—maintaining their rights in the land they had leased by some mechanism like the one that maintained reversionary rights—and thereby annulled the rationale of the term leases. By using tenants as its source of information and judgment, the lord's court gave tenants the power to shape its record. The tenants of St. Albans resented the streamlined, civil-trained baronial council that absorbed much of the traditional business of the manorial court.[163] Their resentment testifies to the advantages the court held for them: it was their ground as well as the lord's. The court depended on the *trewþe* tenants owed to the lord; this left him at the mercy of the *trewþe* tenants owed to each other.

"Stonde manlyche togedyr in trewþe. and helpeʒ trewþe. and trewþe schal helpe ʒowe" (Ball₂): this long chapter has tried to suggest not just what *trewþe* meant, but how it meant, where it got its range of function

---

161. Christopher C. Dyer, "Power and Conflict in the Medieval English Village," in Hooke, ed., *Medieval Villages*, 28.

162. Harvey, *Westminster Abbey*, 252–54.

163. Ada Elizabeth Levett, *Studies in Manorial History*, ed. H. M. Cam, M. Coate, and L. S. Sutherland (New York, 1938), 20–40.

and sense. In Ball's letter, *trewþe* is where the rebels must "stonde," a point of moral reference, but it is also something that needs help, and also something that can offer it. It is a standard of behavior, and the fidelity that creates the standard ("helpeȝ trewþe"), and—bringing the sentence back to the "trinite. fadur and sone and holy gost" with which it began—God himself ("and trewþe schal helpe ȝowe"). The word is a concept only because it is first a social practice; *in trewþe* describes a relation (standing "togedyr") that makes *trewþe* a normative concept to which the rebels can appeal and which also indicates the presence of divine grace: Ball₁ imagines heaven not as a hierarchy but as a community of mutual assistance ("Nowe is tyme lady helpe to iheſu þi sone. and þi sone to his fadur. to mak a gode ende. in þe name of þe trinite. of þat [þat] is begunne"). I have said above that in these sentences, *trewþe* is imagined not as something to be searched for, but as something already possessed; but it is possessed only if it continues to be remade ("helpeȝ trewþe. and trewþe schal helpe ȝowe").

And it is possessed and remade in the countryside. These sentences in Ball₂ lead to a little allegory of the deadly sins: "Nowe regneþ pride in pris. and couetys is hold wys. and lecherye wiþ[outen shame] and glotonye withouten blame Enuye regniþ wiþ tresone. and slouthe is take in grete sesone."[164] Against *trewþe* Ball sets the pride and covetousness and the other evils which the insurgents claim to fight; but the battle is geographically as well as morally articulated, between the villages where *trewþe* lives and the places where *reigning* has been done—halls and courts, seigneurial and royal. Ball₃ draws a corresponding, though not identical, contrast: "bee war of gyle in borugh." What is he talking about? He virtually recapitulates the advice a few lines later: "knoweþ ȝour frend fro ȝour foo." "Frend" is a resonant term of relation in village vocabulary. "Frends" are first of all family,[165] those who give help and support,[166] those near you whom you can count on. This, I

---

164. These verses seem to derive directly from a preacher's jingle on the sins; the differences are discussed in Green, "John Ball's Letters," 182–83. However, in thinking about the conclusions Green draws from differences between Ball's version and the one in Bodl. MS Rawlinson D.893, it must be remembered that the verses must have undergone considerable changes in the course of oral and written transmission.

165. See, for example, William Thorpe, speaking of his family's expense in having him ordained: "But when I came to years of discretion, I had no will to be priest; and therefore my friends were right heavy to me" (*Examination*, 115); and Langland's Will's account of the same thing: "When y ȝong was, many ȝer hennes, / My fader and my frendes foende me to scole" (*Piers Plowman*, ed. Pearsall, C.5.35–36).

166. On the family as an organizing term of social understanding, see Bossy, "Blood

think, makes it clear what Ball's "gyle in borough" is about. *Gyle* is an antonym of *trewþe*,[167] as *vill* is of *borough*. Ball is not concerned with any particular "borough": he is projecting a rhetorical image of village relations as a model for the kind of rule the rising imagined, and a contrast with the kind of rule it opposed. "Gyle" is the plague of the towns; it is also the plague of clerkly administration. Opposed to both is the contractual, face-to-face, communally sanctioned life of the rural village from which the rebels drew their principles of political reform.[168]

The letters embodied a rural political *idiom* distinct from the borough's and the manor's, a vocabulary to embody rural demands. Perambulating the abbey's lands as they would their own, the St. Albans rebels declared them under their own jurisdiction, and under their own *kind* of jurisdiction: the consensual, contractual, truth-pledging jurisdiction of the village community. Building bonfires from documents, rebels throughout England declared that the communities defined by

---

and Baptism," 135–38, and "Mass as a Social Institution." The importance of family, as a sociological category and as an imaginative term in rural England, has of course been contested by Alan Macfarlane, whose study of ownership and the family, *The Origins of English Individualism: The Family, Property, and Social Transition* (Oxford, 1978), has received probably less attention than it deserves because of its polemical preoccupation with the word "peasant." It might be said that although Macfarlane claims that the family was thoroughly subordinated to the individual, his evidence might equally suggest that the medieval bonds of kinship expressed themselves not in the legal status of land (its ownership and heritability) but in the pragmatic manipulation of it. I am also doubtful about the less controverted conclusions of the Toronto-school historians, who assert that the family was subordinated to the individual on the one hand and to the community on the other. They appeal to the virtual nonexistence of intrafamilial pledging; DeWindt, for example, finds that 77 percent of the pledges in Holywell were outside the family (*Land and People*, 249); in Redgrave, the figure was 90 percent (Smith, "Kin and Neighbors," 224). But this evidence is at least ambiguous. The figure of intrafamilial pledges (23 percent in DeWindt's village, for instance, and 10 percent in Smith's) is in a way misleading, for the category is dominated by husbands pledging for their wives. This suggests that, *outside* the obviously exceptional instances of husband-wife pledging, there was a near taboo on pledging for one's own family: to pledge for, say, a brother did not quite count. If family were an unimportant category of relation, then pledging patterns should record an indifferent use of kin and non-kin; the almost complete absence of intrafamilial pledging testifies to the importance of the family rather than otherwise.

167. As it functions, for example, in Trewman: "falsnes and gyle haviþ regned to longe & trewþe. hat bene sette under a lokke."

168. The opposition of town to country calls up a particularly thorny problem; the very idea of such an opposition has been a matter of some controversy. Rodney Hilton provides a neat and subtle taxonomy of the kinds of urban community and suggestions for understanding in what senses it was continuous with the countryside and in what senses it was not ("Towns in English Feudal Society" [1982], rpt. in his *Class Conflict*, 175–86; see also his discussion in *English Peasantry*, ch. 5—which he begins with this line from Ball). The controversy over the economic structure is not really to the point, since as a kind of *local* community structure, it was still available to Ball and the rebels as a type to contrast with the village community that informed their rhetoric.

bonfires would replace the seigneurial government that the documents upheld. These gestures enacted what the St. Albans rebels declared more discursively by pronouncing that "there would be no lord, but only king and commons"; what the Essex rebels evoked by their password "Wyth kynge Richarde and wyth the trew communes"; what Wat Tyler meant by insisting "that there should be no law but the law of Winchester"—that the native forms of rural self-government would now govern the realm at large. The letters give this assertion a self-consciously symbolic cast: the countryside has its own idiom of political judgment, which discloses principles of order and self-rule adequate to ruling a nation.

This is the time to give some substance to an assertion I made back in chapter 1, that the rebels were looking to re-create, not destroy, documentary culture: to ask on the one hand what the political culture of the village had to do with this documentary culture of the commons and realm, and on the other to ask what kind of new documentary culture these spare, odd letters were supposed to represent. "Jakke trewman doþ ȝow to understande þat falsnes and gyle haviþ regned to longe & trewþe. hat bene sette under a lokke. and fal[s]nes regneth in euerylk flokke. no man may come trewþe to. but he syng si dedero." When I first discussed these lines, I cursorily glossed *trewþe* as "justice," but by now its opposition to "falsnes and gyle" should have a more specific resonance. *Trewþe* connotes the rural culture of contractual reliability; yet "trewþe . . . under a lokke" figures the restricted clerical culture of documentary law, locked up in archives and (metaphorically) in Latin and Anglo-French. How could *trewþe* have come to designate these disenfranchising documents in the first place? The answer, I think, is that the rebels believed that *trewþe*—contractual faithfulness; mutual supervision, protection, and enforcement; the whole range of rights and responsibilities and penalties properly overseen by the "common assent and judgment of the whole community"—had been *supplanted* by bureaucratic and judicial writing; taken away, enclosed in alien forms and languages, and locked up. For relations—the social practices of by-laws, pledging, local policing, and above all local memory—lords had substituted parchment, ink, and the money needed to procure them ("speke. spende and spede").

This formulation might seem to imply the straw argument I dismissed in chapter 1: that the destruction of documents was orality's revenge against literacy. But that opposition (always a blunt instrument anyway) would be wholly out of place here. Local memory—the informal archive of the contractual *trewþe* by which the village ran itself—*needed* the written record, even hid behind it to maintain partial independence from seigneurial control. Three examples will show what I mean. Blanchard (as I noted earlier) has said that *quondam* and *nuper* clauses were products of "collective memory."[169] But that is exactly what they were not. Such clauses (recording that B now holds lands once held by A) would have been entered when B took seisin from A. This is not "collective memory"; it is a collective aide-mémoire. If there had been a collective memory capacious enough to recall details of everyone's tenure, villagers would not have needed the *quondam* clauses at all. And they did need them: the ethic of reversionary rights could not have survived the brisk traffic of the peasant land market, could not even have been thought of, without the court rolls. This local principle of village self-rule emerged as it did only because of the lords' documentary practices. The same is true of by-laws. At Great Horwood (Bucks) in 1327, the court roll noted that "all tenants free and customary agree to all the harvest ordinances made in the preceding year, and with the same sanctions, with this addition. . . ."[170] In other words, when the villagers in assembly added to or altered the by-laws that had accumulated over previous years, only the novelties and changes were recorded, without restating existing regulations,[171] so that the court roll was the only usable record of the provisions; indeed, a complete record would have required a search of the rolls. Again, the community treated the rolls as something available to its own use. Finally, the enrollment of land transfers implies the same. A clear record of titles was of no particular concern of the lord, who was satisfied as long as the entry fines were paid, rents and services continued uninterrupted, and his lordship of the holding was not impaired (by sale to an unfeoffed freeman, for example). Peasants enrolled transfers to give proof of title in local disputes, disputes which, though adjudicated in the manorial court, were of concern more to the

169. See n. 133 above.

170. "Omnes liberi et custumarii concedunt omnes ordinaciones autumpnales factas in anno preterito et sub eadem pena et hoc adiunctam" (Ault, *Open-Field Husbandry*, 60).

171. This can be seen in most of the communities whose by-laws Ault has edited. For example, the articles of Great Horwood's by-laws for 1388, 1389, and 1391 concern quite specialized matters, and almost no article in them overlaps with an article in the others; see the entries for 1388, April 1389, August 1389, and August 1391, in Ault, 69–70.

community than to the lord.[172] All these are unofficial uses of the record the lord created, *adaptive* uses, for purposes local to the community.

This chapter began in Bocking, in northern Essex; it ends a little to the west in the village of Thaxted, which also rose in 1381 and burned documents held in the manor house. Twelve years after the rising, the lord had the manor surveyed. Next to the summary of receipts from customary tenants is a curious note:

> And note that as it was said that the tenants have among themselves a custumal other than that destroyed at the time of the rebellion & do not wish to tell the lord's council at present, therefore by the custom of the council now present the custom is that they pay for their works as is above specified, & therefore &c.[173]

It is not immediately clear what this means. The editor speaks of an "attempt of the tenants to concoct a custumal of their own (? after the failure of the rebellion)."[174] But if they had concocted their own custumal, they would have tailored it to their advantage; why then refuse to hand it over ("do not wish to tell the lord's council") once the original had been destroyed and their version was the only record of rents and services? A different explanation makes better sense of their refusal. If what they had was not a custumal of their own devising, but a copy that they had made of the *lord's* custumal, *before* the rebellion, then the lord's council would have had good reason to ask for it, and the tenants good reason to refuse: they had burned the original precisely to erase the memory of the duties it recorded. And if it was indeed the lord's custumal they had copied, they must have done so before rebellion had become even a possibility: why record what you are about to destroy? And if they had copied it well before the rising, they must have felt that they could use it in conducting their collective lives and work, and perhaps in evading the lord's demands.

The village of Thaxted, with their unofficial copy of a document meant to control them, might stand as an emblem for all villages in their variously unofficial uses of official records. To call these uses unofficial

172. "The entry of title in the court rolls was to a customary tenant as a charter was to a free man" (Campbell, "Population Pressure, Inheritance, and the Land Market," 108; and see Faith, "Berkshire," 111).

173. K. C. Newton, *Thaxted in the Fourteenth Century: An Account of the Manor and Borough, with Translated Texts*, Essex Record Office Publications 33 (Chelmsford, 1960), 58; the entire survey is translated pp. 32–66.

174. Newton, *Thaxted*, 32.

is not of course to call them subversive, or even to suggest that the lords would always have minded.[175] But it is to say that local communities adapted the lords' documentation to their own local needs—often without the lords' knowledge—and created practices that depended on it. The villages that rebelled did not need the rebel letters to make them "textual communities," because they already were: the village community shaped its forms of self-rule around the writing in its midst. This political idiom of the countryside had existed around, behind, and under the protective shadow of documentary culture; in 1381, it spoke out loud through documents instead of quietly operating beneath them. "Jon Balle gretyth ȝow wele alle & doþ ȝowe to understande. he haþ rungen ȝoure belle" (Ball₁)—the bell of the parish church, which issued summonses and alarms, the public voice of the village's self-policing. By making that bell a metaphor for the summons he issued in documentary form, Ball transformed village practice into the vocabulary of literate government, announcing not only that the commons were laying claim to documentary culture, but that in doing so, they were revealing a documentary prowess they already, collectively, had.

But who were "they"? The question has haunted the whole book; in a more general form, it has haunted the writing of rural history for a century. Could the English peasantry be sensibly called a class? Or did the most prosperous villagers have more in common with the minor lords than with their fellows? When Hilton speaks of "class conflict" in the middle ages, he means conflict between lords and tenants;[176] when Father Raftis and his Toronto students speak of it, they mean conflict between village elites and their local underlings.[177] And of course both

175. However, Levett's point, which I cited earlier (n. 163 above)—that the councils of the great lords often absorbed business that would ordinarily have been within the competence of their manorial courts—might be explained by the advantage that would accrue to the lords from rationalizing manorial custom, and, more important, removing responsibility for its interpretation and execution from the village community, to block the kind of ambiguities that the villages often exploited through the courts. If this is right, it means that the the the abbot of St. Albans, at least, may have come to suspect that his tenants were using his court in ways he did not approve of.

176. Though not only that: "The stratification of the peasantry was one of the most important developments in the English countryside in the fourteenth and fifteenth centuries, and even in the scanty records of Leicester Abbey we can see how it must have been that the rich peasant and the day labourer became separate agricultural classes of a new type" (Hilton, *The Economic Development of Some Leicestershire Estates in the Fourteenth and Fifteenth Centuries* [Oxford, 1947], 94–95).

177. Keith Wrightson, "Medieval Villagers in Perspective" (review of Britton, *Community of the Vill*), *Peasant Studies* 7 (1978): 209.

are right. The difficulty is particularly vexing with regard to the rising. The holder of a yardland, as I noted before, might use the Statute of Laborers, like a lord, to compel work from his fellows, and Hilton himself has suggested that wealthier peasants may have rebelled in part to break the lords' control of the Statute of Laborers, so that they themselves might enjoy its benefits.[178] Those who led the revolt were in the main those who led the villages, and those who had followed them in more routine matters followed them also in this.[179] But this does not answer the question; it only rephrases it. Did the rising dupe most villagers into fighting for the interests of the prosperous few? Certainly the insurgent hope of extending the forms of local self-government to the government of the realm, if successful, would have dramatically augmented the power of existing leaders. But the most striking thing about the rebel demands—freedom from the statute, freedom from villeinage, low fixed rents—is that they would have benefited the least prosperous as well as the most. Were the most prosperous peasants more like minor lords than like less prosperous peasants? In some ways, yes; but then minor lords did not rebel. To imagine that classes are fixed or given is to imagine that a single standard determines whose interests lie with whose and against whose, that there is a single, natural system of stratification and a single, natural site of conflict over resources. Where we locate class divisions depends on where we look from, how close or distant our perspective and how local or global our questions; but it does not depend only on that. Classes can make themselves by choice.

The rebel letters were a way of making a class. In asserting that literacy existed where it did not belong, they drew the class line, the line that separated the exploited from the exploiters, at exactly the point where writing was controlled: those who in the accepted and public senses *owned* writing—the royal bureaucracy; the manorial bureaucracy; the clerks who served both; the gentry who worked as sheriffs and coroners and escheators; jurors; lawyers—became the enemy, and those who did not closed ranks.

178. Hilton, "Peasant Movements in England Before 1381."

179. "Most of the leading rebels came from the peasant élite. . . . In 1381 the same people continued to act as leaders, now in opposition to authority rather than as collaborators. There were also among the rebels, perhaps even in a majority, poorer people whose names are not commonly recorded, though they are represented among our fourteen by two landless youths, Thomas Draper and William Metefeld junior, and by the Lakenheath alewife, Margaret Wrighte" (Dyer, "The Rising of 1381 in Suffolk," 276).

5

Insurgency Remembered

The story of how the rising was remembered is the story of how it was forgotten, of the cultural and psychic machinery that engaged to keep it in the preterite. What happened in Corpus Christi week finally spilled more ink than blood, and nobody will be surprised that the agencies of power and record moved to transform the rising, to absorb it and use it for their purposes. This process had achieved canonical form by the time the king's chancellor, Michael de la Pole, informed the lords and commons assembled for the Westminster Parliament of 1383 that the sovereign needed readier obedience, since "the rising, as you know, was a rebellion first of all against [the king's] minor servants, then against the greater officers of the realm, then against the king himself. Just as, therefore, such rebellion was, and remains, the source and beginning of mischief and trouble in the realm, so then in true obedience to the king and his servants lies the basis of peace and quiet in the realm, as the obedience the gentles showed the king during the rising demonstrates."[1] Sir Michael's poker-faced tautology (that rebellion was the cause of rebellion) played tactically on local fears for state purposes, making the rising a bogey to scare up parliamentary cooperation. So too the commons in 1381 used the rising in their long struggle against livery and maintenance;[2] bishops and academics to discredit Wyclif;[3] Walsingham

---

1. "Laquel primerement estoit rebell' as ditz petitz Ministres, & puis as grantes Officers del Roialme, & al drain au Roi mesmes, com bien le savez. Et si avant come Rebellion si estoit & est le sours & comencement de meschief & truboill' deinz le Roialme, si est areremain verroi Obeissance au Roi & ses Ministres foundement de tut paix & quietee en mesme le Roialme, sicome clerement apparoit par l'Obeissance qe les gentils firent au Roi en dit Insurrection" (*Rp* 3.150).

2. The commons suggested that the "grevouses oppression en pays par la outrageouse multitude braceours de quereles, & maintenours, qui son come Rois en pays" were among the causes that "firent les dites menues Comunes lour moever, & faire le meschief q'ils firent en dit riot" (*Rp* 3.100).

3. For William of Rymington, see ch. 2, n. 68 above.

to discredit Wyclif;[4] Walsingham to discredit the friars;[5] Walsingham to rehabilitate John of Gaunt, and Knighton to lionize him.[6] But these appropriations, because unsurprising, are not very interesting—virtual memorials of the forgetting, of what about the revolt had to be forgotten before it could be harnessed to rhetorical use. But the more traumatic effects of the rising, its memory *and* its forgetting, were more subtly marked, in the mistakes and evasions that spot its record and in the unattributed adjustments and revisions that reshaped literary and historiographical enterprises at the close of the fourteenth century.

It is curious, or from another perspective most ordinary, that when we speak of the "memory" of the rising we mean how it looked in retrospect to those who were threatened by it, rather than to those who made it. Those rebels who did not lose their lives to a capital sentence took them up again, like John Norford of Childerditch (Essex), who, while continuing to work his lands, avoided the summonses to the lords' court on charges of rebellion until April 1384, when he was fined 4*d.* and returned to work as before; or like Richard Inthehale of Abbess Roding (Essex), who in January 1382, finding himself afferer in the lord's court at the session that charged him with his part in the rising, levied 3*d.* in amercements and a 16*s.* entry fine against himself.[7] Four months after the revolt, the tenants of West Mersea (Essex) were ordered to conduct "a clerk or two appointed by the prior" to record "a new

4. "Nempe cum novissent indigne agere filios suos, Johannem scilicet Wyclife et sequaces ejus, dogmatizando perversam et dampnatam doctrinam Beringarii, de sacramento Corporis et Sanguinis Christi, et, longe lateque per patrias populum maculando, suam praedicationem dilatasse . . . nec fuit ullus cornutus qui volebat, vel audebat, tantis malis occurrere, et filios perfidos correptione debita castigare; missise creditur a multis Deum tribulationem praefatam, eo praecipue tempore quo specialem de transubstantiatione Corporis Christi facit sacrosancta ecclesia mentionem" (*Chronicon*, 311).

5. "Sed jam possessionatis invidentes, procerum crimina approbantes, commune vulgus in errore foventes, et utrorumque peccata commendantes, pro possessionibus acquirendis, qui possessionibus renunciaverant, pro pecuniis congregandis, qui in paupertate perseverare juraverant, dicunt bonum malum [et malum bonum] seducentes principes adulationibus, plebem mendaciis, et utrosque secum in devium pertrahentes" (*Chronicon*, 312).

6. Narrating the dispute that arose between Lancaster and the earl of Northumberland during the rising, Walsingham says, "Tunc primo dux ipse, conversus ad religionem, coepit accusare vitam suam pristinam, non solum privatis sed publicis confessionibus" (*Chronicon*, 328); "Tunc ille cum omni mansuetudine et pietate dedit licentiam suis omnibus, et rogavit ut unusquisque rediret ad propria, ne detrimentum paterentur de bonis suis. At illi ab eo, veluti discipuli a Christo, relicto eo, omnes fugerunt, paucis admodum cum eo remanentibus" (Knighton, *Chronicon*, 145).

7. The records of these cases appear (in translation only) in W. H. Liddell and R. G. E. Wood, eds., *Essex and the Peasants' Revolt: A Selection of Evidence from Contemporary Chronicles, Court Rolls, and Other Sources* (Chelmsford, 1981), fascicle 9 (unpaginated).

extent of all the ancient customs, rents and services and other things,"[8] to replace the extent destroyed in June. What the rising meant in retrospect to them, or to John Norford or Richard Inthehale, we cannot know.

Of course it was always so. We look for the memory of the rebellion among its victims because their memories are available; the record did not belong to those who rebelled; that was their complaint. But just here, in the manorial and shrieval archives, the greatest trauma was suffered: R. G. E. Wood and Andrew Prescott have so far discovered eighty-one manors in Essex alone where the records were destroyed.[9] Later court rolls sometimes refer to June 1381 with the phrase *tempore rumoris et combustionem rotulorum curie*—"at the time of the uproar and the burning of court rolls."[10] The designation does not mark the rebels' constructive enterprise, their desire to create their own documentary culture; no one would expect it to. But this enterprise *was* marked, unwillingly, by those who most articulately denied it: by the chroniclers, Knighton and Walsingham, who recorded the six letters that have made the matter of this book. My first point in my first chapter concerned Knighton's defensive strategy, in looking at letters and seeing speeches. But why did he put himself in the way of needing the defense in the first place? Why did he record the letters at all?

Monastic chronicles were, among other things, archives in narrative, transcribing the charters and writs and letters that secured the privileges and holdings of the houses in which they were composed.[11] The tradition and rationale, even the theory, of the documentary chronicle were perhaps most developed at St. Albans, where in the thirteenth century Matthew Paris had rationalized the practice into a principle of form.[12]

---

8. In Wood, "Essex Manorial Records," 81.

9. Wood, "Essex Manorial Records," 67.

10. See above, ch. 1, n. 82.

11. On this issue, see V. H. Galbraith, *Historical Research in Medieval England*, Creighton Lecture in History 1949 (London, 1951).

12. Matthew, Walsingham's predecessor and exemplar at St. Albans, appended to his mammoth *Chronica majora* a *Liber additamentorum* (volume 6 in the Rolls Series edition) of such muniments. He says concerning a narrative of the harassment of St. Albans by the Picts in the time of Henry III, "Ea in libro Additamentorum, ut hoc volumen deoneretur, annotantur" (*Chronica majora*, ed. Henry Richards Luard, RS 57 [London, 1880], 5:229). Thanks to the meddling editor who felt called to rearrange the documents in the *Liber* chronologically, the RS edition does not allow a sense of the arrangement (though a passing remark suggests that they are arranged by genre). The most impressive aspect of

But it was, with different degrees of tirelessness, an institutional vocation of the major chroniclers: by transcribing important documents in a chronological narrative, they secured extra copies, created a retrieval system for locating them, and provided a controlling context for their interpretation. Fourteenth-century chroniclers such as Knighton and Walsingham assumed a broad portfolio for this archival vocation, preserving and interpreting documents of national political culture as well as of their houses' ownership and privileges. Events of the 1370s gave the chroniclers a new scope for their documentary interests. Whatever the rising itself learned from Wyclif, chroniclers learned from him to document dissent: the lists of condemned articles, papal interventions, and acts of legislation reproduced in Knighton and Walsingham are there to catch out heresy and conspiracy at the point where it emerges— is *forced* to emerge—into public visibility.[13] The chroniclers, like the royal government, saw danger in secrecy;[14] they believed that security

---

Matthew's arrangement is his system of cuing entries in the *Liber* to their narrative context in the main part of the chronicle by means of marginal icons. For example, in the matter of a papal letter Bishop Grosseteste obtained granting privileges over the abbey of Leicester's *spiritualia*, Matthew concludes the account, "Hujus autem impetrationis literae poterunt reperiri ad tale signum [there follows a drawing of a bishop's mitre and crozier] in libro videlicet Additamentorum" (5:96). The effect is to make a book that is at once a series of documentary footnotes to the chronicle's narrative and a collection of documents outlining the royal, seigneurial, and ecclesiastical polities; as Gransden observes, "Matthew had believed that if the rights and privileges, as defined by charters and ancient custom, of all people and institutions were observed, England's political troubles would be ended" (*Historical Writing in England* [Ithaca, 1982] 2:136); he arranged his *Chronica* as a textual example of such order.

13. For example: in Knighton, the heresies and errors defined by the Blackfriars council (158–60); the episcopal letters regarding the heresy, (164–68), and the statement by William Barton, the Oxford chancellor (168–70); the confessions of Hereford and Repingdon and of John Aston (170–71); the list of unascribed heresies (174–76), and of the heresies ascribed to John Aston (176–78) and to John Purvey (179–80).

14. Paul Strohm has commented on the charged meaning of "congregation," "conventicle," "covin," and the like in the politics of the 1380s: "Of particular concern to contemporary commentators was the misuse by such associations of *conjuracion* or debased forms of oath taking to bind people on a non-traditional basis" (*Social Chaucer* [Cambridge, Mass., 1989], 24). But just as important to official concern over such gatherings— which was not new to the last quarter of the century—was the element of secrecy implied. Edward III in the 1350s legislated that "nul Marchaunt ou autre face conspiracie, confederacie, covyne, machination, ou mal engyn, en nul point qe purra tourner a empheschement, destourbance, defesance, ou descrees des dites Estaples" (*SR* 1.342), a very typical example of the fear that the public actions of certain individuals might be secretly coordinated to defeat law and custom. Richard II used the same language writing to the sheriff of Kent (3 July 1381), forbidding (in the light of the recent rebellion) the making of conventicles: "Et si forsan aliqui quicumque hujusmodi ligeos fideles nostros, ad hujusmodi conventicula, congregationes, seu levationes, faciendum seu sustinendum, movere vel excitare praesumant, clam vel palam, quod statim iidem excitatores capiantur, et de eisdem,

lay in discovery and display. Under the year 1382, Knighton's chronicle reproduces a statement of eucharistic doctrine, which he calls a retraction of the heresy of which it is in fact a reaffirmation.[15] Although the document is written in the still quirky and ad hoc vocabulary of early Wycliffite English, and thus leaves some room (not much) for misunderstanding,[16] its very slight obscurity is only an enabling condition of Knighton's misreading. What more obviously provokes his mistake is the mere fact of its formal and public enunciation: if dissent flourishes only in the dark, the only point of speaking it formally and out loud is to renounce it.

Recall how Walsingham said he came by Ball$_3$, found "in the garment of a man about to be hanged";[17] he declares that he is revealing a secreted document. The structure of Knighton's account suggests that he approached the five letters in his chronicles much as Walsingham did his. Knighton narrates the rising twice: first he gives the conventional account of its beginnings and its horrors in London, up through the death of Wat Tyler (whom he calls Jack Straw); then he goes back to the beginning, treating of events around Leicestershire. The *second* narrative ends with the trials of the rebels, especially those under Tresilian at St. Albans. The letters appear at the end of the *first* narrative: in effect, they substitute for an account of the trial by presenting the results of a trial instead, the letters having presumably been brought forward

---

tanquam nostris rebellibus, inimicis et proditoribus fiat indilate, sub forisfactura vitae et membrorum, et omnium aliorum, quae nobis forisfacere poterunt" (Rymer, *Foedera*, 127). The diction in this instance is obviously meant to cover the whole range of activity from conspiracy to open rebellion.

15. Knighton introduces the confession by claiming that Wyclif appeared before Archbishop Courtenay in Oxford "ad respondendum super haeretica pravitate ut prius de praedictis conclusionibus sive opinionibus. *Qui eis omnino renuncians*, nec eas tenuisse, neque tenere se velle protestans, ad maternalis virgae documentum, quod ei antea pro refugio praesto fuerat, advolavit iterum, sub forma quae sequitur" (*Chronicon*, 161–62).

16. If one were not used to the jargon that the early Wycliffites and the examining bishops worked out between them, the affirmation "verray Goddus body in fourme of brede, and if it be broken in thre parties, os the Kirke uses, or elles in a þousand, everylk one of þese parties is þe same Godus body" might mislead, using as it does the characteristic Lollard technique of elaborately affirming the physical presence of Christ in the sacrament (which Wyclif's followers had never denied and were never accused of denying) to swamp the importance of claiming that the bread still remained (their real heresy). But the sentence continues, "and right so as the persone of Crist is verray God and verray man . . ., ryth so as holy Kyrke many hundrith wynter has trowyde, the same Sacrament is *verray Godus body and verray brede*" (*Chronicon*, 161). It is unclear how this document came into Knighton's hands; if we knew, it might help explain his misreading. But the piece clearly enjoyed some circulation, since it appears in a version that seems clearly unrelated to Knighton's in a fifteenth-century miscellany (Bodl. MS 674, fol. 54r).

17. Walsingham, *Chronicon*, 322.

in prosecution. With the single exception of Thomas Baker (of Fobbing), Knighton's list of leaders is merely a list of signatories to the letters, which is his evidence for the identifications: he thinks that he is exposing (or recording the exposure of) those who provoked the largely anonymous violence he has already described. To him the letters are documents, not because the rebels wrote them, but because judicial clerks did: wrote, labeled, and filed them in the course of official business. And so Knighton thought of them as official documents; and so he transcribed them; and so, thinking that his transcriptions exposed secret discourse, he gave these public letters their most lasting publication.

Insofar as the chroniclers thought of themselves as archivists, they remembered the rebellion from the standpoint of its victims: the writs and charters of manorial privileges that they transcribed were what the rebels most characteristically carried away and burned. Walsingham's is the more interesting case in this respect. As the abbey's *scriptorarius* from the 1370s until 1394 (when he left St. Albans for a brief stint as prior at Wymondham), he oversaw bookmaking at a house that took the craft seriously; he compiled the gorgeous *Liber benefactorum* that probably graced the high altar in the abbey church.[18] He supervised the building of the new scriptorium;[19] he gave his last decades to writing and scholarship.[20] Writing the eulogy of his beloved abbot, he thought the quality of Thomas's handwriting worth remarking ("close and crabbed, but quick").[21] He was the man of books in an abbey that took pride in its books. Walsingham described the rising as an antiliterate riot: "[The rebels] worked to give old muniments over to the flames; and lest someone might again be found who would be able to remember the old customs, or new ones, they killed all such. It was dangerous to be known a cleric; much more dangerous to be found with an inkwell: few of those who were, maybe none, escaped their hands."[22] This passage, whose shrillness has something to do with the author's own proximity to inkwells, also promotes the importance of the manuscript culture that St. Albans sponsored and Walsingham oversaw, by portraying the threat to it as nothing less than a threat to order and culture.

18. Galbraith, "Thomas Walsingham," 13–15.

19. *Gesta* 3:303.

20. On his works from these years, see Gransden, *Historical Writing*, vol. 2.

21. "Scriptura sua frequens fuit, et deformis, sed velox, et, propter scribentis sanctitatem et scripturae efficaciam, erat pluribus, etiam magnatibus, pretiosa" (*Gesta* 3:410).

22. Walsingham, *Chronicon*, 308; Latin text above, ch. 1, n. 17.

The political imagination of the great monastic house unfurls from the passage as soon as a corner is pulled. Sudbury's execution, as I remarked before, merely begins the escalating catalogue of the rebels' actions "against the faith" (*in detrimentum fidei*); the point, for Walsingham, was not that the rebels wanted to kill priests or destroy service books or churches, but that they sought to eliminate the twinned disciplines of (Latin) grammar and manuscript production that enabled ecclesiastical culture. Archbishops were easy to come by, and Walsingham did not think Sudbury much of a loss; without "memory"—without writing to codify the "laws and liberties of the church"—the system would lose not so much its supports as its rationale. Those "laws and liberties of the church" conclude the account of the rising in the *Gesta abbatum*, where Walsingham gives his purpose in narrating the insurgency: that monks and abbots to come, "knowing these things, may not collapse but be fortified—should the hour come that they are likewise harassed—after the manner of their elders, and raise themselves up to defend the laws and liberties of the church."[23]

This is an odd passage in a couple of ways. First, it gives formal closure to an episode, which Walsingham does nowhere else; I will take up the implications of that in a moment. Second, it seems contradictory, since, far from acting fortified themselves, Abbot Thomas and his monks were plainly terrified: the prior fled, the abbot capitulated, the community stood paralyzed. The account of their actions hardly belongs to the genre of exemplary narrative, nor does it seem likely to "fortify" anyone. But there is an explanation: the exemplary behavior meant to fortify future monastic readers is not the monks' but Walsingham's. He is referring to the long section that immediately precedes the valediction, where he claims that the rebellion began from a mendacious story that King Offa, when he founded the monastery, also granted liberties to the town. To this claim, he opposes the testimony of a *vita* of St. Ethelwold that the village was then called "Warlamchester" (there was no "St. Albans" for Offa to grant liberties to), and of Matthew Paris that the sixth abbot, not Offa, founded the town. And he concludes with an extraordinary piece of geographical diplomatics, explaining that

23. "Haec de rebellione villanorum breviter commemoravimus, ne nesciant posteri praedecessores suos per eosdem multipliciter fatigatos fuisse, sed semper, dictante justitia, superiores extitisse; ut futuri, videlicet, haec scientes, licet ad horam contingat eos taliter molestari, non tamen concidant, sed more majorum animentur, et se erigant ad libertates et jura Ecclesiae contuenda" (*Gesta* 3:371–72).

the town barely existed then, since its northern stretch was then a fishpool "long and wide" ("a very large ship [was] found in the marsh there at the time of Abbot Michael, and [there is] frequent flooding of the houses of those who live there, from Blackcross to the mill . . . which is still called 'Fischpolstrete'").[24] With these reassuring deductions Walsingham makes himself the exemplary figure: the fortifying example that future monks should observe is the archival research by which he has established the justice of the abbey's privileges.

But (for one thing) Walsingham's researches were possible only because the books were there to be searched—another few days of insurgency and they, and the privileges, and for that matter the author, might not have been; and (for another) he could not sustain his distinction between the textual latinity of the monks and the time-bound illiteracy of the villeins.[25] To prove his point about the fishpool, he depends on the testimony of popular memory (which still called the area "Fishpool Street"). And the larger shape of his demonstration forms a textual repetition of the rebels' perambulation of the bounds ("Wulsinus, the sixth abbot, . . . founded the church of St. Peter to the south, the church of St. Stephen to the north, the church of St. Michael to the west"; "the whole street to the north . . . was empty of residents and uncultivated").[26] His every move to record and contain and refute the rising betrays how close the rebels had come to the monastery's own practices of self-validation.

The manuscript record of the *Gesta* betrays how hard Walsingham found it to quarantine the rising in past time. His refutation of the Offa story and his concluding exhortation occur in what he calls his *recapitulatio*, a final summary of the rising.[27] Just before the *recapitulatio*, the manuscript has a blank column. Why? Up to that point, the narrative has related the trial and execution of William Grindcobbe and his fellows, and the recurrent fractiousness of the villeins left alive, a matter for no little authorial impatience. But the final episode shows something more

24. "Suffragantur huic assertioni quaedam navis reperta in palude praegrandis, tempore Michaelis Abbatis, et aquarum frequens irruptio in domibus eorum qui incolunt locum illum; a Nigra Cruce, videlicet, usque ad molendinum, ea parte qua in praesenti aqua decurrit, quae adhuc dicitur 'Fischepolstrete'" (*Gesta* 3:366).

25. I again rely on Andrew Galloway's description of Walsingham's motives ("Gower and Walsingham on 1381"; see ch. 4, n. 106 above).

26. *Gesta* 3:366.

27. The full rubric is "Recapitulatio malefactorum villanorum Sancti Albani, contra Abbatem et Conventum, ut praemittitur, pluries attentatorum" (*Gesta* 3:365).

than impatience, something more like renewed terror: "Not long after, another tribulation, unheard of before this, befell the abbot, a tribulation great above all other tribulations, which terrified the hearts of those who heard it." One morning, before "our grange of Sandrugge," there appeared "a banner like the ones the insurgents had raised during their revels not long before," hanging from it a "box [*pyxidem*] with linen stubble and a certain letter, with a tally of twenty-one pounds to be paid at Canterbury on a certain day. And if what was asked was not paid, they threatened to take seisin of our manors of Astone and Wyncelowe. And they hung half-burned linen tufts in various places, and tossed balls of linen stubble around the manor of Sandrugge, as a sign that they would burn the grange if the abbot did not fulfill their demands."[28] The mysterious documents claimed to come from the kin of one John Biker, executed for his part in the rising. The abbot does not pay; time passes ("St. Gregory's day came, Easter came"); and then the hogpen and barn at Sandrugge are fired. The same signs are given at Walden the next year; the cowbarn there is fired. Then the mill at Codicote, then houses in the manor of Coumbes (Sussex). Two people confess to the fires, but later retract their confessions.

Then the blank column, then the *recapitulatio*. Blank columns appear now and again in the manuscript of the *Gesta*, always for evident reasons.[29] The reason here is not precisely evident, but it is discernible. Walsingham intended the *recapitulatio* as closure: there, not at the beginning of his account, he relates the original cause of the rising (the mistaken notion about Offa's grant), places the rising in a larger history of sporadic rebellion—fixing it all firmly in the past—and gives his

28. "Non multo post haec, accessit et eidem Abbati et alia tribulatio, hactenus inaudita, tribulatio super omnes tribulationes maxima, et quae terruit cunctorum corda audientium, prae horrore novi facinoris adinventi. Quidam revera, qui praetendebant se fuisse cognatos Johannis Biker, nuper suspensi in insurrectione apud Sanctum Albanum, pro manifestis suis sceleribus, noctu venientes ad praedium nostrum de Sandrugge, erexerunt ante portas quoddam vexillum, quae parum ante insurrectores erexerant dum bacchabantur, et appenderunt pyxidem cum lini stipula, et quamdam litteram, cum tallio viginti et unius librarum eisdem solvendarum Cantuariae, certa die. Et si non solveretur quod petebatur, minabantur se capturos seisinam in maneriis nostris de Astone et de Wyncelowe" (*Gesta* 3:361–62).

29. Most usually to leave space for new material: the illuminated letter *L* which introduces an empty column at fol. 264v, the unfinished story at fols. 287–88, the rubric "Introductio materiae subscriptae" with nothing following at fol. 291r, all indicate that some necessary document was not to hand at the time of copying. Sometimes, too, short blanks are left simply to maintain the visual appeal of the page: at fol. 257v, for example, a fraction of a column remains blank because a new and rather long rubric introduces the next section, which would take up the rest of the column (BL Cotton MS Claudius E.iv).

valediction: the rising was over. But it was not over: that is the message of the blank column. In the banner hung at Sandrugge, the abbey was presented with a written threat, a document that issued from within the tenant community. The juxtaposition of the document at Sandrugge with the symbols of conflagration formed a finely compressed image of the insurgent project that Walsingham everywhere tries to suppress as he narrates Corpus Christi week: burning one written culture to replace it with another. The event showed that the rising could not be called done so readily, for all the chronicler's efforts. Why was the anonymous arson "a tribulation great over all other tribulations," worse even (it seems) that the tribulations of June? Because it was like them, so like them that it seemed part of the same, and therefore continuing, series of events—even the banner was "like the ones the insurgents had raised in their revels not long before"—which suggested that the violence had not, in fact, come to a close. The confessions he relates he does not believe, and he seems as puzzled as Abbot Thomas by the claim that the threat came from Biker's kin.[30] The rubric shows what in fact he suspected and feared: "Concerning the arsonist at the manors of St. Albans commissioned, it is believed, by certain malicious villeins of St. Albans,"[31] a summary that bears close resemblance to the rubrics he uses to describe the rising itself.[32] The blank column in the *Gesta* awaits the conclusion to the story (the discovery of the arsonists and their sponsors and therefore the elimination of the threat), the conclusion that the *recapitulatio* prematurely celebrates.

There is another aspect to Walsingham's difficulty in concluding his account, and that is his uncharacteristic desire to conclude it at all; elsewhere he proceeds from year to year, as chroniclers do. Obviously Walsingham wants to end the story, and to think it ended; but this desire to finish the story is intimately and anxiously related to his desire to tell it in the first place. For Walsingham became a historian only in response to 1381; his first efforts, now a section of "our greater chronicles"

30. "Mirabatur Abbas de hiis praesumptionibus, mirabantur et omnes de suo consilio; et eo maxime, quod nullum unquam Abbas contrarium fecerat cum Johanne Bikir, nec aliquis de familiaribus ejusdem Abbatis; nec et idem Johannes Biker suspensus fuerat ad sectam Abbatis, aut alicujus de suis, sed solummodo ad sectam Regis" (*Gesta* 3:362).

31. "De incendiariis maneriorum Monasterii Sancti Albani, per quosdam malevolos villanorum Sancti Albani, ut creditur, procuratis" (*Gesta* 3:361).

32. In its noting the agency of the abbey's villeins—"Qualiter humiliabantur villani Sancti Albani post mortem Walteri Tylere" (3:314) and their "malice"—e.g., "Continuatio materiae malitiae praenotatae" (3:287 and elsewhere).

(as he called his most elaborate historical work), originally formed a free-standing narrative he called the "tragic history" or "rustic tragedy."[33] "In the foregoing, we have laboriously written, to inform and warn those who come after us, the tragic history [*historiam tragicam*] of the rustics' lordship, the revels of the commons, the madness of the villeins."[34] Thirty years or so later, when he referred readers of his last work to *nostra chronica majora* for a full account of the rising, he used the same title: "Because these matters require their own treatment, I do not include them here, but refer to our greater chronicles those who desire to see the rustic tragedy."[35]

The "tragic history" or "rustic tragedy": it is an intriguing title, bookish and—like *Chronica*, and *Historia*, and *Archana*, and *Ypodigma*, the titles of his major works—Greek. When Chaucer dismisses his "litel tragedye" of Troilus in hopes of turning to "som comedye" (*T&C* 5.1786), he indulges a positively inkhorn taste for the new classicism of Florence and locates his work within a complex and consolidated literary tradition. But Walsingham's is an inkhorn of a different color: neither the humanist nor the Boethian notions of tragedy that inform Chaucer's usage are relevant here. Walsingham was not thinking of drama—in the fourteenth century, almost no one did when thinking of tragedy[36]—nor about the fall of the great or the tragedies of fortune.[37] He was thinking about etymology. Isidore of Seville would have told him that "tragedy" came from *tragos* ("goat"),[38] and he may have known the medieval notion that tragedy is a "goatish song, that is a stinking song: for it concerns the cruelest things, like people killing fathers or mothers or

---

33. This is an unconventional assertion; the universal opinion is that Walsingham began writing in the late 1370s, since the first section of the "greater chronicles" begins with the Good Parliament of 1376. I will offer evidence for my revisionist opinion in a future essay, "Walsingham's Chronicling and the Publication of History."

34. "Scripsimus, non sine labore, in praecedentibus historiam tragicam, ad posterorum notitiam et cautelam, de dominatione rusticorum, debacchatione communium, insania nativorum" (*Chronicon*, 312).

35. "Que quia tractatum expetunt specialem presente compendium non impono remittens ad nostra maiora chronica videre cupientes tragicam rusticam" (*Ypodigma Neustriae*, ed. H. T. Riley, RS 28.7 [London, 1976], 335).

36. See Allen, *Ethical Poetic*, 20. Still, ancient drama was not entirely unknown at St. Albans; there was a manuscript of Terence in the library, now Bodl. MS Auct F.2.13; see N. R. Ker, *Medieval Libraries of Great Britain: A List of Surviving Books*, 2d ed. (London, 1964), 168.

37. I take the latter term from Monica E. McAlpine, *The Genre of Troilus and Criseyde* (Ithaca, 1978), ch. 2.

38. Isidore of Seville, *Etymologiarum sive originum libri XX*, ed. W. M. Lindsay (Oxford, 1911), 8.6.5.

eating their children."[39] Certainly he knew, as Isidore would also have told him, that tragedies "sing the deeds of evil kings,"[40] and there lies the source of Walsingham's wit. Evil *kings*: the title "rustic tragedy" is a mirthless joke whose point lies in its oxymoron: there are no *rustic* tragedies, since the venues of tragedy are the palace and the throne; only ironically might the honor of tragedy be extended to those rustics who "thought to become the equals of their lords."[41] The title *Tragedia* plays on the absurdity of their claims, the absurdity that informs Walsingham's picture of the insurgent forces gathering: "Some with crooks, some with swords enfeebled by rust, some with only axes, a few with bows blackened (because of their age) with soot darker than old ivory and single arrows (and many of these had to be content with a single feather), gathered to conquer the realm. Among a thousand of them you could hardly spot one properly armed, but all of them . . . believed the whole kingdom too weak to resist them."[42]

This is bluster. Walsingham makes the rebels ridiculous in the distance between their martial pretensions and their clownish appearance, though on the other side of the same folio he has said that had God not shown mercy "the kingdom would have been thoroughly destroyed, made a hiss and a derision to all peoples."[43] The dynamics of his repression are so obvious that it would be ungracious to do more than note them: the satirical picture tries to contain the sheer indecorum, the scandal, of the terror by making the rebels doomed and silly from the start. But that is not at all what the rest of his narrative suggests, and his other use of the term *tragedia* signals his inability to contain the memory of the rebellion with wit: "But look! while I write of crimes great and too great done on Friday and Saturday in London, I can barely unravel the *tragedia*; or rather on the same days there occurred similar things to be recorded at St. Albans, as I said before."[44]

39. From the *Catholicon* of John Balbus, quoted in Allen, *Ethical Poetic*, 20.
40. Isidore, *Etymologiae*, 18.45.
41. *Chronicon*, 285.
42. "Quorum quidam tantum baculos, quidam rubigine obductos gladios, quidam bipennes solummodo, nonnulli arcus prae vetustate factos a fumo rubicundiores ebore antiquo, cum singulis sagittis, quarum plures contentae erant una pluma, ad regnum conquirendum convenere. Inter mille vero de talibus, de facili non videndus erat unus armatus, sed omnes, ut magnum numerum confecere, credebant totum regnum illis resistere non valere" (*Chronicon*, 286).
43. "Nisi Deus, misericordiarum Dominus, solito bonitatis intuitu citius compescuisset, et regnum omnino destructum, et factum fuisset cunctis gentibus in sibilum et derisum" (*Chronicon*, 285).
44. "Ecce enim! dum magna et nimis magna facinora scribo, diebus Veneris atque

The desperate troping in the narrative (desperate even for Walsingham) is a protective device, meant to evoke the terror while assuring the doom of its agents. It is appropriate that Walsingham begins his account by imagining England's shame (had the rising succeeded) as a noise, a "hiss" (*sibilum*).[45] His narrative happens in a swirl of noise that obscures agency and ignites violence as an impersonal force, a nightmare of clatters and screams that scare dead metaphors back to life. The rebels are a *turba*;[46] their anger a *furor*;[47] at night their discourse is that of the insanely drunk;[48] they rave;[49] instinct with the devil, they charge the Tower with a terrifying noise.[50] The noise has a visual cognate, only less slightly persistent, in fire: the fire at the Savoy;[51] the fires that consumed the muniments at the Temple and that, "raging," the insurgents set at Clerkenwell (which burned for a full week);[52] the fires they set at Highbury;[53] the fires with which (Walsingham tendentiously claims) Tyler planned to burn down all London.[54] Walsingham's purpose in these tropes becomes nearly explicit at the burning of the Highbury

Sabbati gesta Londoniis, vix eorum explicare possum tragoediam, quin eisdem diebus occurrunt scribenda similia apud Sanctum Albanum, ut praetractum est" (*Chronicon*, 301).

45. *Chronicon*, 285.

46. "Estsaxones suas congregasse turbas" (*Chronicon*, 286); "statuerunt turbam videre collectam" (287); "turba . . . ita inverecunda et insolens habebatur, ut victualia regis, quae ad Turrim vehebantur, diriperet inverecunde. Et insuper, tanta agitabatur insania" (290).

47. "Vulgares, in furorem versi" (288).

48. "Facti fuissent non tam ebrii quam dementes, (nam Londoniarum majores et plebs communis cuncta cellaria illis aperta reliquerant,) coeperunt cum simplicioribus civitatis multa tractare de proditoribus" (288).

49. "Velut amentes cucurrerunt ad locum, et, ignibus in gyro conjectis, destructioni loci vacabant" (289).

50. "Instinctu diabolico portas Turris, ut praetactum est, illi per vias glomeratim et cum clamore terrifico sunt ingressi" (291).

51. "Velut amentes cucurrerunt ad locum, et, ignibur in gyro conjectis, destructioni loci vacabant" (*Chronicon*, 288–89).

52. "Quibus omnibus perpetratis satis malitiose, etiam locum qui vocabatur Temple-barre, in quo apprenticii juris morabantur nobiliores, diruerunt; . . . ubi plura munimenta, quae juridici in custodia habuerunt, igne consumpta sunt. Et amplius insanientes, illam domum nobilem hospitalis Sancti Johannis de Clerkenwell, immisso igne, ardere fecerunt per continuos septem dies" (289).

53. *Chronicon*, 290.

54. "Cogitaverat etenim in ipsa nocte, quia cuncti communes pauperes, videlicet urbis Londoniarum, illis favebant, civitatem despoliasse, occiso prius rege et majoribus sibi adhaerentibus, et eam, quatuor locis injectis ignibus, conflagrasse. Sed qui superbis resistit Deus, humilibusque dat gratiam, non permisit ejus impias imaginationes et affectus ad finem usque perduci; sed gratiose et subito iniquum ejus consilium dissipavit" (295). The nonexplanation for why this plan was never carried out ("God did not permit it") and the very unlikely assertion that the rebels meant to kill the king before meeting him the next day amount to shoulder-shrugging admissions that Walsingham is making the whole thing up for a rhetorical evocation of terror.

manor of the Knights of St. John, where an ambiguity in grammatical antecedence leaves it briefly unclear whether the buildings burn with literal, or the rebels with metaphorical, flames.[55]

This troping let Walsingham suggest, without accountably asserting, that the violence ran the rebels and not the other way around, that a laughable congeries of underequipped rustics could terrorize the kingdom because they were driven by a power unspecified but broadly hinted at. But the troping had a deeper job to do. At one point, just before the execution of Sudbury, Walsingham reflects on the noise he often describes. As the rebels brought Archbishop Sudbury to Tower Hill, he writes,

> they made a hair-raising noise; not like those that humans make, but beyond all measure greater than human noises, rather as the screams of those in hell might be imagined. They made such clamors whenever they beheaded someone, and whenever they threw down buildings, for as long as God left their evils unpunished. No words sounded among their horrifying shrieks; rather, their throats were filled with all sorts of bovine bellows, or—better—with the devilish voices of peacocks.[56]

The ideological work that "noise" does here is clear enough, but a more striking example occurs later on the same folio, when Sudbury meets his death. Deeply suspect in its baroque elaboration,[57] the passage exists (as it were) to silence the words of the rebels (as recorded in another, independent account) by assigning them, with different effect, to Sud-

---

55. The St. Albans rebels, going to London, meet the main body of rebels at Highbury, "qui, immisso igne in editissimas domos, *quo jam ardebant inextinguibiliter*, nitebantur cum diversis instrumentis cuncta, quae incendio dissolvi non poterant, subvertere machinamentis solo tenus" (290). Since the pronoun "qui" governs the plural "nitebantur" that immediately follows the subordinated verb "ardebant," only the rest of the sentence makes it clear that the latter applies to the houses and not to the rebels who fired them.

56. "Quo cum pervenisset, factus est clamor horrendisimus, non similis clamoribus quos edere solent homines, sed qui ultra omnem aestimationem superaret humanos clamores, et maxime posset assimulari ululatibus infernalium incolarum. Qualibus etiam clamoribus usi sunt in omni decapitatione cujuslibet, et prostratione domorum, quamdiu Deus permisit eorum nequitiam impunitam. Non tamen resonabant verba inter horrificos strepitus, sed replebantur guttura multisonis mugitibus, vel quod est verius, vocibus pavonum diabolicis" (*Chronicon*, 292).

57. The grand guignol of Sudbury's execution—after the first stroke he put his hand on his neck, and "nondum manum de loco doloris amoverat, et secundo percussus, summitatibus digitorum amputatis, et arteriarum parte, cecidit; sed nondum occubuit, donec octavo ictu miserabiliter mutilatus in collo et in capite, dignum, ut credimus, martyrium complevisset" (293)—is suspiciously echoed in Walsingham's account of the killing of John Lakingheath at Bury: "in foro publice decollatus est, octies percussus antequam caput esset a corpore separatum" (303), a detail he borrowed (scrambled, really) from the *Electio Timworth*: "spiculator septies eum percussit priusquam amputare potuit ejus caput" (Arnold, ed., *Memorials of St. Edmunds Abbey* 3:129).

bury. According to the *Eulogium* continuator, after the first stroke of
the axe, the rebels cried, "This is the hand of the lord." Walsingham has
Sudbury say, "A! A! It is the hand of the lord,"[58] a peerless example of
the trope of noise at work, displaying the anxious desire that makes
Walsingham tell of those "horrifying shrieks" among which "no words
sounded": it is there to deny, take away, obscure, and otherwise render
inaudible anything the rebels might have *said*—by speech, script, or
purposeful action—and jumble all their words and actions into undifferentiated *sound*.

Walsingham and other writers at the end of the fourteenth century
tried to "forget" the revolt not by forgetting the events, and certainly
not the violence—which they evoked with persistent fascination, but
which was by its nature controllable and (by the time they wrote)
already controlled—but by using the violence to forget something that
more urgently threatened clerical authority and lordly privilege: the
words and gestures by which villeins, artisans, and freeholders had
declared that they understood the clerical bureaucracy that governed
them well enough to imitate it, and that their own local self-government
made much of the bureaucracy superfluous anyway. The troping of
noise in Walsingham's text ensures that what he describes as happening
does in fact, for the reader, happen: that the "cries," "howls," "bellows,"
and the rest keep such words from "sounding" when the rebels open
their mouths.

The noise did not belong to Walsingham alone; it was what literate
England agreed to have heard in June 1381. In the 1390s, Chaucer's one
open reference to the great revolt used the rising as a commonplace of
clangorous disorder. When Chaunticleer is borne off by the fox,

> Ran Colle oure dogge, and Talbot and Gerland,
> And Malkyn, with a dystaf in hir hand;
> Ran cow and calf, and eek the verray hogges,
> So fered for the berkyng of the dogges
> And shoutyng of the men and wommen eeke
> They ronne so hem thoughte hir herte breeke.
> They yolleden as feendes doon in helle;
> The dokes cryden as men wolde hem quelle;
> The gees for feere flowen over the trees;

58. I discuss the difference between the versions, and my reason for preferring that in
the *Eulogium*, ch. 2, n. 92 above.

> Out of the hyve cam the swarm of bees.
> So hydous was the noyse—a, benedicitee!—
> Certes, he Jakke Straw and his meynee
> Ne made nevere shoutes half so shrille
> Whan that they wolden any Flemyng kille,
> As thilke day was maad upon the fox.
> Of bras they broghten bemes, and of box,
> Of horn, of boon, in whiche they blewe and powped,
> And therwithal they skriked and they howped.
> It semed as that hevene sholde falle.[59]

And a commonplace it was: to the contemporaries who recorded it, the rising was The Noise: *rumor, rumor magna, rumor pessima.*

Chaucer, however, was not addressing a commonplace; he was parodying John Gower, who had immediately incorporated a vision of the rising into his encyclopedic political complaint, the *Vox clamantis*:[60] "Some bray in the wild manner of asses," he says of the rebels in one set piece of this poetic dream vision, "some sound the bellows of cattle, some let out the horrid grunts of pigs, at which the earth trembles, the boar froths and makes great tumult, and the wild pig cries out, increasing their noise; wild barking pressed on the air of the city, and the discordant voices of dogs, furious, filled the city. The hungry fox howls, and the wily wolf cries out on high, to call together his partners,"[61] and so on for as many lines again. The governing conceit in book 1 of the *Vox clamantis*, Gower's nightmare dream-vision of the rebellion, is a horrific double metamorphosis. The narrator, who has "thought to go out gathering flowers in the fields" (1.167), instead meets "diverse lots of the vulgar poor wandering in numberless crowds," whom "God's curse, . . . changing their forms, makes . . . beasts"—domestic beasts (asses, cattle, dogs)—who then become furiously wild, refusing service and turning to destruction. After twelve chapters describing their appearance and muster, Gower describes (under the same conceit) their entry into "New Troy" (London), their execution of the "high priest Helenus" (Sudbury), and his own desperate attempts to evade their violence, before he prays, and God finally intervenes to save Gower and the realm.

---

59. *Nun's Priest's Tale*, ll. 3383–3401, in *The Riverside Chaucer*, 3d ed., gen. ed. Larry D. Benson (Boston, 1987). All references to Chaucer's works are from this edition; references to the *Canterbury Tales* in the text will give fragment and line numbers.

60. This was noticed by Ian Bishop, "*The Nun's Priest's Tale* and the Liberal Arts," *RES* ns 30 (1979): 263–64.

61. *Vox clamantis*, in *The Complete Works of John Gower*, ed. G. C. Macaulay (Oxford, 1902), vol. 4, ll. 799–820. Subsequent references are given in the text.

The scene Gower paints is a confusion of furious animal noises, which he renders in his verses (the asses "cry 'heehaw')"[62] and which make the long passage I have just quoted into a string of sputtering ugliness ("Quidam porcorum grunnitus horridiores / Emittunt, que suo murmure terra tremit: / Frendet aper spumans, magnos facit atque tumultus, / Et quiritat verres auget et ipse sonos" [1.801–4]). The satirical and social force of the conceit that produces this ruckus neither requires, nor will bear, much comment; but its purpose does. When the rising erupted, Gower had recently completed the *Vox*,[63] a poem in which he commissioned himself as a public poet, the formal voice of the commons.[64] He added the *visio* on the rising (the present book 1) after the revolt—of which, from his presumptive lodgings in St. Mary Overeys in Southwark, he would have had near tidings. Its purpose was to rescue his vocation as a public poet, and the poem by which he had just claimed it; book 1 of the *Vox* turns a profound threat to his public self-commission into a strategy for extending it.

For the voice he claims in the *Vox* is everybody's. In the first version of the poem—indeed, in the first rubric—Gower explains his title: "He calls this book 'Vox clamantis,' because it is conceived as if from the voice and clamor of all."[65] He introduces his central books by claiming, "I write nothing from my own understanding, but say what the voice of the people [*vox populi*] has reported to me" (4.19–20). The title of the work gives this claim a peculiar inflection, since anyone who could manage Gower's Latin would have been able to complete the phrase *vox clamantis* with its canonical *in deserto*, the isolated voice of John the Baptist prefigured (as the gospel had it) in Isaiah:[66] Gower imagines himself a prophet who declares the consensus of the realm. Eventually, in the *Confessio amantis*, Gower would speak for this general constituency

---

62. "Dum gemiunt solita voca frequenter yha" (1.190).

63. Macaulay, *Works* 4:xxxi–xxxii; John H. Fisher, *John Gower: Moral Philosopher and Friend of Chaucer* (New York, 1964), 101–4.

64. In what follows, I will be using the vocabulary of Anne Middleton's essay "The Idea of Public Poetry in the Reign of Richard II," *Speculum* 53 (1978): 94–114, though the notion of poetic vocation that I trace here looks more desperately and factionally motivated than the literature of public counsel she describes.

65. "Vocat libellum istum Vox Clamantis, quia de voce et clamore quasi omnium conceptus est" (2.prol.rubric). Though in theory it might be chancy to assume that the post-1381 *Vox* faithfully represents the pre-1381 *Vox* minus the narrative of 1381, the later books' silence about the rebellion suggests that Gower did not revise the whole work in adding the present book 1.

66. "Vox clamantis in deserto: Parate viam Domini, Rectas facite in solitudine semitas eius" (Matthew 3.3, quoting Isaiah 40.3).

in its own language, the English vernacular; in the *Vox*, it was precisely his ability to transmute common speech into authoritative Latin that he used to secure his authority to speak for all.[67] "Common" here suggests "commons," those who populate England and do its ordinary business, as distinct from the king and court. As he approaches the poem's *explicit*, he repeats his assertion one last time: "What I have written is the voice of the people [*plebis*], but you will see that where the people cry out, there, often, is God" (7.1467–70). The *plebs* mediates for Gower, and he for it: their common political sense, uncontaminated by insider status in court intrigue, is given the imperative of prophetic form in a Latin poem that translates into the language of the court the sentiments of those excluded from the court. No sycophant (he claims), he speaks for all.

By "all" Gower of course means "some"; he promotes the interests of a particular clientele as the interests of the realm at large (just as the knights of the shire in parliament assumed for themselves the designation of "commons"). He claims to ally himself with the *pauperes* of the realm, but disarmingly acknowledges, at the beginning of the poem, that his *topos* of poverty is only a *topos*: "In my poverty [*pauper*] I give a modest amount from the modest amount I have [*De modicis . . . modica*], and I would rather avail too little than have availed nothing. The person with nothing to give is no miser: if I cannot give gifts [*munera*], I give words" (2.prol.61–64). Gower was no *pauper* by any ordinary measure— certainly not by village standards—and the delicate *modica* admits as much.[68] But the last line ("Si dare non possum *munera*") adopts a scale by which he can call himself poor: he lacks the wherewithal to participate in the system of patronage and retaining, of bribes and gift-giving, through which political influence flows. By that standard, Gower is poor, and so are those for whom he speaks: they lack influence at court, enjoying neither the aristocratic birth nor the great wealth that confer a voice in national politics. Speaking for this middling group, he hits the system at its most vulnerable point: *munera*, however sanctified by usage, became in the last decades of the century the focus of literary and

67. The unity of Gower's vernacular stylistic aspirations with his sense "of the poet's duty to the state, and of the poet as guardian of the common treasure of language" is described in Robert F. Yeager, *John Gower's Poetic: The Search for a New Arion* (Cambridge, Eng., 1990), 9–44, and their strategic origins and historical consequences in David Lawton, "Dulness and the Fifteenth Century," *ELH* 54 (1987): 761–99.

68. See the details of his will in Fisher, *John Gower*, 65–67.

parliamentary attacks on royal misgovernment.[69] By this move, Gower earns moral credit for himself and his clientele, making them the victims of predatory misgovernment, and establishes the attractiveness of his program: to "give words" instead of gifts, in a rational and reformist discourse that declares evils out loud rather than perpetuating them in silence. Obviously the constituency he claims is larger than the audience he expects: the *Vox* speaks *to* those who can read his Latin, but *for* a much wider group altogether.

Thus Gower's "voice" cries out, complaining of social and political corruption: "*Vox clamantis* shall be the name of this volume, which contains the words of new sorrows" (2.prol.83–84). It is obvious how the revolt of 1381 threatened Gower's project. A *populus*, a *plebs*, that complains loudly of social corruption, greed in high places, and misgovernment close about the king—as Gower and his *plebs* do—but in rustic tones, to demand radical reforms (which would put untitled landlords like Gower himself in some jeopardy), threatened to absorb and discredit the discourse of popular complaint by which he claimed cultural status as speaker for the *vox populi*. Their language was simply too like his, and both Gower's political self-positioning and his poetic vocation were potential casualties of the likeness.

But then their language was not like his, because it was English, and this is crucial to Gower's strategy in the *visio*. Ian Bishop notes that Chaucer's fox chase imitates more than Gower's animal noises: the catalogue of names in the *Nun's Priest's Tale* (the animals and people who pursue the fox—"Colle oure dogge, and Talbot and Gerlond, / And Malkyn" [3383–84])—echoes a similar catalogue in the *Vox*. Gower's catalogue, a piece of virtuoso contempt, is closely linked with—indeed immediately precedes—his imitation of the animals' grunts and roars. It needs to be quoted in Latin, and in full:

> Watte vocat, cui Thomme venit, neque Symme retardat,
> Bette que Gibbe simul Hykke venire iubent.
> Colle furit, quem Geffe iuuat, nocumenta parantes,

---

69. *Munera* in this peculative sense is both the Latin equivalent and the ideological point of Langland's Lady Mede: "*Ignis deuorabit tabernacula eorum qui libenter accipiunt munera &c.*" is rendered "fir shal falle & [forbrenne at þe laste] / The hou[s] and [þe] ho[m] of hem þat desireþ / Yiftes or yeresyeues bycause of hire Offices" (B.3.96–100). Gower himself had commented on the phenomenon in the *Speculum*: "Loyalté serra desconfit, / Si tu les douns aras confit / A ces jurours . . . / Ly povres qui n'ad pas d'argent / Se puet doubter de tiele gent / Au fin q'il n'ara pas son droit" (*MO* 25081–83, 25093–95).

> Cum quibus ad dampnum Wille coire vouet.
> Grigge rapit, dum Dawe strepit, comes est quibus Hobbe,
> Lordkyn et in medio non minor esse putat:
> Hudde ferit, quos Iudde terit, dum Tebbe minatur,
> Iakke domos que viros vellit et ense necat:
> Hogge suam pompam vibrat, dum se putat omni
> Maiorem Rege nobilitate fore:
> Balle propheta docet, quem spiritus ante malignus
> Edocuit, que sua tunc fuit alta scola.
> Talia quam plures furias per nomina noui,
> Que fuerat alia pauca recordor ego:
> Sepius exclamant monstrorum vocibus altis,
> Atque modis variis dant variare tonos.
>
>   (1.783–98)

Then the asses bray, the cows bellow, and so on.

Every contemporary account of the revolt reaches this point where the rebel companies are imagined all together (here, the various species convene to attack New Troy), and the writer goes on to name the leaders: in Knighton when he summarizes the revolt,[70] in Walsingham when he moralizes it,[71] in the Dieulacres at the very beginning.[72] The purpose of Gower's naming is different: to display the hopelessly un-discursive character of those who made the revolt rather than the personal responsibility of their leaders. He incorporates the insistently vernacular names of rustic rebels into a poetic register where they do not belong, and shows them to be wholly unassimilable to the language of literary and political discourse. He introduces the catalogue by speaking of these beasts "who lack reason": "*que racione carent*" (1.781–82). This is stock abuse, that the rebels were empty of reason.[73] But *racio* is also measure and the capacity to be measured, pattern and the ability to fit into a pattern. Uninflected, uninflectable, and marked by accent without syllabic quantity, these names are not the stuff from which

---

70. See ch. 1, n. 1 above.

71. The rubric that immediately follows the death of Tyler is "Nomina ductorum communium": "Si quem scire delectat nomina eorum, qui incentores et ductores fuere communium, inveniet hic inserta pro parte. Primus et principalis dicebatur Walterus Tylere; secundus Johannes Strawe; tertius, Johannes Kirkeby . . ." (*Chronicon*, 310).

72. "Anno domini millesimo CCCmo LXXXXIo plebani Cancie Estsex' et aliarum parcium regni vi oppressi inter quos specialiter nominabant sibi duces magna excitacione ut dictum est cuiusdam sacerdotis nephandi Iohannis B., Iak Strawe, Per Plowman et ceteri" (M. V. Clarke and V. H. Galbraith, eds., "The Deposition of Richard II," *BJRL* 14 [1930]: 164).

73. See ch. 1, n. 14 above.

Latin verse could be made, except as the objects of Gower's virtuoso mockery.[74] He places these rural names in a poem to whose language and meter they are plainly inadequate, in effect enclosing them within a political discourse where their utterances cannot sound. Gower can function in both worlds, "recording" their vernacular names as he pursues his Latin complaint, but they cannot, since in his verse their vernacular capacities avail no more than animal inarticulacy; the rebels cannot speak, but only moo. An obvious moral comment on the bestiality of revolt, the transformation of the rebels into beasts also erases any trace of verbal performance on the part of the rebels and disembarrasses Gower's own claim—to represent the popular voice—of a discrediting similarity.

The events of June were a threat to Gower's project, but also an opportunity for it. The rising produced a rare unity of sentiment between those *for* whom and those *to* whom Gower was offering to speak, since all of them were real or potential objects of attack. Whatever else the king, his counselors, magnates, gentry in and out of parliament, religious houses, higher clergy, scribes, and civil servants might have disagreed on, they agreed that the rising was a bad thing.[75] Gower so maneuvered his response in book 1 to make virtue of necessity. The rising forced Gower anxiously to disassociate his "voice crying out" from the voices that cried out in June; by declaring himself a proxy for all those the rebels attacked and by prefacing the rest of the poem with his experience of rebel violence, he was able to assert that he did indeed speak in the common voice—of its victims.

The divine voice that places on Gower the prophet's mantle tells him

74. The indivisibility, the monosyllabic sameness of their names contrasts in particular with Gower's treatment of his own, which he can divide and turn into a discursive signature at the beginning of the book: "Scribentis nomen si queras, ecce loquela / Sub tribus implicita versibus inde latet. / Primos sume pedes Godefridi desque Iohanni, / Principiumque sui Wallia iungat eis: / Ter caput amittens det cetera membra" (1.prol.19–23). This signature does not seem to have been part of the original poem, but was added along with book 1, of which it is a part. (Anne Middleton has suggested to me that Gower models this signature on that of another English prophetic writer, John Erghom, author of the commentary on the *vaticinia* ascribed to John of Bridlington; Thomas Wright, ed., *Political Poems and Songs Relating to English History*, RS 14 [London, 1859], 1:123–215 [the signature appears on 123].)

75. "Factionalism of the most bitter sort might be rampant among the great men of the realm, but in the face of a threat against the system from which all derived whatever power they possessed, they closed ranks to present a solid front" (Richard H. Jones, *The Royal Policy of Richard II: Absolutism in the Later Middle Ages* [Oxford, 1968], 18).

that to *write* (his vision) he must stop *speaking* (his complaints): "Qui silet est firmus, loquitur qui plura repente, / Probra satis fieri postulat ipse sibi" (2041–42). The couplet is merely translated on its way into the *Nun's Priest's Tale*: "God yeve hym meschaunce, / That is so undiscreet of governaunce / That jangleth whan he sholde holde his pees" (VII.3433–35): thus Daun Russell the fox on speech and silence. Bishop, who is right in spotting the fox-chase reference to the *Vox clamantis*, is wrong in thinking it "merely incidental parody."[76] Describing his flight from the rebels' fury, Gower says that "fear added wings to feet, and in my flight I was a bird,"[77] and Chaucer does him the compliment of taking him at his word: for Chauntecleer—bird and singer and dreamer of terrifying beast-dreams—is John Gower, and the tale is book 1 of the *Vox clamantis* in deadpan.[78] Chaucer parallels Gower's diction so closely as in some places virtually to translate it,[79] and he cracks jokes that

76. Bishop, *"Nun's Priest's Tale,"* 264.

77. "Inde ferens lassos aduerso tramite passus, / Quesiui tutam solus habere viam: / Attamen at tantam rabiem pedibus timor alas / Addidit, et volucris in fugiendo fui" (1387–90).

78. Derek Pearsall has hard words for those who would follow Bishop in thinking the "Jakke Strawe" passages a parody: "A desperate plea could be entered that Chaucer is parodying Book I of the *Vox Clamantis*, and that he really had other thoughts about the Revolt that he kept to himself. In this way Chaucer can be allowed his greatness as a poet by being made to share, by imputation, the radical or at least more sophisticated opinions of his modern admirers" (*The Life of Geoffrey Chaucer: A Critical Biography* [Oxford, 1992], 147). I take it that the desperation of which Pearsall speaks concerns not the *presence* of the Gower parody—which seems to me quite irresistible, and which I am suggesting goes well beyond this one passage—but the conclusion that Chaucer therefore somehow sympathized with the rebellion; on the latter point—as will appear—I quite agree with him.

79. Chauntecleer's dream of disaster so frightens him that "for feere almoost I deye" (2906; Gower: "Hec ita cum vidi, me luridus occupat horror, / Et quasi mortifera stat michi vita mea" [1359–60]) and causes his "gronyng" (2907; Gower: "Tunc pariter lacrimas vocemque introrsus abortas, / Extasis exemplo comprimit ipse metus" [1469–70]); Chauntecleer justifies the efficacy of dreams by "olde bookes" (2974; Gower on dreams: "Nos tamen econtra *de tempore preteritorum* / Cercius instructos littera scripta facit" [1.prol.5–6]) that demonstrate "That dremes been significaciouns" (2979; Gower: "significarunt" [prol.7]); books that give the examples of "Daniel" (3128) and "Joseph" (3130), the former of whom did not hold "dremes any vanitee" (3129; Gower: "Ex *Daniele* patet quid sompnia significarunt, / Nec fuit in sompnis *visio vana Ioseph*" [prol.7–8]), the latter showing dreams to be "somtyme" (3131; Gower: "sepeque" [prol.13]) "Warnynge of thynges that shul after falle" (3132; Gower: "prenostica visu" [prol.13]). Chauntecleer enjoys, with Pertelote, "thise blisful briddes how they synge" (3201; Gower: "Milia mille sonant volucrum velut organa cantus" [1.103]) and "the fresssshe floures how they sprynge" (Gower: "Et totidem flores lata per arua fragrant" [1.104]), but his enjoyment comes, as Fortune will have it, to an end, "For evere the latter ende of joye is wo" (3205; Gower: "Tristia post leta, post Phebum nebula, morbi / Tempora post sana sepe venire solent" [1.133–34]). Chauntecleer has "wel read in 'Daun Burnel the Asse'" (3312; Gower: "Burnellus" [1.201]). Chantecleer's capture produces cries greater than those "whan Ylion / Was wonne" (3356–57; Gower:

literalize Gower's figures;[80] he recasts Gower's prophetic vision as barnyard melodrama and turns Gower's *Vox* into Chauntecleer's *voys*. Thus
the cock is introduced ("His *voys* was murier than the murie orgon"
[2851]), and thus, as the singer prophetically dreaming disaster, does he
proxy for the poet of the *Vox clamantis*. As a rooster, Chauntecleer is a
clamans by profession, and the pride he takes in his "voys" becomes his
humiliation. The fox seizes him when he tries to "synge" like his father:

> And for to make his voys the moore strong,
> He wolde so peyne hym that with bothe his yen
> He moste wynke, so loude he wolde cryen.
>
> (3304–6)

The joke, as nasty on Chaucer's part as it is on the fox's, bounces puns
off Gower's pretensions in book 1 of the *Vox*. First, though "wynke"
here means "close his eyes," the word can also mean "sleep,"[81] which is
what the cock would "peyne hym" to do so that he might (if I may
latinize the fox's line) fortify his *Vox*; the suggestion is that Gower's
sleeping song is manifestly contrived and that what Gower calls a
prophetic revelation is just the familiar, willed fiction of the poetic
dream-vision. Second, Gower's song is another contribution to the noise
he deplores ("so *loude* wolde he *cryen*"), a joke secured by the fox's final
flattery: Chauntecleer draws himself up to show his "wisedom and
discrecioun" (3318)—the faculties on which Gower based his image of
the political poet—and "gan to crowe loude for the nones."[82] In fact,
just by rendering him as the cock, Chaucer places Gower among the
animals who rage through the *Vox*, where cocks are already among the
rioters ("the crowd of domestic birds, transformed, was there, whose
leaders were the cock and the gander" [518]); Chauntecleer's comic
fierceness (he "looketh as it were a grim leoun" [3179]) originates in a

---

"Subdita Troiana cecidit victoria victa" [1.989]) and than those at "Cartage" (3365) and
"Rome" (3371; Gower: "Prelia Thebarum, Cartaginis, illaque Rome / Non fuerant istis
plena furore magis" [1.983–84]).

80. Wat Tyler appears in the *Vox* as a crow (*graculus*) "edoctus in arte loquendi" (681);
the Nun's Priest informs us that "thilke tyme, as I have understonde, / Beestes and briddes
koude speke and synge" (2880–81). The moment in Gower when the beasts shake hands
("Complexis manibus mutua pacta ferunt" [726]) is matched by a running joke of Chaucer's
which assigns to the birds appurtenances they lack, as when Pertelote castigates Chauntecleer for having no "mannes herte" to match his "berd" (2920) or Chauntecleer's avowal,
"I hadde levere than my sherte / That ye had radde his legende" (3120–21).

81. Cf. "I wol ben heres, whether I wake or wynke" (*Parliament of Foules*, 482).

82. On Gower's self-image as poet, see A. J. Minnis, "John Gower, *Sapiens* in Ethics
and Politics," *MÆ* 49 (1980), esp. 224–25.

device Gower uses to satirize the foolish ambition of the barnyard rebels (the pigs' "grunts were as the lion's roar" [375]).[83]

In Chaucer's version, Gower dupes himself. For one divinely instructed that "Who is silent, is firm" (or "God yeve hym meschaunce, / That . . . jangleth whan he sholde holde hys pees"), Gower's shrill dream-vision does jangle, so loudly that his strident complaints resemble the cacophony of the rioters he fears and abhors more than the silence of contemplation he enjoins on himself at the end of the poem; the *clamans* of the poem's title resembles too much the *clamor* the animals make, virtually undoing Gower's desire to differentiate the "plebis vox" (7.1469), for whom he claims to speak, from the voice of the "vulgaris . . . plebs" who are his targets in book 1. If the political principle that underwrites your poetic self-commission is that the poet cries with the voice of the people, you will make same the noises they do.

As criticism of Gower's poetic project Chaucer alleges criticism of Gower. The *Vox clamantis* repeatedly blames England's corruptions and disasters, including the revolt, on insufficient love, *amor*: "Wild rusticity is tempered by no love [*nullo . . . amore*], but always does its bitter deeds with a contentious heart" (2101–2).[84] Now Gower had not acquired a wife by the time Chaucer wrote the *Nun's Priest's Tale*; he married only in 1398, when he was seventy or so. He left no heir of the body, and the epitaph he composed for his wife, Agnes Groundolf, praises her "chaste will" (Fisher suggests he was legitimating a live-in nurse).[85] But in the *Tale*, Chaucer fits him with Pertelote, makes him uxorious and oversexed in a way that Gower's persona and, as far as we can tell, Gower himself were not, broadly suggesting that Gower's rhetorical excess and his shrill calls for generalized *amor* bespeak an excess of unformed, sublimated erotic energy.[86] And the object of this energy, Pertelote, proposes Chaucer's most aggressive reflection on the *Vox*. She is the principle of

---

83. See also l. 185, where the asses' "bellies were filled with the fury of lions," and l. 293, "The bull was a lion, a leopard, a bear."

84. And "I judge that there would be no better people from the rising of the sun to its setting, if they had love [*amor*] one for the other" (1.1981–82).

85. Fisher, *John Gower*, 64–65.

86. Gower himself may have felt the force of Chaucer's mockery, since in the *Confessio amantis*, where he takes up again the problems of social "divisioun" that concerned him in the *Vox clamantis*, he makes sexual love the foundation of social love, and appears (in his own words) *fingens se esse amantem*. Richard Axton suggests that Gower learned this lesson from Chaucer ("Gower—Chaucer's Heir?" in Ruth Morse and Barry Windeatt, eds., *Chaucer Traditions: Studies in Honour of Derek Brewer* [Cambridge, Eng., 1990], 21–38).

the body in the tale.[87] Her diagnosis of Chauntecleer's dream rejects his prophetic, Macrobian interpretation in favor of a worldly and medical one;[88] and her prescription for it—"For Goddes love, as taak som laxatyf" (2954)—is a disrespectful version of what Gower proposes for himself at the end of Book I: "Vt michi vox alias que vidi scribere iussit, / Amplius ex toto corde vacare volo." "Since the voice commanded me to write the other things I saw, I desire with all my heart to be more free from distractions" is how Gower might render his meaning, but *vacare*, formally intransitive ("to be empty"; by the usual extension, "to be free of business") can have a more reflexive factitive suggestion: "to empty oneself," a goal to which Pertelote's prescription has a precise if revisionist application.

Chaucer is getting personal here, suggesting that Gower's poetic originated in his psychosexual and intestinal dysfunctions. To trace Gower's *complaint* back to his idiosyncratic *complaints*—to explain the voice by the body of its speaker—is itself a significant criticism of any claim to speak with a common rather than a personal voice. But it is impossible to gauge Chaucer's tone, to decide whether the criticisms are collegial teasing or outright confrontation. The relations between the two poets in the 1390s are rather a crux; around 1393, Gower dropped his commendation of Chaucer from the *Confessio amantis* when he also switched the dedication from Richard II to Bolingbroke.[89] Presumably those able to catch the parody would have known—which is precisely the point. The parody is coterie stuff, aimed at the small group who knew, and maybe participated in, the literary politics of Ricardian London. Chaucer's play on the name of the dogs that chase the fox ("Colle oure dogge, and Talbot and Gerlond" [3383]) aims to elicit a

87. E.g., Sheila Delaney, *Medieval Literary Politics: Shapes of Ideology* (Manchester, 1990), 143.

88. Walter Clyde Curry, *Chaucer and the Medieval Sciences* (London, 1960), 219–20.

89. Fisher suggests that the tension he thinks Gower felt toward Chaucer at the end of the 1380s was a poetic, not a political matter, and that Gower's excision of his commendation of Chaucer, when he switched the dedication from Richard II to Henry Bolingbroke, was more benign than the commendation itself: the lines of commendation were in fact (he says) really a rebuke, while their disappearance shows Gower's refusal to implicate his friend (or former friend) in his own switch of political allegiance (*John Gower*, 199–20). Carolyn Dinshaw has shown how the idea of a "quarrel"—of whatever seriousness and over whatever issue—has offered Chaucerians a masculinist ideological construction of authorship ("Rivalry, Rape, and Manhood: Gower and Chaucer," in R. F. Yeager, ed., *Chaucer and Gower: Difference, Mutuality, Exchange* [Victoria, B.C., 1991], 130–52); at the same time, it is not impossible that a "quarrel," or even the pretense of one, served Chaucer's or Gower's own masculinist construction of authorial identity.

chuckle from literary insiders: a "talbot" was a hunting hound, also known as a "gower"; it appears on the Gower coats of arms.[90] "Colle," on the other hand, is the only name Chaucer's parody incorporates directly from Gower's catalogue, and Chaucer makes him "*oure* dogge" not just because of the homely cast it gives to the scene,[91] but because Colle's companion in the *Vox* is "Geffe" ("Colle rages, and Geffe helps him"),[92] a reference that Chaucer seems delighted to pretend is to himself. The line winks and nudges and nods, reinforcing the coterie's pleasure in belonging.

The audience capable of understanding Chaucer's rough treatment of Gower is a significant issue in understanding the tale, its apparent criticism of the *Vox*, and the memory of the rising in (or at the back of) the minds of those who wrote in its wake. In Fragment VII of the *Canterbury Tales*, which the Nun's Priest concludes, Chaucer meditates extensively on his authorial identity,[93] and—more important—worries the question of reception *as a question of audience*. Reception has already been an issue, in Fragments I and III, where emulation and anger (the Miller's and Reeve's, the Friar's and Summoner's) generate new tales from tales just told.[94] In Fragment VII the hearing of tales produces not more tales, but acts of unsolicited judgment: the Host's silencing of *Sir Thopas* and the Knight's silencing of the Monk's *de casibus* anthology, moments at which the narrators discover to their cost that the social range of their audience is broader than they had allowed for and that literary expectation is shaped by one's place in that range.

The Monk's is an interesting case. If Chaucer harasses Gower with reductive abuse in the *Nun's Priest's Tale*, in the *Monk's Tale* he harasses himself. "First, tragedies wol I telle, / Of whiche I have an hundred in my celle" (VII.1971–72), the Monk announces. "Tragedie" was, as I have said, a bookish term in the fourteenth century (rarer by far than it would be two centuries later), and it is how Chaucer defined the *Troilus* at its

---

90. See Fisher, *John Gower*, 40–41, 40–41nn.; "talbot" and "gower" may in fact have been different kinds of hounds which were confused with each other.

91. See the critical discussions summarized in Pearsall's note (Derek Pearsall, ed., *The Nun's Priest's Tale*, vol. 2, part 9 of *The Variorum Chaucer* [Norman, 1984], 246).

92. "Colle furit, quem Geffe iuuat, nocumenta parantes" (1.745).

93. See Lee Patterson, "'What Man Artow?': Authorial Self-Definition in the *Tale of Sir Thopas* and the *Tale of Melibee*," *Studies in the Age of Chaucer* 11 (1989): 117–76.

94. On the contained and class-specific character of such exchanges, see especially Carl Lindahl, *Earnest Games: Folkloric Patterns in the Canterbury Tales* (Bloomington, 1987), 75–87.

conclusion: "go litel myn tragedie" (*T&C* 5.1786). The Monk, like Chaucer, tells tragedies; like him, he is a devotee of Florentine literary culture who draws his stories from Boccaccio.[95] The last thing the Monk says before *his* tale concludes—that Fortune will "covere hire *brighte face* with a clowde*" from those who trust in her (2766)—quotes the *Troilus*, where Fortune "From Troilus . . . gan hir *brighte face* / Awey to writhe" (*T&C* 4.8–9).[96] Over this line, exasperation carries the Host beyond syntax:

> He spak how Fortune covered with a clowde
> I noot nevere what; and als of a tragedie
> Right now ye herde, and pardee, no remedie
> It is for to biwaille ne compleyne
> That that is doon, and als it is a peyne,
> As ye han seyd, to heere of hevynesse.
>
> (2782–87)

The Knight and the Host agree that the tale is hopeless, but for different, incommensurate reasons. The Knight is not bored; he finds the fall of the great "a greet disese" and would rather hear of a man who "clymbeth up and wexeth fortunat" (2771, 2776). The Host is bored and uncomprehending ("Nere clynkyng of youre belles / . . . / I sholde er this han fallen doun for sleep" [2794–97]), and he suggests a more intriguing topic for the Monk's next narration ("Sir, sey somwhat of huntyng, I yow preye" [2805]).

Here Chaucer imagines the *Troilus* encountered in a context, and by an audience, it was never meant for: it was meant for the courtly audience whose love talk was the vernacular of courteous maneuver

---

95. The rubric ("Heere bigynneth the Monkes Tale De Casibus Virorum Illustrium") gestures toward Chaucer's source in Boccaccio's *De casibus*, and the "modern" stories of Bernabò Visconti and Ugolino of Pisa allusively include Dante and the Visconti protégé Petrarch; on the latter, see David Wallace, "'Whan She Translated Was': A Chaucerian Critique of the Petrarchan Academy," in Patterson, ed., *Literary Practice and Social Change*, 172–76.

96. I assume that the composition of the Monk's Tale—or at least of the last stanza of Croesus—postdates the composition and publication of the *Troilus*. The dating has been, rather pointlessly (in the absence of evidence), a matter of controversy. The Riverside edition note on the tale covers the dispute and its arguments adequately enough to expose its needlessness. The only firmly datable element of the tale is the Bernabò Visconti stanza, which must postdate his death at the end of 1385 (and therefore the *Troilus* as well). The Riverside note blandly comments that Tatlock "gives no decisive reason in support of the late date" (929). But since the only evidence points to a date of 1386 or later, it is the advocates of an *earlier* date who must offer "decisive reasons"—more decisive, certainly, than a circular notion of Chaucer's "development."

("yonge, fresshe folkes, he or she, / In which that love up groweth with youre age" [1835–36]),[97] and for the literati with whom he shared his literary enterprise ("moral Gower" and "philosophical Strode" [1856–57]). It was not meant for Harry Bailly, it was not meant for the Knight, and together they make an impossible audience. The Monk ventures into high literary culture in order to define himself: the Host, requesting a tale, has hinted that he expects bawdy matter from this manly Monk ("oure wyves wole assaye / Religious folk" [1959–60]), a request that disconcerts the Monk into didactic propriety: "I wol doon al my diligence, / As fer as sowneth into honestee" (1966–67), he says, as he decides between "the lyf of Seint Edward" and the tragedies.[98] The Host's later suggestion ("sey somwhat of huntyng") testifies to the inelasticity of his audience's imagination, and after these failures—the audience's to meet the monk, and his to meet the audience—the Host's suggestion prompts a curt refusal: "Nay, . . . I have no lust to pleye. / Now lat another telle, as I have toold" (2806–7).

But the Nun's Priest's own, more accommodating sense of audience creates even greater and more complex pressures. Finding himself ensnared by the question of foreknowledge and necessity—

> Wheither that Goddes worthy forwityng
> Streyneth me nedely for to doon a thyng—
> "Nedely" clepe I symple necessitee (3243–45)—

he eschews the Monk's didactic prolixity—

> I wol nat han to do of swiche mateere;
> My tale is of a cok, as ye may heere—

tumbles straightway into another trap—

> That tok his conseil of his wyf, with sorwe,
> To walken in the yerd upon that morwe
> That he hadde met that dreem that I yow tolde.
> Wommennes conseils been ful ofte colde;
> Wommannes conseil broghte us first to wo
> And made Adam fro Paradys to go,
> Ther as he was ful myrie and wel at ese—

---

97. Green, *Poets and Princepleasers*, ch. 4.

98. See Donald R. Howard, *The Idea of the Canterbury Tales* (Berkeley and Los Angeles, 1976), 280.

backtracks immediately—

> But for I noot to whom it myght displese,
> If I conseil of wommen wolde blame,
> Passe over, for I seyde it in my game—

takes refuge in *auctoritee*—

> Rede auctours, where they trete of swich mateere,
> And what they seyn of wommen ye may here—

and resorts finally to duplicity—

> Thise been the cokkes wordes, and nat myne;
> I kan noon harm of no womman divyne.
>   (7.3251–66)

Like the Monk, the Nun's Priest also reprises the *Troilus and Criseyde*—Troilus' meditations on necessity and foreknowledge in book 4. He wisely cuts himself off (Troilus' meditation lasts 120 lines), *anticipating* Harry Bailly's objections before they can happen, and makes amends with the Host's favorite discourse, the antifeminist complaint.[99] But the instant he does so he finds himself *anticipating* objections from the Wife of Bath; surprised into momentary incoherence, he blames old books and then blames Chauntecleer and at one point—"Passe over, for I seide it in my game"—sounds uncannily like the narrator in Fragment I: "whoso list it nat yheere, / *Turne over the leef* and chese another tale"; "And eek men shal not maken ernest of *game*" (I.3176–77, 3186). Which in turn recalls something the narrator has said still earlier:

> But first I pray yow, of youre curteisye,
> That ye n'arette it nat my vileynye,
> Thogh that I pleynly speke in this mateere,
> To telle yow hir wordes and hir cheere,
> Ne thogh I speke hir wordes proprely. (I.725–29)

The similarities between the Nun's Priest's excuse and the narrator's

---

99. Of Griselde: "By Goddes bones, / Me were levere than a barel ale / My wyf at hoom had herd this legende ones" (IV.1212b–d). Of the Merchant's May: "I have a wyf, though that she povre be, / But of hir tonge, a labbyng shrewe is she, / And yet she hath an heep of vices mo" (IV.2427–29). Of Prudence: "As I am feithful man, / And by that precious corpus Madrian, / I hadde levere than a barel ale / That Goodelief, my wyf, hadde herd this tale! / For she nys no thyng of swich pacience / As was this Melibeus wyf Prudence" (VII.1891–96).

throw the differences into relief. Chaucer's apologiae in Fragment I assume a predictable and familiar audience to whose courtliness ("curteisye") he can appeal and for whom "peasantness" ("vileynye") is other, and offensive. The Nun's Priest, like the Monk, faces a different problem: *multiple* audiences who process his narration in unanticipated ways. The Monk's problem is that he is judged and misunderstood in ways he has never imagined; his tale dramatizes publication, reception not by *a* (unitary) public—what Gower claims to speak for in the *Vox clamantis*—but by *publics*, which include but are not limited to the intended audience of Chaucer's previous works. The Nun's Priest's problem is that he *does* imagine such judgments and misunderstandings. His tale dramatizes diverse, unintended, potential audiences as a nagging awareness at the back of the narrating consciousness, an awareness that reframes his sense of what he says—blocking progress, demanding adjustments, squeezing out apologies, spurring the anxiety that hiccups in the middle of the most virtuoso performance in the *Canterbury Tales*.

The Nun's Priest avoids the trap the Monk falls into, although his vigilance costs him a stumble. But after escaping from one trap, he falls into another, and the problem of unintended audience emerges again, this time without a peep of awareness on the teller's part, directly from the Jack Straw simile. Why did Chaucer name Jack Straw in his single allusion to the rising? Peter W. Travis has brilliantly suggested that the answer lies in the name "Jack."[100] Chaucer traveled "ad partes transmarinas," probably to France, in 1370; to France again, perhaps, in 1376; to Paris and Montreuil in 1377; and to "parts of France" in the same year: he made several visits there in the decade after France's own peasants' revolt, the Jacquerie.[101] Chaucer at least shared mutual acquaintances with Froissart and may have known the *Chroniques*.[102] In any case, he would have known that the French rebels had called themselves the "Jacques"; and he may have guessed (rightly or not) that the English insurgents had modeled their pseudonyms thereupon.[103] He would also

100. Travis, "Chaucer's Trivial Fox Chase and the Peasants' Revolt of 1381," *JMRS* 18 (1988): 216–17.

101. Martin M. Crow and Clair C. Olson, eds., *Chaucer Life-Records* (Oxford, 1966), 31–32, 42–53.

102. On Chaucer's relationship with Froissart, see McFarlane, *Lollard Knights*, 184.

103. What the English rebels knew of the earlier events around Paris is a problem; Mollat and Wolff believe that "les révolutions ne restèrent pas sans influence les unes sur les autres" (*Ongles bleus, Jacques, et Ciompi*, 138). The suggestion that the rebels favored the pseudonym "Jack" because of the Jacques was made to me by Carter Revard.

have known that the Jacques were, more formally, *li Jacques bon-hommes*,[104] Jack Good-Men. So the Nun's Priest unwittingly walks a dangerous way when, within forty lines of "Jakke Straw and his meynee," he exhorts his audience with the time-honored homiletic address— "Taketh the moralite, *goode men*" (3440)—and indeed insists on it: "Now, goode God, if that it be thy wille, / As seith my lord, so *make us alle goode men*" (3444–45). The innocent vocative "goode men," in such discursive proximity to *li Jacques bonhommes*, threatens to become an unintended call to insurgency. The Nun's Priest gives no sense of catching the irony himself. It is precisely the unconsciousness, in this virtuoso narrator, of what his words might mean in another context that demonstrates Chaucer's consciousness that the author cannot control the social reach of the text, and that there are potential though unimagined audiences who might make words spoken in innocence something guilty.

That is the issue in the Jack Straw passage. The wacky testimony of the Dieulacres chronicle that "the perfidious priest John B., Iak Straw, *and Per Plowman*" fomented rebellion in 1381 has an unappreciated significance.[105] In the surviving evidence, Piers Plowman is named as a rebel only in the letters reproduced by Knighton and Walsingham.[106] The chronicle testifies that the rebels' use of his name was known (although Langland's poem was not) even to a chronicler in deepest Cheshire: the letters had been heard of there, if not seen. If they were, they were certainly known too in deepest London. The *Nun's Priest's Tale* registers the existence of those letters—and the claim to rural literacy they stake—in its sense that vernacular narrative might be overheard by this audience which the writer had not expected, or even thought of, but which has suddenly, noisily announced its surprising familiarity with official culture and its determination to seize and reshape it.

---

104. The name came first from the king the rebels made for themselves: "[Ils] avoient fait un roy entre yaus que on clamoit Jake Bonhomme" (Froissart, *Chroniques de France, d'Engleterre, d'Escoce . . .*, ed. Kervyn de Lettenhove [Brussels, 1868], 6:51); in the chilling words with which he introduces his account of the English rising, Froissart recurs to the familiar collective noun: "pour le grant aise et abondance de biens où li menus peuples d'Engletière graoit et vivoit, s'esmut et esleva ceste rebellion, enssi que jadis s'esmurent et eslevèrent en France li Jaque-Bonhomme qui y fissent moult de maulx et par quels incidensses li nobles roiaulmes de France a esté moult grevés" (*Chroniques* 10:386).

105. Clarke and Galbraith, "The Deposition of Richard II," 164; quoted n. 72 above.

106. Galbraith seems to think that some rebel took the name Piers Plowman as some other apparently took the name Jack Trewman: "Jak Strawe is obviously a 'masonic' name, like Piers Plowman" ("Deposition," 161).

Langland found himself in company he did not expect; so might Chaucer.

The anxieties betrayed by Fragment VII sound a new note in Chaucer's poetry, a worry about audiences, heretofore unimagined, that lay beyond the poet's control, audiences who might find his writing and find in it something he had never meant. And these anxieties emerge in the work whose action Chaucer situated beyond the geographical range of city and court. "In Southwerk at the Tabard" (I.20); "And forth we riden a litel moore than paas / Unto the Wateryng of Seint Thomas" (I.825–26); "Lo Depeford, and it is half-wey pryme! / Lo Grenewych, ther many a shrewe is inne!" (I.3906–7); "Loo, Rouchestre stant heer faste by!" (VII.1926); "I bishrewe me, / But if I telle tales two or thre / Of freres er I come to Sidyngborne" (III.845–47). The periodic click of place-names in the frame of the *Tales* marks the poem's place in the landscape of Kent.[107] In the *Book of the Duchess*, the *House of Fame*, the *Parlement*, the *Legend*, the narrator dreams where Chaucer dreamed, in London; the *Troilus*, too, by its triangulated metonymies, sets itself in the city.[108] Chaucer begins his last fiction across Thames; the pilgrimage begins, and would end, outside the city. The geography of the fiction duplicated his own move, in 1385, away from the impacted politics of court and city to Greenwich, where he took up duties as justice of the peace for Kent.[109] And the Kentish geography of the *Canterbury Tales* announced a new project, a new fictional world whose extension along the horizontal axis of the Canterbury road matches its extension along the vertical axis of social stratification.

That the pilgrims take the route the Kentish rebels had taken (going the other direction) during Corpus Christi week is in itself unremarkable; it is the main road between London and Canterbury. But it does mean that the places they pass are potential palimpsests through which

107. The importance of the pilgrimage geography has been discussed only in studies either relentlessly formalist (Charles A. Owen, Jr., *Pilgrimage and Storytelling in the Canterbury Tales: The Dialectic of "Ernest" and "Game"* [Norman, 1977]) or relentlessly empirical (Henry Littlehales, ed., *Some Notes on the Road from London to Canterbury in the Middle Ages* [London, 1898]).

108. With "Troilus" ("little Troy") standing in some relation to London's preferred sobriquet of "Trinovant" ("new Troy"); see D. W. Robertson, Jr., *Chaucer's London* (New York, 1968), 221–22.

109. His appointment, dated 12 October 1385, is printed in Crow and Olson, *Life-Records*, 348–49. On city politics in these years, see Ruth Bird, *The Turbulent London of Richard II*, chs. 5–6; on their relation to literary bureaucrats, see S. Sanderlin, "Chaucer and Ricardian Politics," *Chaucer Review* 22 (1988): 171–84, and Paul Strohm, "Politics and Poetics: Usk and Chaucer," in Patterson, ed., *Literary Practice and Social Change*, 83–112.

the memory of the rising threatens to appear. For example, according to the *Anonimalle*, the king traveled by barge to Greenwich on Corpus Christi Day, where the Kentish rebels, encamped a few paces away at Blackheath, had gone to meet him. In their last recorded act of counsel, Sudbury and Hales dissuaded Richard from granting them audience. The rebels pressed their demand for the traitors; Richard instructed them to meet him at Windsor five days thence. But, warned that they would take him captive, Richard left for the Tower, whereupon the rebel spokesman informed his fellows "that the king had left and that it would be good for them to go on to London to carry out their designs."[110] This is the moment that began the terror for Chaucer and those he knew: the decision to march on London left the capital paralyzed for three days, brought the destruction of the Savoy and the execution of Sudbury, and provoked the opportunistic violence of the city dwellers. Greenwich comes into sight of the Canterbury pilgrims as the Reeve reacts to the slander on himself he has detected in the Miller's tale and meditates sourly on age and anger through the consonantal blockages of his regional speech ("So theek" [3864]). Harry Bailly, in response, gestures toward the approaching towns of Greenwich and Deptford to hurry the tale telling past the threat of violence; he speaks "as lordly as a kyng" (3900). But he fails of his purpose: the Reeve prays a broken neck for the Miller and proceeds to narrative revenge.

What are we to do with these lines? The situation—Greenwich; an angry peasant; a king (an innkeeper speaking as lordly as one); a failed intervention; violence in consequence—almost invites recollection of that crucial moment from which the violence in London flowed. Yet it will not do; Chaucer has seen to it that it will not. The *Canterbury Tales'* most important innovations—the geographical disposition, the social range of tellers and the exchanges between them that shape the telling of the tales themselves—solicit the memory that percolates into the text at the approach of Greenwich, but must ward it off to secure its own continuation. While on one view the range of possible narrative action within the pilgrimage frame is rich and quite varied (partly in consequence of those very innovations; Boccaccio's *brigata* could hardly manage their range), on another it is surprisingly constrained, tolerant only of what will produce further tales: it is simply the logic of the

---

110. "En quel temps le homme appelle yomane avauntdit se hasta a le Blakeheth, criaunt as ses compaignouns qe le roy fuist ale, et bone serroit as eux daler a Loundres persuer lour purpose" (*Anonimalle*, 140).

work, and (as Macherey said) such logic requires certain repressions as part of its routine maintenance.[111] Chaucer's decision to impersonate a reeve and a miller and an entrepreneurial wife, to make them speak tales, exacts its price: they may *only* speak tales, the only events represented will be acts of telling.[112] And so too his decision to include the conditions and estates of men and women in representative individuality, and corporeality, exacts its price: motive is individual motive. Together these imperatives fence out the narration or recollection of collective events, even while the diversity of voices and the geographical specificity invite them in. The Reeve, being a reeve, is presumably a villein;[113] a villein, in fact, from "Biside a toun men clepen Baldeswelle" (I.620) in the northern part of Norfolk, a region distinguished in 1381 for the violence of its insurgency.[114] The "foure gleedes" which the Reeve acknowledges that "we" have—"Avauntyng, liyng, anger, coveitise" (I.3883–84)—are vices commonly attributed to peasants and demesne workers.[115] The Reeve's status, his attributes, the threat of violence, and the approach of Greenwich all seem to gesture toward the memory of 1381, but then to gesture away from it: his "we" means not "we peasants," but "We olde men" (3874), and peasant anger here is the resentment of age rather than of status, its only effect the bitter joke against the Miller.[116]

111. "Thus, the book alone is not self-sufficient; it is necessarily accompanied by a *certain absence*, without which it would not exist" (Pierre Macherey, *A Theory of Literary Production*, trans. Geoffrey Wall [London, 1978], 86).

112. Compare here Lindahl's formulation: "By creating oppositions unresolved by action, Chaucer creates *narrators*, not combatants, for his poem, people who express their differences in words—who tell about crimes, but do not commit them . . .; who talk about, rather than practice, sexual infidelity . . .; who engage in oral rather than in physical battle. . . . The behavior extremes of the *Canterbury Tales* are found within the tales themselves" (*Earnest Games*, 37).

113. Since service as reeve could be used as proof of villeinage, Lindahl's assertion that "it cannot be said with certainty that any of Chaucer's pilgrims" is in the "lowly position" of "partial or total bondage" (*Earnest Games*, 24) is probably wrong (if by "bondage" he means legal unfreedom; it is a puzzling phrase).

114. "La vérité, c'est que la révolte se propagea dans ces comtés [Norfolk and Suffolk] avec une extrême rapidité, qu'elle trouva de l'écho dans les moindres villages, enfin qu'elle ne sévit nulle part, même à Londres, avec plus d'intensité et de violence" (Réville, *Soulèvement*, 54). Réville attributes the exceptional violence in these counties chiefly to their wealth and to the rigor with which lords, especially monastic lords, extracted it.

115. On "liyng" and "coveitise," see ch. 4, nn. 12, 14 above. The peasants' penchant for "anger," one might say, is asserted in every account of the rebellion. "Avaunting" is, in fact, commonly attributed to peasants. Gower found it there: "Ly labourer qui sont truant / Voiont le siecle busoignant / De leur service et leur labour, / Et que poy sont le remenant, / Pour ce s'en vont *en orguillant*" (*MO* 16473–77). And see Jill Mann's discussion, *Chaucer and Medieval Estates Satire: The Literature of Social Classes and the General Prologue to the Canterbury Tales* (Cambridge, Eng., 1973), 163–67.

116. For a different description of the same pattern of defused violence, see Patterson, *Chaucer and the Subject of History*, ch. 4.

John M. Ganim has called one Chaucerian type-scene "the noise of the people": collective speech in which passion destroys policy or ignites violence.[117] He is looking, avowedly, for a Chaucerian politics at a level deeper than topical allusion. But Chaucer's politics, his largest imagination of the possibilities that govern the public world, does not live in such moments: the most interesting thing about Ganim's chapter is how few of them he can find in the Chaucerian oeuvre, and (given their scarcity) his omission of one: the moment in the *Clerk's Tale* when one part of the commons expresses its revulsion at Walter's behavior and at the fickleness of the other part that supports him.[118] No formal marker distinguishes good murmur from bad murmur: like Gower, Chaucer pictures a good common voice and a bad common voice, but offers no clear criterion for differentiating them. The "noyse of peple" is not, in some intrinsic and measurable way, good or bad, but in the social grammar of the *Canterbury Tales* it is exceptional, a solecism. For there is one more point about the "noyse of peple" scenes. In the *Canterbury Tales* they appear only in the tales, never in the frame, where indeed—with its single representatives of various social categories—they would be unimaginable.

Chaucer's politics lives in the form of his fiction. That he uses social types to creates characters (a knight, a squire, a yeoman) and a social microcosm is an observation as old and as tired as Chaucer criticism itself. That this formal choice implied a politics—or at least outlined the form that his politics could take—is a point that still wants to be made. Stephen Knight insists that we should call the pilgrims not "*the* Knight," "*the* Miller," but rather "*a* knight," "*a* miller" (since that is how Chaucer

117. These are "moments when an analogy is made between social disruption and what might be stylistically identified as popular voices, moments that result in narrative crises of one sort or another" (Ganim, *Chaucerian Theatricality* [Princeton, 1990], 108–20). The examples he adduces are the Trojan parliament of *Troilus and Criseyde* (IV.183–96), the fox chase of the *Nun's Priest's Tale*, Saturn's "murmure and the cherles rebellyng" (*CT* I.2459), and (a little curiously) the *Miller's Tale*. He is cautious about tracing the *topos* to the rising, though all the passages he discusses postdate 1381 and there is nothing like the *topos* in any works clearly datable *before* 1381 (the noise of the *House of Fame* is just auditory clutter, an artificial assembly of the world's random talk, not purposeful consensus).

118. On this, see Wallace, "'Whan She Translated Was,'" 200–202. Of the moment when the people anticipate the bride with whom Walter claims he will replace Griselda ("amonges hem they seye / That Walter was no fool, thogh that hym leste / To chaunge his wyf, for it was for the beste" [IV.985–87]), and others among the people rebuke them for their fickleness, Wallace comments that "this critique" of the changeableness of the commons "is voiced by another part of the same social body across a line of rupture drawn by the tyrannical Walter himself" (202). What matters here, however, is that the "voice of the people" is of no particular value and embodies no particular values; it is indifferently good or bad.

introduces them): the characters, he says, are not characters at all, just dumping grounds for class interests and vocational stereotypes.[119] Although the suggestion defeats itself in the making,[120] it does remind us what an odd sort of character Chaucer has created. The pilgrims do representational duty for their classes and professions, their genders and their jobs, in a complex way that leaves Chaucer space for engaged social analysis. The Reeve (since he is most nearly at issue here) is a type, constructed from generalized notions about what reeves did and how they did it, notions we can easily trace back to contemporary sources of all kinds. Ordinarily chosen from within the community of customary tenants, reeves represented the lords' interests within the community and played a cardinal role in the system of delegated authority mentioned in the last chapter. A reeve who did his job well kept a close eye on the fruit of the fields and flocks ("Wel koude he kepe a gerner and a bynne" [I.593]),[121] on the other tenants and servants ("Ther nas baillif, ne hierde, nor oother hyne, / That he ne knew his sleighte and his covyne; / They were adrad of hym as of the deeth" [603–5]),[122] and on his accounts, which he would keep in good order ("by his covenant yaf the rekenynge, / . . . / Ther koude no man brynge hym in arrerage" [600–602]).[123] The Reeve's administrative virtues are drawn from the common wisdom of lords and their counselors. But so are his (clearly if glancingly suggested) vices: a bad reeve turned his office to his personal profit ("He koude bettre than his lord purchace. / . . . / His lord wel koude he plesen subtilly, / To yeve and lene hym of his owene good" [608–11]) and cunningly concealed his delinquencies and embezzlements ("Ther was noon auditour koude on him wynne" [594]). Chaucer's Oswald exists in part to show that the seigneurial versions of reevely vice and reevely virtue might coexist within the same breast, and, more interestingly,

119. Stephen Knight, *Geoffrey Chaucer* (Oxford, 1986).

120. It is impossible to sustain the convention across even a short discussion of the *Tales*, and indeed Chaucer himself does not try to sustain it, even in the General Prologue: "*The* Millere was a stout carl for the nones" (I.545).

121. "E nul cumble de blee ne seyt mes receu de grange en gener pur acreis fere, mes de viii quarters seit pris le ix me de tascurs par dreit mesure pur le acreis, ensy ke nul buscel, ne nul demy bussel, ne nul cantel ne remeyne al provost par les baturs dehors la mesure avantdite" (*Seneschaucy*, in Oschinsky, ed., *Walter of Henley*, 276).

122. "De die claro faciat prepositus in presencia sui vel messoris affros et equos cotidie prebendari. . . . De die dico, ne prebenda noctanter per custodes furetur eisdem" (*Fleta*, 250).

123. On the duties of the reeve, see also T. F. T. Plucknett, *The Mediaeval Bailiff* (London, 1954), 5–8, 27.

how naturally they could do so: the quick calculation, the peripheral vision taking in his lord's tenants and his lord's goods, the virtuosity at accounts—these qualities could produce equally the efficient deputy and the successful embezzler.

The portrait of the Reeve catalogues the qualities traditionally sorted to his kind and questions the assumptions that assigned those qualities. Thus far he is (in Stephen Knight's sense) "*a reeve.*" But he is also "The Reve" (587), with a name ("Osewald" [3860]), a history ("In youthe he hadde lerned a good myster: / He was a wel good wrighte, a carpenter" [613–14]), and a physiognomy ("a sclendre colerik man" [587]). He has a house ("ful faire upon an heeth; / With grene trees yshadwed" [606–7]) and an underemployed phallus ("by his syde he baar a rusty blade" [618]).[124] He has a psychology: choleric, so resentful and vengeful; old and sexually frustrated, so (similarly) resentful and vengeful; resentful and vengeful, so a tyrannically efficient administrator; a tyrannically efficient administrator, so a sublimely expert thief. All this is hardly news: Jill Mann has lucidly argued that the General Prologue uses the materials of estates satire to delineate character.[125] Mann was tracing the literary origins of a specifically literary technique; but the technique has, if not ideological origins, at least ideological effect, defining how Chaucer could (and how he could not) present motivation and agency, what could bring characters to act and what acts they could perform. Using traditional characteristics of particular classes and professions to evoke not groups but individuals, Chaucer traces those characteristics to the idiosyncrasies of the individual rather than to the interests or needs of the group. Nothing would be easier than a flat-footed ideological reading of the Reeve, which might go something like this: enjoying (as reeves could) the opportunities available to the competent peasant who did the lord's work, but finding himself set apart from and against his equals while still offered no exit from their status—isolated, in other words, from both his fellows and his lord—the Reeve eases the sense of

---

124. Compare his own complaint: "For in oure wyl ther stiketh evere a nayl, / To have an hoor heed and a grene tayl, / As hath a leek; for thogh oure myght be goon, / Oure wyl desireth folie evere in oon" (3877–80).

125. "He makes us uncertain of the 'facts' that lie behind their social or professional façades. He uses a sense of past experience . . . to give us the conviction that his characters are not eternal abstractions but are affected by time. . . . Chaucer forces us to feel that we are dealing with real people because we cannot apply to them the absolute responses appropriate to the abstractions of moralistic satire" (Mann, *Chaucer and Medieval Estates Satire*, 189). See also Rosemary Woolf, "Chaucer as a Satirist in the *General Prologue* to the *Canterbury Tales*," *Critical Quarterly* 1 (1959): 150–57.

cognitive dissonance by living and acting purely on his own behalf, exploiting up the social scale and down it at the same time. But the most obvious thing about such a reading is its impertinence. Class does not embitter the Reeve; choler does.

In the narrative idiom of the *Canterbury Tales*, it is as individuals—as bodies, humors, and idiosyncratic personal histories—that characters *have* character. Turn it around and the same thing is true: it is only as individuals that they act, and it is individuals that they act upon. Patterson's argument that Chaucer contains the imagination of insurgency by turning the Miller's rebellion into the Reeve's grudge match is right, with only the reservation that the containment is already implicit in Chaucer's conception. Individuals—even when created to represent a class—still speak and act, from moment to narrative moment, as individuals; the impression that their actions emerge from psychologies and personal histories proscribes even the possibility of mentally substituting the class for its representative. The *Canterbury Tales* has its political purposes (as have some of its narrators), and it stages scenes that it would be silly not to call political. The poem can even gesture metonymically to collective acts, as in the Miller's "rebellion." But it cannot *represent* such acts: a collectivity of one is no collectivity, just a person. In this sense, the *Canterbury Tales* came more than just chronologically after 1381. It can voice relations of power in the encounters of individual characters, ventriloquize discourses from many sites of social experience, engage with the forms and ideologies of popular cultures, but at this particular price: anyone may speak, but no *ones* may speak together.

The pilgrims whom Chaucer used to move his poetry away from the court and city into a Kentish landscape marked by the memory of 1381 were so constructed that the memory of the rising would not be the grim companion of their travel. The one time that memory does emerge into the text, in the fox chase of the *Nun's Priest's Tale*, it emerges in esoteric play. Those who could decode its reference were those who knew the *Vox clamantis* and the Gower coat of arms, who knew that "Colle" was helped by "Geffe," who knew of Gower's claims to public authority and his apparent sexual diffidence—those who had shared with Gower a place in Chaucer's circle. To speak aloud about the rising, Chaucer returns to the cryptic cliquishness of his earlier poetry—the roman-à-clef allegory of the *Book of the Duchess*, the *House of Fame*, the *Parlement*, the *Legend*'s prologue—dispelling and forgetting its threat in the minutely textual encoding of a coterie joke. Chaucer begins the *Canterbury Tales* by announcing that he has moved himself and his poetry outside of London, that his address now extends beyond the court and its satellites; but when he speaks of the rising—which had suggested that there might be a "popular" audience wider than he was perhaps willing to face—he returns to that circle of London readers that he has claimed to have left behind.

Langland's move was more ostentatious, and more ambiguous. For perhaps fifteen of the years he worked at his poem, its governing conceit laid claim to the language, the implements, and the population of the countryside to figure English society and church and to explore the possibility of their reform. His third version, completed sometime in the 1380s (perhaps even the early 1390s),[126] finds him living "in Cornehull," London, "yclothed as a lollare" (C.5.1–2).[127] The autobiographical force of the passage—whether, that is, it has any—is open to doubt,[128] but the force of its gesture is not. The A- and B-versions of *Piers Plowman*, and for that matter the first four passus of the C-version, keep the dreamer unambiguously in the originating West Midlands site of his dream, and suggest throughout that Langland's rustic vocabulary implies rustic origins: he rested his poem on the fiction (at least—we know nothing of his residence during these years) that while extending his vision across all Christendom, the dreamer remains in the countryside from which he draws his authoritative language. But in C.5, he has moved to within a quarter-mile of Chaucer's sometime Aldgate lodgings—but ambiguously: no longer a rural outsider, but not a Londoner either, he lives "yn London and opelond bothe" (44). Thus the Prologue's claim to a geographical inclusiveness (where tillers jostle city

126. The dating of C has received less scholarly attention than that of B; Devlin's suggestion that Usk's *Testament of Love* alluded to C (which would therefore have been written and circulated before Usk's death in 1387) was accepted as recently as Bloomfield; the date has sat there more from convenience than anything else, though most would now acknowledge, I should think, that the presence of C in Usk is illusory, and Malcolm Godden disposes of it in a properly summary fashion (*The Making of Piers Plowman* [London, 1990], 171–72). It will become clear below that I accept a date after 1388, but the reasons are only persuasive, not compelling (see n. 160 below). It is not my purpose to be contentious in describing the C-text as the "third [not the fourth] version" of *Piers Plowman*, but in the absence of any compelling argument for the independent status of Bodley 851 as a separate ("Z") text, I make no use of it; and it is irrelevant to the argument of this book in any case. On the dating of the B-version, see n. 128 below.

127. Citations from the C-text are from Pearsall's edition.

128. On its status as autobiography, see Kane and Burrow, ch. 3, n. 53 above.

merchants) seems to become explicitly a matter of his own experience. But that is not all. Later in C he claims a London residence less ambiguously: "Ich haue yleued in Londone monye long 3eres" (16.286), he says in his colloquy with Liberum Arbitrium (*olim* Charite), defini-tively revising himself out of the countryside and into the metropolis (in B, the assertion is "I haue lyued in londe . . . my name is longe wille" [B.15.152]); but in adopting his city he effaces his signature, the most explicit acknowledgment of the name "Will Langland" he ever made. This is still not all. The earliest surviving manuscripts of *Piers Plowman* are C-version manuscripts, which, more certainly and uniformly than any other family of Langland manuscripts, appear to come from the West Midlands, where they probably enjoyed their earliest circulation.[129] The obvious (though not inevitable) inference is that C first circulated in the vicinity of its author. So Langland was writing in the West Midlands when, for the first time, he avowed a London residence. What was he doing?

The answer must follow a course as vagrant as Langland's own. The Corpus Christi rising challenged Langland more insistently and directly than any other writer, since the world had heard Piers enjoined to provision the rebels and Dowel become a figure for insurgent constancy. Walsingham looked at the rebels and saw monastic culture undone; Langland listened to them and heard himself quoted. He responded, I believe, by thinking back through 1381 and beyond, back to the later 1370s when he had launched *Piers* into the public world,[130] measuring

---

129. On this I depend entirely on Doyle, "Surviving Manuscripts," and M. L. Samuels, "Langland's Dialect," *MÆ* 54 (1985): 232–47.

130. The manuscript evidence for the A-version suggests unmistakably that this version never had, nor apparently was meant to have, the circulation that B achieved; see Doyle, "Surviving Manuscripts," 36–37. I am certain now that I was wrong in "Genres" to assume that B dates from after the papal schism of 1378: the criticism of the papal election in the prologue is manifestly *not* that *some* cardinals have "presumed" to elect an antipope, but that *any* cardinals, being what they are, should presume to elect *any* pope..If the lines do refer to the election in Avignon of Clement VII, why the elaborate pose of caution ("I kan & kan nau3t of court speke more" [prol.111]), since England immediately and almost inevitably sided with Urban VI? Caution would be needed only if the election of which he almost speaks were generally approved around him. All this is complicated by the real ambiguity in what it means to date a work in a manuscript culture, where copies could be made and circulated with or without the author's approval, while the process of composition was still going on. That reservation noted, I now date the B-version at 1376–77, which hardly makes a revolutionary difference in the understanding of literary history but makes some in the understanding of Langland; my evidence is much the same as, though read differently from, that of J. J. Jusserand, *L'Épopée mystique de William Langland* (Paris, 1893); I hope to defend this assertion and discuss the complications of dating in a future essay.

how his voice had sounded once it was beyond recall. In effect, he did something neither Chaucer nor Gower did, something in which he looks at first more like the chroniclers than the poets but finally like none of them: he tried to imagine where the revolt came from—not the events that provoked it, but the discourses that shaped it.

Langland's awareness that Piers had found himself in rebel company was only one warning, though perhaps the most explicit, that his poem was being read to say what he had never meant. Other things had happened to *Piers Plowman* after the mid-1370s, and one of them was Wyclif, whose London preaching in 1376–77 and abortive trial at St. Paul's in 1377 (where Gaunt's high-handed abuse of Bishop Courtenay nearly detonated riots in London)[131] took place just as (I think) copies of the B-version were beginning to circulate. These events made Wyclif's reformist proposals a cause célèbre and began the transformation of "reform" into "heresy." That Wyclif had surely never heard of Langland, and certainly did not allude to his poem, made no difference: changes in the C-version show Langland's realization that his voice had entered the public world along with another, one that sounded uncannily like his and that he had good reason to distance himself from. In his reactions to Wyclif and to the rebels' use of *Piers*, Langland shows an awareness that his poem, structured around the convocation of discordant social voices, could become, through publication, just another one of those voices; that the context into which it issued could harden it into ideology. E. T. Donaldson thought that Langland responded to 1381 by so specifying his meaning as to put it beyond mistake.[132] That is only half the story: Langland's enterprise of principled specificity is the first move in his larger enterprise of principled evasion.

We will never know whether Langland knew of John Ball's Blackheath sermon or of his use of Wit's harangue from B.9. But his minutely attentive changes to the Wit passage in C are among his most obscurely motivated, eliminating apparently harmless stuff quite in harmony with the rest of the poem (a longish passage on Christian responsibility for waifs, for example). Still, Langland recasts the passage in a way that affects specifically, and almost exclusively, the lines and concerns that

---

131. On the inquisition at St. Paul's, see Walsingham, *Chronicon Angliae*, 11–21.

132. Langland "must . . . have been considerably embarrassed by his unwitting mésalliance with John Ball," Donaldson says in explaining the revisions to the prologue (Donaldson, *Piers Plowman: The C-text and Its Poet* [New Haven, 1949], 108; seconded by Middleton, "Public Poetry," 98).

Ball had appropriated from B.9. The bastards are still there, but they are in different company:

> Ho-so lyueth in lawe and in loue doth wel,
> As this wedded men þat this world susteyneth,
> For of here kynde þey come, bothe confessours and martres,
> Prophetus and patriarkes, popes and maydenes.
>
> (C.10.202–5)

The "wedded men" are the lineal descendants of the "trewe wedded libbynge folk" in B. They still "sustain" the world, still give birth as in B. Three things have changed. First, the various estates no longer come "out of o man," as in the B-version line that John Ball used to trace a primal equality back to Adam and Eve. Second, from the list of the progeny of the wedded folk, Langland has excised the "Kynges and kynʒtes, kaysers and [clerkes]" (B.9.113) and replaced them with "Prophetus," "patriarkes," and "popes," so that the C-version lists not social ranks, but the categories of saints on the Roman calendar—removing any temptation to draw conclusions of social equality from the passage. Third, though the folk are "wedded folk" in C, it is no longer clear what else they are. B set "trewe wedded libbynge folk" in apposition to "trewe tidy men þat trauaille desiren," those that "ofgon hir liflode," making the wedded folk *country* folk. But C translates this agricultural lexicon into a clerical metaphor: "Prelates and prestes" replace the "trewe tidy men" of B, and their job is "To tulie þe erthe with tonge and teche men to louye" (C.10.199), a conventional allegory of priesthood and preaching that empties tillage of any material or geographical reference.[133] "Susteyneth," then, is emptied of its agricultural connotations: it now means only that the folk populate the world, where before it had also suggested that their rural "trauaille" sustains with food the population that already exists.

So the C-version passage has shed just those elements that Ball used: the wedded folk remain, but their location (like Langland's own, "in London and opeland bothe") has grown hazy. Likewise with the condemnation of parsimonious bishops that Ball seems to have directed against Sudbury: "*Proditor est prelatus cum Iuda, qui patrimonium christi minus distribuit*" (B.9.91a). This line and its context disappear in C,

---

133. See Stephen A. Barney, "The Plowshare of the Tongue: The Progress of a Symbol from the Bible to *Piers Plowman*," *MS* 35 (1973): 261–93, for the conventional, traditional character of this allegory.

replaced by a new passage that does not so much describe different bishops as it describes the same bishops differently:

> And thenne dede we alle wel, and wel bet ʒut to louye
> Oure enemyes enterely and helpe hem at here nede.
> And ʒut were best to ben aboute and brynge hit to hepe
> That alle landes loueden and in on lawe bileuede.
> Bishopes sholde ben hereaboute and bryng this to hepe,
> For to lese þerfore her lond and her lyf aftur.
> The catel that Crist hadde thre clothes hit were;
> Therof was he robbed and ruyfled or he on rode deyede
> And seth he lees his lyf for lawe sholde loue wexe.
> Prelates and prestes and princes of holy churche
> Sholde nat doute no deth ne no dere ʒeres
> To wende as wyde as þe worlde were
> To tulie þe erthe with tonge and teche men to louye;
> For ho-so loueth, leueth hit wel, god wol nat laton hym sterue
> In meschief for defaute of mete ne for myssyng of clothes.
>
> (C.10.187–201)

I quote this long passage because both its presence and its difficulties show how carefully Langland managed his response to Ball. Pearsall glosses "For to lese" concessively ("Despite the fact that they should lose"); this is grammatically plausible, but hard to reconcile with the lines that conclude the passage, which ask the bishops to become mendicants (for what else might Wit mean by the injunction that they "wende as wyde as þe worlde were" in the trust that "god wol nat laton hym sterue"?). "For to" is less grimly concessive than Pearsall takes it to be: Wit advises the bishops to "bring this to hepe" *to the point of* sacrificing their lands and their lives. The example of Christ, "robbed and ruyfled or he on rode deyede" confirms the reading: his loss of goods and life brought "loue" out of "lawe" and secured redemption. In other words, Wit asks the bishops to disembarrass themselves of their wealth, or (as another might have put it) to disendow themselves. But what prompts the suggestion? How could a mendicant mission, carried by bishops to heathen lands,[134] answer the problems Wit raises in the rest of the passus?

It does not answer them: there is no explaining the contextual point of this passage because it has none. The lines before it discuss "faunto-

---

134. They should see "That *alle landes* loueden and *in on lawe bileued*": these words hardly make sense outside the context of a mission to non-Christians.

kynes and foles þe which þat fauten inwit" (182), the lines after, the
"wedded men þat this world susteyneth" (203). Vagrant, mendicant,
preaching bishops pertain to neither in any obvious way. But they do
pertain to the *original* passage (in B), now imprinted by the events of
Corpus Christi week. When Langland looked again at this page, he saw
what Ball had made of it and perhaps saw its readers seeing what Ball
had made of it; the B-text passage on bishops now meant Sudbury's
execution. C's new advice is that bishops had better get rid of their
goods before others do it for them, as the rebels had purposed to do.
But the rising alone could not have produced this specific proposal for
a missionary episcopacy: after 1381, the prudently reformist mind might
well have thought that poorer bishops would be safer bishops and better
ones, but they might have been allowed to live at home; why does
Langland send them among the heathen?

When Langland wrote B, disendowment was an indistinct lump of
reformist ideology not yet the property of anyone, though it had a
fraternal, even Franciscan flavor;[135] by the time he wrote C, it belonged
so completely to Wyclif that no one else wanted it. Langland offered
his recommendation that bishops become mendicant missionaries in
order to preserve the point of the B-text polemics, to rescue them from
John Ball's appropriations, and to cleanse them of the Wycliffian suggestions that had attached both to the rising and, by another route, to
his own text. While Wyclif had some notion of what a disendowed
episcopacy would look like (it would be poor), he never seems to have
pictured what in particular it was supposed to *do*, without Courts
Christian and excommunications to occupy it. Certainly he did not
picture missions; the landscape of his utopian imagination is English.[136]

---

135. The best-known examples are the disendowment proposal offered in the 1371
parliament by two Austin friars and the arguments by John Mardisley, provincial minister
of the English Franciscans, before the great council in 1373; for the former, see V. H.
Galbraith, "Articles Laid Before the Parliament of 1371," *EHR* 34 (1919): 479–82, and for
the latter, *Eulogium* 3:337–39, and Jeremy I. Catto, "An Alleged Great Council of 1374,"
EHR 82 (1967): 764–71. The history of disendowment is traced in Margaret Aston,
"'Caim's Castles,'" where she uncovers the case of one "frater Johannes" at Oxford, who
recanted a proposal for the disendowment of the secular clergy in 1358 (50). (This may be
the Franciscan about whom Wyclif narrates a similar story in *De veritate* [1:356].) The very
popular disendowment prophecies of the mid-fourteenth-century Franciscan rigorist Jean
de Roquetaillade circulated widely in England; see Kerby-Fulton, *Reformist Apocalypticism*,
23 (a good argument could be made for his influence on Wyclif).

136. On Wyclif's anglocentric ecclesiology, see especially Edith C. Tatnall, "John
Wyclif and *Ecclesia Anglicana*," *Journal of Ecclesiastical History* 20 (1969): 19–59.

Langland assumes a wider scope, maneuvering himself behind Wyclif to recover a notion of disendowment that had become nearly archaic in the 1380s. Wyclif sent no particular thoughts beyond the bounds of Christendom, but the fraternal orders did (the Order of Friars Preachers sprang from Dominic Guzman's realization that ornate papal legates made unpersuasive missionaries; Francis sought the martyr's palm before the sultan). And after a fashion, they still did. Lawrence Clopper has persuasively argued that Anima's complaint in *Piers Plowman* B.15—that the "prelates" of Nazareth, Nineveh, Naphtali, and Damascus "ne wente as crist wisseþ . . . / To be pastours and preche" (15.492–96)—reflects a rigorist Franciscan critique of abusive Franciscan practice: in Langland's lifetime, a fair number of suffragan bishops of such places resided in England, far from their nominal flocks.[137] So Langland perhaps puts these poor, preaching bishops in C.10 to associate himself with the friars, and thereby with the *pre*-Wycliffite disendowment proposals that friars were floating back in the 1370s, when he was still writing B.

In one way, this gesture has distracted us from the rebellion, as Langland probably hoped it would. But in another, indirect and more interesting way, it acknowledges what Gower and Walsingham denied. The rebellion Langland imagines and responds to is neither a kind of historical sport, an isolated eruption without cause, nor the predictable outcome of peasant irrationality. Although he clarifies or effaces details that Ball lifted for the Blackheath sermon, he does not efface the point of Ball's critique: he is still talking about bishops, about their wealth and its spiritual and political dangers. I said earlier that the new passage on bishops relates only to its parent passage in B, not to its context in C, but that is not precisely correct. For if the passage is read *as a revision of B.9*—not, that is, merely for what it says, but against the background of what it no longer says—the logical connections reappear within the C-text passage. In the C-text, Wit arrives at his comments on bishops straight from these comments on imbeciles—

> Ac fauntokynes and foles þe which þat fauten inwit,
> Frendes shal fynde hem and fram folye kepe
> And holy churche helpe to, so sholde no man begge
> Ne spille speche ne tyme, ne myspende noyther

137. This argument appears in Clopper's forthcoming study of Langland's Franciscanism, *Wille Longelonde's Songs of Rechelesnesse*, ch. 2.

Meble ne vnmeble, mete noþer drynke.
And thenne dede we alle wel, and wel bet ȝut to louye
Oure enemyes enterely and helpe hem at here nede
(10.182–88)

On the face of it, the transition from here to the bishops is no transition at all. Such internal coherence as the passage has derives only from the grammatical inevitability of the Dowel, Dobet, Dobest progression (it would be good to take care of each other, better to love our enemies, and bishops could help with the latter by evangelizing the world). But if we read the passage instead as Langland's representation of the internal dialogue between the B-version and the rising,[138] the connections become clearer. "Sholde no cristene creature cryen at þe yate, / Ne faille payn ne potage *and prelates dide as þei sholden*" (B.9.82–83): thus the B-text links the sufferings of "[Fauntes and] fooles" (B.9.68), of whom C also speaks, to episcopal wealth, and prepares for the climactic Latin tag—omitted in C because it had achieved public consequence on Tower Hill in 1381—*Proditor est prelatus cum Iuda qui patrimonium christi minus distribuit.* If these connections from B are supplied to the passage in C—where the fools and beggars lead to the proposal for the self-disendowment of bishops—the rationale for the proposal becomes clear, and the passage becomes a coded dialogue with the rebels' use of Langland's words. Precisely by forcing readers to supply the connection, Langland connects the failure of bishops to relieve the sufferings of the poor with the events that forced him to revise the passage in the first place; the secret that explains the C-text passage is Sudbury's execution. The rebels who killed Sudbury declared why they killed him with a bitter, parodic tableau of the Crucifixion, with his head in Christ's place.[139] Langland deploys the same contrast. Christ was "robbed and ruyfled or he on rode deyede"—despoiled, like the archbishop, and then killed—but in the service of redemption: "seth he lees hys lyf for lawe sholde loue wexe." Not "loue," but more and sterner "lawe" followed Sudbury's execution, which seems in Langland a punishment whose justice he obviously cannot endorse but with which he does not know how to argue.

What this means, finally, is hard to say, which is why I spoke of

138. My vocabulary here is borrowed from P. N. Medvedev, *The Formal Method in Literary Scholarship: A Critical Introduction to Sociological Poetics*, trans. Albert J. Wehrle (Baltimore, 1978).

139. See above, ch. 2.

Langland's "principled evasion." The C-revision, which has always been thought to iron out the complexities of B, only wrinkles them further; his revisions echo back to their origins in B and, I think, were meant to. This is an unconventional assertion, though it does follow (if not inevitably) from some conventional ones; nor is it specific to the rising and its aftermath, which is one aspect of Langland's peculiar achievement. Recently, scholars have noticed that some moments in C read like answers to criticisms of B,[140] answers which assume that B is a public document and that what Langland changes in it will be registered *as* changes by a public that already knows the poem. If this was Langland's sense, he was probably right: the manuscript evidence suggests as much,[141] as does his influence on nearly contemporary poems like *Pierce the Ploughman's Crede* and *The Wars of Alexander*, and even Chaucer's one-line impersonation of *Piers* in the General Prologue and his massive encounter with Langland toward the end of his career.[142] Revision was in part Langland's attempt to reassert control over a literary idea that had become public property. By playing C back against B, adjusting to intervening events, visibly reconfiguring his text to match the reconfigurations of public discourse, Langland in effect registered, without narrating, the contemporary history of attempts to reform social and religious life. When he revised B.9 into C.10, he addressed the rising not as the isolated and monstrous and unique terror it was for the chroniclers, but as one moment in the history of reform. By classifying it with the establishment of the mendicant orders and Wycliffian pro-

140. "If this [Langland's poor reputation among 'lollares of London' avowed in C.5] can be relied upon to be literally true, then Langland had attained something of the reputation of a moralist or reformer already on the basis of the A- and B-texts, albeit a grudging one" (Kerby-Fulton, *Reformist Apocalypticism*, 70; and, on the same passage, Scase, *New Anticlericalism*, 149–50).

141. Kane and Donaldson's introduction to their B-text establishes that Langland had only a relatively corrupt manuscript of B, not his holograph, when he came to write C (98–127). The reasons for his loss of the holograph are of course undecidable—poverty, change of residence, and (why not?) foreign travel are possibilities, besides the generally rejected theory of multiple authorship—but its loss is less interesting than Langland's ability to lay his hand on some other copy of the poem, and a corrupt copy at that: one therefore that had either been executed commercially or been privately copied outside Langland's own supervision.

142. When the narrator of the *Canterbury Tales* allows the Parson's voice to sound in indirect discourse ("And this figure he added eek therto, / That if gold ruste, what shal iren do?" [I.499–500]), he concludes with a virtuoso compassing of Langlandian alliterative style and vocabulary within his own decasyllabic line: "And shame it is, if a prest take keep, / A shiten shépherde / and a cléne shéep" (503–4); Anne Middleton is preparing work on the importance of Langland in redirecting, and finally stalling, the *Canterbury Tales*.

posals for disendowment, he treated it simply as one more discursive event in the attempt to reimagine church and society.

But insofar as he admits the memory of the insurgency into his work, he does so through silences and repressions. It is likely, for example, that Piers' tearing of the pardon in the A- and B-versions disappeared from C in consequence of the great revolt; specifically, I should think, because it seemed in retrospect to confer theological dignity on the destruction of archives. Cutting this scene also removed Piers' fairly contentious assertion of his own theological literacy, when he trades psalter tags with the meddlesome priest; Langland had evidently come to see the two actions, taken together, as a tableau worryingly reminiscent of the rising's ambition to replace old parchment with new parchment. So he erased them; like Walsingham and Knighton and Gower and Chaucer, he suppressed any suggestion of authoritatively literate peasants. But he suppressed with a difference. The chroniclers excised evidences of coherence and planning, leaving only the image of a raging peasant violence; Langland excised the violence. To put it in another and perhaps paradoxical way, by refusing to represent the rising in narrative, Langland refused any attempt to contain it by explanatory cause and effect, and therefore by closure.[143] Chroniclers, poets, chancellors, and bishops all tried to sink the memory of the rebels' discursive ambitions in images of uncontrolled violence, forgetting speech by remembering noise and fire. Langland chose to forget the violence, and thereby left his poem open to a real, though really attenuated, exchange with the claims of the revolt, and to a reconsideration of the sources of his own authority.

The pardon that appears, but is not torn, in C registers in changes both large and small how Langland incorporated the rising into the poem as a discursive event. The most obvious change in C is the addition of two long passages on the discrimination of worthy from unworthy beggars.[144] C inflates beggary out of all apparent proportion, so that it occupies nearly half the pardon's length (now 272 lines) and becomes

---

143. The most dramatic witness to the complexity of Langland's response, and his quirky refusal to represent the rising as the riot of rural appetite, is that it leaves no mark in the one place anyone would expect it to. In the plowing scene of A.7 and B.6, he had already represented precisely the sort of peasant revolt that appears in Walsingham, Knighton, Gower, and the rest: field hands in a violent, boorish assertion of undeserved privilege. But the version of this passus in C.8 shows absolutely no reaction to 1381, no sense that the B passage was prophecy fulfilled by the event.

144. C.9.70–161, 187–282. These passages elaborate B.7.65–99.

its real focus. David Aers gives a fine account of the pardon in *Piers Plowman* B that shows what is at stake. After noting the concern in B with the "wasters" who live luxuriously off the fruits of begging, Aers sensibly asks, "Who actually contributes with such unconditional generosity to fill the bags, bowls, and bellies of such hedonistic vagrants, ones merrily touring post-plague England to waste all that the hard-working winners have produced?"[145] For Aers, the figure of the waster preoccupies Langland as much as it did the nobles and gentry who made and enforced the Statute of Laborers, and it explains his troubled social conservatism: the category of "able-bodied beggar" covered, and covered over, the determination of those who were not (or at least did not want to be) beggars at all to seek higher wages by traveling from manor to manor; it was, Aers says, "an ideological and partisanly class term" meant to help the powerful wring cheap labor from the economically most vulnerable class.[146] Since the rebels did make the statute one of their articulated concerns, this shrewd observation makes it at least plausible that C's massively more detailed interest in the problem (just before Piers, for the first time in three versions, does *not* tear the pardon or quote scripture to the priest) comes in reaction to the revolt (which is, indeed, one of Aers's recurring points of reference). I think it does, but that it performs more complex work than Aers suggests.

The categories of mendicancy are roughly the same in C as in B: there are those who cannot work, and are fit objects of charity; and there are those who can, and are not.[147] What changes is the authority to which Langland appeals when he advocates erring on the side of generosity rather than of caution. The discussion of beggary begins as it does in B:

> Beggares and biddares beth nat in þat bulle
> Bote the sugestioun be soth þat shapeth hym to begge.
> For he þat begeth or biddeth, but yf he haue nede,
> He is fals and faytour and defraudeth the nedy
> And also gileth hym þat gyueth and taketh agayne his wille.
> For he þat gyueth for goddes loue wolde nat gyue, his thankes,

145. Aers, *Community, Gender, and Individual Identity: English Writing 1360–1430* (London, 1988), 36.

146. Aers, *Community*, 40.

147. I am here ignoring the new category Langland adds, the healthy but witless "lunatyk lollares" (9.105–27). The addition of this category has little effect on his fundamental scheme or its originary purposes (though it has a very great effect on Langland's own conception of the poetic vocation).

> Bote ther he wiste were wel grete nede
> And most merytorie to men þat he ȝeueth fore.
> Catoun acordeth therwith: *Cui des, videto.*
> (C.9.61–69)

The passage is, so far, nearly identical to B's.[148] Both versions describe
the ethics of mendicancy in the language of commerce—the false beggar
defrauds the almsgiver—and both cite a classical source, the *Disticha
Catonis*, that advocates suspicion on the donor's part. At this point in B
(in a move that Aers rightly implies is a crucial turn in the poem),
Langland imports another authority—a Christian this time, Gregory
the Great—to oppose to the *Disticha* and suggest that the donor should
lean rather toward charity ("Do not choose on whom you will take
mercy, lest perhaps you pass over one worthy to receive" [B.7.77a]).[149]
Nothing of the sort happens in C: Cato stays, Gregory disappears, but
Gregory's *conclusion* remains, underwritten no longer by an authoritative
text but by an extraordinary and compelling description of suffering
poverty:

> Woet no man, as y wene, who is worthy to haue;
> Ac þat most neden aren oure neyhebores, and we nyme gode hede,
> As prisones in puttes and pore folk in cotes,
> Charged with childrene and chief lordes rente;

148. Which reads:

> Beggeres [and] bidderes beþ noȝt in þe bulle
> But if þe suggestion be sooþ þat shapeþ hem to begge,
> For he þat beggeþ or bit, but he haue nede,
> He is fals wiþ þe feend and defraudeþ þe nedy,
> And [ek g]ileþ þe gyuere ageynes his wille.
> For if he wiste he were noȝt nedy he wolde [it ȝyue]
> Anoþer that were moore nedy; so þe nedieste sholde be holpe.
> Caton kenneþ me þus and þe clerc of stories.
> *Cui des videto* is Catons techyng,
> And in þe stories he techeþ to bistowe þyn almesse:
> *Sit elemosina tua in manu tua donec studes cui des.*
> Ac Gregory was a good man and bad vs gyuen alle
> That askeþ for his loue þat vs al leneþ:
> *Non eligas cui miser[e]aris ne forte pretereas illum qui meretur accipere,*
> *Quia incertum est pro quo deo magis placeas.*
> (B.7.65–77a)

149. This quotation from Gregory, says Aers, is here "submerged in the ethos expressed
by the non-Christian Cato," leaving untouched "the *dominant* tendency of Passus VI and
VII"; but immediately thereafter, in Passus 8 and following, Langland "began a dramatic
disengagement from the newer ethos" that resembles the teaching of Gregory (*Community*,
53).

þat they with spynnyng may spare, spenen it on hous-huyre,
Bothe in mylke and in mele, to make with papelotes
To aglotye with here gurles that greden after fode.

(C.9.70–76)

And so on for another twenty lines. In C the rigorous ethic of almsgiving is dismantled not (as in B) by the authoritative precedence of a Christian over a non-Christian source, but by the empirical force of hunger and its imperatives. That Langland does eventually prop this judgment (in C.11 and following) with the authoritative texts he eschews here does not erase the plain fact that in C.9 he treats rural experience as authority enough to serve in God's own pardon. Langland first legitimates the major turn that Aers notes by acknowledging the force of one complaint the rising launched against lordship, the extravagant cost of the "chief lordes rente."

But is this claim—that Langland substitutes peasant experience and peasant complaint for a textual authority he had already deployed—really plausible? Like B, C insists on the authoritative and documentary status of the pardon as it is given in the first two-thirds of the passus; B.7.5–106 and C.9.4–281 present the pardon itself, marginally annotated and supplemented by explanatory writs (the lines are not "someone's long and enthralling gloss" on the pardon, as Aers thinks).[150] Within the fiction of the poem, the document summarized here *is* the pardon Truth has sent to Piers;[151] it bears the impress of divine authority. So why, in C alone, does Langland wriggle when he introduces the poor folk in cotes ("Woet no man, *as y wene*, who is worthy to haue" [C.9.70]) and then plainly identify experience as his source twenty lines later ("This I woet witterly, *as the world techeth*" [88])? If this document comes from Truth himself, shouldn't Langland's weening and the world's teaching be mere impertinence? At this moment in the poem, God speaks the language of rural experience, or, more precisely and pertinently, rural experience speaks to Langland with the force of divine assertion. Langland has negotiated with the object of his own repression. As he prepared to excise the tearing of the pardon, lest he seem to endorse the rebels' way with documents, he has allowed the rebels'

---

150. Aers, *Community*, 49.

151. Similarly, the pardon also *is* the "two lynes" of the Athanasian creed (B.7.112a, C.9.289a). On the status of the lines summarizing the pardon, and of the two-line version that follows, see David Lawton, *"Piers Plowman*: On Tearing—and Not Tearing—the Pardon," *Philological Quarterly* 60 (1981): 414–22; and my "Genres," 303.

concerns to shape the contents of the pardon itself and found theological authority in the desperation of rural smallholders.

This claim may seem surprising, the more so because Langland promotes rural experience to theological authority in a passage that elaborates (as Aers shows) a limpidly ideological castigation of wandering laborers. Aers assumes that Langland's concern with vagrants betrays anxieties prompted by the events of 1381. But the idea that the landless sponsored or dominated insurgent activity is more an ideologically loaded assumption than a demonstrated fact,[152] and it belongs more to the nineteenth and twentieth centuries than to the fourteenth.[153] Demographic facts aside, the rebels cast themselves, in their public pronouncements, as the settled, smallholding population of the villages. Tyler's demands at Smithfield—that law be the "law of Winchester," that the disendowed goods of the church be divided among "parishioners," and that land be free and of fixed rent—all reflect the interests of the settled village population.[154] The images of the rebel letters—the "post" and "sayles" of Milner's mill, those who gather and "hery[e]þ þe day" or work to "dyȝt . . . corne" (Carter), the "belle" "rungen" by John Ball (Ball₁), Ball's attack on "slouthe" (Ball₂)—locate their authoritative community around the fixtures of the village settlement, and their authority in those who work there. In his condemnation of vagrancy, Langland, as Aers says, is a "traditional moralist";[155] but so were Wat Tyler and the authors of the letters, and villagers themselves: communities themselves thought idleness a threat to their production and survival. "Vagabond" was an insult villagers could direct at one an-

---

152. Dyer states what his collation of indictments with court rolls has shown: "This evidence shows that 100 of 180 rebels from the whole area of rebellion owned goods valued at £1 to £5, and 15 of them were worth more than £5. . . . This is sufficient to show that we are dealing primarily with people well below the ranks of the gentry, but who mainly held some land and goods, not the 'marginals' recently claimed as playing an important part in the revolt" ("Social and Economic Background," 15).

153. Walsingham and Knighton and the continuator of the *Eulogium* and the Monk of Westminster are all quite certain that, however Wyclif or the friars may have fomented rebellion, it was the communities of the villeins who rebelled; so was chancery, whose pardon later in the year spoke of the revolt by "villeins and other malefactors" (*Rp* 3.103). The assumption that it was vagrants who led the violence comes especially from Charles Petit-Dutaillis, "Les prédications populaires: Les lollards et le soulèvement des travailleurs anglais en 1381," in *Études d'histoire du moyen âge dédiées à Gabriel Monod* (Paris, 1896), 373–88.

154. *Anonimalle,* 147.

155. Aers, *Community,* 52–53.

other;[156] village beggars who were "known to the community . . . might fare moderately well at begging," says Barbara Hanawalt, "but strangers were regarded with suspicion."[157]

What John Ball did to Wit's bishops and bastards in B.9 provoked Langland to rethink what he had done to laborers in B.7: his own words became a problem to him once the rebels had presented them as their own. He removed from B.9 the language Ball had taken, but that language did not disappear; it moved, resurfacing in his most explicit moment of reconsideration, the C-text "autobiography" with which I began. A difficult and very troubled passage there brings the bastards and the bishops together once again:

> Hit bycometh for clerkes Crist for to serue
> And knaues vncrounede to carte and to worche.
> For sholde no clerke be crouned but yf he come were
> Of frankeleynes and fre men and of folke ywedded.
> Bondemen and *bastardus* and beggeres children,
> Thyse bylongeth to labory, and lordes kyn to serue
> God and good men, as here degre asketh,
> Somme to synge masses or sitten and wryten,
> Redon and resceyuen þat resoun ouhte to spene.
> Ac *sythe bondemen barnes haen be mad bisshopes*
> *And barnes bastardus haen be erchedekenes*
> And soutares and here sones for suluer han be knyhtes
> And lordes sones here laboreres and leyde here rentes to wedde,
> For the ryhte of this reume ryden aȝeyn oure enemyes
> In confort of the comune and the kynges worschipe,
> And monkes and moniales, þat mendenantes sholde fynde,
> Imade here kyn knyhtes and knyhtes-fees ypurchased,
> Popes and patrones pore gentel blood refused
> And taken Symondes sones seyntwarie to kepe,
> Lyf-holynesse and loue hath be longe hennes,
> And wol, til hit be wered out, or oþerwyse ychaunged.
>
> (C.5.61–81)

This is possibly the most uncompromising assertion of class privilege in the whole poem, and Will sputters his way through it. He meets Reason's question (why do you not labor? aren't you then a vagrant?)

---

156. As the jurors at Broughton called some young rowdies from their own vill (Britton, *Community of the Vill*, 38ff.).

157. Hanawalt, *Ties That Bound*, 236.

with the claim that his clerical status exempts him from work, invoking a picture of social organization that matches labor to villeinage and clergy to freedom—the precise opposite of John Ball's. In a spasm of indignation (parodying, almost, the prophetic parataxis of Reason's speech in the passus before),[158] Will insists that he could be mistaken for a vagrant only because these distinctions (between labor and clergy, villeinage and freedom) have already collapsed: villeins and their bastards sit on the bishop's throne, and knights plow the fields. The undoing of status that the insurgents threatened in 1381 has, Will implies, already happened. In his own defense, he tries to keep stratification rigid, but in doing so, he nonetheless speaks the language of B.9 as Ball had spoken it. Here Will uses (as Ball had used) the population of Wit's speech: the "folke ywedded" (64; compare "trewe wedded libbynge folk" [B.9.110]), their opposites the "bastardus" (65; compare "Wastours and wrecches out of wedlok . . . / Conceyued," [B.9.122–23]), and the deficient "bisshopes" behind it all (70; *"Proditor est prelatus cum Iuda"* [94a]). For Ball, Langland's bastards—wandering, invasive, and oppressive—were a metaphor for the bishops; for Will, they are the very bishops themselves.

But the rigidity cannot so easily protect Will, or Langland, from the charge of vagrancy. At Cornhill, Will lives where vagrants were pilloried;[159] and vagrancy is in any case what Will has been about since the A-text, the poem's model of inquiry. Langland's life and his lifework are both at issue in C.5, which covertly resumes Will's dispute with Imaginatif (in B.12) over the issue of "makyng."[160] The "autobiographical" passage was, Day and Donaldson have suggested, among the last passages Langland added to C,[161] a late attempt to justify his vocation.

---

158. The paratactic structure of these lines in C.5—"Sythe . . . and . . . and . . . "—echoes the "Til . . . and . . . and . . . " of Reason's prophecy:

> "Rede me nat," quod Reson, "no reuþe to haue
> Til lordes and ladies louen alle treuthe
> And hatien alle harlotrie, to heren hit oþer to mouþen hit;
> And tyl Purnele porfiel be put in here whicche . . ."
> (C.4.108–11)

159. See a London ordinance of 1375: "Also,—that no one who, by handicraft, or by the labour of his body, can gain his living, shall counterfeit the begging poor. . . . and that every constable and bedel shall have power to take such persons, and bring them to Cornhulle and put them in the stocks, there to remain according to the Ordinance made thereupon" (Riley, *Memorials of London*, 390; Riley's translation).

160. Kerby-Fulton, *Reformist Apocalypticism*, 70.

161. Donaldson, *C-Text*, 26.

Two things are in his mind as he does it: vagrancy and John Ball. Why these, and why together? Lawrence Clopper and Anne Middleton have independently shown that Reason charges Will with vagrancy under the revised (1388) Statute of Laborers.[162] But why would the statute, the tool of the lords, prompt Langland to his most elaborate self-defense? The answer, I think, is that he had already been charged—by name, so to speak—with the same delinquency, by very different accusers: "lat peres þe plowman my broþur. duelle at home and dyȝt vs corne" (Carter). Through the statute, the lords told those like Langland to cease their wandering; the rebel letters told Piers to cease his. Taken together, the rising and the statute put Langland in an absurd position, facing the same challenge from opposed camps: the rebels who rose against the lords and the lords who wanted a revised statute to prevent any such rebels from rising again.

Another, very minor, lexical revenance in C.5 from Wit's discussion of bastards and marriage shows what defensive anxiety this conjunction of accusers provoked. In B.9, Wit advises "euery maner seculer [man] þat may noȝt continue / Wisely go wedde" (B.9.182–83). Skeat glosses "continue" as "remain chaste," clearly what the context implies. This word, which enjoys no particular prominence in the B-version, becomes a kind of compulsion in C, with particular density and insistence in Passus 5 and a far broader reference than mere chastity. His clerical vocation, Will asserts, is "beste for the body, as the boek telleth, / And sykerost for þe soule, by so y wol *contenue*" (C.5.38–39); and in the autobiographical passage, Reason concludes by exhorting Will to begin "The lyif þat is louable and leele to thy soule," and Conscience chimes in "ȝe, and *contynue*" (103–4). *Continuance*—perseverance—is the minimal condition of an allowable life. While perseverance cannot of itself justify a life, its absence of itself compromises one ("*by so* y wol contenue"). The need to *continue* is the anxiety expressed in Passus 5. The rising showed Langland that his written church might try to come to life and humiliate him; it breached his fictive separation of church from world and of Langland from Will. The rising and the statute *together* showed him that lords and rebels, agreeing in nothing else, agreed that

162. See Clopper, "Need Men and Women Labor? Langland's Wanderer and the Labor Ordinances," in Hanawalt, ed., *Chaucer's England*, 110–29; an essay by Anne Middleton (first written in 1980 but forthcoming in Kerby-Fulton and Justice, *William Langland and Piers Plowman*) locates C.5 in precise response to the reissue of the statute by the Cambridge parliament of 1388.

people like him—wanderers—caused England's problems. But to renounce wandering and therefore authorship would amount to confessing that he had massively "myspened" his time (C.5.93), that his two decades of making had been a flat mistake. How, then, in the face of these accusations, can he "contenue"? How can his wandering be so construed as not to be wandering? So asks C.5.

And so:

> And so y leue yn London and opelond bothe;
> The lomes þat y labore with and lyflode deserue
> Is *pater-noster* and my prymer, *placebo* and *dirige*,
> And my sauter som tyme and my seuene psalmes.
> This y segge for here soules of suche as me helpeth,
> And tho þat fynden me my fode fouchen-safe, y trowe,
> To be welcome when y come, oþer-while in a monthe,
> Now with hym, now with here; on this wyse y begge
> Withoute bagge or botel but my wombe one.
>
> (49–52)

These lines initiate Langland's most urgent defense of poetry, a rethinking of his meditations in B.12.[163] The rising and then the statute told him that his poetic inquiry was mere idleness, or at best unproductive work, and these lines return a most indirect answer. What can it mean to say that he lives "yn London and opeland bothe," and why would he say it?

What can it mean? The aspect of the verb creates difficulties right

---

163. His partial move to London is not the only thing that has changed since the B-text. The "autobiographical" passage in part supplants the inquisition about "making" to which B's Imaginatif subjected Will, and it reverses his assertions there:

> Ac if þer were any wight þat wolde me telle
> What were dowel and dobet and dobest at þe laste,
> Wolde I neuere do werk, but wende to holi chirche
> And þere bidde my bedes but whan ich ete or slepe.
>
> (B.12.25–28)

Where, in B's apologia, bidding his beads would be the welcome consequence of learning Dowel and would signal his farewell to labor, in C's the bidding has already begun and *is* his labor. Writing is not—at least not as it was in B: for the strangest thing about C.5 is how obliquely his writing enters it at all, since it is never quite explicitly mentioned in his long defense. There are, however, the ambiguous lines defining the cleric's proper duties— "Somme to synge masses or sitten and wryten, / Redon and resceyuen þat resoun ouhte to spene" (C.5.68–69)—among whose problems is what sort of writing is under question, and specifically whether or not the following line is meant to be in apposition to it. But though unmentioned it is not absent, since his poetry ("y *made* of tho men as resoun me tauhte" [C.5.5]) provokes the accusations in the first place.

away: he does not say that he has lived, at different times, in different places ("I *have* lived in London and in the country"), or that he now lives on the road ("I am on the move between the city and the country"). He names a residence but locates it (improbably) in two places, one of them ("opeland") so doggedly generic that it implies the very vagrancy he is concerned to deny. He seems to be asserting that the "vagrancy" of the life he describes in *Piers Plowman*, and which Reason interrogates him about, is itself an aspect of domesticity. Once again I take my cue from Middleton. Examination under the statute required the suspect laborer to establish a place of residence: evasive from the beginning of Reason's interrogation, Will gives an answer that is, in the statute's terms, no answer at all. The question was meant to establish where the vagrant laborer should be sent to resume residence and work: its purpose was pragmatic, its pertinent terms geographical. In these terms, Middleton says, Will's answer is simply the prophet's impertinence, a sublime indifference to where he is sent.[164] But are there terms in which Will's would be a real answer? His labor, he says, is the prayer he offers for the souls of those "þat fynden me my fode" and

> fouchen-saf, y trowe,
> To be welcome when y come, oþer-while in a monthe,
> Now with hym, now with here.
>
> (49–51)

This answers the question "Where do you live?" *if* it is inflected "With whom do you live?" His address is not a place but a community, where his position is defined by relations of reciprocity: "This y segge for here soules of such as me helpeth" (48). He has another relation to them as well. "On this wyse y begge / Withoute bagge or botel but my wombe one" (52): he applies to himself the maxim with which lords could describe their villeins—"They have nothing but their bellies," since all they have belongs to the lord—and makes it a claim that he has a job and a residence and an employer, a lord. He is in effect the villein of those from whom he begs, the community of patrons who "welcome" him and collectively hold the place of his seigneur.

---

164. See Middleton's forthcoming essay. Clopper's observation is also pertinent here: "he claims that he needs not labor for his needs because his labor is wandering. . . . He does not admit this as blatantly as I have phrased it because wandering, as we know from elsewhere in the poem, is a disreputable 'occupation'" ("Need Men and Women Labor?" 120).

Why would he say it? The statute, I have suggested, posed the same challenge for Langland that the rising had: he was a vagabond, "useless" in the language the manorial court, a "vagrant" in the language of the statute. But *Piers Plowman* was too deeply invested in a narrative of vagrant inquisition to forgo it without canceling itself altogether: the accusation brought independently by lords and peasants—groups so at odds that they agreed (it must have seemed to Langland) only in suspecting himself—threatened the rationale of his poem by pressing too hard on the figure of the idle wanderer. These accusations forced him to imagine and justify his authorship in terms of a historical self, and to imagine and justify that self in terms of its economic and social relationships, of the community among whom and the lord under whom he lived. If the covert subject of C.5 is Langland's "makyng," then he is speaking not just of his patrons, but of his *audience*. And if he imagines his audience as at once his community and his lord, he assigns that audience the same status the rebels had assigned to themselves as members of village communities: individually they are fellows to each other; collectively they are lords. Coerced by the joint accusation of vagrancy, he chose the insurgent model of community to describe literary production and literary audience.

This move says as much about Langland's response to the revolt as do his excisions and bowdlerizations. Doubtless he retracted the B Prologue's claim that "might of þe communes" undergirds royal authority (B.prol.113) because the rebels seemed to have given it a practical application, and "communes" a meaning, that he did not want; in C, he transferred the basis of rule to "knyghthede" (C.prol.140).[165] But even as he made discursive adjustments to evade his unwitting part in the rising, Langland allowed it to transform his notions of authority and authorship. If he was confronted from two different sides with the accusation of vagrancy, the sides were not exactly symmetrical: the statute would have him recognize a lord, the rebels the lordship of empirical community. He chose the latter, but as much on his own terms as he could, offering the "community" *within* the poem as the community constructed *by* the poem, the community of audience that subtends

165. Pearsall's note: "he may have wished, in C, to remove even the possibility of misinterpretation; the use of Piers Plowman as a rallying call at the time of the Peasants' Revolt . . . may have given him further encouragement to make the change" (note to C.prol.140); Crane brilliantly discusses the ambiguous character of this revision ("Writing Lesson," 211–13).

authorship and becomes a community thereby. Thus Langland acknowl-edged—tenuously, evasively, and by analogy only—what no other poet or chronicler was willing to: that the commons who rose in 1381 defined themselves too as textual communities.

In 1432, Nicholas Bishop, a secular clerk in Oxford, compiled a private cartulary that recorded holdings in and around Oxford, especially those of the abbey of Oseney.[166] Toward the end, without further explanation and immediately following a conventional documentary entry, he copied a vernacular rhyme:

> man be war and be no fool
> þenke a pon þe ax and of þe stool
> þe stool was hard þe ax was scharp ·
> þe iiij. ȝere of kyng Richard.[167]

Twenty years or so after Bishop made his cartulary, a monk of Bury St. Edmunds copied a similar verse into a small tabular chronicle of the kings of England and the abbots of Bury. He made two mistakes. Here is the verse in its context:

Richard II succeeded him [Edward III], for this king died without issue. In the fourth year of Richard II, the vulgar of Kent rose in rebellion. In the fifth year, the great bridge at Oxford fell. In the fourteenth year there was a great wind on the feast of St. Paul. This king was crowned in his tenth year, and directly succeeded his grandfather Edward to the throne of England. At the time of this king, the commons of Kent rose in rebellion, and came to the city of London and burnt the mansion of the Duke of Lancaster, called the Savoy. At the same time the insurgents of Kent, with their evil helpers, cruelly killed the duke of Gloucester and the count of Arundel.

> The ax was sharpe the stokke was harde
> in the xiiij. yer of kyng Richarde.[168]

---

166. He prefaces the book with a vernacular narrative of his property dispute with the abbot of Oseney, which led him to compile the cartulary in the first place; this is printed in Sanford B. Meech, "Nicholas Bishop, an Exemplar of the Oxford Dialect of the Fifteenth Century," *PMLA* 49 (1934): 443–59.

167. CUL MS Dd.14.2, fol. 312r.

168. "Cui successit Ricardus secundus qui quidem rex obiit absque liberis. anno iiijo Ricardi secundi insurrexerunt vulgares cantie. anno vo magnus pons oxonie cecidit. anno xiiijo fuit magnus ventus sancti pauli. Iste rex anno etatis sue xo coronatus est in regem & inmediate post avum suum viz Edwardum in regnum Anglie successit. huius regis tempore surrexerunt communitates cantie et ad civitatem london' venerunt ibidemque mansionem

The first error—the "xiiij."—is a problem, but not a serious one: the context refers unambiguously to the rebellion, and the "xiiij.," certainly a relic of the "fourteenth year" that saw the great wind ("a° xiiij° fuit magnus ventus"), is merely a scribal miscopying, not a construal (or misconstrual) of the poem's reference.[169]

The second error is more interesting. The duke of Gloucester (Thomas of Woodstock, the king's uncle) and the earl of Arundel (Thomas Fitzalàn) long outlasted 1381; both died in 1397, Richard's late vengeance for their opposition in 1386–1388. The chronicler has mistakenly substituted their names for those of Archbishop Sudbury and Sir Robert Hales, the chancellor and treasurer whom the rebels beheaded,[170] and this mistake suggests what the Bury monk, at least, thought was the real application of the verse. Scholars have casually assumed that it recalls the executions of rebels and warns anyone meditating a second rebellion what fate might await him.[171] Though most of the rebels were not beheaded but hanged, as befitted their station, this is plausible enough: the verse sounds like nothing so much as the "verses in sermons" that Siegfried Wenzel has collected and studied. The Bury chronicler, on the other hand, thinks that the poem describes the executions the rebels performed, not those they suffered.

---

ducis Lancastrie Savoy nomine combusserunt. Eodem tempore insurrectores cantie cum suis iniquis auxiliis ducem Gloucestrie et comitem de Arundel crudeliter necaverunt. The ax was sharpe the stokke was harde in the xiiij. yere of kyng Richarde" (St. John's College, Oxford, MS 209, fol. 56r).

169. Though he thinks the rhyme properly refers to 1381, Robbins assumes that this scribe thought it referred to 1391 (14 Richard II was June 1390–June 1391; Robbins, *Historical Poems*, 273); apparently he did not look at the manuscript, but only at the printed catalogue, which transcribes the verses (H. O. Coxe, *Catalogus codicum mss. que in collegiis antique Oxoniis hodie adservantur* [Oxford, 1852], pars 2, p. 73). Likewise Kenneth Sisam, who edits the verse from this manusript under the title "On the Year 1390–1," in *Fourteenth Century Verse and Prose* (Oxford, 1921). John H. Pratt notes that 1381 was the fourteenth year of King Richard's *age*; "The 'Scharpe Ax' of Richard II," *Neuphilologische Mitteilungen* 77 (1976): 80–84. But regnal-year dating was so universal and conventional that a scribal error is more likely.

170. Gail MacMurray Gibson has suggested to me that what motivated the slip was the mysterious death in 1447 of Humphrey, the more recent duke of Gloucester, while in the custody of the chronicler's own monastery of St. Edmunds.

171. See Robbins, *Historical Poems*, 54, with which Dobson concurs (*Peasants' Revolt*, 305); Theo Stemmler produces a slightly different version of the same reading: that the rhyme is a friendly address to "the lower classes of society, the potential participants in a new rising," meant to warn against "a useless rising" ("The Peasants' Revolt of 1381 in Contemporary Literature," in Ulrich Broich, Theo Stemmler, and Gerd Stratmann, eds., *Functions of Literature: Essays Presented to Erwin Wolff on his Sixtieth Birthday* [Tübingen, 1984], 30–31).

The chronicler was right, though he got the names wrong. The verse first appears, in a late fourteenth-century hand, in a collection of canon law;[172] then in Bishop's cartulary, perhaps forty years later; then in the Bury chronicle, twenty years later still. None of these manuscripts could conceivably have been the exemplar for any of the others; it is almost impossible to imagine any vanished intermediary texts that might have carried it from one to the next: these three manuscripts are independent witnesses and attest to the poem's wide circulation. More interesting is the sort of manuscripts they are. The audience for canon law was narrowly defined: universities, bishops, and monastic houses, for the most part. The Bury chronicle, similarly, was an in-house production for the monks themselves (its chief purpose was to record the abbots of Bury, its monks, and its privileges).[173] And Nicholas Bishop evidently found the verse more or less as and where he reproduced it, among the charters of Oseney Abbey that he made it his chief business to copy;[174] and if there is anything more usually private to the clerical and lordly classes than a canon-law treatise or a house chronicle, it is a cartulary.

So the poem does not appear where we should expect it if it were aimed at those who might rebel; it is found in no sermon collections, no devotional books, no manuscripts with material meant to reach, directly or indirectly, a lay audience. It does appear, however, just where we should expect it (as the Bury chronicler thought) if it was aimed at those who would suffer most—suffer *again*—in a second rebellion. It does not warn villagers not to rebel; it warns landholders what posses-sionate privilege, unchecked, can push people to: load your tenants too heavy, and they will cut off your head (it was a lesson the prior of Bury—hunted, captured, and beheaded by the Suffolk rebels—might

172. BL Cotton Cleopatra D.3, fol. 134r. This copy of the verse is printed, without further information, in Siegfried Wenzel, "Unrecorded Middle English Verses," *Anglia* 92 (1974): 70. There is a discussion of this manuscript in Z. N. Brooke, *The English Church and the Papacy from the Conquest to the Reign of John* (Cambridge, Eng., 1931), 243.

173. Fol. 35a contains the note, "Anno Domini M.cccc.lviij. in festo Apostolorum Phillippi et Jacobi Thomas Croftis habitum recepit cum aliis tribus." The chronicle also transcribes a charter Richard II granted regarding the much-contested manor of Milden-hall (fol. 73b). The last item in the manuscript, not noted in the public catalogue, is a life of St. Edmund, patron of the abbey.

174. It is true that elsewhere Bishop includes material that sits oddly in a cartulary—a metrical chronicle (beginning on fol. 260v) and the *Prophecies of Merlin* (beginning on fol. 291r)—but these nonce items hold their own, distinct place together, and the cartulary resumes at the end of the latter. The "ax was sharp" verse, by contrast, is a scribble among the charters.

have wished he had learned before 1381).[175] And it appears in the kind of documents, concerned with the maintenance of landed privilege in great religious houses, that the insurgency aimed to destroy, inscribes its warnings on the material embodiments of clerkly prerogative. The poem shows lords saying to themselves what they would not say out loud; it marks a return of the repressed.

175. Riley, ed., *Memorials of St. Edmund's Abbey* 3:127–28; Réville, *Soulèvement*, 69–71.

Epilogue

So what happened?

Throughout this book, I have ignored one conventional question: why did the rising happen? I now all but ignore another: what happened in consequence? This question has preoccupied historians: most agree that the rising put paid to the idea of a poll tax; they agree on little else.[1] But I would like to point to several things can be asserted without question to have happened in consequence: the first book of the *Vox clamantis*; the "Jakke Strawe" passage of the *Nun's Priest's Tale*; some of Langland's last revision; the "ax was sharp" verse; and the chronicle accounts—in Walsingham and Knighton, the *Anonimalle* and the *Eulogium*, the Westminster and Dieulacres and Kirkstall chronicles—on which this book has so largely depended.

In other words, *texts* happened in consequence, which assumes more generally that texts do *happen*—that they do not just *mean* or *exist*. This is a matter of some importance to my practice throughout the book. I have insisted (uncontroversially) that all written records of the rebellion serve large and distorting ideological interests; that the chronicles and the judicial records emerged from the very institutions that the insurgents set out to capture and revise, and (in their different ways, and by their different mechanisms) narrate a version of the rising that is as suspect in its least detail as in its grandest *récit*. And yet I repeatedly treat those details as usable testimony about the words and actions of the rebels. I would not be surprised to hear myself enjoined that I cannot serve two masters, cannot have it both ways.

I would reply that *we* cannot have it—for "it" here is historical knowledge—in any fewer than two ways. The chronicles and the indictments simply *are* the rebellion for us, because they alone record it. To be sure, we could follow the Essex road to Mile End, trace the

---

1. A useful summary of answers to these and other historiographical questions can be found in Dobson, "Remembering the Peasants' Revolt."

foundations of the Savoy, find the shape of the Bocking fields cut into the soil; that is, we could invoke nontextual evidence in reconstructing the rebellion. But without textual evidence, we would not know what to reconstruct, or even conceive of reconstructing it.

There are two expedients by which we could choose *not* to have it both ways. We could credit the chronicles (or the judicial records, or both) generally and take their accounts roughly at face value, making adjustments to account for discrepancies between them and the quality of their information; in this case we would write more or less the history that Stubbs, Oman, and Petit-Dutaillis have written, of undisciplined and ignorant peasants venting inarticulate rage at the scapegoats nearest to hand. Or we could refuse to credit the sources altogether, decide that they are so deeply compromised that we can learn from them only their own purposes and ideologies; in this case we would write no history of the rebellion at all (we would have no rebellion to write about) and would thereby suppress its memory more thoroughly than the chroniclers and justices did. Otherwise we must have it both ways. We must begin from those texts that are, without question, distorted by interest and ideology, and we must begin from the distortions themselves.

Derek Pearsall has worried that we cannot be sure of finding anything that the chronicles have not distorted or invented for their purposes. Of the "old chair" from which the *Anonimalle* says the king's bill was read to the rebels, he says, "This has the air of something seen, not invented: the arbitrariness of the old chair carries authenticity. Yet is it entirely arbitrary? Does not the old chair carry some impression of impropriety and indignity which enhances the image of the reversal of order?"[2] But take a similar moment from Walsingham's *Gesta*, quite simple and on the whole inconsequential. Abbot Thomas, after hearing the demands and the threats of the St. Albans insurgents, reluctantly handed over the documents they required, giving them the charters and rolls of the house, which "they consumed in the flames" (*flammis consumpserunt*). But they continued to pursue the ancient charter of Offa:

> These did nothing to satisfy the unruly populace; no, they demanded a certain ancient charter confirming the liberties of the villeins, with capital letters, one of gold and the other of azure; and without that, they asserted,

2. Pearsall, "Interpretative Models for the Peasants' Revolt," in Patrick J. Gallacher and Helen Damico, eds., *Hermeneutics and Medieval Culture* (Albany, 1989), 67.

they would not be satisfied with promises. The abbot assured them that he knew of no such charter, had not even heard of it before; but he asked them to be patient for the moment, since they had obtained all he could confer on them, and he had refused none of their demands. He would search for the charter among the abbey's documents himself, to see if it could be found anywhere, and give it to them without deceit, if only they would now cease from their rage.[3]

One can do to the "capital letters, one of gold and the other of azure," what Pearsall does to the old chair. Does this detail not carry some impression of the uncomprehending awe the rebels evince before the written word; of their sense that an ideal past is somehow contained in a document they could not read and that, if released, it would somehow magically restore that past in the present; some impression, therefore, of their ignorance?

It does. But could Walsingham have invented this detail, which he found so useful? He cannot have invented it, he could not even have understood it, because it potentially disconfirms the very idea of the rebels' ignorance and the abbey's innocence that it is meant to support.[4] For the words he reports ("capital letters . . . of gold and of azure") describe the decorated capitals that did in fact appear on royal charters, and they therefore imply that someone—some rebel, some acquaintance of the rebels, some ancestor of the rebels—had seen one. But such charters were not to be found everywhere; around St. Albans, where might such a thing have been seen? The abbey, most probably. Correct or not, that is a conclusion Walsingham could not allow a reader to entertain, because it could suggest that the insurgents' belief in an ancient charter of liberties rested on some knowledge of the abbey's archives. If there were any such charter of liberties, then the abbot had suppressed it, had not acted *sine fraude*; and Walsingham is eager to

---

3. "Sed ista sufficere non valebant indisciplinato populo, quin quamdam chartam antiquam reposcerent de libertatibus villanorum, cujus litterae capitales fuerunt, de auro una, altera de azorio, sine qua non posse satisfieri votis populi asserebant. Abbas autem affirmavit se nullam talem chartam scire, nec quidem de illa audisse perante; sed contentos eos esse rogavit ad praesens, quod omnia obtinuerant ab eo quae potuit conferre eis, et nihil negaverat quod duxerant postalandum; velle se chartam inter munimenta requirere, si uspiam inveniri posset, et eis sine fraude resignare, tantum jam quiescerent a furore" (*Gesta* 3:308).

4. It happens, adventitiously, that there is evidence suggesting that Walsingham did not invent the detail, since it appears in the complaint the abbey lodged with the king and council after the rising ("demaunderent del dit Abbe une Chartre de lours libertez, com ilz dissoient, dount une lettre fuit dor, et une autre dasor" [*Gesta* 3:291])—unless, of course, Walsingham wrote the complaint.

show that the abbot, unlike the rebels, attended meticulously to legal precedent and documentary witness.[5] My point is not that some such charter did exist, but that Walsingham would not have invented a detail which might suggest it did. But neither would he have *reported* such a detail—not if he understood it. He did not understand the request for a charter "with capital letters, one of gold and one of azure." And if he did not understand it, he did not invent it. He did not understand it because he could not connect the request with the one thing he "knew" for certain about peasants: that writing was simply a mystery to them.

But this assumption—that the rebels could not think informedly about texts or act with the rationality that texts represent—*is*, for most scholars, the chronicles' central ideological distortion.[6] The distortion here does not baffle, *but enables*, our attempt to know what the rebels did and said. Ideology determines what authors (or anyone else) can say by determining what they can see and understand. When it most powerfully and completely dictates an author's narrative, that author is most likely to include material she or he does not comprehend, whose consequences she or he cannot see. Later in his account, Walsingham could narrate how the rebels made perambulation "without waiting for the charter [that Abbot Thomas had just granted] to be sealed,"[7] because to him, with a monk's assumptions about peasants, the "meaning" of their action was simply its demonstration that they did not know what seals were for. For him, these assumptions made all the insurgents' actions into evidence of incoherence and irrationality, which he could then cite as such. But by citing details that seemed incoherent or pointless to him, he made them available to other and later readers who might find their coherence and their point.

The notion that sources can be most informative when most compromised is at least counterintuitive. But what, exactly, compromises these sources? Many scholars have assumed that the chroniclers narrated the rebellion as they did in order to discredit it.[8] But that is incredible:

---

5. See the exchange between Abbot Thomas and the rebel spokesman Richard of Wallingford that begins ch. 4 above.

6. See Patterson, *Chaucer and the Subject of History*, 262–70; Ronan, "1381"; Crane, "Writing Lesson," 208–9; Strohm, *Hochon's Arrow*, 42–51.

7. Walsingham, *Gesta* 3:320; see ch. 4, n. 104 above.

8. Mostly recently, Crane, "Writing Lesson," ("the writers' attempt to condemn the revolt and make good sense of its repression"), 208; Strohm, *Hochon's Arrow* ("their texts . . . serve clerical partisanship, bolster royal authority, and uphold hierarchy and vested privilege"), 33.

could Walsingham (or Knighton or the *Eulogium* continuator) have thought that any conceivable reader of Latin chronicles—another monk or cleric, most usually—needed to be told that the rising was a bad thing? For such writers and readers, the insurgency was self-discrediting from the moment arrows flew at Brentwood. In public discourse—in parliament, for example—it was mentioned precisely because everyone (everyone who counted) already condemned it, so that it could be used to condemn other people and other practices.[9] When we do find deliberate distortions and inventions in the chronicles, they operate in just this way, as when Walsingham includes the supposed "confession of Jack Straw," which someone (maybe Walsingham himself) had confected with luridly polemical intent.[10] According to this "confession," the rebels planned to kill Richard's knights, to kill all the greater lords, and then (having used his person to recruit adherents) to kill the king; and they planned to drive from the realm all possessionate clergy, bishops, monks, canons, and parish priests, leaving only the mendicant friars to celebrate the sacraments. The last item is the point of this tendentious little piece: its purpose was not to damn a rising that hardly needed damning, but by its means to damn the friars (and perhaps Wyclif as well; *possessionati* was his favored term for wealthy religious). No chronicle reader would have sympathized with the rebels; but some might have sympathized with Wyclif or the friars, and Walsingham used the rebellion to urge them to better thoughts.

The realization that the chroniclers did not need to discredit the rising can help us make sense of their accounts, both of their distortions and of what the distortions betray. If we want to agree with Strohm that the chroniclers' principal strategy was to portray the insurgents "as yokel interlopers, as shifty manipulators of traditional oaths and understandings, as a purposely undisciplined rabble,"[11] then we must assume that the chroniclers really knew better—actually saw the insurgents as a rational and disciplined community with a coherently articulated program—and suppressed their knowledge for interested purposes. It makes better sense to assume that undisciplined and shifty yokels were simply *what they saw* when they looked back on the rebellion.[12] They did not

9. See ch. 5, nn. 1–5 above.

10. Walsingham, *Chronicon*, 309–10.

11. *Hochon's Arrow*, 34.

12. This assumption can also make better sense of some of the evidence Strohm himself cites. For example, discussing the habit of the chroniclers to describe the rebels as the

need to invent incriminating details, because (to their minds) the details they knew incriminated perfectly well without their help. This is not to say that the chroniclers did not invent and embroider, that fancies and mistakes and ill-founded reports do not disfigure their texts. It is to say that for them the insurgency was so obviously and unquestionably evil as to leave them free of any need to distort consciously and programmatically; that their texts may be interpreted to discover not just the representation they constructed, but also the historical materials from which they constructed it. Their writing of course served their own interests (whose does not?) and was of course distorted by their own ideologies (whose is not?). But they could not foreclose its possible uses, even uses contrary to their intent (who can?); in part *because they could not anticipate them.* Chaucer, I have suggested, knew this well when he wrote Fragment VII of the *Canterbury Tales*, and so did Gower when he wrote book 1 of the *Vox clamantis* to glue his poem back together; the deracinated character of literary discourse, which had no firm institutional location or warrant, left such poets aware that they might be misread in ways that they could only partly anticipate. But peasants, too, knew it well: no form of writing served lordly interests and ideology more surely and directly than the manorial custumal, yet the tenants of Thaxted were able to use their lord's, copied apparently without his knowledge, to purposes of their own.[13]

And we ought to know it too. I have operated throughout on the difficult assumption that we can know fourteenth-century rural culture more thoroughly than its clerical contemporaries could know it. But that is really not so surprising, for the kind of literary and historical analysis that we bring to the study are among the uses of their texts that those writers could not anticipate or foreclose. When I was writing the first chapters, I thought I was trying to give the rebels back their own voices. That seems to me now an unfortunate way to put it. They had

---

meanest of peasants, he says that, nonetheless, "telltale traces of a largely effaced alternative linger to affirm the imaginary nature of their interpretive schemes"; these are the "fragmentary admissions" of Walsingham and the Westminster chronicler that there were other, more prosperous rebels (*Hochon's Arrow*, 37). But there is nothing fragmentary about the Westminster chronicler's mention of certain "nobiliores de villa" who took part in the St. Albans rising; it is a flat assertion. If these chroniclers were pursuing a strategy of characterizing the rebels as the lowest serfs, why would they have admitted these details and qualifications at all—since these are not just "traces" that "linger," but authorial choices? I would suggest that the chroniclers were so completely and unreflectively certain of the rebels' uniformly low status that evidence of the alternative could not affect their certainty.

13. See above, pp. 190–91.

voices and used them (they do not need my advocacy, and are past caring); and the writers who chronicled their actions did not efface those voices, because they could not understand them well enough to efface them. Most of us perhaps can allow ourselves to listen to those voices only because we are not threatened by them, as Walsingham and Knighton were; and since we have that advantage, we may as well make use of it. We might learn something; and one thing we might learn is that official culture need not be read as it wishes.

Bibliography

TEXTS

MANUSCRIPTS

Cambridge University Library   Dd.14.2
London, British Library   Cotton Claudius E.iii
                                 Cotton Claudius E.iv
                                 Cotton Cleopatra D.iii
                                 Cotton Tiberius C.viii
                                 Royal 13.E.ix
Oxford, Bodleian Library   Bodley 158
                                 Bodley 316
Oxford, St. John's College   209

PRINTED WORKS

The Anonimalle Chronicle, 1333–1381. Ed. V. H. Galbraith. Manchester, 1927.

Ault, Warren. O. *Open-Field Husbandry and the Village Community: A Study of Agrarian By-Laws in Medieval England.* Transactions of the American Philosophical Society 55.7. Philadelphia, 1965.

Becon, Thomas. *The Displayeng of the Popishe Masse.* In John Ayre, ed., *Prayers and Other Pieces.* Parker Society 4. Cambridge, Eng., 1844.

Bolland, William Craddock, ed. *Select Bills in Eyre A.D. 1292–1333.* SS 30. London, 1914.

Brinton, Thomas. *The Sermons of Thomas Brinton, Bishop of Rochester (1373–1389).* Ed. Sister Mary Aquinas Devlin. 2 vols. London, 1954.

Caesarius of Heisterbach. *Dialogus miraculorum.* Ed. Joseph Strange. 2 vols. Cologne, 1851.

Calendar of Close Rolls. London, 1902–.

Calendar of Patent Rolls. London, 1901–.

Chaucer, Geoffrey. *The Riverside Chaucer.* Ed. Larry D. Benson. Boston, 1987.

Clarke, M. V., and V. H. Galbraith, eds. "The Deposition of Richard II." [Dieulacres chronicle.] *BJRL* 14 (1930): 125–81.

The Court Rolls of Ramsey, Hepmangrove, and Bury, 1268–1600. Ed. and trans. Edwin Brezette DeWindt. Toronto, 1990.

Court Rolls of the Abbey of Ramsey and of the Honor of Clare. Ed. Warren Ortman Ault. New Haven, 1928.

Court Rolls of the Manor of Hales. Ed. John Amphlett. 3 vols. Oxford, 1910.

Coxe, H. O. *Catalogus codicum mss. que in collegiis Oxoniis hodie adservantur.* Oxford, 1852.

Crow, Martin M., and Clair C. Olson. *Chaucer Life-Records.* Oxford, 1966.

Dahmus, Joseph Henry, ed. *The Metropolitan Visitations of William Courtenay, Archbishop of Canterbury 1381–1396.* Urbana, Ill., 1950.

DeWindt, Anne Reiber, and Edwin Brezette DeWindt, eds. *Royal Justice and the Medieval English Countryside.* Toronto, 1981.

Dieulacres chronicle. *See* Clarke and Galbraith.

Eulogium (historiarum sive temporis). Ed. Frank Scott Haydon. RS 9. London, 1863.

Fasciculi zizaniorum magistri Johannis Wyclif cum tritico. Ed. W. W. Shirley. RS 5. London, 1858.

Flaherty, W. E. "The Great Rebellion in Kent of 1381 Illustrated from the Public Records." *Archæologia Cantiana* 3 (1860): 65–96.

———. "Sequel to the Great Rebellion in Kent of 1381." *Archæologia Cantiana* 4 (1861): 67–86.

Fleta. Ed. H. G. Richardson and G. O. Sayles. 3 vols. SS 72. London, 1955.

Froissart, Jean. *Chroniques de France, d'Engleterre, d'Escoce. . . .* Ed. Kervyn de Lettenhove. Brussels, 1868.

Galbraith, V. H. "Articles Laid Before the Parliament of 1371." *EHR* 34 (1919): 479–82.

[Gosford, John. *Electio Johannis Tymworth.*] "Collectanea fratris Andreae Astone, Hostiarii Sancti Edmundi." In *Memorials of St. Edmund's Abbey.* Ed. Thomas Arnold. Vol. 3. RS 96. London, 1896.

Gower, John. *The Complete Works of John Gower.* Ed. G. C. Macaulay. 4 vols. Oxford, 1899.

Gross, Charles, ed. *Select Cases from the Coroners' Rolls A.D. 1265–1413.* SS 9. London, 1896.

Hall, Hubert. *A Formula Book of English Official Historical Documents.* Cambridge, Eng., 1908.

Hart, William Henry, and Posonby A. Lyons, ed. *Cartularium Monasterii de Rameseia.* RS 79. London, 1884.

[Hereford, Nicholas.] Forde, Simon, ed. "Nicholas Hereford's Ascension Day Sermon, 1382." *MS* 51 (1989): 205–41.

Higden, Ralph. *Polychronicon Ranulphi Higden.* Ed. C. Babington. London, 1896.

Historia vitae et regni Ricardi secundi. Ed. George B. Stow, Jr. Philadelphia, 1977.

Hudson, Anne. *English Wycliffite Sermons.* Vol. 1. Oxford, 1983.

———. *Selections from English Wycliffite Writings.* Cambridge, Eng., 1978.

Illingworth, William. "Copy of a Libel Against Archbishop Neville." *Archaeologia* 16 (1812): 80–83.

Isidore of Seville. *Etymologiarum sive originum libri XX.* Ed. W. M. Lindsay. Oxford, 1911.

Kingsford, C. L., ed. *Chronicles of London.* Oxford, 1905.

The Kirkstall Abbey Chronicles. Ed. John Taylor. Leeds, 1952.

Knighton, Henry. *Chronicon Henrici Knighton*. Ed. Joseph Rawson Lumby. RS 92. London, 1895.

Langland, William. *Piers Plowman: The B Version*. Ed. George Kane and E. Talbot Donaldson. London, 1975.

———. *Piers Plowman: An Edition of the C-Text*. Ed. Derek Pearsall. Berkeley and Los Angeles, 1979.

Liddell, W. H., and R. G. E. Wood, eds. *Essex and the Peasants' Revolt: A Selection of Evidence from Contemporary Chronicles, Court Rolls, and Other Sources*. Essex Record Office Publications 81. Chelmsford, Eng., 1981.

Luard, Henry Richards, ed. *Annales monastici*. RS 36. 3:3–420. London, 1866.

Maitland, F. W., ed. *Select Pleas in Manorial and Other Seignorial Courts*. SS 2. London, 1889.

———, ed. *Select Pleas of the Crown*. Vol. 1, *A.D. 1200–1225*. SS 1. London, 1888.

Maitland, F. W., and William Paley Baildon, eds. *The Court Baron, Being Precedents for Use in Seignorial and Other Local Courts*. SS 4. London, 1891.

Mannyng, Robert, of Brunne. *Handlyng Synne*. Ed. Idelle Sullens. Binghamton, 1983.

Map, Walter. *De nugis curialium*. Ed. M. R. James. Oxford, 1914.

Matthew Paris. *Chronica majora*. Ed. Henry Richards Luard. RS 57. 7 vols. London, 1874–1883.

Minor Poems of the Vernon MS. Ed. Carl Horstman. EETS os 98. London, 1892.

Mirk, John. *Instructions for Parish Priests*. Ed. Gillis Kristensson. Lund, 1974.

———. *Mirk's Festial: A Collection of Homilies*. Ed. Theodor Erbe. EETS es 96. London, 1905.

Nichols, John F. "An Early Fourteenth Century Petition from the Tenants of Bocking to Their Manorial Lord." *EcHR* 2 (1930): 300–307.

Palmer, W. M., and H. W. Sanders. *The Peasants' Revolt of 1381 as It Affected the Villages of Cambridgeshire*. Documents Relating to Cambridgeshire Villages 2. Cambridge, Eng., 1926.

Postan, M. M., and C. N. L. Brooke, ed. *Carte nativorum*. Northamptonshire Record Society 20. Oxford, 1960.

Powell, Edgar, and G. M. Trevelyan. *The Peasants' Rising and the Lollards: A Collection of Unpublished Documents*. London, 1899.

Powicke, F. M., and C. R. Cheney. *Councils and Synods, with Other Documents Relating to the English Church*. Vol. 2, *A.D. 1205–1313*. Oxford, 1964.

Registrum Johannis Trefnant episcopi Herefordensis. Ed. William W. Capes. London, 1916.

Registrum Ricardi Mayew, Episcopi Herefordensis A.D. MDIV–MDXVI. Ed. A. T. Bannister. CYS 27. Canterbury, 1921.

Riley, Thomas Henry, ed. *Memorials of London and London Life in the Thirteeth, Fourteenth, and Fifteenth Centuries*. London, 1868.

Robbins, Rossell Hope, ed. *Historical Poems of the Fourteenth and Fifteenth Centuries*. New York, 1959.

Rotuli parliamentorum; ut et petitiones et placita in parliamento. London, 1767–1777.

Rymer, Thomas. *Foedera, conventiones, litterae, et cujucunque generis acta publica.* . . . New ed. Ed. Adams Clarke, Frederic Holbrook, and John Caley. 4 vols. London, 1869.

Sayles, G. O., ed. *Select Cases in the Court of King's Bench under Edward II.* SS 74. London, 1957.

Sisam, Kenneth, ed. *Fourteenth Century Verse and Prose.* Oxford, 1921.

Sparvel-Bayly, J. A. "Essex in Insurrection, 1381." *Transactions of the Essex Archaeological Society* ns 1 (1878): 205–19.

Statutes of the Realm; Printed by Command of His Majesty George the Third. . . . [London,] 1810.

Stow, John. *Survay of London, Contayning the Originall, Antiquity, Increase, Moderne Estate, and Description of that Citie.* . . . London, 1598.

Thorne, William. *Chronica de rebus gestis abbatum sancti Augustini Cantuariae.* In Roger Twysden, ed., *Historiae anglicanae scriptores decem.* London, 1652.

Thorpe, William. *The Examination of Master William Thorpe, Priest.* . . . In Alfred W. Pollard, ed., *Fifteenth Century Prose and Verse,* 97–174. New York, n.d.

Walsingham, Thomas. *Chronicon Angliae.* Ed. Edward Maunde Thompson. RS 64. London, 1874.

———. *Gesta abbatum monasterii Sancti Albani.* Ed. Henry Thomas Riley. RS 28. London, 1869.

[———.] *Johannis de Trokelowe et Henrici de Blaneforde . . . chronica et annales.* RS 28.4. London, 1866.

———. *Ypodigma Neustriae.* Ed. H. T. Riley. RS 28.7. London, 1976.

Walter of Henley and Other Treatises on Estate Management and Accounting. Ed. Dorothea Oschinsky. Oxford, 1971.

Wenzel, Siegfried. "Unrecorded Middle English Verses." *Anglia* 92 (1974): 55–78.

The Westminster Chronicle 1381–1394. Ed. and trans. L. C. Hector and Barbara F. Harvey. Oxford, 1982.

Wilkins, David. *Conciliae Magnae Britannie et Hibernie.* 4 vols. London, 1737.

Wright, Thomas, ed. *Political Poems and Songs Relating to English History.* . . . RS 14. 2 vols. London, 1859.

Wrottesley, G., ed. "The Burton Chartulary." *Collections for a History of Staffordshire* (William Salt Archaeological Society) 5 (1884): 1–101.

Wyclif, John. *De apostasia.* Ed. Michael Henry Dziewicki. London, 1889.

———. *De blasphemia.* Ed. Michael Henry Dziewicki. London, 1893.

———. *De civili dominio.* Ed. R. L. Poole and J. Loserth. 4 vols. London, 1885–1904.

———. *De officio regis.* Ed. Alfred W. Pollard and Charles Sayle. London, 1887.

———. *De veritate sacre scripture.* Ed. Rudolf Buddensieg. 3 vols. London, 1905.

———. *Dialogus sive Speculum ecclesie militantis.* Ed. Alfred W. Pollard. London, 1886.

———. *Opera minora.* Ed. Johann Loserth. London, 1913.

———. *Polemical Works in Latin.* Ed. R. Buddensieg. 2 vols. London, 1883.

———. *Trialogus, cum Supplemento trialogi.* Ed. G. Lechler. Oxford, 1869.

STUDIES

Adamson, J. W. "The Extent of Literacy in England in the Fifteenth and Sixteenth Centuries: Notes and Conjectures." *The Library*, 4th ser., 10 (1929): 363–93.

Aers, Davis. *Chaucer, Langland, and the Creative Imagination*. London, 1980.

———. *Community, Gender, and Individual Identity: English Writing 1360–1430*. London, 1988.

Alford, John. "The Role of the Quotations in *Piers Plowman*." *Speculum* 52 (1977): 80–99.

Allen, Judson Boyce. *The Ethical Poetic of the Later Middle Ages: A Decorum of Convenient Distinction*. Toronto, 1982.

———. "Langland's Reading and Writing: *Detractor* and the Pardon Passus." *Speculum* 59 (1987): 342–62.

Astill, Grenville. "Rural Settlement: The Toft and the Croft." In Astill and Annie Grant, eds., *The Countryside of Medieval England*, 36–61. Oxford, 1988.

Aston, Margaret. "'Caim's Castles': Poverty, Politics, and Disendowment." In R. B. Dobson, ed., *The Church, Politics, and Patronage in the Fifteenth Century*, 45–81. Gloucester, 1984.

———. *Laws Against Images*. Vol. 1 of *England's Iconoclasts*. Oxford, 1988.

———. *Lollards and Reformers: Images and Literacy in Late Medieval Religion*. London, 1984.

———. "Wyclif and the Vernacular." *SCH* subsidia 5 (1987): 281–330.

Aston, T. H., and C. H. E. Philpin, eds. *The Brenner Debate: Agrarian Class Structure and Economic Development in Pre-Industrial Europe*. Cambridge, Eng., 1985.

Ault, Warren O. *The Self-Directing Activities of Village Communities in Medieval England*. Boston, 1952.

———. "Village By-Laws by Common Consent." *Speculum* 29 (1954): 378–94.

Austin, J. L. *How to Do Things with Words*. Cambridge, Eng., 1975.

Axton, Richard. "Gower—Chaucer's Heir?" In Ruth Morse and Barry Windeatt, eds., *Chaucer Traditions: Studies in Honour of Derek Brewer*, 21–38. Cambridge, Eng., 1990.

Baker, Alan R. H. "Open Fields and Partible Inheritance on a Kent Manor." *EcHR*, 2d ser., 17 (1964): 1–23.

Baker, Denise N. "From Plowing to Penitence: *Piers Plowman* and Fourteenth-Century Theology." *Speculum* 55 (1980): 715–25.

Bakhtin, Mikhail. *Rabelais and His World*. Trans. Hélène Iswolsky. Bloomington, Ind., 1984.

Baldwin, Anna. *The Theme of Government in Piers Plowman*. Cambridge, Eng., 1981.

Barney, Stephen A. "The Plowshare of the Tongue: The Progress of a Symbol from the Bible to *Piers Plowman*." *MS* 35 (1973): 261–93.

Barron, Caroline. *Revolt in London: Eleventh to Fifteenth June 1381*. London, 1981.

Baüml, Franz. "Varieties and Consequences of Medieval Literacy and Illiteracy." *Speculum* 55 (1980): 237–65.

Bellamy, J. G. *Crime and Public Order in England in the Later Middle Ages.* London, 1973.

———. *The Law of Treason in England in the Later Middle Ages.* Cambridge, Eng., 1970.

Bird, Brian, and David Stephenson. "Who Was John Ball?" *Essex Archaeology and History*, 3d ser., 8 (1977 for 1976): 287–88.

Bird, Ruth. *The Turbulent London of Richard II.* London, 1949.

Bishop, Ian. "*The Nun's Priest's Tale* and the Liberal Arts." *RES* ns 30 (1979): 257–67.

Blanchard, Ian. "Industrial Employment and the Rural Land Market 1380–1520." In Smith, ed., *Land, Kinship, and Life-Cycle*, 227–75.

Bloch, Marc. "The Advent and Triumph of the Watermill." In his *Land and Work in Medieval Europe: Selected Essays*, 136–68. Trans. J. E. Anderson. Berkeley and Los Angeles, 1967.

Bloomfield, Morton. *Piers Plowman as a Fourteenth-Century Apocalypse.* New Brunswick, 1962.

Bossy, John. "Blood and Baptism: Kinship, Community, and Christianity in Europe from the Fourteenth to the Seventeenth Centuries." *SCH* 10 (1973): 129–43.

———. *Christianity in the West 1400–1700.* Oxford, 1985.

———. "The Mass as a Social Institution 1200–1700." *Past and Present* 100 (1983): 29–61.

Bourquin, Guy. *Piers Plowman: Étude sur la génèse littéraire des trois versions.* 2 vols. Paris, 1978.

Bowers, John R. *The Crisis of Will in Piers Plowman.* Washington, D.C., 1986.

Brenner, Robert. "Agrarian Class Structure and Economic Development in Pre-Industrial Europe." In Aston and Philpin, eds., *Brenner Debate*, 10–63.

———. "The Agrarian Roots of European Capitalism." In Aston and Philpin, eds., *Brenner Debate*, 213–327.

Brentano, Robert. *Two Churches: England and Italy in the Thirteenth Century.* 1968; rpt. Berkeley and Los Angeles, 1988.

Britton, C. E. *A Metereological Chronology to A.D. 1450.* London, 1937.

Britton, Edward. *The Community of the Vill: A Study in the History of the Family and Village Life in Fourteenth-Century England.* Toronto, 1977.

Brooke, C. N. L. "Religious Sentiment and Church Design in the Later Middle Ages." *BJRL* 50 (1967): 13–33.

Brooke, Z. N. *The English Church and the Papacy from the Conquest to the Reign of John.* Cambridge, Eng., 1931.

Brooks, Nicholas. "The Organization and Achievements of the Peasants of Kent and Essex in 1381." In H. Mayr Harting and R. I. Moore, eds., *Studies in Medieval History Presented to R. C. H. Davies*, 247–70. London, 1985.

Brown, A. L. "Parliament, c. 1377–1422." In Davies and Denton, eds., *The English Parliament in the Middle Ages*, 109–40.

Burdach, Konrad. *Der Dichter des Ackermann aus Böhmen und seine Zeit.* Vol. 3

of *Vom Mittelalter zur Reformation: Forschungen zur Geschichte der deutschen Bildung*. Berlin, 1926.

Burke, Kenneth. *A Grammar of Motives*. Berkeley and Los Angeles, 1969.

Burrow, J. A. "The Audience of *Piers Plowman*." *Anglia* 75 (1957): 373–84.

———. *Autobiographical Poetry in the Middle Ages: The Case of Thomas Hoccleve*. London, 1982.

Butcher, A. F. "English Urban Society and the Revolt of 1381." In Hilton and Aston, eds., *English Rising*, 84–111.

Calkin, Susan Woolfson. "Alexander Neville, Archbishop of York (1373–1388): A Study of His Career with Emphasis on the Crisis at Beverley in 1381." Ph.D. diss. University of California, Berkeley, 1976.

Cam, Helen M. "The Community of the Vill." In her *Law-Finders and Law-Makers in Medieval England: Collected Studies in Legal and Constitutional History*, 71–84. London, 1962.

Campbell, Bruce M. S. "Agricultural Progress in Medieval Society: Some Evidence from Eastern Norfolk." *EcHR*, 2d ser., 36 (1983): 26–46.

———. "Population Pressure, Inheritance, and the Land Market in a Fourteenth-Century Peasant Community." In Smith, ed., *Land, Kinship, and Life-Cycle*, 87–134.

Camporesi, Piero. *La casa dell'eternità*. Milan, 1987.

Carruthers, Mary. *The Search for Saint Truth: A Study of Meaning in Piers Plowman*. Evanston, 1973.

Catto, Jeremy I. "An Alleged Great Council of 1374." *EHR* 82 (1967): 764–71.

———. "Wyclif and the Cult of the Eucharist." *SCH* subsidia 4 (1985): 269–86.

Certeau, Michel de. *The Practice of Everyday Life*. Trans. Steven F. Rendall. Berkeley and Los Angeles, 1984.

Christ, Karl. *The Handbook of Medieval Library History*. Trans. Theophil M. Otto. Metuchen, N.J., 1984.

Churchill, Irene Josephine. *Canterbury Administration: The Administrative Machinery of the Archbishop of Canterbury Illustrated from Original Records*. London, 1933.

Clanchy, M. T. *From Memory To Written Record: England, 1066–1307*. Cambridge, Mass., 1979.

Clark, Elaine. "Debt Litigation in a Late Medieval English Vill." In J. Ambrose Raftis, ed., *Pathways to Medieval Peasants*, 247–79. Toronto, 1981.

Clark, J. W. *Libraries in the Medieval and Renaissance Periods*. Cambridge, Eng. 1894.

Clark, Peter. *The English Alehouse: A Social History 1200–1830*. London, 1983.

Clarke, Maude V. "Henry Knighton and the Library Catalogue of Leicester Abbey." *EHR* 45 (1930): 103–7.

Clopper, Lawrence. "Need Men and Women Labor? Langland's Wanderer and the Labor Ordinances." In Hanawalt, ed., *Chaucer's England*, 110–29.

Coleman, Janet. *Piers Plowman and the "Moderni."* Rome, 1981.

Crane, Susan. "The Writing Lesson of 1381." In Hanawalt, ed., *Chaucer's England*, 201–21.

Cressy, David. *Literacy and the Social Order: Reading and Writing in Tudor and Stuart England.* Cambridge, Eng., 1980.

Crook, David. "Derbyshire and the English Rising of 1381." *Historical Research* 60 (1987): 9–23.

Cross, Claire. "'Great Reasoners in Scripture': The Activities of Women Lollards 1380–1530." *SCH* subsidia 1 (1978): 359–80.

Curry, Walter Clyde. *Chaucer and the Medieval Sciences.* 2d ed. London, 1960.

Dahmus, Joseph W. *The Prosecution of John Wyclyf.* New Haven, 1952.

Davenport, Frances G. "The Decay of Villeinage in East Anglia." *TRHS* ns 14 (1900): 123–41.

Davies, R. G., and J. H. Denton, eds. *The English Parliament in the Middle Ages.* Philadelphia, 1981.

Dawson, James Doyne. "Richard FitzRalph and the Fourteenth Century Poverty Controversies." *Journal of Ecclesiastical History* 3 (1983): 315–44.

Delaney, Sheila. *Medieval Literary Politics: Shapes of Ideology.* Manchester, 1990.

DeWindt, Edwin Brezette. *Land and People in Holywell-cum-Needingworth: Structures of Tenure and Patterns of Social Organization in an East Midlands Village 1252–1457.* Toronto, 1972.

Dinshaw, Carolyn. "Rivalry, Rape, and Manhood: Gower and Chaucer." In R. F. Yeager, ed., *Chaucer and Gower: Difference, Mutuality, Exchange,* 130–52. Victoria, 1991.

Dobson, R. B. *The Peasants' Revolt of 1381.* London, 1970.

———. "Remembering the Peasants' Revolt 1381–1981." In Liddell and Wood, eds., *Essex and the Great Revolt,* 1–20.

Donaldson, E. Talbot. *Piers Plowman: The C-Text and Its Poet.* New Haven, 1949.

Douie, Decima L. *Archbishop Pecham.* Oxford, 1952.

Doyle, A. I. "Remarks on Surviving Manuscripts of *Piers Plowman.*" In Gregory Kratzman and James Simpson, eds., *Medieval English Religious and Ethical Literature in Honour of G. H. Russell,* 35–58. Cambridge, Eng., 1986.

DuBoulay, F. R. H., and Caroline M. Barron, eds. *The Reign of Richard II: Essays in Honour of May McKisack.* London, 1971.

Duby, Georges. *Rural Economy and Country Life in the Medieval West.* Trans. Cynthia Postan. Columbia, S.C., 1968.

Du Cange, Charles du Fresne, Sieur. *Glossarium mediae et infimae Latinitatis.* Nova editio. Niort, 1885.

Dyer, Christopher C. "The Causes of the Revolt in Rural Essex." In Liddell and Wood, eds., *Essex and the Great Revolt,* 21–36.

———. "Documentary Evidence: Problems and Enquiries." In Grenville Astill and Annie Grant, eds., *The Countryside of Medieval England,* 12–35. Oxford, 1988.

———. *Lords and Peasants in a Changing Society: The Estates of the Bishopric of Worcester, 680–1540.* Cambridge, Eng., 1980.

———. "Power and Conflict in the Medieval English Village." In Hooke, ed., *Medieval Villages,* 27–32.

———. "The Rising of 1381 in Suffolk: Its Origins and Participants." *Proceedings of the Suffolk Institute of Archaeology and History* 36 (1988): 274–87.

———. "The Social and Economic Background to the Rural Revolt of 1381." In Hilton and Aston, eds., *English Rising*, 9–42.

———. *Standards of Living in the Later Middle Ages: Social Change in England c.1200–1520*. Cambridge, Eng., 1989.

Eagleton, Terry. *Walter Benjamin, or, Towards a Revolutionary Criticism*. London, 1981.

Eberhard, Oscar. *Der Bauernaufstand vom Jahre 1381 in der englischen Poesie*. Anglistische Forschungen 51. Heidelberg, 1917.

Edwards, Sir Goronway. *The Second Century of the English Parliament*. Oxford, 1979.

Erzgräber, Willi. *William Langlands Piers Plowman: Eine Interpretation des C-Textes*. Heidelberg, 1957.

Faith, Rosamond. "Berkshire: Fourteenth and Fifteenth Centuries." In P. D. A. Harvey, ed., *The Peasant Land Market in Medieval England*, 106–77. Oxford, 1984.

———. "The 'Great Rumour' of 1377 and Peasant Ideology." In Hilton and Aston, eds., *English Rising*, 42–73.

First Report of the Royal Commission on Historical Manuscripts. London, 1870.

Fisher, John H. *John Gower: Moral Philosopher and Friend of Chaucer*. New York, 1964.

Fortescue, Adrian. *The Mass: A Study of the Roman Liturgy*. 2d ed. London, 1955.

Foucault, Michel. *Language, Counter-Memory, Practice: Selected Essays and Interviews*. Trans. Donald F. Bouchard and Sherry Simon. Ithaca, 1977.

Fowler, David C. *Piers the Plowman: Literary Relations of the A and B Texts*. Seattle, 1961.

———. "Poetry and the Liberal Arts: The Oxford Background of *Piers the Plowman*." *Arts libéraux et philosophie au moyen âge*. Actes du Quatrième congrès international de philosophie médiévale, 715–19. Montréal, 1969.

Frank, Robert Worth, Jr. "The Art of Reading Personification Allegory." *ELH* 20 (1953): 237–50.

———. *Piers Plowman and the Scheme of Salvation*. New Haven, 1957.

Friedman, Albert B. "'Whan Adam Delved . . .': Contexts of a Historic Proverb." In Larry D. Benson, ed., *The Learned and the Lewed: Studies in Chaucer and Medieval Literature*, 213–30. Ed. Larry D. Benson. Cambridge, Mass., 1974.

Fryde, E. B. *The Great Revolt of 1381*. Historical Association General Series 100. London, 1981.

Fryde, E. B., and Natalie Fryde. "Peasant Rebellion and Peasant Discontents." In Edward Miller, ed., *The Agrarian History of England and Wales*, vol. 3, *1348–1500*, 744–819. Cambridge, Eng., 1991.

Fumagalli, Mariateresa Brocchieri-Fumagalli. *Wyclif: Il comunismo dei predestinati*. Florence, 1975.

Gabel, L. C. *Benefit of Clergy in England in the Later Middle Ages*. London, 1928.

Galbraith, V. H. "The Chronicle of Henry Knighton." In D. J. Gordon, ed., *Frit Saxl . . . A Volume of Memorial Essays*, 136–48. London, 1957.

———. *Historical Research in Medieval England*. Creighton Lecture in History 1949. London, 1951.

————. Introduction to *The St. Albans Chronicle, 1406–1420*. Oxford, 1937.

————. *Studies in the Public Records*. London, 1948.

————. "Thomas Walsingham and the Saint Albans Chronicle, 1272–1422." *EHR* 47 (1932): 12–30.

————. "Thoughts about the Peasants' Revolt." In DuBoulay and Barron, eds., *The Reign of Richard II*, 46–57.

Galloway, Andrew. "Gower and Walsingham on 1381 and the Profession of the Late Medieval Author." Paper delivered to the Medieval Association of the Pacific, Tucson, March 1988.

Ganim, John M. *Chaucerian Theatricality*. Princeton, 1990.

Godden, Malcolm. *The Making of Piers Plowman*. London, 1990.

Gradon, Pamela. "Langland and the Ideology of Dissent." *Proceedings of the British Academy* 66 (1980): 179–205.

Gransden, Antonia. *Historical Writing in England*. Vol. 2. Ithaca, 1982.

Graus, F. "The Late Medieval Poor in Town and Countryside." In Sylvia L. Thrupp, ed., *Change in Medieval Society: Europe North of the Alps*, 314–24. New York, 1964.

Green, Richard Firth. "John Ball's Letters: Literary History and Historical Literature." In Hanawalt, ed., *Chaucer's England*, 176–200.

————. *Poets and Princepleasers: Literature and the English Court in the Late Middle Ages*. Toronto, 1980.

Gurevich, Aron. *Medieval Popular Culture: Problems of Belief and Perception*. Trans. János M. Bak and Paul A. Hollingsworth. Cambridge, Eng., 1988.

Hall, G. D. G. "The Abbot of Abingdon and the Tenants of Winkfield." *MÆ* 28 (1959): 91–95.

Hanawalt, Barbara A. "Men's Games, King's Deer: Poaching in Medieval England." *JMRS* 19 (1988): 175–93.

————. *The Ties That Bound: Peasant Families in Medieval England*. Oxford, 1986.

————, ed. *Chaucer's England: Literature in Historical Context*. Minneapolis, 1992.

Hanna, Ralph, III. "Pilate's Voice/Shirley's Case." *South Atlantic Quarterly* 94 (1992): 793–812.

————. "Will's Work." In Steve Justice and Kathryn Kerby-Fulton, eds., *William Langland and Piers Plowman*. Forthcoming.

Hansen, Harriet Merete. "The Peasants' Revolt of 1381 and the Chronicles." *Journal of Medieval History* 6 (1980): 393–415.

Harding, Alan. *The Law Courts of Medieval England*. London, 1973.

————. "Plaints and Bills in the History of English Law, Mainly in the Period 1250–1350." In D. Jenkins, ed., *Legal History Studies, 1972*, 65–86. Cardiff, 1972.

————. "The Revolt Against the Justices." In Hilton and Aston, eds., *English Rising of 1381*, 165–93.

Hartung, Albert, ed. *A Manual of the Writings in Middle English*. Vol. 5. New Haven, 1975.

Harvey, Barbara A. *Westminster Abbey and Its Estates in the Middle Ages.* Oxford, 1977.

Harwood, Britton J. "Dame Study and the Place of Orality in *Piers Plowman.*" *ELH* 57 (1990): 1–17.

———. "Imaginative in *Piers Plowman.*" *MÆ* 44 (1975): 249–63.

———. "Langland's *Kynde Wit.*" *JEGP* 75 (1976): 330–36.

———. "*Piers Plowman*: Fourteenth-Century Skepticism and the Theology of Suffering." *Bucknell Review* 19 (1971): 119–36.

Hatcher, John. *Plague, Population, and the English Economy 1348–1530.* London, 1977.

Hewitt, H. J. *The Organization of War under Edward III, 1338–62.* Manchester, 1966.

Hilton, Rodney H. *Bond Men Made Free: Medieval Peasant Movements and the English Rising of 1381.* New York, 1973.

———. *Class Conflict and the Crisis of Feudalism: Essays in Medieval Social History.* London, 1985.

———. "A Crisis of Feudalism." *Past and Present* 80 (1978): 3–19.

———. *The Decline of Serfdom in Medieval England.* London, 1969.

———. *The Economic Development of Some Leicestershire Estates in the Fourteenth and Fifteenth Centuries.* Oxford, 1947.

———. *The English Peasantry in the Later Middle Ages.* Oxford, 1975.

———. "Feudalism in Europe: Problems for Historical Materialists." *New Left Review* 147 (1984): 84–93.

———, ed. *Peasants, Knights, and Heretics: Studies in Medieval English Social History.* Cambridge, Eng., 1976.

Hilton, R. H., and T. H. Aston, eds. *The English Rising of 1381.* Cambridge, Eng., 1984.

Hilton, R. H., and H. Fagan. *The English Rising of 1381.* London, 1950.

Hoare, Christobel M. *The History of an East Anglian Soke: Studies in Original Documents, Including Hitherto Unpublished Material Dealing with the Peasants' Rising of 1381, and Bondage and Bond Tenure.* Bedford, 1918.

Hobsbawm, Eric. *Primitive Rebels: Studies in Archaic Forms of Social Movement in the Nineteenth and Twentieth Centuries.* New York, 1959.

Holloway, Julia Bolton. *The Pilgrim and the Book: A Study of Dante, Langland, and Chaucer.* New York, 1987.

Holmes, G. A. *The Estates of the Higher Nobility in Fourteenth Century England.* Cambridge, Eng., 1957.

Homans, George C. *English Villagers of the Thirteenth Century.* 1947; rpt. New York, 1975.

Hooke, Della, ed. *Medieval Villages.* Oxford University Committee for Archaeology Monograph 5. Oxford, 1985.

Howard, Donald R. *The Idea of the Canterbury Tales.* Berkeley and Los Angeles, 1976.

Hudson, Anne. "Epilogue: The Legacy of *Piers Plowman.*" In John A. Alford, ed., *A Companion to Piers Plowman,* 251–66. Berkeley and Los Angeles, 1988.

————. *Lollards and Their Books*. London, 1985.

————. "A Lollard Sermon-Cycle and Its Implications." *MÆ* 40 (1971): 142–56.

————. *The Premature Reformation: Wycliffite Texts and Lollard History*. Oxford, 1988.

————. "Wyclif and the English Language." In Anthony Kenny, ed., *Wyclif in His Times*, 85–103. Oxford, 1986.

Hughes, Jonathan. *Pastors and Visionaries: Religion and Secular Life in Late Medieval Yorkshire*. Woodbridge, Suffolk, 1988.

Hyams, Paul R. *King, Lords, and Peasants in Medieval England: The Common Law of Villeinage in the Twelfth and Thirteenth Centuries*. Oxford, 1980.

————. "The Origins of a Peasant Land Market in England." *EcHR*, 2d ser., 23 (1970): 18–31.

James, Mervyn R. "Ritual, Drama, and Social Body in the Late Medieval English Town." *Past and Present* 98 (1983): 3–29.

Jameson, Fredric. *Marxism and Form: Twentieth-Century Dialectical Theories of Literature*. Princeton, 1974.

————. *The Political Unconscious: Narrative as a Socially Symbolic Act*. Ithaca, 1981.

Jenkinson, C. Hilary, and Mabel H. Mills. "Rolls from a Sheriff's Office of the Fourteenth Century." *EHR* 43 (1928): 21–32.

Jennings, Margaret, C.S.J. "Piers Plowman and Holy Church." *Viator* 9 (1978): 367–74.

Jones, Richard H. *The Royal Policy of Richard II: Absolutism in the Later Middle Ages*. Oxford, 1968.

Jungmann, Joseph A., S.J. *The Mass of the Roman Rite: Its Origins and Development*. Trans. Francis A. Brunner, C.SS.R. 2 vols. New York, 1955.

Jusserand, J. J. *L'Épopée mystique de William Langland*. Paris, 1893.

Justice, Steven. "The Genres of *Piers Plowman*." *Viator* 19 (1988): 291–306.

Kaeuper, Richard W. "Two Early Lists of Literates in England: 1334, 1373." *EHR* 99 (1984): 363–69.

————. *War, Justice, and Public Order: England and France in the Later Middle Ages*. Oxford, 1988.

Kane, George. *The Autobiographical Fallacy in Chaucer and Langland Studies*. London, 1965.

————. "Some Fourteenth-Century 'Political' Poems." In Gregory Kratzmann and James Simpson, eds., *Medieval English Religious and Ethical Literature: Essays in Honour of G. H. Russell*, 82–91. Cambridge, Eng., 1986.

Kerby-Fulton, Kathryn. *Reformist Apocalypticism and Piers Plowman*. Cambridge, Eng., 1990.

Kerr, N. R. *Medieval Libraries of Great Britain: A List of Surviving Books*. 2d ed. London, 1964.

King, Archdale A. *Eucharistic Reservation in the Western Church*. London, 1965.

King, Edmund. *Peterborough Abbey 1086–1310: A Study in the Land Market*. Cambridge, Eng., 1973.

Kirk, Elizabeth D. "Langland's Plowman and the Recreation of Fourteenth-Century Religious Metaphor." *YLS* 2 (1988): 1–21.

Knight, Stephen. *Geoffrey Chaucer*. London, 1986.

Knowles, Dom David. *The Religious Orders in England*. 3 vols. Cambridge, Eng., 1957.

Kriehn, George. "Studies in the Sources of the Social Revolt in 1381." *AHR* 7 (1901): 254–85, 458–84.

Lambrick, Gabrielle. "The Impeachment of the Abbot of Abingdon in 1368." *EHR* 82 (1967): 250–76.

Lawton, David. "Dulness and the Fifteenth Century." *ELH* 54 (1987): 761–99.

———. "Lollardy and the *Piers Plowman* Tradition." *MLR* 76 (1981): 780–93.

———. "*Piers Plowman*: On Tearing—and Not Tearing—the Pardon." *Philological Quarterly* 60 (1981): 414–22.

———, ed. *Middle English Alliterative Poetry and Its Literary Backgrounds: Seven Essays*. Cambridge, 1982.

Leff, Gordon. *Paris and Oxford Universities in the Thirteenth and Fourteenth Centuries: An Institutional and Intellectual History*. New York, 1968.

Levett, Ada Elizabeth. *Studies in Manorial History*. Ed. H. M. Cam, M. Coate, and L. S. Sutherland. New York, 1938.

Liddell, W. H., and R. G. E. Wood, eds. *Essex and the Great Revolt of 1381: Lectures Celebrating the Six Hundredth Anniversary*. Essex Record Office Publications 84. Chelmsford, 1982.

Lindahl, Carl. *Earnest Games: Folkloric Patterns in the Canterbury Tales*. Bloomington, 1987.

Littlehales, Henry, ed. *Some Notes on the Road from London to Canterbury in the Middle Ages*. London, 1898.

Lubac, Henri de. *Corpus mysticum: L'eucharistie et l'église au moyen âge. Étude historique*. Paris, 1949.

Lytle, Guy Fitch. "The Social Origins of Oxford Students in the Late Middle Ages: New College, c. 1380–c. 1510." In Jozef Ijsewijn and Jacques Paquet, *The Universities in the Late Middle Ages*, 426–54. Leuven, 1978.

McAlpine, Monica E. *The Genre of Troilus and Criseyde*. Ithaca, 1978.

Macfarlane, Alan. *The Origins of English Individualism: The Family, Property, and Social Transition*. Oxford, 1978.

McFarlane, K. B. *John Wycliffe and the Beginnings of English Nonconformity*. London, 1952.

———. *Lancastrian Kings and Lollard Knights*. Oxford, 1972.

McHardy, A. K. "Liturgy and Propaganda in the Diocese of Lincoln During the Hundred Years War." *SCH* 18 (1982): 215–27.

Macherey, Pierre. *A Theory of Literary Production*. Trans. Geoffrey Wall. London, 1978.

McIntosh, Angus, M. L. Samuels, and Michael Benskin. *A Linguistic Atlas of Late Middle English*. 4 vols. Aberdeen, 1986.

McIntosh, Marjorie Keniston. *Autonomy and Community: The Royal Manor of Havering, 1200–1500*. Cambridge, Eng., 1986.

McKisack, May. *The Fourteenth Century 1307–1399*. Oxford, 1959.

Maddicott, J. R. "The County Community and the Making of Public Opinion in Fourteenth-Century England." *TRHS*, 5th ser., 28 (1978): 27–43.

——. *The English Peasantry and the Demands of the Crown, 1298–1341. Past and Present* Supplement 1. Oxford, 1975.

——. *Law and Lordship: Royal Justices as Retainers in Thirteenth- and Four-teenth-Century England. Past and Present* Supplement 4. Oxford, 1978.

——. "Parliament and the Constituencies, 1272–1377." In Davies and Denton, eds., *English Parliament*, 61–87.

——. "Poems of Social Protest in Early Fourteenth-Century England." In W. M. Ormrod, ed., *England in the Fourteenth Century: Proceedings of the 1985 Harlaxton Symposium*, 130–44. Woodbridge, Suffolk, 1986.

Maitland, F. W. "The Crown as Corporation." In his *Collected Papers*, ed. H. A. L. Fisher, 3:244–70. Cambridge, 1911.

Mallard, W. "Dating the *Sermones Quadraginta* of John Wyclif." *Medievalia et Humanistica* 17 (1966): 86–105.

Mann, Jill. *Chaucer and Medieval Estates Satire: The Literature of Social Classes and the General Prologue to the Canterbury Tales*. Cambridge, Eng., 1973.

Medvedev, P. N. *The Formal Method in Literary Scholarship: A Critical Introduction to Sociological Poetics*. Trans. Albert J. Wehrle. Baltimore, 1978.

Meech, Sanford B. "Nicholas Bishop, an Exemplar of the Oxford Dialect of the Fifteenth Century." *PMLA* 49 (1934): 443–59.

Middleton, Anne. "The Audience and Public of *Piers Plowman*." In Lawton, ed., *Middle English Alliterative Poetry*, 101–23.

——. "The Idea of Public Poetry in the Reign of Richard II." *Speculum* 53 (1978): 94–114.

——. "Narration and the Invention of Experience: Episodic Form in *Piers Plowman*." In Larry D. Benson and Siegfried Wenzel, eds., *The Wisdom of Poetry: Essays in Early English Literature in Honor of Morton W. Bloomfield*, 91–122. Kalamazoo, 1982.

——. "William Langland's 'Kynde Name': Authorial Signature and Social Identity in Late Fourteenth-Century England." In Patterson, ed., *Literary Practice*, 15–82.

Miller, Edward, ed. *The Agrarian History of England and Wales*. Vol. 3, *1348–1500*. Cambridge, Eng., 1991.

Minnis, A. J. "*John Gower, Sapiens* in Ethics and Politics." *MÆ* 49 (1980): 207–29.

——. *Medieval Theory of Authorship: Scholastic Literary Attitudes in the Later Middle Ages*. 2d ed. Philadelphia, 1988.

Miskimin, Harry A. *The Economy of Early Renaissance Europe, 1300–1460*. Englewood Cliffs, 1969.

Mollat, Michel, and Philippe Wolff. *Ongles bleus, Jacques, et Ciompi: Les révolutions populaires en Europe aux XIVe et XVe siècles*. Paris, 1970.

Moran, Jo Ann Hoeppner. *The Growth of English Schooling 1340–1548: Learning, Literacy, and Laicization in Pre-Reformation York Diocese*. Princeton, 1985.

Morris, William Alfred. *The Early English County Court*. Berkeley, 1926.

Murray, Alexander. *Reason and Society in the Middle Ages*. Oxford, 1978.

Muscatine, Charles. *Poetry and Crisis in the Age of Chaucer*. Notre Dame, 1972.

Newton, K. C. *Thaxted in the Fourteenth Century: An Account of the Manor and*

Borough, with Translated Texts. Essex Record Office Publications 33. Chelmsford, 1960.

Olson, Paul A. *The Canterbury Tales and the Good Society.* Princeton, 1986.

Oman, Sir Charles. *The Great Revolt of 1381.* Oxford, 1906.

Ong, Walter J. *Orality and Literacy.* London, 1982.

Orme, Nicholas. *Education and Society in Medieval and Renaissance England.* London, 1989.

———. *English Schools in the Middle Ages.* London, 1973.

Ormrod, W. M. "The Peasants' Revolt and the Government of England." *Journal of British Studies* 29 (1990): 1–30.

Orwin, C. S., and C. S. Orwin. *The Open Fields.* 3d ed. Oxford, 1967.

Owen, Charles A., Jr., *Pilgrimage and Storytelling in the Canterbury Tales: The Dialectic of "Ernest" and "Game."* Norman, 1977.

Owen, Dorothy. *Church and Society in Medieval Lincolnshire.* Lincoln, Eng., 1971.

Palmer, Robert C. *The County Courts of Medieval England 1150–1350.* Princeton, 1982.

Parkes, M. B. "The Influence of the Concepts of *Ordinatio* and *Compilatio* on the Development of the Book." In J. J. G. Alexander and M. T. Gibson, eds., *Medieval Learning and Literature: Essays Presented to R. W. Hunt,* 115–41. Oxford, 1975.

———. "The Literacy of the Laity." In David Daiches and A. Thorlby, *The Medieval World,* 555–77. London, 1973.

Patterson, Lee. *Chaucer and the Subject of History.* Madison, 1991.

———. "On the Margin: Postmodernism, Ironic History, and Medieval Studies." *Speculum* 65 (1990): 87–108.

———. "'What Man Artow?': Authorial Self-Definition in the *Tale of Sir Thopas* and the *Tale of Melibee.*" *Studies in the Age of Chaucer* 11 (1989): 117–76.

———, ed. *Literary Practice and Social Change in Britain, 1380–1530.* Berkeley and Los Angeles, 1990.

Pearsall, Derek. "The Alliterative Revival: Origins and Social Backgrounds." In Lawton, ed., *Middle English Alliterative Poetry,* 34–53.

———. "Interpretative Models for the Peasants' Revolt." In Patrick J. Gallacher and Helen Damico, eds., *Hermeneutics and Medieval Culture,* 63–70. Albany, 1989.

———. *The Life of Geoffrey Chaucer: A Critical Biography.* Oxford, 1992.

———, ed. *The Nun's Priest's Tale.* Vol. 2, part 9 of *The Variorum Chaucer.* Norman, 1984.

Petit-Dutaillis, Charles. "Les prédications populaires: Les lollards et le soulèvement des travailleurs anglais en 1381." In *Études d'histoire du moyen âge dédiées à Gabriel Monod,* 373–88. Paris, 1896.

———. *Studies and Notes Supplemental to Stubbs' Constitutional History.* Vol. 2. Manchester, 1915.

Phythian-Adams, Charles. "Ceremony and the Citizen: The Communal Year at Coventry." In Peter Clark and Paul Slack, eds., *Crisis and Order in English Towns 1500–1700: Essays in Urban History,* 57–85. Toronto, 1972.

———. *Local History and Folklore: A New Framework.* London, 1975.

Pimsler, Martin. "Solidarity in the Medieval Village? The Evidence of Personal Pledging at Elton, Huntingdonshire." *Journal of British Studies* 17 (1977): 1–11.

Pirenne, Henri. "L'Instruction des marchands au moyen âge." *Annales* 1 (1929): 13–28.

Plucknett, T. F. T. *The Mediaeval Bailiff.* London, 1954.

Pollock, Frederick, and F. W. Maitland. *The History of English Law Before the Time of Edward I.* 2 vols. Cambridge, Eng., 1926.

Poos, L. R. "The Social Context of Statute of Labourers Enforcement." *Law and History Review* 1 (1983): 27–52.

Postan, Michael M. *The Medieval Economy and Society: An Economic History of Britain 1100–1500.* Berkeley and Los Angeles, 1972.

Postan, Michael M., and John Hatcher. "Population and Class Relations in Feudal Society." In Aston and Philpin, eds., *Brenner Debate,* 64–78.

Powell, Edgar. *The Rising of 1381 in East Anglia.* Cambridge, Eng., 1896.

Pratt, John H. "The 'Scharpe Ax' of Richard II." *Neuphilologische Mitteilungen* 77 (1976): 80–84.

Prescott, Andrew J. "Judicial Records of the Rising of 1381." Ph.D. thesis. Bedford College, University of London, 1984.

———. "London in the Peasants' Revolt: A Portrait Gallery." *London Journal* 7 (1981): 125–43.

Putnam, Bertha Haven. *The Enforcement of the Statute of Laborers During the First Decade after the Black Death, 1349–1359.* New York, 1908.

———. "Maximum Wage-Laws for Priests after the Black Death, 1348–1381." *AHR* 21 (1915): 12–32.

Quin, W. F. *A History of Braintree and Bocking.* Lavenham, 1981.

Quirk, Randolf. "Langland's Use of 'Kind Wit' and 'Inwit.'" *JEGP* 52 (1953): 182–88.

———. "Vis Imaginativa." *JEGP* 53 (1954): 81–83.

Raftis, J. Ambrose. "Social Change Versus Revolution: New Interpretations of the Peasants' Revolt of 1381." In F. X. Newman, ed. *Social Unrest in the Late Middle Ages,* 3–22. Binghamton, 1986.

———. *Tenure and Mobility: Studies in the Social History of the Medieval English Village.* Toronto, 1964.

———. *Warboys: Two Hundred Years in the Life of an English Mediaeval Village.* Toronto, 1974.

Rayner, Doris. "The Forms and Machinery of the 'Commune Petition' in the Fourteenth Century." *EHR* 56 (1941): 198–233, 549–70.

Réville, André. *Le Soulèvement des travailleurs d'Angleterre en 1381.* Paris, 1898.

Richardson, H. G. "The Commons and Medieval Politics." *TRHS* 28 (1945): 21–45.

———. "Business Training in Medieval Oxford." *AHR* 46 (1941): 259–80.

———. "Heresy and the Lay Power under Richard II." *EHR* 51 (1936): 1–28.

Richardson, H. G., and G. O. Sayles. "The Early Statutes." *Law Quarterly Review* 50 (1934): 201–24, 540–71.

————. *The Governance of Medieval England from the Conquest to Magna Carta.* Edinburgh, 1963.

————. "The Parliaments of Edward III." *BIHR* 8 (1930): 65–77; 9 (1931): 1–18.

Richter, Michael. "A Socio-linguistic Approach to the Latin Middle Ages." *SCH* 11 (1975): 69–82.

Robbins, Rossell Hope. "The Arma Christi Rolls." *MLR* 34 (1934): 415–21.

————. "Middle English Poems of Protest." *Anglia* 78 (1960): 193–203.

Roberts, B. K. "Village Patterns and Forms: Some Models for Discussion." In Hooke, ed., *Medieval Villages*, 7–25.

Roberts, Eileen. "St. Albans' Borough Boundary and Its Significance in the Peasants' Revolt." In *The Peasants' Revolt in Hertfordshire: The Rising and Its Background*, 126–34. Stevenage Old Town, 1981.

Robertson, D. W., Jr. *Chaucer's London.* New York, 1968.

Robertson, D. W., Jr., and B. F. Huppé. *Piers Plowman and Scriptural Tradition.* Princeton, 1951.

Ronan, Nick. "1381: Writing in Revolt. Signs of Confederacy in the Chronicle Accounts of the English Rising." *Forum for Modern Language Studies* 25 (1989): 304–14.

Roseberry, William. *Anthropologies and Histories: Essays in Culture, History, and Political Economy.* New Brunswick, 1989.

Rubin, Miri. "Corpus Christi Fraternities and Late Medieval Piety." *SCH* 23 (1986): 97–109.

————. *Corpus Christi: The Eucharist in Late Medieval Culture.* Cambridge, Eng., 1991.

Samuels, M. L. "Langland's Dialect." *MÆ* 54 (1985): 232–47.

Sanderlin, S. "Chaucer and Ricardian Politics." *Chaucer Review* 22 (1988): 171–84.

Sayles, G. O. "Richard II in 1381 and 1399." *EHR* 103 (1988): 820–29.

Scase, Wendy. *Piers Plowman and the New Anticlericalism.* Cambridge, Eng., 1989.

Scattergood, V. J. *Politics and Poetry in the Fifteenth Century.* London, 1971.

Schmidt, A. V. C. "A Note on Langland's Conception of 'Anima' and 'Inwit.'" *Notes and Queries* ns 15 (1968): 363–64.

————. "A Note on the Phrase 'Free Wit' in the C-Text of *Piers Plowman*." *Notes and Queries* ns 15 (1968): 168–69.

Searle, Eleanor, and Robert Burghardt. "The Defense of England and the Peasants' Revolt." *Viator* 3 (1972): 36–88.

Simpson, James. "The Constraints of Satire in 'Piers Plowman' and 'Mum and the Sothsegger.'" In Helen Phillips, ed., *Langland, the Mystics, and the Medieval English Religious Tradition: Essays in Honour of S. S. Hussey*, 11–31. Cambridge, Eng., 1990.

————. *Piers Plowman: An Introduction to the B-Text.* London, 1990.

Smith, R. M. "Kin and Neighbors in a Thirteenth-Century Suffolk Community." *Journal of Family History* 4 (1979): 219–56.

————, ed. *Land, Kinship, and Life-Cycle.* Cambridge, Eng., 1984.

Spiegel, Gabrielle. "History, Historicism, and the Social Logic of the Text in the Middle Ages." *Speculum* 65 (1990): 59–86.

Stemmler, Theo. "The Peasants' Revolt of 1381 in Contemporary Literature." In Ulrich Broich, Theo Stemmler, and Gerd Stratmann, eds., *Functions of Literature: Essays Presented to Erwin Wolff on his Sixtieth Birthday*, 21–38. Tübingen, 1984.

Stock, Brian. *The Implications of Literacy: Written Language and Models of Interpretation in the Eleventh and Twelfth Centuries*. Princeton, 1983.

Streeter, Burnett Hillman. *The Chained Library: A Survey of Four Centuries in the Evolution of the English Library*. London, 1931.

Strohm, Paul. "Politics and Poetics: Usk and Chaucer." In Patterson, ed., *Literary Practice and Social Change*, 83–112.

———. *Hochon's Arrow: The Social Imagination of Fourteenth-Century Texts*. Princeton, 1992.

———. *Social Chaucer*. Cambridge, Mass., 1989.

Stubbs, William. *The Constitutional History of England in Its Origin and Development*. 3d ed. Oxford, 1883.

Tanner, Norman. *The Church in Late Medieval Norwich 1370–1532*. Toronto, 1984.

Tatnall, Edith C. "John Wyclif and *Ecclesia Anglicana*." *Journal of Ecclesiastical History* 20 (1969): 19–59.

Taylor, Andrew. "Playing on the Margins: Bakhtin and the Smithfield Decretals." Paper delivered at the International Congress of Medieval Studies, Kalamazoo, May 1992.

Thirsk, Joan. "The Common Fields." 1964. Rpt. in Hilton, *Peasants, Knights, and Heretics*, 10–32.

———. "The Origin of the Common Fields." 1966. Rpt. in Hilton, *Peasants, Knights, and Heretics*, 51–56.

Thomas, Keith. *Religion and the Decline of Magic*. New York, 1971.

Thomson, Williell R. *The Latin Writings of John Wyclyf: An Annotated Catalogue*. Toronto, 1983.

Thorndike, Lynn. "Elementary and Secondary Education in the Middle Ages." *Speculum* 15 (1940): 400–408.

Tierney, Brian. *Medieval Poor Law: A Sketch of Canonical Theory and Its Application in England*. Berkeley and Los Angeles, 1959.

Tillotson, J. H. "Peasant Unrest in the England of Richard II: Some Evidence from Royal Records." *Historical Studies* (University of Melbourne) 16 (1974–75): 1–16.

Titow, J. Z. *English Rural Society 1200–1350*. London, 1969.

———. "Some Differences Between Manors and Their Effects on the Condition of the Peasant in the Thirteenth Century." *Agricultural History Review* 10 (1962): 1–13.

Tout, Thomas Frederick. *Chapters in the Administrative History of Mediaeval England*. Manchester, 1928.

———. "Parliament and Public Opinion, 1376–1388." In *The Collected Papers of Thomas Frederick Tout*, 173–90. Manchester, 1934.

Travis, Peter W. "Chaucer's Trivial Fox Chase and the Peasants' Revolt of 1381." *JMRS* 18 (1988): 185–220.

Turner, Ralph V. "The *Miles Literatus* in Twelfth- and Thirteenth-Century England: How Rare a Phenomenon?" *AHR* 83 (1978): 928–45.

Turville-Peter, Thorlac. *The Alliterative Revival.* Cambridge, Eng., 1977.

Voloshinov, V. N. *Marxism and the Philosophy of Language.* Trans. Ladislav Matejka and I. R. Titunik. New York, 1973.

von Nolcken, Christina. "*Piers Plowman,* the Wycliffites, and *Pierce the Plowman's Creed.*" *YLS* 2 (1988): 71–102.

Wake, Joan. "Communitas Villae." *EHR* 37 (1922): 407–13.

Wallace, David. "'Whan She Translated Was': A Chaucerian Critique of the Petrarchan Academy." In Patterson, ed., *Literary Practice and Social Change,* 156–215.

Weisheipl, James. "The Curriculum of the Faculty of Arts at Oxford in the Early Fourteenth Century." *MS* 29 (1964): 143–85.

Wells, J. E. *Manual of Writing in Middle English 1050–1400.* New Haven, 1916.

White, Allon, and Peter Stallybrass. *The Politics and Poetics of Transgression.* Ithaca, 1986.

White, Beatrice. "Poet and Peasant." In DuBoulay and Barron, eds., *The Reign of Richard II,* 58–74.

White, Lynn, Jr. *Medieval Technology and Social Change.* Oxford, 1962.

Wilkinson, Bertie. "The Peasants' Revolt of 1381." *Speculum* 15 (1940): 12–35.

———. *Studies in the Constitutional History of the Thirteenth and Fourteenth Centuries.* Manchester, 1937.

Williams, Raymond. *The Country and the City.* Oxford, 1973.

Wilson, R. M. *The Lost Literature of Medieval England.* 2d ed. London, 1970.

Wood, R. G. E. "Essex Manorial Records and the Revolt." In Liddell and Wood, eds., *Essex and the Great Revolt,* 85–98.

Woolf, Rosemary. "Chaucer as a Satirist in the *General Prologue* to the *Canterbury Tales.*" *Critical Quarterly* 1 (1959): 150–57.

———. "Some Non-Medieval Qualities of *Piers Plowman.*" *Essays in Criticism* 12 (1962): 111–25.

Workman, Herbert B. *John Wyclif: A Study of the English Medieval Church.* 2 vols. Oxford, 1926.

Wright, A. R. *British Calendar Customs: England.* London, 1938.

Wrightson, Keith. "Medieval Villagers in Perspective." *Peasant Studies* 7 (1978): 203–17.

Yeager, Robert F. *John Gower's Poetic: The Search for a New Arion.* Cambridge, Eng., 1990.

Index

Note: I have alphabetized medieval names, wherever possible, under the family name, or our equivalent of it. At times, though, this sounded too strange to my own ears. "Plowman, Piers" was of course an impossibility, but neither could I bring myself to enter "Seville, Isidore of" or "Straw, Jack." Nobility—with the single exception of John of Gaunt, who appears thus—appear under their most usual title (e.g., "Arundel, Thomas Fitzalan, earl of").